Conservation in Africa
people, policies and practice

Conservation in Africa
people, policies and practice

EDITED BY
DAVID ANDERSON
Department of History, Birkbeck College, University of London

AND

RICHARD GROVE
African Studies Centre and Clare Hall, University of Cambridge

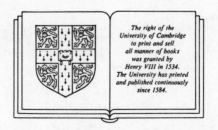

The right of the
University of Cambridge
to print and sell
all manner of books
was granted by
Henry VIII in 1534.
The University has printed
and published continuously
since 1584.

CAMBRIDGE UNIVERSITY PRESS

CAMBRIDGE

NEW YORK   PORT CHESTER   MELBOURNE   SYDNEY

Published by the Press Syndicate of the University of Cambridge
The Pitt Building, Trumpington Street, Cambridge CB2 1RP
40 West 20th Street, New York, NY 10011, USA
10 Stamford Road, Oakleigh, Melbourne 3166, Australia

First published 1987
First paperback edition 1989

Printed in Great Britain at the University Press, Cambridge

British Library cataloguing in publication data
Conservation in Africa : people, policies and
practice.
1. Conservation of natural resources –
Africa
I. Anderson, David II. Grove, Richard
333.7'2'096   S934.A35

Library of Congress cataloguing in publication data
Conservation in Africa.
1. Nature conservation – Africa. 2. Conservation of
natural resources – Africa. I. Anderson, David,
1957– . II. Grove, Richard (Richard H.)
QH77.A4C66 1987   333.7'2'096   87-8053

ISBN 0 521 34199 X hard covers
ISBN 0 521 34990 7 paperback

CONTENTS

PREFACE

This book owes its origins to an exploratory seminar held at Queen Elizabeth House, Oxford, in October 1983. During the course of this seminar three historians, approaching the subject from very different backgrounds, found that their ideas about the problems of conservation and resource management in Africa were converging to a surprising degree. Furthermore, the participants at the seminar shared the view that a more comprehensive exploration of conservation orthodoxies would be both academically fruitful and practically useful. Consequently, a much larger workshop was organised and held under the auspices of the African Studies Centre at Cambridge University. This workshop took place in April 1985. Biological scientists, social scientists and historians were all well represented at this meeting, at which more than one hundred participants discussed 26 papers covering a very wide range of interests within the general theme of 'Conservation in Africa'. Thirteen of the papers from that workshop have been revised for publication in this volume, while a further three chapters have been subsequently added.

With the aim of continuing the dialogue between the biological and social scientists that the workshop so successfully stimulated, an interdisciplinary seminar series was begun in 1985 at the African Studies Centre, Cambridge, under the title 'Reconciling Conservation and Development'. Both the seminar series and this volume aim, quite deliberately, to consolidate and promote a commitment to an interdisciplinary approach to the study of the environmental problems of Africa.

In coordinating the Cambridge workshop and in making this book possible, the editors would particularly like to thank the staff of the African Studies Centre, Paula Munro, Janet Seeley, Ludgard De Decker and A.T. Grove. We would also like to thank Bill Adams, William Beinart, Kathy Homewood, Paul Howell, Jeff Lewis, Robin Pellew, John Scherlis, Richard Waller, and the late Con Benson for their encouragement, inspiration and advice.

David Anderson
Richard Grove

CONTRIBUTORS

William M. Adams, Department of Geography, University of Cambridge, Downing Place, Cambridge

David M. Anderson, Department of History, Birkbeck College, University of London, Malet Street, London WC1E 7HX

Olusegun O. Areola, Department of Geography, Faculty of the Social Sciences, University of Ibadan, Ibadan, Nigeria

William Beinart, Department of History, University of Bristol, 13–15 Woodland Avenue, Bristol BS8 1TB

Richard H.V. Bell, Luangwa Integrated Resource Development Project, PO Box 510249, Chipata, Zambia

David Brokensha, Department of Anthropology and Environmental Studies, University of California, Santa Barbara, California 93106, USA

David Collett, Assistant Curator, National Museums and Monuments, Private Bag 9158, Masvingo, Zimbabwe

Maknun Gamaledinn, African Studies Centre, University of Cambridge, Free School Lane, Cambridge

Richard Grove, Research Fellow in History, Clare Hall, Cambridge CB3 9AL

Richard Hogg, Department of Social Anthropology, University of Manchester, Roscoe Building, Brunswick Street, Manchester M13 2PL

Katherine Homewood, Department of Anthropology, University College, Gower Street, London WC1E 6BT

Paul P. Howell, Emeritus Fellow, Wolfson College, Cambridge

Francine M.R. Hughes, Department of Geography, University of Cambridge, Downing Place, Cambridge

Keith Lindsay, Department of Applied Ecology, University of Cambridge, Pembroke Street, Cambridge

Peter D. Little, Institute for Development Anthropology, 99 Collier Street, Suite 302, PO Box 818, Binghamton, New York 13902, USA

John M. Lonsdale, Trinity College, Cambridge CB2 1TQ

John MacKenzie, Department of History, Furness College, Bailrigg, University of Lancaster, Lancaster LA1 4YG

John McCracken, Department of History, Stirling University, Stirling FK9 4LA

Andrew C. Millington, Department of Geography, University of Reading, PO Box 227, Whiteknights, Reading RG6 2AB

William A. Rodgers, Wildlife Institute of India, PO New Forest, Dehra Dun, India

David Turton, Department of Social Anthroplogy, University of Manchester, Roscoe Building, Brunswick Street, Manchester M13 2PL

The scramble for Eden: past, present and future in African conservation

DAVID ANDERSON AND RICHARD GROVE

There is no doubting the seriousness of environmental and agrarian problems in Africa today in the eyes of the developed world. Human life, natural habitat, soils and species are all thought to be endangered in the continent to an extent never known before. The 'crisis' in Africa, whether enunciated in terms of sheer human suffering and the tragedy of famine, the threat to wildlife or the spread of desertification, is becoming a commonplace of academic and popular culture throughout the industrialised world and, not least, among urbanised Africans themselves. The western media, and television especially have helped to catalyse this development and, while often distorting and misrepresenting the issues, have linked the African predicament, at least temporarily, to the mainstream of European concerns. Even the very name 'Africa', it might be argued, has come to be equated with notions of doom and despondency that have very little to do with older connotations of Africa in the European mind. The more hopeful idea of Africa as a natural habitat teeming with spectacular wildlife has much older antecedents than the image conferred on the continent in the 1980s by famine. Equally the European interest in conserving the wildlife and habitats of Africa has a long history, much of it entirely ignorant of the long-established and successful ways in which Africans have ensured their own survival and that of the soils, plants and creatures which they need in order to live (Worthington, 1958; Darling, 1960; cf. Brokensha, Warren & Werner, 1980; Richards, 1985) and which form a basic part of the texture and meaning of rural, non-industrial existence.

In recent years, however, 'conservation' has come to much greater prominence in the context of the perceived crisis in Africa and it is in the light of this development that the purpose of this book was conceived. Conservation is a much used term, its meanings ranging through a variety of contexts. In the African context, the view that has commonly identified conservation with the protection of species and habitats, with movements to preserve wildlife and wilderness, is giving way to a broader discussion

1

linking conservation to the process of rural development and the survival of agrarian societies in Africa. This book is about the manner in which conservation practices and policies in Africa today relate to the process of rural development and social change, and about the significance of past conservation strategies in shaping the way that present problems are viewed and tackled. Prescriptions for environmental management of all kinds, for wildlife, soils and water are now being put forward, mainly by Europeans (e.g. Harrison, 1984), as panaceas for coping with an ecological crisis in the same way in which advisors to post-war colonial governments in Africa put forward 'development' plans, many of which had a substantial 'conservation' component, to deal with the manifest poverty of the continent (see Worthington, 1983). This connection is not an accidental one and the links between conservation and development ideologies and their contribution to the difficulties of Africa today are an important underlying theme of this book.

It is now being recognised in much of the social science literature that the development policies pursued by colonial and post-colonial governments and their 'experts' have not only been economically unsuccessful in many respects, they have also frequently been extremely harmful to the natural environment and thereby to the prospects of human survival in Africa in the long term (Redclift, 1984; Timberlake, 1985). More specifically, much of the work of development economists has been sadly lacking in critical sociological insights into the potential impacts of their programmes on rural African populations (Mair, 1984; Hill, 1986). These 'experts', who have so far had a wide environmental impact upon Africa because of the scope and finance they have been allowed, have often failed to understand not just the social context but the wider ecological context as well. This is particularly important since rural development strategies often amount, in practice, to unintentional forms of environmental policy quite independent of the socio-economic transitions they aspire to achieve (Chambers, 1983). Part of the message of this collection of essays is to warn that many of the prescriptions for environmental management, and for conservation in particular, which are continuing to be made for Africa by development 'experts' may well prove as hazardous for the people and wildlife of Africa as recent policies for rural economic development have been.

Many of those conservationists currently advocating conservation programmes for Africa, whose views are given considerable currency in the immediacy of the apparent environmental crisis of the 1980s, also threaten merely to pay lip service to the social context within which they propose to operate their systems of management (e.g. IUCN, 1980;

Allen, 1980; WWF/IUCN, 1983). Despite the superficially attractive approach of such international initiatives as the World Conservation Strategy (IUCN, 1980) in seeking to enlist the integration of development goals with conservation objectives and the participation of local people, some of the underlying assumptions they perhaps unconsciously embody are disturbing; at root, the World Conservation Strategy simply implies that the conservationists' vision of society must predominate. But, as Redclift (1984) laments, the World Conservation Strategy 'does not even begin to examine the social and political changes that would be necessary to meet its conservation goals'. Thus, we read in one guide to the World Conservation Strategy, that 'ultimately the behaviour of entire societies towards the biosphere must be transformed if the achievement of conservation objectives is to be achieved' (Allen, 1980). Such propaganda for global social manipulation implicitly arrogates the determination of basic modes of social intercourse with the environment to itself in a way that goes beyond even the most dramatic 'social engineering' ambitions of the colonial state in Africa after 1945.

The fact that most government conservation and rural economic development programmes in Africa have been applied without an awareness of the broader social implications they embody has been largely due to the prominent role of specialists in designing those schemes – most commonly biologists in the case of measures for the protection of species and the preservation of habitats, and economists in the case of rural development projects. The objectives of these programmes have tended to reflect the very narrowly conceived academic or ideological preoccupations of the specialists concerned, and to be framed and dominated by European views of the need for and nature of conservation or rural development. As the state in Africa has become increasingly interventionist, the risks which have devolved from this characteristic relationship between government and 'expert' in Africa, itself a direct legacy of the colonial period, have become more apparent. It has become more and more difficult for rural people in Africa to escape from or to ignore the agrarian and environmental dictates imposed upon them by governments. At the same time, the conservation methods that have been implemented in Africa have been distorted by environmental priorities which have been specific to the predicament and perceptions of the industrialising parts of Europe and North America (Freud, 1921; Graham, 1973; Passmore, 1974; Brandt, 1977). Most of these perceptions have had little relevance to the realities of the environmental changes experienced by most Africans since colonisation. Nevertheless, they have to be understood in order to explain the aims of conservationists and

attitudes towards conservation in Africa today, if only because of the
strong continuity between the conservation policies of the colonial state
in Africa and those of independent African governments. Moreover, it
remains true that Europeans and their ideas exert an undiminished, even
increasing influence over the African environment today (Smith, 1980;
Mazrui, 1980).

Because of the dominant role of European ideas in shaping conservation policies in Africa in the past and the present, we have to make some
effort to understand the wider psychological function of the African
environment in the European mind. This difficult task has already been
usefully attempted by several writers (see Curtin, 1964; Graham, 1973;
Marnham, 1980). The problem is rooted in the nature of the colonial
relationship itself, which allowed Europeans to impose their image of
Africa upon the reality of the African landscape. Much of the emotional
as distinct from the economic investment which Europe made in Africa
has manifested itself in a wish to protect the natural environment as a
special kind of 'Eden', for the purposes of the European psyche, rather
than as a complex and changing environment in which people have
actually had to live. The desire to maintain and preserve 'Eden' has been
particularly pronounced in eastern and southern Africa, where European
ambitions have extended to permanent settlement. Here, at its crudest,
Africa has been portrayed as offering the opportunity to experience a
wild and natural environment which was no longer available in the domesticated landscapes of Europe. At a practical level, Europeans were able
to exploit their technological superiority to control access to the African
environment, and to seek for themselves, quite literally, pastures new
and a 'promised land'. Whether Boer trekker or Kenya pioneer, the
principle was the same: a journey was being made out of the constraints
of European economic and mental constriction. The writings of Elspeth
Huxley (1959; 1962), Ernest Hemingway (1936) and Karen Blixen (1937)
bear eloquent witness to the function of Africa as a wilderness in which
European man sought to rediscover a lost harmony with nature and the
natural environment (Marx, 1964; Olwig & Olwig, 1980). Much of conservation thinking in Africa, as defined and exercised by Europeans,
has therefore been directed to sustaining an image of Africa which forms
a part of a European mythology. Europe no longer exerts direct political
control over Africa, but the mythology of the African environment and
the symbol of Africa as a yet unspoilt Eden continues to stimulate many
of those who wish to intervene in the way the environment is managed
in Africa. Some of these powerful motivations have been best summed

up in the writings of Bernard Grzimek, possibly the most influential European post-war publicist of African wildlife:

. . .men are easily inspired by human ideas but they forget them just as quickly. Only Nature is eternal, unless we senselessly destroy it. In fifty years' time nobody will be interested in the results of conferences which fill today's headlines . . . but fifty years from now when a lion walks into the red dawn and roars resoundingly, it will mean something to people and quicken their hearts . . . they will stand in quiet awe, as for the first time in their lives, they watch 20,000 zebra wander across the endless plain . . . is it really stupid to work for the zebras, lions and men who will walk the earth in a hundred or two hundred years' time?   (*Grzimek & Grzimek, 1965*).

Nature's eternity was symbolised in Africa, with its herds of wildlife, not in the plain artificiality of industrialised urban society in Europe.

This perceptual polarisation of a 'despoiled' Europe and a 'natural' Africa has held sway since the nineteenth century. Indeed, it was in the African colonies that early environmentalists were first able to lobby government and exert an influence inhibiting environmental changes they did not like, long before this was politically practicable in Europe (Grove, 1987). Paradoxically, it was also in the colonial context, in Australia and North America as well as in Africa, that the natural environment was first perceived as threatened specifically by European economic forces and where governments first incorporated conservation as part of their accepted role (Nash, 1967; Powell, 1976; Grove, 1987). The very early development of conservation ideas in the colonies helps to draw our attention to the fact that conceptions of environmental crisis in Africa are also not new. They have an historical dimension which cannot be overlooked (Beinart, 1984; Anderson, 1984; Johnson & Anderson, 1987). Even a cursory examination of this dimension indicates that the idea of a 'crisis' in Africa has as much to do with the history and development of European perceptions of Africa as it has to do with the undeniable reality of environmental degradation engendered directly and indirectly by the penetration of western economic forces, technology and medicine.

The image of Africa as a refuge from the technological society of Europe has frequently been reinforced by the broad notion that the conservation of the African environment is an entirely apolitical affair, a global value that no prejudice could undermine. Thus, another influential crusader for the cause of African conservation, Laurens van der Post, has couched his imperatives in terms of a war uniting all mankind:

We must come to grips with the need for the survival of life on this planet and one of the most essential of these needs is the preservation of large areas of

wilderness . . . it is a war in which we are engaged . . . it is a subject which is
not political, but beyond politics, sociology and material ideals.

(quoted in Vance, 1982)

This naïve and idealised picture of apolitical conservation in Africa, or
anywhere else for that matter, is faintly absurd. As a rallying call to
humanity to gather round the standard of environmentalism it has proven
to be fatally flawed, failing to appreciate that, to rural societies in Africa,
conservation is a *very* political issue. Attempts to manage the African
landscape for conservation or development invariably involve direct
interventions in the relationship between man and his environment (i.e.
between rural man and his means of production). The impact of these
interventions often extends geographically far beyond the intention of
the deliberate plan, being carried through wide networks of social link-
age. In this sense any intervention in the rural environment represents
a far more serious undertaking to the subsistence economy than it does
to one which possesses the safety net of an industrial base. In rural
Africa the management and ownership of land, as both the dwelling
place and means of production of the majority of the population, therefore lies at the core of the political agenda (Richards, 1983). Consequently, in the essays which follow we set out, quite deliberately, to
explode the myth that conservation in Africa can be apolitical in objective
or method, and to assert the importance of sociological factors and
material ideals in determining the sort of conservation that will be attainable in Africa.

The call for conservation has become ever louder with the extraordinary growth of environmentalism in the West since the Second World
War, and more especially over the past two decades. This flowering of
interest in conservation has been generated by sharpened perceptions
of the prospects for a global ecological 'crisis'. Public concern in western
Europe and North America has expressed itself in the burgeoning of
environmental pressure groups and the spread of an interest in the natural
world as a wider element of European culture (Allen, 1976; Lowe &
Goyder, 1983). Part of this new awareness has stressed the vulnerability
of nature as a paradigm of man and has emphasised the conviction that
society as a whole may be becoming more vulnerable to technologically
caused risks (Lowe, 1980). Many of these preoccupations have been
global in their scope: nuclear power, tropical rainforest destruction,
excessive use of fossil resources, artificially induced climatic changes,
and marine pollution are all seen as threatening global ecological stability.
While environmental concerns of this type are of much greater longevity
than is commonly realised, it is only recently that important elements

of western society, including some governments, have become so recep-
tive to the language of the advocates of conservation and environmental
management that they have been ready to consider the radical interventionist ideas of the 'environmentalists' who have consistently foretold a
global ecological crisis (O'Riordan, 1976; Redclift, 1984). It is important
to bear in mind that the growth of this global environmentalism has
been based in perceptions and values of the environment that are closely
connected with the functioning and social dynamics of western society
(Douglas & Wildavsky, 1982).

It is against this background of the growing influence of environmentalism in the West that the more recent diagnosis of a crisis in Africa
needs to be more critically examined. Western environmentalists have
characteristically used the threat of 'eco-catastrophe' as a lever for highly
interventionist physical and social prescriptions (Cotgrove, 1976; Lowe,
1980; Brass, 1986). In some ways, the crisis in Africa serves as a surrogate
for the disaster that environmentalists have long claimed to be threatening. The potency of this crisis scenario has been boosted by the very real
spectacle of famine and environmental degradation which has served to
shatter – though perhaps only temporarily – the image of the wild Eden
in Africa. The imagery of desertification has served an important purpose
in this respect: Eden threatens, quite literally, to dry up, through the
agency of human misuse. This diagnosis accordingly provides an opportunity for western experts, be they environmentalists or developers, to
impose their preferred environmental solutions on rural Africa. In this
setting definitions of a broad environmental rather than strictly human
crisis allow programmes for the conservation of soil, water, forests and,
to a lesser extent, wildlife to prove quite as attractive as any rural development strategy, particularly when combined with the latter (see Timberlake, 1985).

Present-day propagandists for more government conservation have
often failed to realise that, historically, the conservation strategies which
have found favour in African states have seldom been based upon the
participation or consent of the communities whose lives they affect.
Thus, conservation in Africa has frequently meant the simple exclusion
of rural people from national parks and forest reserves, in the interests
of the protection of large animal species and preservation of habitats.
Where measures have been introduced that relate directly to systems of
land husbandry, such as the soil conservation programmes and resettlement schemes of the late-colonial government, these have been inspired
by European notions of the 'improvement' of rural Africa (Beinart, 1984;
Anderson, 1984) and imposed upon an often reluctant population. The

majority of conservation programmes, however, have either been directed at protecting the narrow interests of non-subsistence agriculture or have been utilised for exercising an enhanced degree of social control by the state. In other words, the exclusion or the social control of people has been the pragmatic guiding principle if not the original motivation of these policies. For these reasons, the history of conservation in Africa has a legacy which remains important in framing the attitudes of rural communities towards any conservation initiatives now proposed. The use of the term 'alienation' in referring to this kind of conservation says, perhaps unintentionally, as much as needs to be said about its basic philosophy.

Confronted by the reality of famine and immense human tragedy in Africa in the 1980s, the ideologies and programmes of traditional conservationists and modern environmentalists have been found wanting. Just as development economists have had to reassess their plans for Africa in the context of an ecological crisis they had not bargained for, the scientists who promote conservation have been forced to look beyond the narrow confines of their own disciplines. The impact of the diagnosis of crisis in Africa has therefore had the effect of widening the debate on conservation, bringing the social context within which any conservation strategy must be implemented to much greater prominence, its significance having been given emphasis by the essentially human dimension of famine and by the perceived enormity of the environmental task at hand in the continent. The principal aim of this book, then, is to contribute to this broadening approach to conservation in Africa by stimulating a greater dialogue between scientists and social scientists all of whom are concerned, in their different ways, with aspects of conservation. Above all, these essays seek quite deliberately to assert the social context that has been missing from so much that has been written about conservation in Africa.

The essays gathered in this volume therefore share a common perspective, although they are written by people with widely differing academic backgrounds and training, ranging from anthropologists and historians to ecologists and zoologists. The organisation of the book has grouped chapters around themes, and not disciplines. Each of the four parts of the book is prefaced by a short introduction, which seeks to highlight the broader themes and significance of the chapters that follow. The chapters in Part One of the book deal with past and present conservation ideologies in Africa, from the earliest introduction of conservation legislation at the Cape in the mid-nineteenth century to the present debates about the need for new forms of conservation policy. Part Two of the book considers conservation in the context of wildlife and game parks, and in relation to the African pastoralists who make use of those same rangelands. These chapters examine and question prevailing perceptions of pastoralist land-use, and look at the practical human problems in implementing game park policies. Part Three moves on to look at conservation priorities for rural communities, with chapters dealing with indigenous and imposed resource management systems, conflicts over forest conservation and fuelwood provision, and policies towards soil conservation. Finally, in Part Four, conservation is considered in its present relationship to development. These case studies indicate the pressing need for conservation to be incorporated within the planning and implementation of rural development, the unwillingness of developers to learn from past mistakes, and the ultimate futility of development without conservation. Throughout the book the importance of an historical perspective in understanding the origins and evolution of present attitudes and approaches towards conservation in Africa is given prominence, and the social context of conservation is stressed.

While historians and social scientists cannot offer neat solutions to the problems of Africa, they can contribute to the explanatory work that now needs to be done to try to forestall the recurrence of famine and failed intervention. Although much has been written about the technical side of ecological change and about conservation methods since early colonial times, little has been written that assists in the critical task of integrating an ecological or scientific understanding of the present African environment with an equally sophisticated understanding of the processes of social change that affect the people who live in rural Africa (but see Chambers, 1983; Marks 1984; Richards, 1985). While in various parts of Africa the gross external pressures of war, borehole drilling and enforced resettlement programmes continue to subvert indigenous responses to natural environmental stresses (Timberlake, 1985; Sinclair & Fryxell, 1985), it is likely that the debate about the management of the African environment will continue to be provoked by further images of 'crisis'. Evolving European environmental prejudices are therefore likely to continue to exercise influence over the objectives and the geographical claims which conservation programmes and rural development projects make in Africa. At the same time, while many African governments now consider conservation to be 'a good thing', policies for National Parks, game reserves, forest protection and soil conservation programmes are unlikely to be successfully implemented if they fail to involve the participation and cooperation of the rural people whose lives they will invariably alter.

There exists an absolute necessity for scientists, social scientists, historians, development planners and the governments and agencies they advise, to begin to learn to speak to each other, and to become mutually aware of the full complexity of the social dynamics that operate in rural Africa. Discussions about the future of the African environment must therefore also comprehend a debate about the future of African rural society. This debate will continue to be destructively one-sided until a time comes when African rural people participate directly in the process of decision-making that affects the environment in which they live. In future one might hope that the essential complementarity of ecological and sociological analyses of the African rural environment will be kept firmly in focus.

References

ALLEN, D. (1976). *The Naturalist in Britain: a social history.* London: Allen Lane.

ALLEN, R. (1980). *How To Save The World: strategy for world conservation.* London: Kogan Page.

ANDERSON, D.M. (1984). Depression, Dust Bowl, Demography and Drought: the Colonial State and soil conservation in East Africa during the 1930s. *African Affairs*, **83** (332), 321–43.

BEINART, W. (1984). Soil erosion, conservationism, and ideas about development in Southern Africa. *Journal of Southern African Studies*, **11** (2), 52–83.

BLIXEN, K.C. (1937). *Out of Africa.* London: Putnam.

BRANDT, A. (1977). Views – surprise: environmentalists and industrialists are brothers under the skin. *Atlantic Monthly*, **240**, 40–9.

BRASS, P.R. (1986). The political uses of crisis: the Bihar famine, 1966–7. *Journal of Asian Studies*, **45** (2), 245–67.

BROKENSHA, D., WARREN, D. & WERNER, O. (1980). *Indigenous Knowledge and Development.* Washington: University of America Press.

CHAMBERS, R. (1983). *Rural Development: putting the last first.* Harlow: Longman.

COTGROVE, S. (1976). Environmentalism and Utopia. *The Sociological Review,* **18**, 23–42.

CURTIN, P. (1964). *The Image of Africa.* Oxford: Oxford University Press.

DARLING, F.F. (1960). *Wildlife in an African Territory.* Lusaka: Game and Tsetse Control Department, Govt of Northern Rhodesia.

DOUGLAS, M. & WILDAVSKY, A. (1982). *Risk and Culture: an essay in the selection of technical and environmental dangers.* Los Angeles: University of California Press.

FREUD, S. (1921). *The Future of an Illusion.* London: Hogarth Press.

GRAHAM, A.D. (1973). *The Gardeners of Eden.* London: George Allen & Unwin.

GROVE, R. (1987). Conservation and Colonialism: the development of environmental attitudes and conservation policies in the British Imperial context, with special reference to India, Mauritius, and the Cape Colony, 1814–1914. Unpublished Ph.D. thesis, University of Cambridge.

✶ GRZIMEK, B & GRZIMEK, M. (1965). *Serengeti Shall Not Die*. London: Hamish Hamilton.

HARRISON, P. (1984). *Inside the Third World: the anatomy of poverty*. London: Penguin.

HEMINGWAY, E. (1936). *The Green Hills of Africa*. London: Jonathan Cape.

HILL, P. (1986). *Development Economics on Trial: the anthropological case for a prosecution*. Cambridge: Cambridge University Press.

✓ HUXLEY, E. (1959). *The Flame Trees of Thika*. London: Chatto & Windus.

HUXLEY, E. (1962). *The Mottled Lizard*. London: Chatto & Windus.

IUCN (1980). *World Conservation Strategy*. Gland, Switzerland: International Union for the Conservation of Nature and Natural Resources.

JOHNSON, D.H. & ANDERSON, D.M., ed. (1987). *The Ecology of Survival: Case Studies from Northeast African History*. London: Crook Academic Press.

LOWE, P.D. (1980). Ecology as Ideology. In *Rural Sociology of Advanced Societies*. ed. F. Buttel, F. Cavazzani & H. Newby. London: Croom Helm.

LOWE, P.D. & GOYDER, J.M. (1983). *Environmental Groups and Politics*. London: George Allen & Unwin.

MAIR, L. (1984). *Anthropology and Development*. London: Macmillan.

MARKS, S. (1984). *The Imperial Lion: human dimensions of wildlife management in Africa*. Epping: Bowker.

✓ MARNHAM, P. (1980). *Fantastic Invasion: Despatches from Contemporary Africa*. London: Jonathan Cape.

✓ MARX, L. (1964). *The Machine in the Garden: technology and the pastoral ideal in America*. Oxford: Oxford University Press.

MAZRUI, A. (1980). *The African Condition: a political diagnosis*. Cambridge: Cambridge University Press.

NASH, R. (1967). *Wilderness and the American Mind*. New Haven, Connecticut: Yale University Press.

OLWIG, K.F. & OLWIG, K. (1980). Conflicting perceptions of nature in an 'American Paradise': the problems of American-style National Parks in the Third World. Unpublished typescript, Department of Geography, University of Copenhagen.

O'RIORDAN, T. (1967). *Environmentalism*. London: Pion Press.

PASSMORE, J. (1974). *Man's Responsibility for Nature: ecological problems and western traditions*. London: Duckworth.

POWELL, J.M. (1976). *Environmental Management in Australia, 1788–1914: Guardians, Improvers and Profit: an introductory survey*. Melbourne: Oxford University Press.

REDCLIFT, M. (1984). *Development and the Environmental Crisis: red or green alternatives?* London: Methuen.

✓ RICHARDS, P. (1983). Ecological change and the politics of African land-use. *African Studies Review*, **26** (2), 1–72.

RICHARDS, P. (1985). *Indigenous Agricultural Revolution*. London: Hutchinson.

SINCLAIR, A.R.E. & FRYXELL, J.M. (1985). The Sahel of Africa: ecology of a disaster. *Canadian Journal of Ecology*, **63**, 987–94.

SMITH, A. (1980). *How Western Culture Dominates the World*. New York: Oxford University Press.

TIMBERLAKE, L. (1985). *Africa in Crisis: the causes, the cures of environmental bankruptcy*. London: Earthscan.

VANCE, M. (1982). *Wilderness*. Moray: Findhorn Press.

WORTHINGTON, E.B. (1958). *Science in the Development of Africa*. Paris: Commission for Technical Cooperation in Africa South of the Sahara.

WORTHINGTON, E.B. (1983). *The Ecological Century: a personal appraisal*. Oxford: Clarendon Press.

WWF/IUCN (1983). *World Wildlife Fund/International Union for the Conservation of Nature*, Occasional Paper no. 1. Godalming: WWF/IUCN.

PART ONE

Conservation ideologies in Africa

Introduction

WILLIAM BEINART

Conservation, as the conference discussion of the chapters collected here revealed, means different things to different people. Those working within scientific and technical disciplines tended to see the conservation of Africa's natural resources as a necessary and urgent task in which experts should play a central role. Some emphasised aesthetic and scientific values, as well as man's responsibility to the future, and displayed a certain humility in the confrontation with nature. They warned of the dire long-term consequences of the destruction of particular natural environments and advocated that these be protected. Others felt that the intensity of the demand for resources in rural Africa, and the creeping process of privatisation, would ultimately lead to the failure of protectionist strategies. Conservationists, they argued, should run with the tide. Game would be more securely protected by commercial game farming for meat and hunting; this would also necessitate the preservation of natural habitats in which the animals could survive. In the agricultural sphere, private gain would provide the incentive for longer-term maintenance of soil fertility and watersheds under changing conditions; interventions should be planned accordingly.

But a number of the social scientists raised more fundamental questions about the motivations for and results of conservation policies. Some suggested that major schemes, involving extensive land-use planning, or the reservation of game parks, or controlled irrigated farming, had totally or partly failed because they were insensitive, or directly inimical to the interests of local people (Collett, Chapter 6; Hogg, Chapter 14). Local practices with regard to the exploitation of natural resources had seldom been studied closely enough; ideas about ecology, land use plans and concepts such as the carrying capacity of grazing land had been imposed inflexibly from outside (Homewood & Rodgers, Chapter 5; Little & Brokensha, Chapter 9).

Papers and discussions along these lines – some of which are included in this Part – were far less sanguine about the role of outside experts.

15

They raised questions about what was being conserved, by whom, for whom, and from whom. Those investigating the history of conservationist thinking and policy argued that these ideas had deep roots in the colonial encounter: many of the solutions now canvassed had been widely debated and even implemented in earlier decades. They suggested that technical experts needed to be far more self-conscious about the background and social context of their disciplines, and about previous attempts at intervention. Past policy and schemes should be analysed not only in order to evaluate which had been successfully implemented, but also for insights into the implications and legacy of earlier scientific ideas and conservationist 'ideologies'.

One significant point which emerges from the chapters in this Part, as well as other recent research, is that the history of ideas about conservation is multi-faceted. Colonial concern about forests and afforestation, the slaughter of game, soil erosion, desertification and overstocking, for example, arose at different times and in different contexts. Certainly some Victorian protagonists of conservation, like John Croumbie Brown at the Cape whose important but largely forgotten work is being investigated by Grove (Chapter 1), conceived of a more holistic approach. And, in broad terms, those arguing for conservation in all these spheres might be said to have been against overexploitation of natural resources for immediate gain, and in favour of some degree of control by the state. But each phase of colonial rule in different countries, as well as shifts in technical thinking and scientific disciplines, brought new problems, priorities and solutions to the fore.

Game preservation is a case in point, and its history also serves well to raise questions about some of the motives behind, and problems with, conservationist ideas. As MacKenzie illustrates in Chapter 2, Victorian attitudes to African animals were, to put it mildly, predatory. Vast quantities of animals were slaughtered, whether for profit, or for meat to feed settlers and their bearers, or for 'sport'. Yet by the turn of the twentieth century, the increasing scarcity of larger game animals especially in southern Africa contributed, along with more general social and economic changes, to produce a significant shift in attitudes. Hunting for subsistence and gain gave way, amongst the growing colonial élite, to 'the Hunt' as a socially exclusive pleasure pursuit. Concern amongst settler landowners to retain some wild animals on their farms coincided with the wider growth of scientific and aesthetic interest in game. Those without property who attempted to claim natural rights to hunt increasingly became defined as poachers and acted against as such (Vaughan, 1978; Trapido, 1983). It is a deep irony of colonial history that some of the most ardent game conservationists came from the same social group of travellers, settlers and officials which a generation earlier had produced some of the most bloodthirsty hunters.

It was at this time also, in the early twentieth century, that game reserves were first demarcated on a significant scale. Local African people found themselves deprived not only of a former supplement to their diet and income but also sometimes of seasonal grazing lands and even arable plots. And, as McCracken illustrates in Chapter 3, the demarcation of game reserves, together with other colonial measures which probably had the effect of allowing game numbers to increase in the early decades of the century, facilitated the spread of tsetse belts in colonial Malawi. McCracken does not, however, suggest that conservationist imperatives were mainly responsible for the spread of the fly. Culling of game to control tsetse was hampered more by lack of finance and state capacity than by official desire to protect animals; this strategy was, in any case, insufficient by itself.

In more recent years, the ideas behind reserves have again shifted. In theory they have become open to all to view animals. And, as social concern has impinged on conservation thinking, some attempts have been made to integrate herders and cultivators into controlled areas – seen not only as game reserves but as complete natural habitats – rather than to exclude them completely. But, although such areas might prove to be assets considered valuable by local people in the longer term, access remains rather restricted and conflicts over resources are by no means resolved. Tourists, those with cars, and the scientific and media communities who study and publicise the contents of the parks are still the main viewers of game. The success of the international and national wildlife organisations in inserting African animals into the imagination of the western world draws on old-established strands in ideas about Africa: a contradictory set of attitudes that would at once see Africa developed and wild. Africa is seen to provide wildernesses for the world at large – especially in developed countries where land and natural resources have been exploited more intensively for longer periods and conservation programmes have been initiated from a less 'natural' baseline.

Ideas shaping soil conservation policies have a rather different history (Anderson, 1984; Beinart, 1984). The 1930s, when the American dust bowl catapulted the problem of soil erosion into international consciousness, is generally recognised as the period in which colonial administrations in Africa launched more extensive investigations and remedial works. Soil conservation became seen as an urgent necessity and, in the context of the colonial world, much of the blame was laid on African farming practices and African attitudes to cattle in conditions of 'land shortage'. It has, however, been suggested that concern about soil conservation in Africa had far deeper roots and was not merely a sudden response to the perceived crises of the early 1930s. Some officials, in southern Africa particularly, attempted to alert settler farmers to the dangers of soil erosion and the 'mining' of land as agricultural production expanded in the previous few decades. As in the case of game preservationists, they wished to control the capacity of private individuals to destroy the natural environment for private gain – and to ensure the longer term viability of agrarian accumulation.

Grove's work points to an even earlier conservation lobby in the Cape and India in the nineteenth century. Control of forests was sometimes deemed necessary in order to assure supplies of wood for naval and other strategic and public uses. Research into, and classification of, plant species by medical officials and botanists enabled them to see at first hand the destructive effects of new agricultural practices and alerted them to the need for protection. By the second half of the nineteenth century, the linkages between tree cover, the incidence of rainfall, the holding of soil and water in watersheds, and soil erosion were being more widely canvassed. Forestry became seen as a more integral part of agricultural improvement in the wider sphere. This was especially so in drier environments with highly seasonal rainfall patterns and where irrigation projects were being investigated. Nineteenth-century imperial concern, Grove argues, shaped the way in which the problem of soil conservation was later conceived; the legislation passed in the Cape – innovative in the context of the empire as a whole – was drawn on in African colonies and elsewhere.

One feature of these early interventions – which bears comparison with ideas about game preservation – was the commitment to protectionist strategies implemented by the state. Especially from the 1930s, however, far more emphasis was laid on the need to change methods of farming and stock-keeping rather than just to exclude agriculturalists from forests, watersheds and stream banks. Terraces, ridges, grass strips and bunds, rotational systems of grazing and cropping, and cattle culling all came into favour in various colonies; the increasing size, capacity and expertise of agriculture departments made such radical measures seem possible for the first time. But these much more interventionist strategies, which directly affected the way in which peasants used their land, pushed conservation to the heart of political conflicts between peasants and colonial states. The experiments with, and attempts to introduce, more total land use planning after the Second World War served to intensify opposition to conservation measures. This legacy of political conflict over agricultural schemes survived the transition to independence.

Some of the interventions in African agriculture were not without success. But the problems experienced, especially in major schemes, have persuaded some technical experts to reconsider their strategies and call for 'conservation with a human face'. Bell, in Chapter 4, again points to the potential for conflict between conservationist and planning ideals on the one hand, and the requirements of local communities on the other. He also emphasises the need for far greater sensitivity to African methods of coping with their environment, and with ecological crises. It could be argued that the question of whose world is being planned by whom, and to what end, must be asked even more forcefully in the current context, as drought and starvation have gripped large swathes of the continent. Overarching intervention seems a vital and urgent task: many African communities, especially in East Africa, seem bereft of resources with which to respond; total dislocation might suggest that reconstruction can be built on completely new foundations. Popular opinion in the West, fuelled by Band Aid, demands that something be done not only to feed Africa but to 'develop' it and protect its natural resources. But those who have investigated the history of conservation and agricultural planning may find this new call to action rather ingenuous. While the social concern is admirable, and technical experts must surely play a central role, many of the following chapters suggest that this burst of enthusiasm should be tempered by a clear understanding of the politics of conservation and the history of outside intervention.

References

ANDERSON, D.M. (1984). Depression, Dust Bowl, Demography and Drought: the Colonial State and soil conservation in East Africa during the 1930s. *African Affairs*, **83** (332), 321–43.

BEINART, W. (1984). Soil erosion, conservationism, and ideas about development in Southern Africa. *Journal of Southern African Studies*, **11** (2), 52–83.

TRAPIDO, S. (1983). Poachers, proletarians and gentry in the early twentieth century Transvaal. Institute of Commonwealth Studies Seminar Paper, London.

VAUGHAN, M. (1978). Uncontrolled animals and aliens: colonial conservation mania in Malawi. Staff Research Seminar Paper, History Department, University of Malawi.

1

Early themes in African conservation: the Cape in the nineteenth century

RICHARD GROVE

By the later part of the eighteenth century European colonial expansion and economic penetration in North America, southern Africa and India had begun to cause major environmental changes. Industrialisation in Europe, and especially in Britain, helped to accelerate this process. The nature and timing of these changes is still the subject of debate, but it is clear that by the turn of the century deforestation was already taking place at an unprecedented pace in many colonial territories, as well as in China and the United States (Goudie, 1981; Richards *et al.*, 1985). Although the environmental impact of European expansion caused trepidation among contemporary observers throughout the colonies, accounts of the way in which embryonic environmental anxieties were transformed into fully-fledged conservation policies have so far been confined to the United States (Hays, 1959; Nash, 1967; Worster, 1977). As a result, major misconceptions have arisen with respect to the derivation of conservation ideas outside the United States. One commentator, for example, tells us that 'Conservation has often been hailed as one of America's major contributions to world reform movements, in that its ideas were eventually exported to Great Britain and other nations. All this is true. . .' (Worster, 1977). American influences have recently been further stressed in relation to the transfer of twentieth-century American preoccupations with soil erosion and conservation to the African colonies (Beinart, 1984; Helms & Flader, 1985). These views have, in some respects, discouraged attempts to look further back into African colonial history for the antecedents of twentieth-century conservation policies, or to understand the intellectual exchanges which took place between individual colonies from the 1830s (Grove, 1987a).

This chapter examines the significance of the colonial context in shaping conservation policies, by taking a closer look at the perceptions of the Victorian observers of the African environment in the Cape Colony. Nineteenth-century fears of ecological disaster in the Cape Colony were largely locally derived in origin and based chiefly on empirical observations of rapid deforestation and increased frequency of flood occurrence and soil erosion. These anxieties first surfaced in the 1840s, but gathered momentum in the period of social reassessment and philosophical turmoil in the natural sciences during the years leading up to and in the decade after the publication in 1859 of Darwin's *The Origin of Species*. They were paralleled in other parts of the Empire outside Africa. In India, for example, environmental concerns were translated into government action with forest conservation policies in the Madras and Bombay Presidencies in 1847 and 1857 respectively, and there were analogous developments in Mauritius (Grove, 1987b). These interventionist policies in the colonies had evolved well before the publication of *Man and Nature* by G.P. Marsh in 1864, the event normally connected with the beginnings of government conservation efforts in the United States. The purpose of this survey is to identify the intellectual components of the early conservation propaganda wielded at the Cape, and to point to the importance of conceptual milestones in early Cape conservation.

In studying the derivation of conservation ideas and policy in Africa, particular attention must be paid to the personal beliefs and actions of the early colonial scientist or expert. In the evolution of colonial environmental attitudes and policies a whole gamut of scientific and other arguments has been used by scientists to promote particular social strategies or even idiosyncratic enthusiasms. Once a body of environmental attitudes became firmly established, selected scientific arguments were canvassed according to both their social expediency and their capacity to be politically convincing and to mirror, often temporarily, governmental or societal preoccupations. In the context of a perceived crisis, these scientific arguments were often taken over by propagandists, some of them scientists, as expedients to mobilise government action. Public statements of the time influenced the colonial response to ecological change in Africa, but they do not offer the best guide to longer-term environmental perceptions affecting policy. The intellectual antecedents and allegiances of the propagandists themselves are important in this respect, although often difficult to elucidate. The consensus required to initiate an environmental policy in the colonies was narrower than in metropolitan societies, and the role of a very few interested individuals could therefore easily come to acquire considerable significance. Partly for this reason, nineteenth-century environmental ideas nurtured in the European mind found their field of prosecution (often quite literally), as did hunting ideologies, in the colonial rather than the metropolitan context (MacKenzie, Chapter 2). Interventionist conservation policies were, in a very real sense, much easier to experiment with in the colonies.

This transfer of the environmental costs of early European industrialisation to the colonies only makes the need to examine the characteristics of conservation policies in the colonial situation more urgent. Much of the ideology of modern conservation thinking actually emerged out of colonial rather than metropolitan conditions (Grove, 1987a), and in this context the Cape experience is of particular importance.

The origins of conservation at the Cape, 1811–54

The first phase of a conservationist debate about the uses of the Cape environment arose in connection with the fate of the larger forests along the southern coast, following the reservation in 1811 of forests at Plettenberg Bay for the use of the Royal Navy (Sim, 1907; cf. Ribbentrop, 1899). The subsequent decision of the Navy Board that these Cape woods were unsuited for Navy use, particularly for masting needs, provoked a public debate involving government, settlers, and the Cape newspapers, about the management and ownership of the forests. This catalysed a wider discussion about the role of government in managing both forest and veldt (Darnell, 1866). By 1846 haphazard exploitation of forests had become obviously destructive of large areas of timber, while the state of pastures and scrubland surrounding Cape Town was the subject of public comment. It seems that once settler opinion had become conscious of the lack of management in one area, attention could then be easily shifted to defining other environmental problems. Public opinion at the Cape was sufficiently vocal by 1846 to ensure the passing of an Ordinance dedicated to 'the better preservation of the Cape Flats and Downs' (Sim, 1907). From this measure, designed in the first place to check soil erosion and sand blow in the Cape Flats, the continuance of a concerted measure of urban-based and essentially aesthetically derived environmental thinking can be dated.

Much of the lobbying to establish the 1846 Ordinance was carried out by Dr Ludwig Pappe, an Austrian surgeon who had already established himself in a non-stipendiary role as the 'Cape Botanist', at a time when the only other similar post in the Empire was held by Dr Fraser as Colonial Botanist in New South Wales (Powell, 1976). Pappe, who earned his living as a medical practitioner and surgeon, brought to the Cape that connection between environmental concern and the medical profession which was instrumental in the development of state conservation in India (Grove, 1987b). In 1846 he had commenced a correspondence with the Director of Kew, Sir William Hooker, on the state of the Cape flora, a flora which Hooker held to be second only to that of India, by

reason of its high degree of speciation. This alliance between the Cape
scientist and botanical science in Britain was to prove important in terms
of government influence. From 1846 until 1858 the increasing prominence
of Pappe as a lobbyist for protectionist policies and as a scientist formally
consulted by Government ostensibly on matters to do with 'economic
botany' meant that, apart from the interest of Cape Town European
opinion in urban amenities, at least three elements were present in the
debates about Cape land use; the protection of forests, the role of a
botanic garden for disseminating scientific knowledge, and the protection
of plant and animal species.

The institutional role of the botanic garden became central to the
emergence of conservationist ideas at the Cape. The original botanic
garden at Kaap Stad had been set up as the 'Governor's Garden' by the
Netherlands East India Company in 1685, for the cultivation of useful
imported plants (Lighton, 1973). After the cession to the British in 1806
the garden fell into disuse and by 1828 Whitehall had rejected the idea
of resurrecting the garden on the grounds that 'beautifying a garden'
could not justify large public expenditure.[1] In 1845 the question of reestablishing it was raised once again in a letter to the Cape Government,
signed by various individuals including Pappe and members of the
Agricultural Society of Swellendam, one of the foremost settler farming
societies. Hooker also wrote from Kew at the instigation of Pappe,
suggesting a new site for a botanic garden on Table Mountain. Opinions
at this stage were divided about the purpose of a botanic garden. The
Cape Mail, in an editorial, stressed the economic advantages the garden
could bring.[2] By contrast, a four-man Commission appointed by the
Cape Government to consider the question, stressed the aesthetic and
amenity aspects of the garden. Pappe himself, in a further letter to
Hooker, highlighted the advantages for public education, and was later
in 1848 to state publicly the economic potential of the botanic garden
for the exchange of plants with other colonies. In the context of the
micro-environment which the botanic garden represented, a discussion
about environmental values had already begun, in which the economic
value was traded against the aesthetic. However, for the rest of the 1840s
proper funding was not forthcoming for the botanic garden and Pappe
eventually resigned from the Commission.

At the behest of Hooker, Pappe devoted himself after 1846 to compiling
the standard work on Cape trees and shrubs, the *Silva Capensis* (Pappe,
1862). The work involved extensive travelling during the course of which
Pappe was further able to monitor the depredations being made on
forests, particularly in the old cedar forests of the Cedarberg. The writings

of other observers heightened Pappe's awareness of the speed of deforestation, and he was certainly familiar with Alexander's comment that Cape forests were 'fast disappearing under the destroying hand of man . . . no one takes charge of the trees, nor is a word spoken to save them' (Alexander, 1838). Such perceptions encouraged Pappe to adopt the *Silva Capensis* as a vehicle for spreading the conservationist gospel, his introduction to the first edition dwelling at length on the loss of huge areas of woodland by fire damage from the spread of seasonal veldt fires both on Table Mountain and around the Cedarberg.

The beginnings of intervention, 1854–66

The advent of the Cape Legislative Assembly in 1854 transformed the status of the embryonic conservation lobby, which until that date lacked legislative credibility. Without such a political shift it is doubtful whether comprehensive conservation measures would have emerged. Specifically, the existence of a representative House of Assembly allowed both pro- and anti-conservationist settler opinion to be more quickly mediated and transmuted into legislative action. In 1854 a Commission appointed by the House of Assembly ended the legacy of indecision about the administration of the Cape forests and condemned the structure of existing property rights and timber concessions worked by private owners. In February 1856 Conservancies were set up in the forests of the George region. Hesitating in its egalitarian enthusiasm, however, the Assembly decided that private property rights should be retained in part. This was a strategy, encouraging the competition of Government and private interests, of a type which was eventually to be decisively rejected by the Government of India in 1861 (Stebbing, 1922). In allowing competition between state and private interests the Assembly created the germ of future problems which were to destroy the first phase of Cape Government conservation by 1866, the year in which H.B. Darnell, an Assembly member, wrote that 'Government entered into competition with the private interests, ruinous to both' (Darnell 1866). Significantly enough, the Cape Government, many members of which during the 1850s were enthusiasts for natural history, adopted a hostile attitude to private ownership of the larger forests. Thus, the suggestion of the Assembly that private owners should be compensated for loss of forest rights was condemned by a report of the Auditor-General which spoke of 'the noble natural forest'. So from 1855 to 1866 both the Government and the Assembly, though the latter somewhat less consistently, supported a thoroughgoing conservation policy.

Much of the impetus for this may be related to the influence of Pappe and a few other individuals, above all Rawson W. Rawson, the ex-Colonial Secretary of Mauritius. Rawson had succeeded to the Cape Governorship in 1853 and brought with him both a keen anxiety about the consequences of deforestation (which was much more acute in Mauritius) and an interest in natural history. The latter led him to co-author a book on the ferns of the Cape Colony together with Ludwig Pappe (Pappe & Rawson, 1858). The relationship between Pappe and Rawson was an important one for the evolution of conservation legislation at the Cape. Essentially their acquaintance represented the union of two distinct types of environmental preoccupation. Pappe was principally taken up by the possibility of species extinctions and it was partly in this respect that the high rate of forest clearance worried him. Rawson, on the other hand, was a close intellectual associate of Louis Bouton, the Secretary of the Mauritius Royal Society.[3] Bouton, a keen advocate of the theories of Humboldt and Boussingault, had long preached the risks of deforestation and its supposed connections with rainfall decline (Grove 1987a). Rawson felt that the risks at the Cape were just as great. Furthermore his letters to Bouton from the Cape indicate his high regard for Pappe's intimate knowledge of the situation at the Cape. It was not surprising, then, that, as Governor, Rawson should have supported Pappe's demand for government intervention to prevent further deforestation and veldt deterioration.

In 1858 Pappe was officially appointed Chief Botanist of the Cape Colony. In practice, although not on paper, his official duty was to promote conservation ideas, in a very broad sense, throughout the colony. His wide, although still vague, remit had no real precedent and he was quick to take advantage of this. The first-fruit of his efforts to cultivate a consciousness of the conservation needs of the colony was the Forest and Herbage Preservation Act no. 18 of 1859. The successful passage of the Act owed much to the efforts of Sir William Hooker, whose help had been enlisted by Pappe, and it remained the basis for conservation legislation in South Africa until the Union, surviving in a slightly modified form as the Forestry Act no. 22 of 1888. This legislation, the most comprehensive form of conservation legislation passed in British colonies during the nineteenth century, owed a great deal to the controversy which had surrounded the Knysna forests. The initial passage of the law was enabled by the hard lobbying of a few scientists and an Assembly determined to put an end to the anarchical forest situation which had arisen as a legacy of past partial and ambiguous regulations, which had their origins in early Dutch timber rules.

The appointment of a Colonial Botanist in 1858 was only part of a wide picture of growing environmental regulation. In 1858 Government Notice 263 was issued concerning the 'Preservation of Elephants and Buffaloes'. This formalised a latent (and mainly urban) interest in the protection of the remaining isolated population of large mammals in the South Cape forests, which had been heavily reduced by ivory hunting. Indeed, exports of ivory had reached a peak in 1858 (Kerr, 1886). Simultaneously, the government had begun to set up what were effectively the first "state' game reserves in Africa, in the Knysna and Tsitsikamme forests. These measures probably reflected an urban-based interest in animal protection, which paralleled contemporary moves towards animal protectionism in Britain at the time (Turner, 1981). Their enforcement proved extremely difficult, given both bad communications and hostile rural attitudes to forest and game protection. A stream of correspondence on the obstacles encountered by Forest Conservators based at Uitenhage, who had to administer the Game Preservation laws, ensued between the conservators and the Governor's office.[4] Although the government enjoyed enthusiastic Cape Town press support for its protection policies in the pages of the *Cape Mail*, tension between Forest Conservators and farmers owning land adjacent to the forest reserves remained high and the poaching problem insoluble.

The rapid evolution after 1858 of conservation regulations proved the value of government sanction in protecting the landscape. The Official Reports of the Colonial Botanists published annually between 1859 and 1866 amounted to a developing and coherent programme for soil, water, forest and species conservation, generally in that order of priority (Cape Government, 1859–66). In his 1860 Report, Pappe concentrated on the risks of forest destruction in relation to rainfall incidence, though emphasising the aesthetic, botanical and economic value of the woods which were being destroyed (Cape Government, 1860). In the formal adoption of a climatic argument for the first time in the Cape he was influenced by the successful use of this argument by the East India surgeon–botanists of the Bombay and Madras Presidencies. These had culminated in the presentation at the British Association in 1851 of a Report on the economic consequences of tropical forest destruction (British Association, 1852) which helped to lead to the adoption, in principle, of an integrated state Forest Conservancy policy for the whole of India by Governor Dalhousie in 1854 (Grove, 1987a). Worried as they were by the prospects of species disappearing, the strength of the arguments used by conservationists in India during the 1840s lay not in the fear of species extinction (which carried little weight with government, anyway) but in the connections new developments in the life sciences were allowing them to make between deforestation and the incidence of famine. Extensive deforestation, they argued, would certainly increase the likelihood of famine. Implicitly therefore, if the state did not protect forests, it could be held responsible for an increased incidence of famine, with all the social consequences that this entailed. It was this dour message which accounted for the success of medical botanists in India in persuading an initially very reluctant government to commence large-scale forest conservation. As surgeons and botanists (and thus as early scientists), the staff of the East India Company Medical Service could rely on their high social status with government (Grove, 1987b). These arguments strengthened the case of the Colonial Botanists at the Cape, and as a medical botanist Pappe enjoyed a similar standing to his Indian colleagues. The humanistic ideological basis of early Indian conservation was thus inherited by Pappe. However, as a public justification for conservation at the Cape, this was soon to give way to more prominent considerations, in a manner again following the pattern of Indian experience.

The recurrence of drought at the Cape was a matter of persistent concern for both settlers and scientists. A serious drought in 1847 had caused considerable alarm, but the severity of the 1862 drought was to have significant consequences for the conservation ideologies then evolving at the Cape. This drought coincided with the death of Pappe and the appointment of a Scotsman, John Croumbie Brown, as second Colonial Botanist. The appointment was recommended by a member of the Legislative Assembly, Saul Solomon, who had known Brown during an earlier posting with the London Missionary Society in the Cape. Both men shared a concern for social reform and held pronounced humanitarian convictions, as well as sharing an interest in conservation (Gladstone–Solomon, 1948). Solomon was already an advocate of plantation forestry as a safeguard to water supplies in degraded semi-arid areas, having witnessed the successful application of such schemes on his native St Helena, and on Ascension Island after their initiation by the East India Company during the 1820s.

Brown had observed the 1847 drought, and later reported his shock at the effects the famine brought in its wake to the more remote parts of the Cape:

I witnessed the privations to which the inhabitants were subjected through the aridity of the climate . . . my recollections of the journey call up vividly even now oft-recurring visions of bones of oxen at varying distances along the road – the bones of men which had succumbed by the way of travelling, in a land where no water is. . .   *(Brown, 1875)*

Brown was a self-confessed aesthete in the contemporary Scottish intellectual tradition which was at that time nurturing a splendid neo-Roman-
ticist school of landscape painting. He waxed lyrical over the Knysna
scenery which he found 'truly grand and lovers of the beauties of nature
will find themselves fully repaid for any inconvenience which may have
been the result of a rough voyage'. The connection between the development of a conservation policy in the Cape and the Scottish Romanticist
proclivities of Brown was a significant one. However, it was not a unique
connection. John Muir and Hugh Cleghorn, both key figures in the
cultivating of a consciousness of environmental issues in the United
States and India respectively, seem to have inherited the same cultural
preoccupations as Brown (Nash, 1967; Grove, 1987b). As colonial officials Cleghorn and Brown also shared a fear of the effects of famine on
social stability. On his appointment, in the midst of the 1862 drought,
Brown toured the whole of the colony and its dependency of British
Kaffraria and then wrote in somewhat millennial terms:

It was thus that I was led . . . to means by which a more satisfactory treatment
of the remaining forests might be secured and that the disastrous consequences
of what had been done might be averted.   *(Brown, 1875)*

The 1862 drought marked a perceptive turning point among the whole
settler community and produced a willing and attentive audience of
white farmers, as Brown set about an extraordinary programme, presenting to scientific and agricultural societies during 1863–5 hundreds of
educational lectures and seminars on the dangers of veldt burning, forest
destruction and the consequences which it might have for soil erosion
and flooding. Many of these addresses, amounting almost to one-man
agricultural extension courses, are detailed in his Official Reports. He
also began a voluminous correspondence not only with settler farmers,
eliciting information on drought conditions, but with botanists on almost
every continent, comparing notes on botany, environmental aridification,
and many other subjects (e.g. Brown, 1866). His 1863 Official Report
shocked the House of Assembly into realising the need to back its 1859
legislation with rigorous agricultural advice (Cape Government, 1863).

In 1864 an Assembly Select Committee on soil erosion, drought and
associated problems was set up, to which Brown was invited to give
evidence in 1865.[5] Brown's recommendations to the Committee listed
five main measures as a basis for the strengthening of existing legislation:

1. ' An attempt to arrest the desiccation of the soil and climate which has been
and is being occasioned by the burning of the veldt, by the partial or entire
abandonment of the prevalent practice.

2.   An attempt to counteract the desiccation of soil and climate which has already been effected by the destruction of herbage and bush in time past by the general and extensive planting of forest trees.

3.   An attempt to increase still further the humidity of the climate which has already been affected by the formation of inland sheets of water, either with or without appliances for the irrigation of arable land.

4.   The establishment of an experimental farm where the possibility of profit being realised by the culture of different crops and the utilisation of their products may be tested and whence information on practical subjects connected therewith may be supplied to all requiring it.

5.   The procuring from other countries of information over and above what is accessible in the colony, in regard to arboriculture and forest economy, in regard to methods of conducting experimental farms and in regard to markets which are open for our products, the uses to which these products are applied and the possibility of presenting them in a state calculated to secure a greater demand or higher prices.

Here, for the first time, particular emphasis was placed on the protection of semi-arid pasturage, which had emerged as pre-eminent in importance in the Cape agrarian economy, with the emphasis on forest protection somewhat reduced. The specific linking of issues of soil deterioration and climate extended Pappe's enlistment of Indian and Mauritian climatic concerns, once again, for the purpose of encouraging a deeper degree of state intervention across the whole field of agricultural operation, and outside the formally established Forest and Game Reserves. Even in their details Brown's recommendations presage those made by the South African Drought Commission of 1922 and later by the Colonial Office in recommending the establishment of experimental farms (Drought Commission, 1922; Beinart, 1984). Indeed, among others, Hall, writing in the *South African Journal of Science* (Hall, 1934) copiously acknowledged the debt owed by twentieth-century scientists to the foresight and imaginative vision of Brown in his warnings for the future of pastoral agriculture in southern Africa, which at the time he considered were still going largely unheeded.

Brown was, indeed, a man ahead of his time. He does not appear to have anticipated how deeply his proposals would be opposed both by white settler farming groups and, more especially, by Cape Town timber traders. By 1866 the memory of the 1862 drought was fading and the perceived ease of settler expansion towards the east had become apparent, lessening the sense of resource shortage and crisis. In this altered context the climatic hazard argument lost its efficacy, and Brown, always more outspoken and less of a diplomat than Pappe, lost his support in the Cape Assembly. Aspersions were cast upon his scientific professionalism. It was suggested that he had overreached his remit as Colonial Botanist and that he should have confined himself to botanical collecting. Such sentiments had not been heard in 1862, but in 1866 one bolder Assembly member remarked that:

The country has been thrown back by many years, nor does there seem to be any prospect of improvement while the forest lasts. Instead of being a source of wealth to the people, it is a mockery, a delusion, and a snare and will continue to be a burden upon the colony so long as it is thought necessary to keep up the farce of conservation. *(in Sim, 1907)*

On 18 December 1866, among a flurry of economic retrenchment measures, funding for the Office of Colonial Botanist was withdrawn and Brown was forced into bitter and premature retirement, a victim of his own success as an advocate of state conservationism. Brown left the Cape Colony almost immediately, despite the implorings of Saul Solomon, who believed, probably correctly, that the post, if not the policies, could be retrieved by patient lobbying. After his return to Scotland, Brown went on to produce a stream of books and articles on forest and water conservation in southern Africa and elsewhere. He also maintained a wide correspondence in the Cape and further afield with those whose acquaintance he had made as Colonial Botanist, and so continued to exert a major innovatory influence over the development of colonial conservation policies (Brown, 1881, 1885, 1887).

Conservation intervention after 1866

A significant, almost global, intellectual exchange on the environmental problems of the Empire had begun to take shape among the British scientific community by 1852 with, for example, the publication of the British Association report on tropical forest destruction (British Association, 1852). It was beginning to be translated by 1866 into a pattern of state intervention co-ordinated at a metropolitan level with reference to more than one colony. In a sense the process had been begun after 1840 by William and Joseph Hooker, father and son, as Directors of Kew. The East India Company Court of Directors Despatch to Indian local government officials on the subject of tree cover and climatic change in 1847 had been another instance of the type of environmental information gathering facility which the colonising role allowed (Government of India, 1880). These had remained somewhat rarefied in application, however, the one relating specifically to the acquisition of scientific material and the other to the solution of one particularly threatening problem. Nevertheless the precedent was established, and was first used on an Empire-wide scale in 1876 when Whitehall circularised all colonies and even some non-colonial territories to obtain information on existing models of game and wildlife protection legislation. This search for models was probably made at the instigation of Alfred Newton, Professor of Zoology at Cambridge, and progenitor of the first British bird protection legislation of the 1860s (Grove, 1987a).

Both Kew and the British Association played a major part in advocating centralised encouragement of conservation ideas. The departure of Brown from the Cape, and the subsequent depredations on the Cape forests by railway timber interests, had temporarily put a stop to state conservation at the Cape, demonstrating how critical the presence of trained scientists was both in assessing qualitatively the consequences of colonial economic penetration and in ensuring that solutions were attempted. The progress in forest conservancy which had taken place in India had been originated and guided by medical staff present as an integral part of the colonial infrastructure. Their continued official role was not dependent, as Brown's had been, on the whim of a Representative Assembly. Joseph Hooker was well aware of this problem and, furthermore, of the need for continuity of policy. In 1872, for example, he quoted Brown's descriptions of land degradation in the Cape widely in his lobbyings of government for the formal training of Forest Conservation officers for the whole of the colonial service. India, he considered, was the only colonial territory in which a satisfactory situation pertained (Hooker, 1872).

It was, however, in southern Africa itself that Brown's post-redundancy propagandising first took effect, stimulated by his publication of *The Hydrology of South Africa* in 1875. Brown had, in fact, been encouraged to write this book, the first summary of his own extensive research, by G.P. Marsh, whose writings are widely held to have stimulated the initial growth of the conservation and national park movement in the United States. Brown's first comprehensive explanatory treatise on environmental degradation in the Colony in the form of his Official Reports had, in fact, appeared some time before Marsh published *Man and Nature* in 1864.

Given prominence by the coordination of conservation ideology outside Africa, it was not long before Brown's writings were put into practice in the colonies and in southern Africa in particular. In 1876 the Umhlanga Planters' Association of Natal took up Brown's views, 'a very interesting paper being read before the Association on the subject of forests in relation to rain' (Government of Natal, 1880). Following on this, the Governor of Natal was prevailed upon by the small white settler community (in much the same way as the Cape Governor had been pressured to set up a botanic garden Commission by the Agricultural Society of Swellendam in 1845) to set up a 'Commission to enquire into and report upon the extent and condition of the forest lands in the colony'. The Commission was not actually formally instituted until 1878, but its report was published by the end of 1880 (Government of Natal, 1880). The report was a remarkable *tour de force*, being a thorough and scholarly survey of the conservation literature available at the time. Particular prominence was allotted to Brown's views on the need to reform agricultural methods and promote small-scale irrigation schemes, and to institute forest conservancy. Forest protection and water pollution legislation passed in Mauritius during 1865–75 was referred to as worthy of imitation while legislation contemplated in the Australian colonies (where the prolific Hooker protégé Von Mueller had occupied the post of Government Botanist since 1854) and New Zealand was also mentioned.

The basic scientific literature was cited and the report drew special attention to the work of Humboldt and Boussingault, the two men whose warnings of the possible climatic effects of deforestation had first attracted the notice of East India Company Surgeons Alexander Gibson and Edward Balfour (Grove, 1987b), and then been so assiduously cultivated (and, it must be said, somewhat coloured, exaggerated and simplified) by Pappe and Brown for their own conservation propaganda purposes.

The Natal Forest Commission marked a watershed in conservation thinking. It recommended intervention on several fronts, but particularly in the rapid gazetting of forest reserves and the promotion of exotic-tree planting policies. It was also noteworthy in assigning blame for forest clearance and subsequent soil erosion to both European planters and African agriculturalists. The most remarkable feature of the report occurs in relation to its comments on the process of land alienation and the consequent psychological impact on African farmers. Commenting on the proposal that conservation measures should be imposed on Zulu farmers at a time when eviction was commonplace the Commissioners noted that:

The consideration of this portion of the question would be incomplete if it did not include the individual interest the native has in the land itself which he is thus so summarily called upon to improve with foresight and still his power of imitation enables him to borrow from his European neighbour. It will indeed be unreasonable to impose upon him conditions affecting permanency of agriculture and homestead formed upon civilised modes, and at the same time withhold the security of title to the land which promises in perpetuity the fruits of his work.

(Government of Natal, 1880)

These more enlightened references to the predicament enforced on peasant farmers, though prophetic in more ways than one, were, not surprisingly, largely ignored by the Natal Government. The risks in alienating the white farming community by attending to peasant interests were too great. Forest conservation was a much less contentious course to follow and involved a lower risk of confrontation with European farmers. Thus, by 1882 the Commission Report had, at the very least, helped to ensure the appointment of Indian-trained forest conservators to the Cape Colony and Natal.

Metropolitan British interests after 1860 and until at least 1914 were, in effect, more concerned with encouraging the mania for game reserves of the ex-hunter and species protectionists than with fostering the kinds of extensive land and water supply protection policies which had first been pursued at the Cape (Vaughan, 1978). However, the lack of metropolitan interest did not prevent the widespread application of pre-1866 Cape precepts much further afield. The 1858 and 1888 Forest and Herbage Preservation Acts were used in attempts to control and penalise the incursions into the Bechuanaland forest lands of timber-hungry Rand traders based in Johannesburg and catering for the needs of the new mining industry.[6] Later, they were also used as models for legislation in Rhodesia, which remained in force until 1945.[7] Further north, the gazetting of early forest reserves for water catchment purposes in Nyasaland followed both Indian and Cape precedents (Grove, 1987a).

The pattern established by the Natal Commission failed to address many of the soil conservation problems which had been forecast by Brown. However vehemently the desiccationists, of whom Brown was the forerunner in Africa, should argue, attention continued to be focused mainly, and quite inappropriately, on the small patches of remaining forest land. These were mostly located in relatively infertile upland areas on the peripheries of which African peasant farmers had been forced to seek refuge when not confined to the worst eroded grasslands. Perhaps here lie the roots of the sudden need, in the twentieth century, to react to this pattern and seek conservation policies which were appropriate to non-forest areas. The scientific conservation arguments used by Brown had been taken up selectively and on the basis of expedients suitable to the settler farming interests and those of the erstwhile game-hunters.

Conclusion

By about 1880 a conservation structure deriving from a *mélange* of Indian and Cape Colony philosophies had been established in southern Africa. It remained to inheritors of that tradition, such as E.P. Stebbing, the historian of Indian forests and a forester with experience in both India and latterly West Africa, to make the direct connection between the desiccation arguments of the 1850s and those so widely advocated in the 1930s (Stebbing, 1922, 1935). Put at its most simplistic, the conversion of a European conservation ethic, evolved in southern African conditions into a conscious and comprehensive policy of state intervention in the Cape Colony, seems to have been sanctioned by the coincidence of a triangle of interests. These were, firstly, those of a lobby promoting the interest of scientific botany, aesthetic and amenity enthusiasms; secondly, the anxieties of a white settler farming community; and thirdly, the concerns of a government fearful of external security considerations and anxious to secure the future of a settler agrarian economy which it understood to be threatened by drought. The responses of the white settler community bulked large in this equation. At first, underlying all these factors lay a fundamental and subliminal anxiety about the ability of the European settler to survive in an alien land, or indeed, his right to do so. However, as soon as scientists could no longer make the drought threat credible the temporary support of the settler community came to an end and state intervention, at least temporarily, collapsed. Thus the first colonial conservation initiatives in Africa contrasted strongly with parallel initiatives in India. In India success was more assured because of the extent to which scientists could maintain credibility with, or indeed threaten, a colonial government whose main security consideration was dictated by the stability of a peasant and not a settler population. In British colonial Africa, on the other hand, it was only when the interests of peasant agriculture became politically paramount, as they did during the 1930s, that the influence of the 'experts' could reassert itself and enlist the anxieties and the commitment of central government to conservation policies which extended beyond forest and game reserve alienation. In this sense the ideology of the scientific expert was allowed to resurface because it was once more convenient to government.

It might be thought that the main significance of the early Cape conservation policies lies merely in their precocity and, undoubtedly, in an antiquarian sense, there is an intrinsic interest in perceptions and policies which predated those of the United States or Europe. But the implications of Cape policy extend further. The deeper motivations underlying perceptions of hazard and even aesthetic tastes change slowly. If modern ideas of conservation did emerge initially as a direct response by a coterie of humanitarian scientists to the environmental consequences of colonialism, as seems increasingly likely, a substantial revision of some of the premises of contemporary environmentalist thinking will be necessary. Currently several attempts are being made, without the aid of any substantial historical perspective, to reconcile the ideologies of development and conservation on the assumption that they have had very different objectives (Redclift, 1984; Robertson 1985). A knowledge of the Cape experience leads one to suggest instead that both development and conservation ideas have had substantially similar origins, both deriving from utilitarian concepts of 'improvement'. In particular the primacy of large animal protection (often so inimical to 'development' thinking) as a part of the evolution of a colonial conservation ethic in Africa emerges as a distinctly secondary development. In this respect, the main lesson of early Cape conservation lies not so much in its precocity but in the fact that it failed, in its original form, to establish itself as a part of the function of African colonial government. The reason for this was that the implications of the conservation policies proposed by the Colonial Botanists had begun to pose a serious threat to the uninhibited activities of European settler land-users, particularly those whose capital-intensive activities were dependent on deforestation continuing. This was in spite of the fact that senior officials in the Cape Government had associated themselves with wide-ranging conservation objectives and anxieties. The relatively holistic ideology which the Colonial Botanists evolved and propagandised, initially with government help, strongly reflected its Humboldtian antecedents. Such an ideology was difficult to reconcile with the driving interests of local European capital, which the British colonial State in Africa was far less in a position to contradict than it was in India. Therein lay the downfall of early colonial conservation in Africa. Although elements of conservation regulation which were pioneered in the Cape in terms of forest protection and game reservation remained politically palatable for colonial governments after 1866, the application of those parts of the Cape legislation which were more concerned with overall environmental processes than with the protection of the biologically unique have only found their counterparts in more recent times. Indeed, taking a long evolutionary perspective, those as yet embryonic contemporary conservation ideologies which identify with the basic needs of peasant populations have much in common with the ideas of Pappe and Brown. They have much less in common with the

Nimrodic obsessions and land-alienation strategies of the colonial conservation policies of the intervening period. In this sense, the wheel may have come full circle.

Notes

1   Letter from Downing Street to Cape Government, 3 March 1828, no. GH1/6b, Cape Provincial Archives.
2   *Cape Mail and South African Commercial Advertiser*, Editorial, 8 January 1859.
3   Correspondence of the Secretary, Société des Arts et des Sciences, Archives; Mauritius Sugar Research Institute, Le Reduit, Mauritius.
4   Forest Rangers letters, esp. no. 62, 1859, Cape Provincial Archives.
5   Minutes of evidence taken before the Select Committee on the Colonial Botanist's Report, p.23, Committee Report (1865), Cape Town.
6   Correspondence, 16 February 1892, between Resident Magistrate, Vryburg and the Administrator, Vryburg, no. 117R Forestry File, Botswana Government Archives, Gaberone.
7   Forestry Files, GF categories, National Archives of Zimbabwe, Harare.

References

ALEXANDER, J.E. (1838). *An Expedition of Discovery into the Interior of Africa*. London: H. Colborn.

BEINART, W. (1984). Soil erosion, conservationism, and ideas about development in southern Africa. *Journal of Southern African Studies*, **11** (2), 52–83.

BRITISH ASSOCIATION (1852). Report of the Committee appointed by the British Association to consider the probable effects in an economical and physical point of view of the destruction of the tropical forests, by Dr Hugh Cleghorn, Prof. Forbes Royle, R. Baird Smith and Capt. R. Strachey, pp.22–45, *Report of the Proceedings of the British Association*.

BROWN, J.C. (1866). *Circular from the Colonial Botanist relative to the South African Plants desired by the directors of the Botanic Gardens in Europe and elsewhere*. Cape Town: Office of the Colonial Botanist.

BROWN, J.C. (1875). *The Hydrology of South Africa*. Edinburgh: Henry King.

BROWN, J.C. (1881). A British School of Forestry, present position of the question. *Journal of Forestry and Estate Management*, April–May, 4–12.

BROWN, J.C. (1885). An argument for the organisation of a National School of Forestry. *Proceedings of the British Association*, 421–8.

BROWN, J.C. (1887). *The Crown Forests at the Cape of Good Hope*. Edinburgh: Oliver & Boyd.

CAPE GOVERNMENT. (1858–66) *Annual Reports of the Colonial Botanists*. Cape Town: Govt Printer.

DARNELL, H.B. (1866). *The Past, Present and Future Condition of the Forests of the George, Knysna and Uitenhage Districts*. Cape Town: Govt Printer.

DARWIN, C. (1859). *The Origin of Species*. London: J. Murray.

DROUGHT COMMISSION (1922). *Interim Report of the South African Drought Investigation Commission*. Cape Town: Govt Printer.

GLADSTONE-SOLOMON, W.E. (1948). *Saul Solomon*. Oxford: Oxford University Press.

GOUDIE, A.S. (1981). *The Human Impact: Man's Role in Environmental Change*. Oxford: Oxford University Press.

GOVERNMENT OF INDIA (1880). *Report of the Famine Commission*. Calcutta: Govt Printer.

GOVERNMENT OF NATAL (1880). *Report of the Commission enquiring into the Extent and Condition of the Forest Lands of the Colony*. Pietermaritzburg: Govt Printer.

GROVE, R.H. (1987a). Conservation and Colonialism: the development of environmental attitudes and conservation policies in the British Imperial context, with special reference to India, Mauritius and the Cape Colony, 1814–1914. Unpublished Ph.D. thesis, University of Cambridge.

GROVE, R.H. (1987b). Surgeons, forests and famine: the emergence of the conservation debate in India, 1788–1852. *Indian Social and Economic History Review*. (In press.)

HALL,T.D. (1934). South African pastures: retrospective and perspective. *South African Journal of Science*. **31**, 23–46.

HAYS, S. (1959). *Conservation and the Gospel of Efficiency: The Progressive Conservation Movement. 1890–1920*. Cambridge, Mass: Harvard University Press.

HELMS, D. & FLADER, S.L. (1985). *The History of Soil and Water Conservation*. Washington, DC: Agricultural History Society.

HOOKER, J.D. (1872). Forestry. *Journal of Applied Science*. August, 221–3.

LIGHTON, C. (1973). *Cape Floral Kingdom: the story of South Africa's wildflowers*. Cape Town: Juta Press.

MARSH, G.P. (1864). *Man and Nature: or Physical Geography as modified by Human Action*. New York: G. Scribner.

NASH, R. (1967). *Wilderness and the American Mind*. New Haven, Connecticut: Yale University Press.

PAPPE, L. (1862). *Silva Capensis, or a description of South African forest trees and arborescent shrubs*. Cape Town: Van de Standt, De Villiers & Co.

PAPPE, L. & RAWSON, R.W. (1858). *Filicum Africae Arboralis, or an enumeration of the South African ferns hitherto known*. Cape Town: S.Solomon Steam Printing Office.

REDCLIFT, M. (1984). *Development and the Environmental Crisis: Red or Green Alternatives*? London: Methuen.

RIBBENTROP, B. (1899). *Forestry in British India*. Calcutta: Govt Printer.

RICHARDS, J.F., HAGEN, J.R. & HAYNES, E.S. (1985). Changing land-use in Bihar, Punjab and Haryana, 1850–1970. *Modern Asian Studies*, **19**(9), 699–732.

ROBERTSON, A.F. (1985). *People and Planning: the anthropology of development*. Cambridge: Cambridge University Press.

SIM, T.R. (1907). *The Forests and Forest Flora of the Cape Colony*. Aberdeen: Taylor & Henderson.

STEBBING, E.P. (1922). *The Forests of India*, 3 vols. London: J.Lane.

STEBBING, E.P. (1935). The Encroaching Sahara: the threat to the West African Colonies, *Geographical Journal*. **85**, 506–24.

TURNER, J. (1981). *Reckoning with the Beast*. Baltimore: Johns Hopkins Press.

VAUGHAN, M. (1978). Uncontrolled animals and aliens: colonial conservation mania in Malawi. Staff Research Seminar Paper, History Department, University of Malawi.

WORSTER, D. (1977). *Nature's Economy. A History of Ecological Ideas*. Cambridge: Cambridge University Press.

2

Chivalry, social Darwinism and ritualised killing: the hunting ethos in Central Africa up to 1914

JOHN M. MACKENZIE

The central significance of the Hunt in the ideology of late nineteenth-century imperialism has never been fully realised. The importance of the Hunt can be identified at every level of the theory and practice of the imperial ethos. It played a part in popular imperialism in Britain. In Africa it acted as a vital point of interaction between Africans and Europeans. Explorers, prospectors, missionaries and pioneers were also hunters. The ivory-hunting frontier in southern Africa was at one and the same time a prime impulse to the interior and the marker of the white advance. Most early colonial administrators were hunters as were the majority of European settlers. The Hunt was extolled by the military as the vital preparation for and adjunct of war. As African access to hunting was progressively reduced, the Hunt became not only the symbol of European dominance, but also the determinant of class within that dominance. As conservation policies developed at the turn of the century, the Hunt became the preserve of famous travellers, high-ranking officers, politicians, royalty and aristocrats, as it had been in India for some time. Conservation was promoted, in part, because these hunters deprecated the plain man's hunting, whether the unbridled depredations of the settler, or, above all, the commercial activities or survival techniques of Africans.

This connection between hunting and imperialism was made by Hugh Gunn in an article on 'The Sportsman as an Empire Builder' in 1925:

> The early training and the instincts of the hunter have had much more to do with the expansion of the Empire than is generally realised.
>
> (Gunn, 1925: 137–8)

The British have been extolled, Gunn went on, for their sea-sense, as hardy navigators, but

> the spirit of the chase has been equally responsible for the adventures and enterprises that have led, hand in hand with trade and commerce, to the exploration and settlement of unknown and pagan lands.

While in India the soldier and the big game hunter were often synonymous, in Africa the missionaries and explorers were also hunters. Robert Moffat and David Livingstone hunted with famous hunters like Cumming, Oswell, and Murray.

For Gunn, however, all hunting was sport: he made no attempt to distinguish the various types of hunting that had gone into 'Empire building' in southern and Central Africa. In fact, three principal phases can be identified in the extension of European hunting in the region. The first of these was purely commercial hunting for ivory and skins. The second was hunting as a subsidy for the second level of European advance, the period of acquisition, conquest, and settlement. The third was the transformation of hunting into the Hunt, when it came to be surrounded by ideology and ritual. Its objectives then were the collection of trophies and natural history specimens, the establishment of records, and the pursuit of manliness and moral edification through 'sportsmanship'. The first two were the periods of massive destruction of African game. They were conducted in league with African practitioners of hunting and Africans acquired vast quantities of meat in a brief bonanza associated with the destruction of elephant, buffalo, and antelope herds. In the first the meat was largely incidental. In the second the meat was the crucial protein supplement to the low – or non-existent – wages offered by pioneers, prospectors, miners, settlers, and town and railway builders. The gun had become a vital part of the payroll. Subsidies from hunting also helped to pay the first colonial administrators and keep the more penurious companies – like the African Lakes and the Imperial British East Africa – alive. It was only in the third phase that notions of conservation came to the fore.

It is therefore the third phase, with all its attendant belief systems, which will be treated most extensively in this chapter. It is, however, necessary to establish first the distinction between African and European hunting, the scale of destruction which took place in the earlier phases, the role of hunting in the relationship between African and European, and its significance as an imperial subsidy.

Commercial hunting

There is ample evidence that hunting was an annual activity in many African societies. Hunting for meat has received very little attention among students of the pre-colonial economy, but it is clear that in societies with a basically carbohydrate diet there was a constant search for protein supplement. Given the fact that cattle were so seldom slaughtered for meat, some (but by no means all) pastoral societies also turned to game. The nineteenth-century sources abound with descriptions of a wide variety of African hunting techniques (MacKenzie, 1987a, b). Hunting was often an important part of boyhood training and it frequently involved the deployment of large forces under chiefly control. The great annual elephant hunts of Sepopa and Lewanika or the mass hunts of the Ndebele under Mzilikazi and Lobengula were celebrated events. Through them the kings attempted to control trade and the activities of white hunters, as well as enhance their power through the distribution of firearms and the resulting large quantities of meat. Royal hunting reserves, some attempts at conservation of endangered species through the introduction of the concept of royal game, and even new rituals associated with the Hunt, all seem to have developed at this time.

In attempting to control white elephant hunters, however, African rulers were riding the tiger of European advance. White hunters appeared in Central Africa from the 1850s and by the 1870s and 1880s they had become very nearly a flood. Both Mzilikazi and Lobengula tried to limit the entry of white hunters into their kingdom, but with little success. At the beginning of his reign, Lobengula issued hunting regulations restricting white hunters to a particular route and charged a licence fee of a gun (to the value of £15) and ammunition (Wallis, 1946; Cobbing, 1976). White hunters were restricted to the outer regions of the kingdom in an effort to protect Ndebele hunters from competition. Nevertheless, favoured hunters became convenient conduits for the flow of ivory from Lozi and Ndebele territory, aids in diplomacy, and a useful source of firearms and ammunition. Sepopa formed a close relationship with George Westbeech, who spent almost eighteen years in Lozi country hunting and trading, after several years hunting south of the Zambezi (Coillard, 1897; Gann, 1964; Clay, 1968). Westbeech survived the upheavals of the Lozi state and maintained his influence under Lewanika. Thomas Baines, George Phillips, and Frederick Selous all, at different times, exercised influence at Lobengula's court (Wallis, 1946).

The figures for the export of ivory and the consequent destruction of elephants in this period are staggering. The hunter William Finaughty, active between 1864 and 1875, shot 95 elephants in one trip in 1868 yielding 5,000 lb of ivory (Finaughty, 1916). Henry Hartley killed between 1,000 and 1,200 elephants in his career. Karl Mauch's bag for one season in 1867 was 91 elephants yielding 4,000 lb of ivory (Bernhard, 1971); in the same year Jan Viljoen shot 210 elephants in one trip and Petrus Jacobs was alleged to have achieved yet more prodigious feats with the

gun (Selous, 1881; Millais 1918). All of these hunters hunted from horse-
back, but with the slaughter of the 1860s, elephants retreated to the 'fly'
country where they could only be hunted on foot. It was at this point
that Phillips and Westbeech adopted the system which maximised ivory
exports while minimising risks to themselves, a technique already used
by the Boer hunting community in the Zoutpansberg (Daly, 1937;Wagner,
1980).Westbeech and Phillips operated as ivory entrepreneurs employing
large numbers of African hunters (as many as 50 at times), supervised
by young Boer and mixed-race hunters (Tabler, 1963; Clay, 1968). It was
by this technique that Westbeech sent out no fewer than ten to fifteen
tons of ivory each year between 1871 and 1888. Mauch's average was
44 lb per animal; Finaughty's 52 lb. Using the mean of these Westbeech's
annual figure represents the destruction of 470–700 elephants each year.
In 1876, 40,000 lb of ivory were traded on the Zambezi in one season,
representing about 850 elephants (Millais, 1918). In the following year
the figure declined to 25,000 lb, illustrating the increasing difficulties in
finding elephants. By 1886, Lewanika was lamenting that the riches of
his kingdom in ivory were almost all spent (Mackintosh, 1908). By the
time Frederick Selous arrived in Central Africa in 1872, the elephant
herds were already retreating to the remoter areas, and he devoted the
later part of his career to the largely unsuccessful search for a new
elephant-hunting ground (Millais, 1918).

This decline of ivory resources reduced the black kings' bargaining
power. Westbeech succeeded in reorientating the Lozi country's trade
away from the Ovimbundu traders of Angola and did much to ensure
the acceptance of missionaries like François Coillard at the Lozi Court
(Gann, 1964). Elephant hunters helped the concession hunters of the
1880s to achieve their ends, and Selous played a crucial role in guiding
the British South Africa Company's (BSAC) Pioneer Column into
Mashonaland in 1890.

Hunting as subsidy

Ivory now acted as an important subsidy to the second level of the
imperial advance. If the great hunters and traders were only interested
in the personal fortune that could be secured from ivory, others were
concerned to use it to finance other objectives. The London Missionary
Society (LMS) missionary, Thomas Morgan Thomas, who arrived at
Inyati in northern Matabeleland in 1859, hunted and traded to finance
his mission (Thomas, 1873). In 1870 he was expelled from the LMS for
these activities, but he returned to found an independent mission which

he subsidised from his hunting exploits between 1874 and 1884. The Moir brothers, who founded the evangelical trading concern, the African Lakes Company (ALC), to pursue Livingstone's favoured combination of Christianity and commerce, used ivory as a means of furthering their ambitions. As F.L.M. Moir put it in his memoirs, the large sums realised from ivory kept the Company going, 'and so enabled it to carry on the work for which it had been founded' (Moir, 1923). Soon the missionary Robert Laws was lamenting the fact that the herds of elephants Livingstone had seen in the Shire and Nyasa areas had all disappeared (Laws, 1934). Both Karl Mauch and Thomas Baines funded their prospecting expeditions on the proceeds of ivory sales (Baines, 1877; Wallis, 1946; Bernhard, 1971). To this end, Baines and Mauch (on different trips) joined forces with the celebrated elephant hunter, Henry Hartley, who had first noticed gold workings while hunting. Many publicists for hunting trips into the interior pointed out that such trips could be financed by the shooting of a few good elephants (Tabler, 1963).

The exploits of Frederick Lugard illustrate the manner in which hunters, campaigners, and administrators fused in the years just before and after the establishment of white rule. When Lugard arrived in Africa as a penniless adventurer in 1888 he was taken on by the ALC as a combined elephant hunter and expedition leader against the Swahili traders on Lake Nyasa. In East Africa both Lugard and Frederick Jackson mixed campaigning with elephant hunting and partly financed the former from the latter, a highly advantageous arrangement for the Imperial British East Africa Company (IBEAC) (Lugard, 1893: Vol.1). Geoffrey Archer (later Governor of Somaliland, Uganda and the Sudan) considered becoming a professional hunter, but became instead an administrator in Kenya's Northern Frontier District, augmenting his salary by annual elephant hunting. Alfred Sharpe (later Governor of Nyasaland) was an elephant hunter, as was Robert Coryndon, BSAC administrator in Northern Rhodesia and later Governor of Uganda and Kenya (Sharpe, 1921; Archer, 1963). All the BSAC administrators in North Western Rhodesia were eager hunters who encouraged Lewanika's increasingly ritualised taste for the hunt in the early years of colonial rule.

If the hunt for ivory led to a rapidly retreating elephant frontier, the hunting of other forms of game soon led to a dramatic contraction of the game zone. Buffalo, antelope and zebra herds, already largely destroyed south of the Limpopo, were to be ruthlessly exploited during the last two decades of the century by professional hunters, sportsmen, and the pioneers of the New Imperialism in Central Africa. Just as ivory provided, and continued to provide even in much reduced circumstances,

a subsidy to other concerns, missionary and commercial, exploratory
and administrative, so did game constitute a vital support system for
the often exiguous survival of European pioneers. All pre-colonial hunters, prospectors, traders, explorers and missionaries lived off the land.
That represented no mean subsidy when large numbers of porters, beat-
ers and servants had to be fed. Both before and after the imposition of
colonial rule, trading, natural history and administrative expeditions
invariably required as many as 100 carriers and other followers.
Moreover, a supply of meat could 'sweeten' the local population among
whom the intruders were travelling or settling (Waller, 1880; Tabler,
1963). Missionaries found that they were welcome less for the gospel
than for the gun. Thomas Morgan Thomas related how at the end of a
sermon his African listeners sought their reward for patience by demanding that he shoot some game for them (Thomas, 1873). Another missionary reported that the delight of a people on hearing he was to establish
a mission in their territory seemed to be primarily related to the fact
that he would hunt for them (*Central Africa*, 1916). The works of Coillard,
Arnot, Donald Fraser and others amply demonstrate that the successful
missionary in Africa had also to be a successful hunter.

But hunting soon became much more than a 'sweetener'. Africans
exhibited an insatiable demand for meat and badgered expedition leaders
and missionaries to provide it. Europeans soon realised that labour could
be attracted and held in this way. While ivory was an important overt
subsidy for the imperial advance, meat was a concealed subsidy, difficult
to quantify, but crucial none the less. Again missionaries led the way.
Bishop Knight-Bruce and Isaac Shimmin, both notable hunters, supplied
large quantities of meat to their followers (Blennerhasset & Sleeman,
1893; Brown, 1899). One missionary was said to have built his church
by paying his labour in meat.[1] Donald Fraser fed his mission – including
a school of some seventy catechists – by trading meat for foodstuffs with
the surrounding population (Fraser, 1934). Such trade represents another
vital area of the meat subsidy. Even the very grand expedition of Lord
Randolph Churchill traded meat for grain (Churchill, 1893). The
archaeologist, J. Theodore Bent, employed a young hunter called Harrington to keep his party in meat when excavating the Zimbabwe Ruins
in 1891 (Bent, 1892).[2]

Many of the members of the BSAC's Pioneer Column of 1890 themselves described the manner in which they were lured northwards by the
complex myth of Central Africa, incorporating gold, adventure and the
Hunt. Several were influenced by the popular literature of the period,
including the works of Henty, Rider Haggard, and Selous (Finlason,

1893).[3] The interlinking of these cultural influences is perfectly reflected in the fact that Haggard modelled Allan Quatermain on Selous and Captain Good on Frederick Jackson, who taught the novelist a great deal about hunting and fed him incidents for fictional reworking (Jackson, 1969). When the pioneers fanned out from Fort Salisbury in late 1890 their main desire was to 'get rich quick' on the alleged gold reserves of the territory and return home as soon as possible. In persuading Africans to take them to the many gold shafts excavated by medieval miners they were free in distributing arms as rewards. These arms were partly used in hunting and were to be turned against the whites in the 1896–7 revolt.[4] The pioneers also hunted daily to feed such labour as they could secure, trade for grain with the locals, and, sometimes, subsidise their prospecting from the sale of skins and trophies.

Although the pioneers were provided with farms as well as gold concessions, few (except the Boers among them) wished to be farmers. One transport rider remarked that he had yet to meet a Rhodesian farmer who actually grew anything (Hyatt, 1914). Nevertheless, some staked out their putative farms, hoping to secure labour from the Africans resident upon them, and find profit in a process of asset-stripping combined with the hope that the land would rapidly accrue in value. This asset-stripping involved the removal of timber for sale to townships, mines and railway companies, and the shooting-out of all game.

The building of the railways further contributed to the massive asault upon game. Railway engineers, like missionaries, had to be good shots to keep their labourers and staff in meat. Supplying meat to large numbers of workers was a vital subsidy to the tight financing of railway lines like the Beira–Mashonaland or the trans-Zambezi route to Northern Rhodesia, both of which passed through game-rich regions. H.F. Varian, one of the most distinguished of the railway engineers was an excellent shot who kept his men well supplied (Pauling, 1926; Varian, 1953). Once the lines were built, they brought in a fresh flood of rather less intrepid hunters, some of whom were known, in the early days of the railway, to shoot at the teeming game of the Pungwe Flats in Mozambique from the windows of railway carriages (Alderson, 1898). It was not long before it teemed no more.

The rich game resources of Central Africa were also to prove an essential supply element in time of war. In both the war against the Ndebele in 1893 and the revolt of the Shona and Ndebele in 1896–7, as well as several other campaigns north of the Zambezi, the provisioning of troops and settlers was a considerable problem. But colonial troopers and local and British officers were as proficient in the hunt as they were in the prosecution of war. Indeed, the accounts of these campaigns invariably contain more on hunting than on fighting. Baden-Powell described several columns in 1896 as being saved by the shooting of game when other supplies were running short, and there was also time for hunting as sport (Baden-Powell, 1897).

The supply difficulties of the 1896–7 revolt had been massively exacerbated by the rinderpest epidemic which broke out early in 1896, destroying hundreds of oxen in transport spans throughout the country, as well as entire cattle herds, before proceeding like a bush fire through Bechuanaland and the South African territories, reaching Cape Town before the end of the year. Studies of rinderpest have generally concentrated on its effects on cattle, but it was no less devastating in its onslaught on game (van Onselen, 1972; Kjekshus, 1977). Elephant, hippopotamus and rhinoceros were immune, but entire buffalo herds were destroyed. The large antelope like kudu and eland seem to have been particularly susceptible, although none of the buck were free of the scourge. As the rinderpest spread southwards, hunters, warriors and settlers commented with alarm upon this dramatic destruction of the game. Baden-Powell lamented not only the transport difficulties but also the reduction in the quantities of meat available to his troops (Baden-Powell, 1897). Since all game regulations were suspended for the duration of the revolts, the game were subjected to unrestricted hunting at the moment of their greatest vulnerability. H.F. Varian noted that in the rinderpest's 'full toll of game throughout South-East Africa, buffalo were especially hard hit' (Varian, 1953). Alfred Sharpe suggested that the vast herds of buffalo he had seen on the Congo-Northern Rhodesia frontier in 1890 were totally wiped out (Sharpe, 1921). Selous' biographer, J.G. Millais, claimed that in 1896 nine-tenths of kudu, eland and buffalo were carried off by the rinderpest in the Pungwe district of Mozambique and similar effects occurred in Southern Rhodesia (Millais, 1918).

By the time the rinderpest struck, however, the game frontier, like the elephant before it, was already in rapid retreat. The game had long since departed from the high veld plains of the Orange Free State and the Transvaal. The decline in the numbers of game had already been noted in the last decades of the independent Ndebele kingdom, and Lobengula had forbidden hunters, white or black, to shoot cow elephants or take ostrich eggs. In 1883, he fined the hunters Selous and Martin for shooting hippopotamus against his wishes (Cobbing, 1976). Ndebele hunters found that they had to move further and further from the heartland of their state in order to secure game of any sort. Traditional African hunting and been relatively inefficient, but the acquisition of modern guns by Africans had changed all that. Lobengula's efforts to control hunting can well be understood in the light of the scale of the bags of the well-known hunters. Selous, in an appendix to his book *A Hunter's Wanderings* proudly listed his kills. Between 1877 and 1880 he shot 548 head, of which only twenty were elephants. With high-velocity rifles in the later 1890s, Europeans were to become even more devastatingly competent. Wherever game was disturbed by hunters it lost its innocence and its curiosity. The animals steadily retreated from all lines of communication and the settlements of the white invaders.

There are many graphic descriptions of this process. When the BSAC column assembled at Macloutsie in Bechuanaland, the presence of so many men soon ensured that no game was to be had anywhere in the vicinity (Leonard, 1896). Hugh Marshall Hole described the column as giving 'the big game animals of Mashonaland a scare from which they never fully recovered' (Hole, 1928). Once the column arrived at Fort Salisbury, the professional hunter and natural history collector, William Harvey Brown, was sent out to secure meat for the new settlement. He described his wonder at finding great herds of game on the Gwibi flats little more than ten miles from Salisbury (Brown, 1899). By the following year, Lord Randolph Churchill's party proceeded to exactly the same area and found no game at all (Churchill, 1893). Churchill travelled with a famous hunter, Hans Lee (who was aided, as so many hunters had been, by Bushmen trackers) and it is clear that the expedition, which was supposed to be primarily an investigation of the economic potential of Rhodesia, was in fact almost entirely taken up with daily hunting exploits. Churchill certainly devoted more space to hunting than to economics in his book on the journey. He described the manner in which, when an area rich in game was found, the party would settle there for several days until the game had been driven off by the daily depredations of his party. Everywhere Africans emerged to take advantage of the meat abandoned in the search for trophies. The figures of daily bags reflected a veritable orgy of killing and Churchill's party often heard the shots of other hunting groups nearby.

The Hunt

Churchill's expedition perfectly symbolises the movement of hunting into its third, less practical, phase. The distinction between hunting and the Hunt is an important one which is best charted through the changing tone of hunting publications. The famous southern African hunting works of the middle decades of the nineteenth century, like those of Cornwallis

Harris (1852), R. Gordon Cumming (1850) and W.C. Baldwin (1863), are essentially unselfconscious and more or less tedious accounts of daily hunting exploits. (cf. Faulkner, 1868; Rouillard, 1936).They are unencumbered by any philosophical or ideological approaches to hunting except insofar as hunting represented a free, roving, adventurous and individualist way of life. All hunters in the later nineteenth century testified to the great influence of these works in taking them to Africa, whether as commercial hunter, pioneer and natural historian like Selous, settler/sportsman like Denis Lyell, or wealthy international hunter like Theodore Roosevelt. But the writings of these later hunters make it clear that they were indulging in the Hunt, a symbol of white dominance, a marker of 'manliness' and the moral worth of 'sportsmanship', at one and the same time a ritual and a scientific pursuit as well as a practical activity. And the proportion of the practical to the ritualistic had a tendency to decline. This was no accident, for conservation policies tended to emphasise the legitimacy of this form of hunting over all others. While none of these hunters doubted their own right of access to extravagant killing, they argued for conservation policies and the need to restrict the access of others. They extolled the work of the hunter/naturalist administrators like Sir Alfred Sharpe and Sir Harry Johnston who had begun to set up protected hunting marshes and forests like those of the medieval kings.[5]

The medieval analogy is not fanciful: it is a significant component of the late nineteenth-century Hunt. The contemporary rediscovery of medieval chivalry and its transformation into a moral code for the age in literature, education, the iconography of book illustrations, stained glass and popular art, and in extolling the virtues of horsemanship, the ritualised warring of the tournament, and the valour and violence involved in vanquishing foes animal, human, or mythological was an important constituent in the thinking of imperial hunters in Africa, particularly those educated in the public schools (Girouard, 1981). It was precisely the universality of this code which made hunting the common experience of missionary, prospector, pioneer, explorer, soldier and administrator. The chivalric complex involved the severe separation of the male and female worlds, as did war and imperialism. The medieval tournament ritualised warfare and killing and facilitated the emergence of the fittest, who would be hailed as heroes by both the crowd and the ladies in whose honour the tournament was held. The element of sexual selection implied in the tournament was not lost on an age increasingly obsessed with social Darwinism and notions of eugenics. Moreover, the tournament obscured, at least for the nineteenth-century if not the medieval mind, the violent realities of warfare and its very real horrors for the lower orders, social and racial. Again the connections with imperialism are apparent.

These connections, usually implicit but sometimes explicit, are particularly apparent in juvenile literature. An examination of the works of Henty, on which so many white hunters in Africa were brought up, will soon make this apparent (MacKenzie, 1984, 1986). But Henty was only one, if the most famous, of a large number of writers for children who gave all their work a powerful ideological twist. Hunting stories became a prime staple of all juvenile literature. R.M. Ballantyne's frequently lurid descriptions of hunting made this a respectable part of writing for children. Journals like the *Boy's Own Paper*, which secured such a remarkable popularity in this period, were full of hunting stories and extraordinarily graphic descriptions of taxidermy. Books of heroes, often presented as school and Sunday school prizes, tended to equate heroism in some instances with hunting exploits.[6] Many hunters noted the effects of such writings in their boyhood and the manner in which they turned to small-scale hunting in their own local environments, fantasising about the big game that would eventually come their way (Lyell, 1923).

The imperial Hunt also fed back into ideas on the moral training and socialisation of youth in the twentieth century. Baden-Powell's Boy Scouts were of course the prime example, but several other youth organisations, including the Empire Youth Movement, founded in the 1930s, took up the chivalric/hunting/warfare complex (MacKenzie, 1984). For Baden-Powell the connections were quite clear. In the opening pages of *Scouting for Boys*, one of the twentieth century's best sellers, he argued for the training of British youth in the use of guns, so that they could be like Boer boys (Baden-Powell, 1908). His use of animal names and sounds, training in woodcraft and spooring, his distinctions between war and peace scouts were all of course derived as much from his experience of the Hunt as from warfare. Among the 'peace scouts' he held up for emulation were 'North American trappers' and 'Central African hunters'.

Indeed, B-P repeatedly emphasised the connections between hunting and war in all his writings – peace scouts were after all constantly prepared for war. Hunting, he wrote, 'tests, develops and sustains the soldier's best service qualities and stands without rival as a training-school for officers' (Baden-Powell, 1900). He described the 'ecstasy of a fighting gallop' in pig-sticking in India, where officers and men took their appropriate places in the Hunt. He put these techniques to good use in the Mashonaland and Matabeleland campaigns of 1896–7. In *Sport in War* he described the work involved in military operations as sporting in itself, particularly the chase for 'wild beasts of the human kind', which offered 'plenty of excitement and novel experience' among the kopjes and broken country of Rhodesia (Baden-Powell, 1900). Elsewhere he remarked that 'the longest march seems short when one is hunting game. . . lion or leopard, boar or buck, nigger or nothing' (Baden-Powell, 1897).

E.A.H. Alderson also wrote a book on the connections between hunting and campaigning (Alderson, 1900), and his account of the suppression of the Shona rising was a combination of sport and war in which the sport tended to predominate. He was gratified to find that all his officers in Mashonaland were devotees of the Hunt and a wide range of hunting metaphors came easily to his pen. Hunting the Shona was compared to chasing the fox, rabbiting from bolt holes, shooting snipe, and scaring rooks. On one occasion he told his men to treat an attack as an August Bank Holiday outing. When the Acting Administrator of Mashonaland, Judge Vintcent, joined Alderson's column, Alderson described him as being 'like a schoolboy out hunting in the holidays at the idea of having a go at the Mashonas' (Alderson, 1898). Thus the line between animals and humans was blurred. The thorough acceptability of hunting helped to obscure the generalised violence of the colonial situation. Throughout the region those on hunting trips were readily turned aside to punitive expeditions in which they could apply their skills to manhunting. A soldier who devoted his entire life to sport, Sir Claude Champion de Crespigny, combined hunting with fighting in East Africa in 1905 when he led a column against the Sotik. After a successful day's campaigning he wrote of his bag of men: 'Sotiks killed, 50. The last item we had hoped to make 500' (Crespigny, 1925). Soldier, hunter and naturalist, C.H. Stigand entitled a chapter in one of his books 'Stalking the African' (Stigand, 1913).

Hunters often showed more squeamishness about the hunting of animals than they did in the killing of Africans. Nevertheless, evolutionary ideas abound in the literature of the Hunt and are linked to concepts of 'sportsmanship'. Crocodiles, at a less advanced stage of evolution, were fair game for slaughter. More highly evolved animals, like antelopes and elephants, deserved a more sportsmanlike approach. The injured animal should be spoored and shot at all costs. Waiting up for animals, concealed in a tree or a hide for example, shooting them from trains or river steamers, going for the leg shot to cripple rather than a head or heart shot to kill were all considered unsportsmanlike.

Hunters also anthropomorphised animals in an attempt to suggest a degree of equality in the contest and therefore emphasise the physical endurance and courage required in the Hunt. Every hunter celebrated his own survival with gory but admiring tales of those who had been killed by elephant, buffalo and lion (Daly, 1937). The elephant provided the greatest exhilaration through its sheer bulk, intelligence, and difficulty in obtaining a mortal shot, with of course the added tang of profit. The rhinoceros, on the other hand, was described as witless, choleric, dyspeptic and unsociable, and its virtual extermination in southern Africa was often explained, and by implication justified, on the grounds of its unpleasant character. Other animals were similarly provided with personalities, and the most 'wary' among them, the most difficult to hunt and kill were described as the most sporting, while those which most vigorously resisted death were 'plucky'.

What was fair in the Hunt was not, however, fair in war. Africans apparently lost all claims to sporting consideration because revolt was itself unsportsmanlike. A wide variety of social Darwinian comment can be found in all the works of this period. E.S. Grogan claimed to find illustrations of human evolution everywhere he looked in Africa and contrived to incorporate his naked anti-semitism into his repeated animadversions on race (Grogan & Sharpe, 1909). For Theodore Roosevelt, part of the excitement of Africa was that it brought the hunter face to face with the Palaeolithic past, with his remote evolutionary ancestors, with a raw wildness unimaginable in the civilised world (Roosevelt, 1910). There was of course a problem in all of this. Imperial man may have seen himself as at the other end of the evolutionary spectrum from the hunting and gathering Bushmen, but as imperial man the hunter he deeply respected their incomparable skill as trackers and utilised their knowledge and powers of observation to the full. The only way in which the late nineteenth-century hunter could separate his activities from those of the Bushmen – apart from the massive contrast in technology – was by comparing the sheer necessity of the one with the sportsmanship of the other. Many practitioners of the Hunt wrote of the astonishment of their followers that they could ignore and refuse to kill much meat on the hoof while spending many exhausting hours going for one particular trophy (Stigand, 1913). While the expertise of the Bushman was amply acknowledged, other peoples, both black and white, were judged according to their capacity in the Hunt. Most hunter/writers compared the hunting abilities of different African peoples and were contemptuous of many of them.

Hunting was also used as an important criterion in social Darwinian comment relating to Europeans. In this respect the 'internal' social Darwinism of Herbert Spencer was mixed with the 'external' of Benjamin

Kidd and Karl Pearson. For Denis Lyell, as for most practitioners of the Hunt, the fittest were created through the rugged individualism of the Hunt with its pitting of man against elephants and other dangerous game (Lyell, 1923). The hunter's exploits were constantly contrasted with the activities of weaklings at home, who should be allowed to go to the wall. The same contrast emerges in B-P's characterisation of cigarette-smoking street-loafers in *Scouting for Boys*. B-P, Selous, de Crespigny, and a host of boys' writers transferred the notions of sexual selection they constantly saw at work in the wild to human affairs: the brave hunter ought to, and did, get the prettiest girl. The Hunt was also the marker of national character. The Portuguese were despised because they did not hunt; the Germans were admired because they hunted to great effect (Selous, 1893; Grogan & Sharpe, 1909; Lyell, 1923).

The best hunters also prided themselves on being natural historians, and it was this that gave pseudo-scientific authority to their observations on human behaviour. Roosevelt rightly noted the absence of such theorising in the earlier hunting classics of southern Africa, and remarked upon the extraordinary craze for natural history in late Victorian and Edwardian times. The Natural History Museum in South Kensington, in the full glory of its Alfred Waterhouse terracotta plumage, opened its doors in 1881. The museums of Washington, New York, every capital of Europe, Cape Town, Pretoria, and a host of lesser towns, soon became stuffed with stuffed animals in the succeeding decades. Selous, W. Harvey Brown, Denis Lyell, and Marcus Daly all hunted for the leading museums, while Roosevelt led a massive expedition to East Africa to collect for the National Museum in Washington immediately after he relinquished the Presidency. Roosevelt, his son, two naturalists, and a vast army of camp followers, succeeded in bagging between 150 and 200 species, usually many examples of each. The precise number is difficult to gauge because of the propensity of natural historians of the time to proliferate species and subspecies. The expedition was exempted from the game laws by the Acting Governor of Kenya, Sir Frederick Jackson, himself a famous big game hunter, who later deplored the carnage wrought by Roosevelt's party (Jackson, 1969).

The discovery and classification of a species (often artificial subdivisions resulting from regional variants) was a great prize for any explorer or hunter. In the early period it was comparatively easy to be honoured in this way, but even the hunters from the second and third phases managed it. The railway engineer, H.F. Varian, had two types of small antelope named after him (Varian, 1953). Alfred Sharpe attached his name to a duiker and E.S. Grogan named a new species after his girl friend (Grogan & Sharpe, 1909). The frantic search for specimens in this third, natural history, phase of the hunting onslaught on Africa actually placed some species at risk. Robert Coryndon shot what were then thought to be the last two white rhinoceros in Mashonaland in 1893 (Hole, 1928). They were carefully mounted and sold, one to the Rothschild Collection, the other to the Cape Town Museum, no doubt at suitably inflated prices for their rarity value.

The Rothschild Museum, housed at Tring – now part of the Natural History Museum – was the largest in private hands, matched only by those of Selous and Roosevelt. But all hunters made collections of skulls, horns and skins as trophies, and the masters of many country houses were bitten by the craze. The Bowes-Lyons at Glamis, the Dukes of Atholl and Sutherland at Blair and Dunrobin Castles, and Powell-Cotton at Quex House in Kent filled their homes with skins, heads, and horns from around the world. The third and fourth Lords Egerton of Tatton Park in Cheshire covered the walls of their vast tenants' hall with African trophies and entertained both tenants and estate servants amidst the symbols of their hunting exploits.[7] It was a notable expression of surplus wealth, an opportunity for conspicuous expenditure which coincided precisely with the conversion of vast acreages in Scotland from sheep runs to deer forests (Orr, 1982). This curious taste rubbed off on those who did not hunt. Skins and horns became a feature of many middle-class houses as stay-at-homes attempted to bask in the reflected glory of the Hunt. Millions of skins were traded from southern Africa in the last decades of the nineteenth century. Rhodesian pioneers found a ready market for skins and trophies when all other forms of economic activity failed (Millais, 1918).

The pseudo-scientific activities of the natural historians and specimen seekers gave rise to an obsession with records. The taxidermist and publisher Rowland Ward published almost annual lists of animal and horn size which inevitably stimulated emulation. C.H. Stigand and Denis Lyell published works on the spoor and droppings of game to help other hunters (Stigand & Lyell, 1906; Ward, 1923, 1935; Lyell, 1929). Lyell and Roosevelt made a study of bullets they retrieved from carcases in order to assess the impact of different calibres on the anatomies of various animals (Roosevelt, 1910; Lyell, 1923).

The groups of hunters who justified their activities on scientific grounds were the most vigorous proponents of a conservation policy. They all lamented the retreat of the game frontiers and the extermination or near-extermination of some species, a process in which they themselves had often participated. Observers of this decline searched for scapegoats, preferably as distantly related to themselves as possible. Disease could be depicted as an 'act of God', although rinderpest had of course been introduced by human agency. Marcus Daly offered an evolutionary explanation for the disappearance of the quagga and black wildebeest from southern Africa (Daly, 1937). He denied that unbridled Boer hunting was at fault. The problem was an excess of bull calves and the fact that neither of these species, unlike buffalo, eland and other large antelope, excluded defeated bulls from the herd. The absence of adequate sexual selection, and the 'fact' that offspring took their prime characteristics from the weaker parent, ensured decline and extinction.

Selous, embittered by his failure as an elephant hunter, pinned the blame for decline on African hunters, but most observers were realistic enough to recognise the incompatibility of white settlement and the survival of game (Selous, 1908). Lord Randolph Churchill urged in 1891 that the BSAC territories should be preserved as a happy hunting ground for commercial killer and gentleman sportsman and not as a field for settlement (Churchill, 1893). E.S. Grogan implied that settlers should be kept out of Africa, although he subsequently became one (Grogan & Sharpe, 1909). The American big game photographer, Cherry Kearton, another friend of Roosevelt, roundly attacked settlers as the main enemy of game (Kearton, 1913). H.F. Varian, however, saw hunting parties of the Churchill type as the prime villains, often securing, he suggested, bags of 300 head on trips of three months or less (Varian, 1953).

Nevertheless, the effect of game regulations was to restrict hunting to the gentleman sportsman, administrator and soldier. Thus the cultural concept of the Hunt was underpinned by conservation legislation. Although there had been a number of conservation regulations at the Cape from the 1820s (Grove, Chapter 1), the first adequate legislation for game conservation came with the Cape Act for the Preservation of Game, 1886.[8] This Act was extended to the BSAC by Proclamation of the High Commissioner in 1891. It was subsequently modified by a succession of Company regulations during the 1890s. The game laws were consolidated and amended in 1899 and again in 1906. Through these laws Africans were entirely excluded from hunting. Licences were set at a price well beyond their reach. Rights were given to landowners which placed them in an exceptionally powerful position over game on their land. Elsewhere, instructive exemptions were made until 1906. 'Prospectors, farmers, and travellers' were exempt provided they were shooting for their own consumption only. The BSA Police were exempt in order to be able to feed their men. There were also exemptions for *bona fide* scientific and farming purposes. The close season was from the end of October to April, that is precisely coinciding with the rains when specimen and sporting hunting were unlikely to take place, when animals would be widely dispersed in the bush, and African gardens would be most at risk. In 1906 many exemptions were removed, licence fees were increased, and the status of Royal Game was extended to more animals. The transformation of hunting into the Hunt was almost complete.

Two reservations must be made about this neat picture. Game laws were notoriously difficult to enforce among settlers, while some government officials made no attempt to enforce the laws and ignored them themselves (Eliot, 1905; Hyatt, 1914; Hole, 1928). As tourist hunting increased, the Union-Castle guides to South and East Africa annually encouraged hunters with the remark that game laws were very difficult to enforce particularly in remoter districts (*Castle Guide*, 1899–1900). Game regulations were largely irrelevant to Africans: their access to game was denied through the operation of gun laws, together with the fact that game became extremely scarce in areas of dense human settlement like the reserves.

Although some chiefs were permitted to keep old tower muskets as symbols of status and as a means of scaring such game as still invaded their gardens, it was administrators who became the defensive hunters in African areas.[9] The connection between the prestige of the ruler and his prowess in the Hunt had come to be firmly transferred to whites. They shot game to protect African and European lands, for their own sport, and to feed their men. They also shot out game in the name of tsetse control: as the herds of buffalo and antelope recovered from the devastation of rinderpest they were subjected to repeated government culls.

When famine struck Southern Rhodesia in 1922, game meat was no longer available as a hedge against starvation. In this and in all subsequent periods of failed rains, Africans had neither the opportunity nor the means to turn to the protein bounty bestowed upon their forefathers. One rare African source, the history of Manyika written by an employee of the Methodist Episcopal Mission Press in Umtali (Mtare), Jason Machiwanyika, lamented the removal of meat from the African diet:

Europeans took all guns from Africans and refused to let them shoot game. But Europeans shoot game. Africans have to eat relish only with vegetables. If an African shoots an animal with a gun, the African is arrested and the gun is confiscated.[10]

Rather earlier, Sir Frederick Jackson had expressed surprise that the Administration of the East Africa Protectorate had not attempted to alleviate the Kamba famine of 1899 by permitting hunting (Jackson, 1969). The disappearance of game was one of the characteristics of the changing landscape most frequently identified by elderly informants in an oral research project in the 1970s.[11]

Hunting had been to Africans a significant route into the international economy through ivory, a source of meat and skins, and, if it had been a means for the enhancement of chiefly power and privilege, it had also acted as a route to meritocratic advance for the able hunter. For whites, hunting had provided an irresistible lure to the interior, a convenient subsidy to other white activities during the difficult years of the white advance, a source of pride, power, prestige and popularity to the early administrators, and finally a rich man's diversion in the remoter corners of Africa (cf. Churchill, 1908). Ideas about conservation emerged in the third phase of the Hunt and were closely bound up with the myths, ideologies, and pseudo-scientific practices of that period. The need for a white subsidy being past, the need to feed Africans not yet recognised, the link between conservation and the Hunt lay in the demarcation of the privilege and power of the new rulers of Africa.

Notes

1   National Archives of Zimbabwe Historical Manuscripts Collection (NAZ Hist. MSS Coll.), Reminiscences of William Edwards (ED6/1/1).

2   Bent employed large numbers of Africans on his excavations, presenting considerable commissariat problems (papers of H.T. Harrington, HA5/1/1, and the reminiscences of L.C. Meredith, uncatalogued, NAZ Hist. MSS Coll.).

3   Correspondence of H.J. Borrow (BO11/1/1) and papers of W.I.S. Driver (Misc DR2) in NAZ Hist. MSS Coll.

4   Papers of J.J.F. Darling (DA6/3/2), NAZ Hist. MSS Coll.

5   On the setting up of the reserves, see the reports of Sir H. Johnston and Sir A. Sharpe on the Trade and General Condition of the British Central Africa Protectorate, 1895–6, 1896–7, 1897–8. Parliamentary command papers C8254 (vol. LVIII, 423), C8438 (vol. LXII, 15), C9048 (vol. LXIII, 237).

6   See, for example, *Pictorial Sport and Adventure, forming a compendium of natural history*, London, n.d., but late 1890s, in which killing animals, hunting and heroism are clearly equated. A copy in the author's possession was given as a Sunday school prize in 1900.

7   The hunting diaries of the Egertons are now deposited in the Cheshire County Records Office, Chester.

8   The Game Law Amendment Ordinance of 1886, Cape Colony. Game licences were stipulated in the BSAC Charter of 1889 and the regulations were extended in the Game Law Amendment Ordinance no. 7 of 1893,

Ordinance no. 6 of 1894, regulations 198 and 199 of 1898, and a long series of regulations in 1899, the Statute Law of Southern Rhodesia.

9   All the early native commissioners were hunters and the first Chief Native Commissioner, Brabant, seems to have been appointed largely on his hunting and veldcraft capacities, since he was subsequently discovered to be barely literate (Papers of M.E. Weale, WE3/2/5, NAZ Hist MSS Coll). In later years the native commissioner H.N. Hemans refused promotion and always insisted on being sent to the remote Gokwe District because it was one of the few areas where hunting remained good. Hemans also emphasised the importance of hunting to the administrator's prestige (Hemans, 1935: 5, 83).

10   Jason Machiwanyika (uncatalogued), NAZ Hist. MSS Coll.

11   Some eighty interviews, which included questions on hunting, were collected by myself in the Chibi, Gutu, Wedza, Mrewa, Mtoko, Godhlwayo, and Matobo districts of Zimbabwe in 1973–4. They are deposited in the oral evidence collections of the Department of History of the University of Zimbabwe.

References

ALDERSON, E.A.H. (1898). *With the Mounted Infantry and the Mashonaland Field Force.* London: Methuen.

ALDERSON, E.A.H. (1900). *Pink and Scarlet, or Hunting as a School for Soldiering.* London: Heinemann.

ARCHER, Sir G. (1963). *Personal and Historical Memoirs of an East African Administrator.* Edinburgh: Oliver & Boyd.

BADEN-POWELL, R.S.S. (1897). *The Matabele Campaign.* London: Methuen.

BADEN-POWELL, R.S.S. (1900). *Sport in War.* London: Heinemann.

BADEN-POWELL, R.S.S. (1908). *Scouting for Boys.* London: C.A. Pearson.

BAINES, T. (1877). *The Gold Regions of South East Africa.* London: Chatto & Windus.

BALDWIN, W.C. (1863). *African Hunting and Adventure from the Natal to the Zambezi, from 1852 to 1860.* London: Bentley.

BENT, J.T. (1892). *The Ruined Cities of Mashonaland: being a record of excavation and exploration in 1891.* London: Longman.

BERNHARD, F.O., ed. (1971). *Karl Mauch.* Cape Town: Struik.

BLENNERHASSET, R. & SLEEMAN, L. (1893). *Adventures in Mashonaland, by two hospital nurses.* London: Macmillan.

BROWN, W.H. (1899). *On the South African Frontier.* Reprinted 1970, Bulawayo: Books of Rhodesia.

CASTLE GUIDE (various). *Castle Guide (later Union-Castle Guide) to South Africa* 1899–1900, and subsequent editions.

CENTRAL AFRICA (1916). *Central Africa, a monthly record of the work of the Universities Mission to Central Africa,* vol. 24.

CHURCHILL, Lord Randolph (1893). *Men, Mines and Animals in South Africa.* London: Sampson, Low.

CHURCHILL, W.S. (1908). *My African Journey.* Reprinted 1962, London: Holland Press/Neville Spearman.

CLAY, G. (1968). *Your Friend Lewanika*. London: Chatto & Windus.

COBBING, J.R.D. (1976). The Ndebele under the Khumalos, 1830–96. Unpublished Ph.D. thesis, University of Lancaster.

COILLARD, F. (1897). *On the Threshold of Central Africa*. London: Hodder & Stoughton.

CRESPIGNY, Sir C.C. de (1925). *Forty Years of a Sportsman's Life*. London: Mills & Boon.

CUMMING, R.G.G. (1850). *Five Years of a Hunter's Life in the Far Interior of South Africa*. London: John Murray.

DALY, M. (1937). *Big Game Hunting and Adventure, 1897–1936*. London: Macmillan.

ELIOT, C. (1905). *The East African Protectorate*. London: Edward Arnold.

FAULKNER, H. (1868). *Elephant Haunts, being a Sportsman's Narrative of the Search for Dr. Livingstone*. London: n.p.

FINAUGHTY, W. (1916). *The Recollections of William Finaughty*, ed. G.L. Harrison. Reprinted 1973, Bulawayo: Books of Rhodesia.

FINLASON, C.E. (1893). *A Nobody in Mashonaland*. London: G. Vickers.

FRASER, Agnes (1934). *Donald Frazer*, London: Edward Arnold.

GANN, L.H. (1964). *A History of Northern Rhodesia*. London: Chatto &Windus.

GIROUARD, M. (1981). *The Return to Camelot: Chivalry and the English Gentleman*. New Haven: Yale University Press.

GROGAN, E.S. & SHARPE, A.H. (1909). *Fron the Cape to Cairo*. London: T. Nelson.

GUNN, H. (1925). The sportsman as an empire builder. In *The Book of Red Deer and Empire Big Game*, ed. J. Ross & H. Gunn. London: Simpkins, Marshall, Hamilton, Kent & Co.

HARRIS, W.C. (1852). *The Wild Sports of Southern Africa*. 5th edn London: Bohn.

HEMANS, H.N. (1935). *The Log of a Native Commissioner, a record of work and sport in southern Rhodesia*. London: H.F. & G. Witherby.

HOLE, H.M. (1928). *Old Rhodesian Days*. London: Macmillan.

HYATT, S.P. (1914). *The Old Transport Road*. London: Andrew Melrose.

JACKSON, Sir Frederick (1969). *Early Days in East Africa*. 1st edn 1930. London: Edward Arnold.

KEARTON, Cherry (1913). *Photographing Wildlife Across the World*. London: Cassell.

KJEKSHUS, H. (1977). *Ecology Control and Economic Development in East African History*. London: Heinemann.

LAWS, R. (1934). *Reminiscences of Livingstonia*. London: Oliver & Boyd.

LEONARD, A.G. (1896). *How We Made Rhodesia*. London: Kegan Paul.

LUGARD. F.D. (1893). *The Rise of Our East African Empire*, 2 vols. London: Blackwood.

LYELL, D.D. (1923). *Memories of an African Hunter*. London:T. Fisher Unwin.

LYELL, D.D. (1929). *The Hunting and Spoor of Central African Game*. London: T. Fisher Unwin.

MACKENZIE, J.M. (1984). *Propaganda and Empire*. Manchester: Manchester University Press.

MACKENZIE, J.M., ed. (1986). *Imperialism and Popular Culture*. Manchester: Manchester University Press.

MACKENZIE, J.M. (1987a). Hunting in East and Central Africa in the late nineteenth century with special reference to Zimbabwe. In *Sport in Africa* ed. W. Baker & J.A. Mangan. (In press).

MACKENZIE, J.M. (1987b). *Imperialism and the Hunting Ethos*. Manchester: Manchester University Press. (In press).

MACKINTOSH, C.W. (1908). *Coillard of the Zambezi*. London: T. Fisher Unwin.

MILLAIS, J.G. (1918). *The Life of F.C. Selous*. London: Longman.

MOIR, F.L.M. (1923). *After Livingstone, an African Trade Romance*. London: Hodder & Stoughton.

ONSELEN, C. van (1972). Reactions to rinderpest in South Africa, 1896–7. *Journal of African History*. **13** (3), 473–88.

ORR, W. (1982). *Deer Forests, Landlords and Crofters*. Edinburgh: John Donald.

PAULING, G. (1926). *Chronicles of a Contractor*. London: Constable.

ROOSEVELT, T. (1910). *African Game Trials*. London: Murray.

ROUILLARD, Nancy ed. (1936). *Matabele Thompson: an autobiography*. London: Faber & Faber.

SELOUS, F.C. (1881). *A Hunter's Wanderings in Africa*. London: Bentley.

SELOUS, F.C. (1893). *Travel and Adventure in South-East Africa*. London: Rowland Ward.

SELOUS, F.C. (1908). *African Nature Notes and Reminiscences*. London: Macmillan.

SHARPE, Sir Alfred (1921). *The Backbone of Africa*. London: H.F. & G. Witherby.

STIGAND, C.H. (1913). *Hunting the Elephant in Africa and other Recollections of Thirteen Years Wandering*. London: Macmillan.

STIGAND, C.H. & LYELL, D.D. (1906). *Central African Game and its Spoor*. London: Horace Cox.

TABLER, E.C. (1963). *Trade and Travel in Early Barotseland*. London: Chatto & Windus.

THOMAS, T.M. (1873). *Eleven Years in Central South Africa*. London: n.p.

VARIAN. H.F. (1953). *Some African Milestones*. London: George Ronald.

WAGNER, R. (1980). Zoutspanberg: The dynamics of the hunting frontier. In *Economy and Society in Pre-Industrial South Africa*, ed. S. Marks & A.T. Atmore, pp.313–49. London: Longman.

WALLER, H., ed. (1880). *The Last Journals of David Livingstone, from 1865 to his death. vol. 1*. New York: Harper & Brothers.

WALLIS, J.P.R., ed. (1946). *The Northern Goldfields Diaries of Thomas Baines*, 3 vols. London: n.p.

WARD, R. (1923). *The Sportsman's Handbook*, 11th edn. London: Rowland Ward.

WARD, R. (1935). *Records of Big Game*, 10th edn. London: Rowland Ward.

3

Colonialism, capitalism and the ecological crisis in Malawi: a reassessment

JOHN McCRACKEN

One of the most important recent developments in the historiography of East Central Africa has been the growing interest displayed by historians in the process of ecological change. Pioneered in the 1970s by Helge Kjekshus and Leroy Vail, this approach challenged established orthodoxies by suggesting that, prior to the late nineteenth century, African communities were able to sustain viable ecological control systems with a considerable degree of success (Ford, 1971; Kjekshus, 1977; Vail, 1977, 1983; Iliffe, 1979). From the 1890s, however, so Vail writes in his study of eastern Zambia, 'The dual impact of expanding capitalism and colonial administration . . . resulted in a major ecological catastrophe.' The 'finely balanced relationship between man and his environment that had existed in the area prior to the mid-nineteenth century was undermined, involving it in a process of underdevelopment still unreversed today' (Vail, 1977:130). Colonial-induced diseases, colonial warfare, labour recruitment and colonial policies of control combined to bring about a breakdown of the 'man-controlled ecological system', the spread of previously limited tsetse fly belts, the eruption of sleeping sickness, the destruction of men and cattle and the permanent impoverishment of large parts of the East Central African hinterland. The process is eloquently described in Vail's most recent survey, charting the impact of capitalism in Mozambique, Malawi and Zambia:

The daily realities of colonial control, labour migrancy and village consolidation interacted with the natural disasters of the 1890s to precipitate an ecological collapse. Fields and gardens deserted in the nineteenth century and pasture emptied of cattle by the rinderpest epidemic reverted to bush. The compulsory consolidation of the villages and the general shortage of male labour caused these areas to remain unused. At the same time, wild game made a rapid comeback, much aided by colonial legislation . . . The spread of tsetse fly and sleeping sickness occurred widely and further impoverished the people when it appeared in areas where it had hitherto been unknown and killed their cattle.

(Vail, 1983: 228–9)

The aim of this chapter is to assess the validity of the Vail/Kjekshus thesis as it related to the spread of tsetse fly belts in Nyasaland (colonial Malawi). In certain respects, the Malawian example may be seen as an exception to East Central African norms. Despite the mountainous configuration of much of the country, the relatively high rainfall and easy access to regular water supplies provided by the Shire River and Lake Malawi have ensured that population densities in the Malawi region have always been significantly higher than among her neighbours: an estimated 42.6 per square mile in 1935–6, for example, compared with 4.7 per square mile in Northern Rhodesia and 14.3 per square mile in Tanganyika (Hailey, 1938: 108; Webster, 1980). Pastoralism, in consequence has never played as substantial a role in Malawi as it did in the economies of the Zimbabwean plateau to the south or the East African plains to the north. By the 1880s the only Malawian communities owning substantial herds were the Ngoni and Ngonde in the north. Nevertheless, if Malawi's experiences were in some ways different from those of the rest of the region, in others they were very much the same. As I have demonstrated elsewhere, there was a similar advance of tsetse belts in the first two decades of the twentieth century; a similar eruption of trypanosomiasis and sleeping sickness, the former killing cattle, the latter men; a similar series of generally ineffective attempts by colonial technocrats to halt the advance of the fly (McCracken, 1982). Lessons from Malawi should not be applied uncritically to other often very different environments. But neither are they totally lacking in more general validity.

The tsetse fly, which carries parasites fatal to domestic animals, two of which are capable of infecting men with sleeping sickness, is probably the most dangerous vector of disease in the *miombo* woodland regions of Central Africa. The precise distribution of tsetse in pre-colonial Malawi is unknown, but there is evidence to suggest that in the 1890s it was confined mainly to the Lower Shire Valley south of Chikwawa, to the Upper Shire Valley south of Fort Johnston (Mangoche) and to a substantial belt covering the Phalombe plain between Lake Chilwa, Zomba and Mulanje. Further north, tsetse was found in patches in the lowlands adjacent to Lake Malawi stretching from Domira Bay in the south to some forty miles south of Karonga, and there was also a substantial patch stretching from the Vwaza Marsh west to the Luangwa Valley. But in the northern uplands south through the Mzimba and Kasungu districts to the Lilongwe plain and beyond there appear to have been no tsetse at all[1] (Johnston, 1897: 377–8) (see Fig. 3.1).

From the early years of the twentieth century, however, Malawi, in

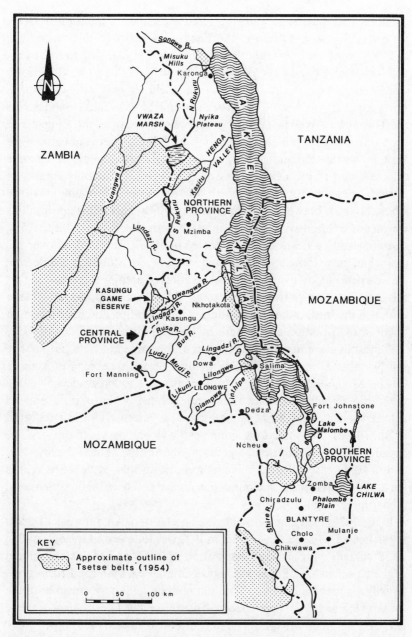

Fig. 3.1. Malawi showing the distribution of tsetse flies. 1954. (Adapted from Mitchell & Steele (1956).

common with her neighbours, suffered a dramatic expansion in tsetse fly belts. No tsetse existed in the Kasungu District in 1900, according to Dr George Prentice, founder of the Livingstonia Mission station there, and 'cattle and horses could be taken about freely'. But by 1907 tsetse were making significant advances from the Luangwa Valley to within thirty miles of the Free Church station and by 1914 had spread across the Dwangwa River in the north and nearly as far as the Lingadzi in the south.[2] On the lakeshore plain north of Salima herds of cattle were kept in various locations. But in 1904 substantial numbers became infected, and in the next five years 'the tsetse . . . steadily spread up towards the hills and to the north and south until now [in 1909] the whole country between the Lake and the hills, including the foothills which are covered with bush is infested with them'.[3] In 1908 the first cases of sleeping sickness were detected in the district. By 1913 over 160 cases had been officially confirmed, though Dr Meredith Sanderson, who carried out an investigation in the affected area, was convinced that this was a tiny proportion of the total.[4] Most victims preferred to take refuge in the bush rather than suffering incarceration and almost certain death in the isolation camps built by the authorities.

Almost as alarming were the reports of the spread of tsetse into northern Ngoniland, one of the major centres of cattle-keeping in Malawi. 'In the Mombera's district trypanosomiasis was found to occur among the cattle in villages along the course of the Rukuru river and its tributaries as far north as the main road', a veterinary officer reported in April 1915. 'The infections among cattle as one passes to the west are found to be more extensive, a great number of the animals having died and in some cases all that remains to indicate that cattle were kept is the khola which once sheltered the animals' (Nyasaland Agricultural Department, 1914–15).

In the 1920s the expansion of tsetse accelerated. An outbreak of sleeping sickness on the Kasungu plain in 1922 was followed by the evacuation of 58 villages with an adult population of 2,800 and the establishment of the Kasungu Game Reserve (now National Park) in the *Brachystegia* woodlands they had vacated. This did nothing to halt the advance of the fly. Moving at an average speed of nearly seven miles a year, a tsetse belt over 40 miles wide progressed southwards towards Lilongwe, crossing the Rusa River in 1924 and the Ludzi River in 1926 and reaching the outskirts of Fort Manning (Mchinji) in 1927.[5] Between Kasungu and Nkhota Kota the eastern and western belts met thus cutting off northern cattle from markets in the south. In 1923 cattle died of trypanosomiasis in no less than eight districts in the Protectorate. 'We have more to fear from this disease as a hindrance to the development of the Protectorate as a whole than any other disease, political condition or change in market values of the raw products which we can produce', the Chief Veterinary Officer commented. Tsetse, he claimed, was responsible for the reversion to bush of at least one third of the total uninhabited land in the territory (Nyasaland Agricultural Department, 1923).

It is one thing to chronicle the process of ecological change and another to demonstrate its relationship with the impact of capitalism. As a working hypothesis, there is good reason to accept the view (emphasised by Vail but rejected by Kjekshus) that the initial spread of tsetse was connected with changes in settlement patterns that go back to the mid-nineteenth century (Vail, 1977:132–3; Kjekshus, 1977: 9–25). Prior to that time villages tended to be dispersed on fertile ground, along valleys and within easy reach of water. However, with the eruption of the Ngoni into the northern Malawi region from the 1850s and the intensification of slave and ivory trading further south, the situation dramatically altered. In the Lower Shire Valley, so Mandala demonstrates, the dual agricultural system based upon the *dimba* floodland and *mphala* dryland zones was disrupted as people took refuge on the small islands of the Shire River and within the surrounding marshes (Mandala, 1983). In the Shire Highlands, bush and game reclaimed the Blantyre–Zomba plain, with most people taking refuge in fortified mountain sanctuaries or on Chisi island in Lake Chilwa (Vaughan, 1981; White, 1984:516). Similarly, in northern Malawi, the large concentrated villages established by the Ngoni were surrounded by a bush-covered belt of depopulated territory fifty miles wide in some sections (Vail, 1981: 240–1; Thompson, 1982: 19–20). The Henga valley, formerly a centre of Tumbuka population, 'was made a wilderness . . . the favourite resort of game and beasts of prey'. Stockaded villages in the Kasungu district were clustered in clearings a few miles in radius beyond which the bush stretched as far as the horizon (*Aurora*, 1897, 1900).

The ending of raiding following the establishment of colonial rule created the conditions for a further advance of the fly. The movement of dispersed populations away from places of sanctuary to land long abandoned to the bush resulted in the interpenetration of natural and managed ecosystems, the ideal environment for animal diseases. The expansion of tsetse in the Dowa District may be used to illustrate the point. 'In the beginning of 1903', the Assistant Resident noted, 'the Angoni from the hills began to move down to the plain near the lake in search of better soil for their gardens and settled on the lower Lipimbi and Lingadzi rivers also near the Sanjoka dambo and thus disturbed the

Buffalo, Eland and other large game which up to that time had been in undisputed possession of those districts and which had not moved far from the rivers where there was always water and good feeding. The game then began to move across the main road from Domira Bay to the Kuti and Sanjoka Dambos but were again disturbed by new native settlements and moved back carrying with them the Tsetse.' By 1909 game and tsetse had spread 'all over the plain and up to the foothills from where the natives have moved'. Villages were 'built in the bush, without more clearing than has been absolutely necessary with the result that the fly is prevalent actually in the villages'.[6] Whether the sleeping sickness that resulted was an indigenous disease or introduced from elsewhere remains a matter of dispute. But there can be no question that once it erupted, it spread with terrifying speed.

For Vail and Kjekshus it was colonial administrative policies, preventing the re-emergence of a rational settlement pattern and depriving Africans of the means to defend themselves against animals, that turned the setbacks of the nineteenth century into the ecological collapse of the twentieth. In Malawi, however, the story is somewhat different. As in other parts of Eastern Africa, the state made periodic attempts to force people against their will into consolidated villages, but more often than not it lacked the means to ensure that its demands were met. The first concerted campaign began in March 1915 when the decision was taken to apply the 1912 District Administration Native Ordinance in those parts of the Shire Highlands most affected by the Chilembwe Rising 'with the object of facilitating the concentration of huts and generally providing for more effective powers of control over the native population.'[7] Orders were given that no fewer than twenty huts were to constitute a village, and for some months a vigorous policy of concentration was pursued with Yao chiefs actively assisting the *askari* in forcing their 'Anguru' subjects into villages (White, 1984: 526–30). Yao chiefs south of Lake Malawi also encouraged the reconstruction of consolidated villages as did chiefs and headmen in northern Ngoniland, where a ban was imposed on the founding of isolated settlements on the Vipya plateau.[8]

From 1918, however, the ineffectiveness of the government's policy became increasingly clear. At one council meeting after another, Yao chiefs in the South Nyasa District bemoaned the tendency of their subjects 'to drift away from the concentrated villages to erect their huts in the gardens or on new sites in the forest'. Officials in the Mzimba District complained in vain that villagers had taken to living permanently in garden huts remote from the influence of the tax gatherer. In Chiradzulu in 1921, 'The practice of groups separating from their original village and establishing small villages of their own' had become sufficiently common to arouse the concern of the District Officer.[9] Occasionally, as when villages were moved from an area as a defence against sleeping sickness, genuine consolidation did take place. The 58 villages moved from west Kasungu in 1922 were reduced to a total of 24 averaging the large number of 72 huts each. [10] More frequently, however, consolidation was conspicuous by its absence. Writing in 1928, a senior official in the Secretariat admitted 'that since the war for various reasons e.g. shortage of staff, frequent changes of Residents . . . inexperienced officers . . . this matter has perhaps not always received the consistent attention it deserves'. Over the greater part of the Southern Province and in the Henga Valley too, the official policy had been largely abandoned, so Sir Charles Bowring, the Governor, believed.[11]

From the late 1920s, the Provincial Commissioner for the Southern Province, actively supported by Bowring, launched a new drive to consolidate villages, but once more it proved unsuccessful. For a few short years, district officers were bombarded with circulars warning them of the dangers to social control that were resulting from 'the breaking up of native villages into scattered communities'; chiefs were implored to take action against persistent offenders.[12] But with Bowring's departure in 1930, the policy ran out of steam. When the District Commissioner for Dedza argued in 1931 that in his view concentration was agriculturally inefficient, the new governor, Sir Shenton Thomas, surprised officials by minuting 'So do I'.

Fresh instructions ordering the abandonment of concentration were therefore hastily circulated to district officers; chiefs were informed, sometimes to their chagrin, that offenders should no longer be charged.[13] After over twenty years of periodic harassment, the large number of scattered villages still surviving in the country were finally left in peace. Only in areas where the coercive powers of the government were strongest, notably around Blantyre and Zomba, had the policy of consolidation met with even limited success. Elsewhere, there is little evidence to suggest that it had influenced settlement in more than a marginal manner.

A more difficult question to determine is how far colonial policies aimed at arms control and game preservation influenced the spread of tsetse. There can be no dispute that from 1891, when a gun tax was imposed, the Nyasaland government systematically attempted to limit African control of firearms while preventing the unrestricted killing of game. But it is questionable how effective these policies were. Under

Harry Johnston, the selling of guns and gunpowder to Africans without government approval was made illegal and game licences costing up to £25 per annum were introduced (Great Britain, 1894). All Africans owning firearms – 501 in 1914 – were required to obtain a licence, and this practice was tightened on the outbreak of the First World War, when arms of precision were withdrawn. All serviceable rifles and revolvers belonging to Africans were officially confiscated in the aftermath of the Chilembwe Rising. Residents were informed 'that until further notice no permits are to be issued to any native to import or purchase any firearm whatever, whether breech-loading or muzzle-loading and whether rifles or shot guns'. Only 727 guns were legally owned by Africans in the two northern provinces in 1935, many being of quite ancient vintage.[14]

It is when one moves the focus of attention from the aim of these policies to their effects that doubts begin to surface. Arms control was undoubtedly easier to impose than the concentration of villages, but game control was not. Reports from a variety of districts in the early years of the century tell of 'a good deal of illegal hunting . . . by the natives', and this trend accelerated after the First World War, helped by the substantial number of firearms retained illegally by ex-*askari*.[15] In the absence of a strong police force and in the face of opposition from Native Authorities, it was difficult to prevent the game laws becoming a dead letter, the Northern Provincial Commissioner noted in 1935. 'Of the 727 guns owned by natives in the Province, it may be assumed that at least half are used for the killing of game.' Large-scale, centrally-organised hunting expeditions of the type employed by Yao and Ngoni chiefs during the nineteenth century virtually disappeared with the establishment of colonial rule. But trapping and snaring continued unabated – the main constraint being the new demands made on men's labour time through the creation of a wage economy.[16]

For the authorities, moreover, the security gained through control of firearms required to be balanced against the popular resentment that the imposition of such laws aroused. Their readiness to respond with a measure of flexibility was demonstrated as early as 1904 when permission was granted for Mbelwa's Ngoni to hunt free of licence throughout virtually the whole of the Mzimba District – a privilege that they continued to exercise as late as 1939.[17] In other areas, village meetings frequently became the venue for intense bargaining between local councillors and district officers, with the former emphasising the damage caused to crops by elephants and other animals and the latter agreeing to supply Principal Headmen and councillors with Martini Henry rifles in order to limit the damage. From the late 1920s, professional African hunters were employed in the South Nyasa District to protect gardens from the depredations of elephants; this scheme was extended to the Lower Shire District in 1936.[18]

The effect of these policies on the animal population of Nyasaland is extremely difficult to determine. In certain areas, notably in the Kasungu District and on the south east shores of Lake Malawi, it may well be that colonial occupation was marked by an increase in the number of wild animals. ('Wild Africa of ten or twelve years ago is tame when compared with wild Africa of to-day', Dr Prentice commented from Kasungu in 1913.) In the Misuku Hills of the North Nyasa District, game was still a major hazard in the late 1920s, with lions and leopards killing several hundred cattle a year, and elephants, antelope, pigs and monkeys causing enormous damage in gardens.[19] As with cattle, wild animals recovered quickly from the rinderpest epidemic of 1892–4, though it seems unlikely that the absence of game laws by itself would have seriously checked the advance. Over much of the country, however, the growth of human population and the increasing colonisation of the land in the 1930s appears to have been accompanied by some decline in the number of animals. By 1935 it was only in the Fort Manning, Kasungu and Nkhota Kota districts of the Northern and Central Provinces that game was numerous, the Provincial Commissioner declared. The great herds of reedbuck, zebra and eland that had once inhabited the Henga Valley had retreated to the Nyika plateau. 'Elephants', it was claimed, 'harry the maize gardens of Lilongwe and Dowa no longer.'[20] For most farmers, depredations by animals remained an important irritant, but probably not an increasing one.

From the early years of the century, it was an article of faith among critics of colonial game policies that the spread of tsetse could have been halted by the systematic shooting of game: 'Game brings tsetse. Tsetse carried the trypanosome. Trypanosomes produce Sleeping Sickness. Clear out the game and you clear out the tsetse' (Letter to *The Livingstonia News*, April 1911: 33). Arguing that 'This increase of fly is due entirely to the European policy of game protection,' Dr Prentice repeatedly demanded the introduction of free shooting zones in which Africans should be allowed to hunt without hindrance. The introduction of free shooting in the Kasungu District in May 1915, however, illustrated some of the difficulties involved. Within a year over 1,200 head of game had been shot, but with distinctly unfavourable results. In an area of sparse population, the unrestricted shooting of wild animals simply scattered them to new regions, thus accelerating the advance of the fly.[21]

Fresh experiments with free shooting followed in the early 1920s, but in the opinion of the government entomologist, Dr W.A. Lamborn, they were equally ineffectual. No doubt there were some devotees of the 'Artemis cult' in Nyasaland convinced on ideological grounds that the shooting of wild animals should remain a European preserve (Ford, 1979). More important in the shaping of policy, however, was the belief, based on the experiences of R.W. Jack in Southern Rhodesia, that the cost of destroying all animals was so high as to make it prohibitively expensive.[22] In theory, at least, the elimination of elephants was a practical proposition. But as wild pig and warthogs were the major hosts of tsetse, that in itself would have done little to reduce the problem. As late as 1954, one of the heaviest concentrations of tsetse in Nyasaland lay in an area two miles from Fort Johnston from which virtually all animals except for warthogs had been eliminated (Mitchell & Steele, 1956).

If the impact of colonial administration has been oversimplified in accounts of the spread of tsetse, so too have been the effects of the emergence of the capitalist economy. This is not the place to attempt an assessment of the impact of labour migration in Nyasaland except to say that in the Kasungu District, with a population density among the lowest in the country, the spread of tsetse was intimately related to the flood of labour to the south. After the First World War, hut tax collection increased and in the absence of an economic alternative, the drain of labour began. In some villages by 1925 'hardly a single able-bodied man was kept at home', gardens were no longer cultivated, fields had reverted to bush.[23] Cattle and men were retreating under the inexorable advance of the fly.

Yet while capitalist development stimulated the expansion of tsetse, it also created the conditions in which the advance was brought to a halt. Prior to 1927 a succession of colonial experts had struggled in vain to control the movement of the fly, but from that year the expansion of African tobacco growing in the Central Province began to take effect (McCracken, 1983). Initiated in 1922 by A.F. Barron, tobacco cultivation proved so popular that in 1928 over 25,000 growers were registered in the Province and some 1,342 tons of tobacco were produced. Barron, Conforzi, Wilmot-Smith and other settlers purchased leasehold estates on the tsetse-infested land in the vicinity of the Bua, Mudi and Ludzi rivers, and as immigrants flooded in to take up tenancies, the bush was cut back, increasing amounts of land were put under cultivation and the advance of tsetse was halted. Visiting the Dowa and Fort Manning districts in 1929, Lamborn 'was greatly impressed at the great economic development of the region to the immediate south of the tsetse area that has taken place during the late rains, on the Dowa side of the Bua in particular'.[24] He applauded 'the stroke of policy which afforded Mr Barron on attractive terms a very large holding . . . on the north side of the Mudi', in consequence of which 'the tobacco patches became larger and larger annually'. Two years later the retreat of tsetse was well under way and Lamborn was trumpeting the virtues of commercial agriculture:[25]

The economic opening up of the country within the past few years has been prodigious. Patches cleared by natives for the cultivation of tobacco have become noticeably larger and more numerous even within the past eighteen months, and the rapid deforestation that is proceeding has become more and more evident, the demand for fuel for curing purposes being considerable. More and more motor roads and tracks are being developed and more natives are coming in as tenants to assist in opening up European-owned estates . . . Furthermore there is general agreement among Europeans and natives alike that the game is fast vanishing south of the reserve and has actually gone in the vicinity of the tobacco-growing centres. This accords with my own recent experience, for I saw very few evidences indeed of the presence of game. Such is the combination of factors that seem to be determining the withdrawal of the fly.

By 1937, 400 square miles of previously infested land had been cleared; none existed south of the Ludzi and Mudi rivers, and with the exception of a couple of small patches, none could be found up to ten miles north of the Ludzi.[24] In both the Lilongwe and Dowa districts, cattle were being cautiously reintroduced to land from which they had previously been removed. Subsequent progress was erratic, but the trend towards the withdrawal of tsetse was maintained. When a committee investigated the distribution of the fly in Nyasaland in 1954, it found that in the two northern provinces tsetse was restricted to the Kasungu Game Reserve and to three substantial patches near the lakeshore with a thinner subsidiary area further north spreading out from the Vwaza Marsh (Mitchell & Steele, 1956). On the Zomba-Mulanje plain the increase in population, much of it composed of Lomwe immigrants, had resulted in the virtual eradication of game and the consequent elimination of tsetse. Increasingly, the most serious focus of tsetse was to be found in the Lower Shire Valley where the remarkable expansion of cattle-keeping by a minority of rich peasants from the late 1930s had been hindered by the activities of the fly. And the problem of that area was that the tsetse formed part of a large belt stretching from Mozambique over which Malawians had little control (Schoffeleers, 1985).

In his penetrating study of capitalism, ecology and society in the Lower Shire Valley, Elias Mandala criticises conventional accounts of ecological change in East Central Africa by suggesting that they concentrate almost exclusively on how capitalism dominates specific ecosystems rather than how it interacts with them (Mandala, 1983: 261–2). The main conclusion in this chapter is to support Mandala's proposition. Vail's analysis is a stimulating one throwing new light on an important theme in a persuasive, well-documented manner. But it errs, as far as Nyasaland is concerned, both in assuming that the colonial administration was a great deal more powerful and effective than it was and also in its failure to depict capitalist penetration in its full complex and contradictory character – impoverishing African societies and economies on the one hand while providing the means to escape from, or at least to struggle with, historical poverty on the other (Iliffe, 1979: 2–3). What seems now to be required in the study of ecological change is a more flexible approach, giving due weight to the expansion of the market and the impact of colonial policies, but also taking account of those basic features studied by entomologists, botanists and geologists in the 1920s and 1930s – 'changes in composition and behaviour of vegetation and soils, of the wild fauna and of the tsetses which live upon them' (Ford, 1979: 272). A retreat into ecological determinism is clearly to be avoided. But it is worth paying serious attention to the vegetational and altitudinal requirements of *Glossina morsitans*, the major species of tsetse in Malawi, and more generally to the relationship that exists between the soils and vegetation of a particular area on the one hand and the distribution of particular types of mammals and insects on the other (Mulligan, 1970). The investigation conducted into the spread of tsetse south from the Kasungu area by B.D. Burt, the botanist attached to the prestigious Department of Tsetse Research in Tanganyika in 1937, may be used to illustrate the point. Burt did not deny that the opening up of land for tobacco growing in the vicinity of the Bua and Mudi rivers was a factor in explaining the halt in the advance of the fly. But he placed equal emphasis on the movement of tsetse away from their ideal habitat, the close canopy *Brachystegia* or miombo woodland interspersed with marshy grasslands that existed in a broad belt in the Kasungu area into the more open, less suitable habitat provided by the *Combretum–Acacia* woodlands of the Lilongwe plain. Furthermore, he suggests that in expanding south towards Dedza Mountain, the fly was beginning to reach its altitudinal limits – some 4,500 feet in Nyasaland as compared with 5,000 feet at latitude 5°S in Tanganyika (Mitchell & Steele, 1956).[27]

Such factors in themselves do not explain the process of ecological change. But they provide the context in which that change takes place.

Notes

1   S. Simpson, 'Report on the Agricultural Resources of Nyasaland', 6
     October 1908, Public Record Office, Colonial Office (PRO C.O.) 525/24.
2   R.H. Keppel-Compton, memorandum on 'Tsetse Fly in the Kasungu
     District', June 1926, Malawi National Archives, (MNA) M/2/23/4; W.A.
     Lamborn, 'The Tsetse Fly Problem in the Northern Province', paper read
     to the Nyasaland Branch of the British Medical Association, Blantyre,
     10 July 1936, MNA M2/23/3; Livingstonia Mission Report for 1907, p.37.
3   Assistant Resident, 'Report on the spread of Tsetse fly in the Dowa
     sub-district during the last seven years', 1909, MNA GFT 1/5/1.
4   Dr Meredith Sanderson, 'Preliminary Report on the Occurrence of cases
     of Trypanosomiasis in the Dowa sub-district', 1910, MNA M1/1/1; Sum-
     mary of proceedings of the 12th session of the Legislative Council, 4–5
     November 1913, *Nyasaland Government Gazette*.
5   Lamborn, 'Tsetse fly Problem'; Annual Report for the Northern Province,
     1922–3, MNA S1/1712/23; Kasungu District Book, vol.1, 'Sleeping Sick-
     ness'; B.D. Burt, 'A brief investigation of the country in the neighbour-
     hood of the advance of Glossina Morsitans to the Bua River in Nyasaland',
     June 1937, MNA M2/23/3.
6   Assistant Resident, 'Report on the spread of Tsetse fly', 1909; Meredith
     Sanderson, 'Preliminary Report on Occurrence of cases of
     Trypanosomiasis', 1910.
7   Hector Duff, Chief Secretary, to Resident, Blantyre, 22 March 1915,
     MNA NSB 1/2/1.
8   Fort Johnston District Book, vol.2, summary of proceedings of District
     Council, 29 October 1918, November 1919; Mzimba District Book, vol.1.
9   Fort Johnston District Book, vol.2, summary of proceedings of District
     Council, November 1919; Mzimba District Book, summary of meetings,
     2 September 1919, 18 February 1927; Chiradzulu District Book, vol.2,
     summary of proceedings of District Council, 10 August 1921.
10   Annual Report for the Northern Province to March 1923, MNA S1/1712/
     23.
11   Acting Assistant Chief Secretary, 'Note on Concentration of Native huts
     and villages', 12 August 1928; and memo by Sir Charles Bowring, 10
     September 1928, both MNA S1/1150/28.
12   W.B. Davidson-Houston to all PCs, DCs and Commissioner of Police, 1
     September 1928, MNA S1/1150/28; Mzimba District Book, summary of
     proceedings of District Council, 30 November 1929, 30 August and 18
     December 1930.
13   Annual Report for Dedza District for 1931, with notes by the Governor,
     MNA S1/61/A–E/32; Mzimba District Book, summary of proceedings of
     District Council, 3 June 1931; Annual Report for Mombera District, 1931,
     MNA S1/61FJ/32.
14   George Smith, Governor, to the Secretary of State for the Colonies, 16
     May 1914, PRO C.O. 525/56; Hector Duff to all Residents, 12 February,
     10 May 1915, MNA NSB 1/2/1.

15   Dr J.S. Old to Principal Medical Officer, Zomba, 10 October 1910, MNA
      M/1/1; Hector Duff, Acting Governor, to Secretary of State for the Col-
      onies, Secret, 22 May 1919, PRO C.O. 537/845.
16   Annual Report on the Northern Province for 1935, MNA S1/80/36.
17   Mzimba District Book, vol.1; Annual Report on the Northern Province
      for 1938, MNA NC 2/1/9.
18   Fort Johnston District Book, vol.4; Annual report on the Southern Pro-
      vince for 1935, MNA NS 3/1/5.
19   Livingstonia Mission Report for 1913, p.26; Interim Report of Native
      Reserves Commission (North Nyasa District), 1929, PRO C.O. 525/139.
20   Annual Report on the Northern Province for 1935, MNA S1/80/36;
      Mzimba District Book, vol. 1.
21   Livingstonia Mission Report for 1907, p.37; Kasungu District Book, vol.1,
      Ngara sub-district 1907–20. In 1915–16, 1, 152 head of game were killed in
      this area by European hunters alone; Lamborn, 'Tsetse Fly Problem',
      1936; Principal Medical Officer, Zomba, to R. Wood, 27 March 1926,
      MNA GFT 1/5/1.
22   Principal Medical Officer to Wood, ibid.; W.A. Lamborn, 'Further Report
      on the Tsetse Control Scheme', 22 April 1927, MNA GFT 1/5/1.
23   Annual Report on the Northern Province to March 1926, MNA S1/920/26.
24   W.A. Lamborn, 'First Report on the Tsetse Fly problem in the Dowa and
      Fort Manning Districts', 9 May 1929, MNA GFT 1/5/1.
25   W.A. Lamborn, 'Further Report on the Tsetse Fly Problem', 1931, MNA
      M2/23/3.
26   W.A. Lamborn, 'Report no.1 for 1937', 15 December 1937, MNA M2/23/3.
27   B.D. Burt, 'A brief investigation of the country in the neighbourhood of
      the advance of Glossina Morsitans to the Bua River in Nyasaland', June
      1937, MNA M2/23/3.

References

AURORA, 1 December 1897, and 1 October 1900.

FORD, J. (1971). *The Role of Trypanosomiases in African Ecology.* Oxford:
    Oxford University Press.

FORD, J. (1979). Ideas which have influenced attempts to solve the problems
    of African Trypanosomiasis. *Social Science and Medicine*, **13B** (4), 269–75.

GREAT BRITAIN, (1894). *Report by Commissioner Johnston on the First Three
    Years' Administration.* Command Paper, Cmd.7504. London: HMSO.

HAILEY, Lord (1938). *An African Survey.* London: HMSO.

ILIFFE, J. (1979). *A Modern History of Tanganyika.* Cambridge: Cambridge
    University Press.

JOHNSTON, H.H. (1897). *British Central Africa.* London:

KJEKSHUS, H. (1977). *Ecology Control and Economic Development in East
    African History.* London: Heinemann.

LIVINGSTONIA NEWS. April, 1911.

MANDALA, E.C. (1983). Capitalism, ecology and society: the Lower Tchiri
    (Shire) Valley of Malawi, 1860–1960. Unpublished Ph.D. thesis, University
    of Minnesota.

McCRACKEN, J. (1982). Experts and expertise in Colonial Malawi. *African Affairs*. **81** (322), 101–16.

McCRACKEN. J. (1983). Planters, peasants and the Colonial State: the impact of the Native Tobacco Board in the Central Province of Malawi. *Journal of Southern African Studies*, **9** (2), 172–92.

MITCHELL, B.L. & STEELE, B. (1956). *A Report on the Distribution of Tsetse Flies in Nyasaland and some Recommendations for Control*. Zomba: Govt Printer.

MULLIGAN, H.W., ed. (1970). *The African Trypanosomiases*. London: Halsted.

NYASALAND AGRICULTURAL DEPARTMENT (1914–23). Annual Reports. Blantyre: Govt printer.

NYASALAND GOVERNMENT GAZETTE. (Nov. 1913). Summary of proceedings of the 12th session of the Legislative Council. Blantyre: Govt Printer.

SCHOFFELEERS, M. (1985). Economic Change and Religious Polarization in an African Rural District. In *Malawi – An Alternative Pattern of Development*. Edinburgh: Centre of African Studies.

THOMPSON, T.J. (1982). The origins, migration, and settlement of the Northern Ngoni. *Society of Malawi Journal*, **34** (1).

VAIL, L. (1977). Ecology and history: the example of Eastern Zambia. *Journal of Southern African Studies*, **3** (2), 129–55.

VAIL, L. (1981). The making of the 'Dead North': a study of Ngoni rule in northern Malawi, *c.* 1855–1907. In *Before and After Shaka: Papers in Ngoni History*, ed. J.B. Peires. Grahamstown: Rhodes University.

VAIL, L. (1983). The political economy of East–Central Africa. In *History of Central Africa*, vol.2, ed. D. Birmingham & P.M. Martin. London: Longman.

VAUGHAN, M. (1981). Social and economic change in Southern Malawi: a study of rural communities in the Shire Highlands and Upper Shire Valley from the mid-nineteenth century to 1915. Unpublished Ph.D. thesis, University of London.

WEBSTER, J.B. (1980). Drought, migration and chronology in the Lake Malawi Littoral. *Transafrican Journal of History*, **9** (1) and (2), 70–90.

WHITE, L. (1984). 'Tribes' and the aftermath of the Chilembwe Rising. *African Affairs*, **83** (333), 511–41.

4

Conservation with a human face: conflict and reconciliation in African land use planning

R.H.V. BELL

'Africa is on the brink of ecological collapse.' So said a senior World Bank official at a development conference at Tananarivo in November 1985, and most people seemed to believe him. This type of belief has long given licence to government and international intervention in African rural development, and particularly to conservationist lobbies to promote a conservationist programme in Africa. The outlines of this programme are stated in the World Conservation Strategy published by the International Union for the Conservation of Nature and Natural Resources (IUCN) in 1980. The primary objectives of this strategy are as follows (IUCN, 1980):

(i)   to maintain essential ecological processes and life-support systems (i.e. atmosphere, soil and water cycles);
(ii) to preserve genetic diversity (including preventing extinctions and preserving representative biotic communities);
(iii) to ensure the sustainable utilisation of species and ecosystems.

The conservationist programme is a strategy of limitation of resource use and human population increase. As such it inevitably embodies conflict between short-term individual interests and long-term communal interests. Any programme that emphasises long-term communal benefits at the expense of short-term individual benefits will meet with resistance. The problems and costs of conservation are proportional to the extent of the conflict between these two sets of interests (Bell, 1986a). For a conservationist programme to develop and survive without external enforcement, the benefits conferred must be real and they must not be long delayed.

The conservationist programme has certain features in common with centrally planned socialist economic systems. Both systems are intended to ensure equable access to resources, communism by social classes living in parallel at one time, conservation by successive generations through time. Both involve conflicts between individual and communal interests, creating characteristic categories of illegal activity, communist systems

79

their pervasive 'economic crimes' and conservationist programmes their 'ecological offences'; both are most readily implemented by means of government enforcement. It is no accident, therefore, that in both cases there is a trend towards reconciling the conflict between the individual and the community by introducing individual rewards into the system. Some communist systems are edging towards mixed economies, while some conservation programmes are testing, with equal caution, the concept of conservation with a human face.

The costs and benefits of conservation

The balance between the various costs and benefits of conservation varies considerably between different sectors of society, both national and international. The costs in terms of alienated land, restrictions on resource use and damage to life and property are mainly carried by rural populations, particularly those at the interface between settlement and conservation areas. The political and financial costs of administering conservation programmes are carried mainly by national governments. The benefits of aesthetic and recreational experiences and scientific opportunities are enjoyed mainly by foreigners. The benefits of national prestige are enjoyed mainly by national governments as, currently, are most of the revenues from the use of wildlife resources. The rural interface communities who carry much of the cost derive few benefits. At present, then, costs and benefits are unevenly distributed.

For both costs and benefits there are two distinct classes which may be called direct and indirect respectively. A direct benefit is one that directly fulfils a human need that cannot be fulfilled in any other way; an indirect benefit is one that provides the means of fulfilling some other need. Thus for those who want to see wild elephants, wild elephants only will suffice as a direct benefit; however, wild elephants provide the indirect benefit of cash from ivory to buy fertiliser. A direct cost is one that cannot be neutralised by substituting some other commodity, whereas an indirect cost can be so neutralised. For example, when people are relocated to vacate land for a national park, the loss of access to ritual sites is a direct cost, whereas loss of agricultural land is an indirect cost which can be compensated by payment or allocation of alternative land. The primary direct benefits of conservation are aesthetic (including prestige) and intellectual (i.e. scientific), while the primary indirect benefits are utilitarian and monetary. The same may be said of costs. In this they resemble works of art, of which the direct benefits derive from their artistic value, while their indirect benefits are due to their potential as financial investments.

In the conservation arena, public discussion of costs and benefits is couched almost exclusively in terms of the indirect class, that is, of the utilitarian and monetary consequences of conservation or the lack of it. This tendency is well illustrated by the World Conservation Strategy (IUCN, 1980), in which, for example, preservation of genetic diversity is justified principally on the grounds of maintaining crop production and of the potential of wild organisms as sources of useful products. This emphasis on the indirect, utilitarian values of conservation is no doubt due to the feeling that the direct, aesthetic values are frivolous and will carry insufficient weight with governments and rural interface populations. Nonetheless, I consider the utilitarian justification of conservation to be opportunistic, unrealistic and potentially counterproductive. It is opportunistic because it is used as a stalking horse for motivations which are in reality aesthetic (cf. Bell, 1983). It is unrealistic because it cannot account for the scale of the commitment to conservation in Africa or elsewhere in relation to any critical accounting of its utilitarian returns. It may be counterproductive to the conservationist programme because, if conservation is justified on the grounds of utilitarian benefits, anything else that produces more of those benefits, must take precedence over conservation (Clarke, 1972; Bell, 1983).

This brings us back to the question of whether Africa is on the brink of ecological collapse. If the answer is yes, this can be taken as a powerful utilitarian justification of a strong conservationist programme. The benefits, in terms of living standards, will be real and immediate, so that in theory the programme should meet with little resistance. If it does meet with resistance, the argument runs, it may be necessary to impose the programme from above, the end justifying the means. If, on the other hand, Africa is not on the brink of ecological collapse, the benefits may be less immediately evident and a more gradual approach may be indicated.

Africa's ecological crisis

It is fashionable to describe the status and trend of man–environment relations in Africa in terms of concern and alarm. The scenario is presented as follows, for example by Timberlake (1985), Myers (1984) and Soulé (1984) among others: the rate of human population increase is the highest of any continent at about 3.5 per cent per year, and exceeds 4 per cent in Kenya and possibly Nigeria, Botswana and Malawi (Myers, 1980). Populations are increasing more rapidly than food supplies and services such as hospitals and schools, so that living standards are declining (Timberlake, 1985). Agriculture is expanding at the expense of natural vegetation into unsuitable land, leading to soil loss and erosion. Livestock numbers continue to increase; cattle increased by 30 per cent between 1965 and 1980 in sub-Saharan Africa, while small stock increased by 60 per cent in the same period (World Bank, 1984). These trends are leading to a steepening spiral of degradation and, ultimately, desertification. Africa is on the brink of ecological collapse.

Is this scenario realistic? Let us take each component in turn.

Human population increase. Firstly, it is probable that the published rates of human increase are inflated as a result of progressive improvements of census technique (M. Norton-Griffiths, personal communication). Secondly, admitting that the rates of increase are still high, what do they mean? They mean that Africa's human populations are not encountering serious constraints such as shortage of land, food, other resources and facilities. They mean that Africa's human populations are not yet approaching the ecological carrying capacity of the continent (see Caughley, 1977; Bell, 1986b, for the definition of ecological carrying capacity). If the population is still below carrying capacity even though it has been increasing rapidly for at least the last half century, it follows that, at the onset of the colonial era, the population must have been a small fraction of the carrying capacity.

Why was the population of Africa so low? My own view is based on that of Ford (1971). It is that the majority of the African population is derived from relatively recent immigrants and is thus vulnerable to the hostile disease environment (Hartwig & Patterson, 1978; Ranesford, 1983); that the primary defence has been cultural, involving the formation of disease-free centres by means of dense settlements eliminating wild vectors; that this pattern allowed the buildup of large populations during the Iron Age (perhaps 300 BC to about AD1700); that this cultural resistance was fractured by the opening up of Africa from about 1700 to 1930, involving political conflicts, the slave trade, major tribal movements such as that of the Ngoni, a general improvement of communications after 1900, and the introduction of external diseases; and that this fracturing re-exposed the population to endemic disease vectors and pests (such as tsetse fly and even elephant), all factors combining to cause a population crash. Ranesford (1983) quotes figures from the Belgian Congo, for example, suggesting a decline in population from 40 million in 1880 to 9.25 million in 1933. A summary of the continental situation is given by Curtin *et al.* (1981).

Livestock. The situation here is similar. The majority of livestock types have probably been introduced to Africa within the last 10,000 years

(Epstein, 1971; Klein, 1984), and most are vulnerable to a series of vector-borne diseases. Over 90 per cent of the African cattle population was eliminated at the start of the colonial era by the rinderpest pandemic introduced to Eritrea in 1887 and reaching the Cape in 1900 (Ford, 1971). Since then, the livestock population has increased steadily, to the alarm first of colonial administrators (e.g. Kenya Land Commission, 1934), and later of international advisers (e.g. Le Houerou & Skouri, 1980). These two statements of concern, made 47 years apart, are practically identical. Still the livestock population continues to increase (World Bank, 1984), in spite of two major droughts. Again this can only mean that Africa has yet to reach its ecological carrying capacity for livestock.

Land availability. Hunter (1979) estimated photogrammetrically that in Malawi, the fifth most densely populated country in Africa, 33 per cent of the land area was under 'natural vegetation', over and above National Parks and Game Reserves (11 per cent), Forest Reserves (9 per cent), agriculture (36 per cent) and urban developments (11 per cent). Norton–Griffiths (Ecosystems, 1985) whose company Ecosystems has carried out quantitative land-use surveys of over 700,000 km^2 in Tanzania, Kenya, Uganda and Sudan, estimates that even within the more densely settled strata, less than 30 per cent of available land is currently under cultivation. Grimsdell & Bell (1975) found that in the Bangweulu margin and islands, the most densely settled part of rural Zambia, 41 per cent of cultivable land was fallow. We conclude that the proposition that Africa is facing an immediate shortage of arable land is open to question, except on a limited local basis.

Degradation Can Africa continue to support the existing and foreseeable human and livestock populations without degradation significantly reducing the carrying capacity of affected areas? Quantitative data are hard to obtain. It is generally accepted that African soils under continuous cultivation commonly lose fertility and crop productivity (Nye & Greenland, 1960; Lal & Greenland, 1979). However, as Young (1976) points out, the result is a state of low-level equilibrium, in which humus and nutrient levels remain constant and crop yields are stabilised at a low level. It is not a catastrophe scenario. Similarly with livestock, Western (unpublished data) has shown that grass productivity falls initially in response to livestock buildup, then settles at a low plateau that is stable over a wide range of stock densities until it is finally eliminated by hoof action at concentration points such as bomas and waterpoints.

These low-level equilibrium models may explain the fact that the catastrophes regularly predicted rarely occur. For example, Trapnell (1953), on the basis of a survey of the ecology and land-use of North-Eastern

Rhodesia (Zambia), concluded that extensive areas were overpopulated, suffering from degradation and erosion, and were approaching ecological collapse. Now, forty years later, the collapse has not occurred, and land-use planners are discussing the accommodation of ten times the population present in 1943 (Oscarsson, 1984). Again, the Kapata Peninsula in the Bangweulu basin was estimated by Trapnell (1953) on the basis of a 1938 census, to contain about 43 people per km^2, making it one of the densest populations of rural Zambia. Trapnell considered the area 'to have been cultivated beyond recognition of (its) former state . . . land shortage is acute . . . soil depletion is marked . . . and provides the most serious population problem in Northern Province'. On the basis of the 1969 census, Jackman & Davies (1972) estimated the density in the area to be over 190 per km^2, a figure confirmed by Grimsdell and Bell (1975) by aerial photography of houses. This example makes two points: firstly that the 1938 estimate was almost certainly too low, implying an inflated rate of increase of over five per cent per annum to reach the 1969 figure, and secondly that the apparently critical ecological situation did not lead to collapse, nor has it done so now, twelve years later. Such instances are commonplace. It is much more difficult to find substantiated cases of degradation due to overpopulation or overstocking leading to reduced densities or even to reduced standards of living.

Desertification

Semi-arid and arid zones are amongst the most fragile ecosystems on earth. They can very quickly undergo irreversible degradation at the hand of man: their threshold of critical injury is reached after only a moderate or even marginal modification through human activities. Desertification is now thought to be overtaking 60,000 km^2 per year . . .   *(Myers, 1984)*

The 'settlement–overgrazing' hypothesis of desertification has recently been restated by Sinclair & Fryxell (1985). However, several aspects of this hypothesis remain open to question. Firstly, through the Quaternary, the Sahelian climate has been both drier and wetter than it is now, and the desert correspondingly larger and smaller (Grove, 1968; Grove & Warren, 1968; Rzoska, 1976; Klein, 1984). Reduction of rainfall without human intervention is thus a sufficient explanation of desert expansion, although this does not rule out human and livestock involvement in the present situation. Secondly, analysis of the Sahel rainfall records indicates a drying trend from the late 1950s to the present (Lamb, 1982; Nicholson, 1983; Kerr, 1985). Thirdly, the albedo theory of a positive feedback between vegetation reduction and diminishing rainfall remains subject to dispute (Otterman, 1974; Charney *et al.*, 1977; Nicholson, 1983; Sinclair & Fryxell, 1985), while it cannot account for the linkages between

Sahelian and broader weather patterns (i.e. Kidson, 1977). Fourthly, the recovery of Sahelian vegetation following reduction of grazing pressure (Wade, 1974; Le Houerou, 1976; H.F. Lamprey, personal communication), shows that herbivore use modifies vegetation structure (as it always does as herbivores approach carrying capacity, Caughley, 1977; Bell, 1986c), and that this change is not irreversible, as implied by Myers (1984) and Sinclair & Fryxell (1985). It does not, however, show that current changes in Sahelian vegetation are independent of rainfall capacities for humans of the Sahel, under livestock densities that would allow vegetation states that would satisfy conservationists. Finally, measurements of primary production on satellite imagery at a number of 'desertified' sites in eastern Africa, showed no difference in production in years of equivalent rainfall before and after drought spells (M. Norton-Griffiths, personal communication). We may conclude, therefore, that a climatic drying trend is the primary cause of Sahelian desertification, while the contribution of settlement and overgrazing is unclear.

Famines. There is no doubt that there are periodic and serious shortfalls in food production in parts of Africa, for example in the recent Ethiopian–Sahelian drought and in Mozambique. The questions are: are these food shortfalls the consequences of modern trends in man–environment reltions, and are they density-related?

The first question can be answered quite clearly in the negative. For Ethiopia, for example, Hancock (1985) quotes Pankhurst (1966, 1972) as listing 30 occasions on which the country was affected by famine between the years 1540 and 1900. Most famines were related to drought, although one of the worst, that of 1888–92, was compounded by the first rinderpest pandemic which killed most of the cattle and, according to Pankhurst, may have led to the deaths of 75 per cent of the human population. Droughts and famines are characteristic of arid environments and are not the consequence of modern developments in the Sahel. Rainfall variability is highest in arid areas (Norton-Griffiths, Herlocker & Pennycuick, 1978; Nicholson, 1979), so that the carrying capacity fluctuates widely, allowing populations to build up beyond the bottleneck values imposed by periodic droughts.

The current droughts may be unusual in one important respect. This is that the traditional response of humans and livestock, that of movement, is now to some extent constrained by the rigid political boundaries of modern nation states. Even so, as the latest Sahelian drought eases, the estimated mortality toll has been much smaller than predicted (Ingram, 1985) and will not affect the generally increasing trend of Africa's human population.

The second question, is food shortfall density-related, is more difficult to answer without detailed statistical analysis taking into account other variables such as rainfall and soils. However, a casual survey suggests the opposite, that living standards are either independent of density or actually positively correlated, as in the highlands of Kenya and northern Tanzania, southern Nigeria, Malawi, etc. World Bank (1984) statistics indicate that food production in Ruanda, the most densely populated country in Africa, is keeping pace with, or outstripping, population growth. Food shortfalls that are unrelated to drought, then, are almost without exception related to civil disturbances, as in Mozambique, Uganda and eastern Zaïre. Frequently disturbance-induced shortfalls are exacerbated by emphasis on cash crops at the expense of food crops (Hancock, 1985; Timberlake, 1985). These are political and economic, rather than ecological problems.

The status of wildlife and wildlife conservation

Africa has reached the present with a relatively modest level of Quaternary extinctions (Klein, 1984), and with its ecological communities relatively intact. Exceptions are the moist forests which are species-poor compared with those of tropical America and Asia; this is probably due to periodic fragmentation by climate changes rather than to human interference (McKinnon, unpublished data). The status of ecosystem conservation has been reviewed for eastern Africa by Lamprey (1975) and IUCN (1976), while the Afro-tropical realm as a whole is currently under review (McKinnon, unpublished data); a workshop reached the following preliminary conclusion (IUCN, 1985):

While Africa south of the Sahara has allocated a relatively high proportion of its land to protected areas, and while many African countries possess extensive, representative and well managed protected area systems, there is no room for complacency on the overall conservation situation. The fundamental problem is recognised as the rapid human population increase. The immediate shortcomings are of two types. Firstly, there are important omissions or deficiencies in the representation of biotic communities in protected area systems. Secondly, there are serious shortcomings in the management of existing protected area systems, due to constraints of funding, trained manpower, equipment and political support . . .

Clarke (1981) estimated, on the basis of the United Nations List of National Parks and Equivalent Reserves (Anon, 1980), that 3.5 per cent of sub-Saharan Africa was allocated to protected areas of this status. The current figure is probably at least 4 per cent. This proportion compares favourably with other global regions, being significantly surpassed only by North America (12.6 per cent) and the Oceanic islands (10.3 per cent) (Clarke, 1981). Several African countries, including Botswana, Malawi, Tanzania and Zambia, have allocated over 10 per cent of their land area to national parks or equivalent reserves. Using a figure of 4 per cent for sub-Saharan Africa, the total area of National Park is possibly around 850,000 km^2 (Bell & Clarke, 1986a). In addition to the national parks and equivalent reserves is a significant area of Forest Reserve as well as mixed-use conservation areas. The number of national parks and equivalent reserves gazetted has more than doubled since the independence of most African states in the 1960s, with a particularly rapid phase of land acquisition in the mid-1970s (Harrison, unpublished data). In general, then, the protected area situation in Africa is relatively favourable. However, certain ecosystems are under-represented or under-protected (IUCN, 1985): lowland and montane forests, deserts, swamps, seashore, freshwater and alkaline lakes, succulent karoo and lowland *fynbos*.

There are, in addition, a considerable number of endangered and threatened species, including a large number of plant species (IUCN, 1984), about 180 species of birds (Collar & Stuart, 1984) and several other species of vertebrate. In the latter category, conspicuous members are the scimitar-horned oryx (*Oryx dammah*), possibly already extinct in the wild (Newby, 1986), and the northern white rhinoceros (*Ceratotherium simum cottoni*) (AERSG, 1985). The black rhinoceros (*Diceros bicornis*) has also been drastically reduced over the last decade as a result of illegal hunting for horn (Bradley Martin, 1980, 1983; Bradley Martin & Bradley Martin, 1983). The present number is probably around 8,000 (AERSG, 1985). Much attention has also been given to the decline of the African elephant (*Loxodonta africana*) as a result of illegal hunting for ivory. Certainly its numbers and range have been reduced over the last decade, but the total population is currently estimated at between about 740,000 (Douglas-Hamilton's, 1984, lower estimate) and 1,180,000 (Martin, 1986c), and can scarcely be considered endangered or even threatened, except on a local basis (Parker & Amin, 1983). The situation of the elephant is not atypical of the situation of African wildlife as a whole, that is, it is more optimistic than the media would have us believe. This is backed up by Prescott-Allen's (1984) analysis of the IUCN *Red Data Book* (IUCN, 1978, 1979a, b), which indicates that of 25 countries with 20 or more vertebrate species known to be threatened, only two (South Africa and Cameroon) are in mainland Africa, while of 13 countries with 10 or more endemic vertebrate species known to be threatened, only one (South Africa) is on the continent.

The commitment of most African governments to wildlife conservation cannot be doubted. The massive allocation of land, frequently as great or greater after independence than before, speaks for itself. So does the allocation of funds. Bell & Clarke (1986a) estimate, on the basis of data collated by Cumming, Martin & Taylor (1984) and other sources, that the total financial allocation to wildlife conservation in Africa other than South Africa in 1981 was about $75 million, with about as much again being spent in South Africa. The majority of these funds is derived from national government subventions rather than from external donations. Given the responsibilities of conservation agencies outside national parks, this works out at roughly $50 per km^2 of national park on average.

There can equally be no doubt as to the reality of the conflict with local interests. Most conservation agencies are paramilitary armed and uniformed organisations, in which the majority of expenditure is devoted to law enforcement and public relations. Under existing wildlife legislation in many African countries, normal rural existence is nearly impossible without breaking the law (Marks, 1976). Most such offences are minor and undetected, but in many countries extensive enforcement takes place. For example, in Malawi around 500 persons per year are charged on wildlife-related counts, while in 1981, 239 people were arrested in and around Kasungu National Park alone (Bell, 1984). In many African countries, armed confrontations between 'poachers', that is those acting contrary to wildlife legislation, and enforcement staff, are commonplace and deaths and injuries on both sides are regular occurrences. In some countries, infringement of wildlife legislation on a large scale, such as residence within protected areas and extraction of products such as meat, ivory, rhinoceros horn, skins and timber, is common, as in the Ivory Coast (Hall-Martin, unpublished data), Sudan (AERSG, 1985) and Mozambique (J. Tello, personal communication); here, no serious attempt is made to enforce wildlife legislation.

The crisis: another viewpoint

The human population in Africa is increasing rapidly, but the overall population density is still relatively low except in certain localised concentrations. Extensive surveys indicate the availability of considerable areas of usable land. Crop production per area is roughly constant. Frequent predictions of soil exhaustion and catchment degradation are rarely fulfilled. Livestock numbers continue to increase although there have been localised die-offs due to droughts. Undisturbed natural biotic communities remain in considerable quantities both inside and out: protected areas. The protected area system is large and generally resentative of Africa's biotic communities. Africa's fauna has been relatively lightly affected by Pleistocene and recent extinctions, and spectacular large mammal communities exist in many countries. A small number of large mammal species is seriously endangered mainly due to illegal hunting for high cash value products such as rhinoceros horn.

We appear, then, to be faced with a paradox. On the one hand the human population is increasing very rapidly, but on the other hand the overall ecological situation seems generally satisfactory with considerable room for further human increase without either ecological collapse, elimination of major biotic communities or extinction of many species. The key to this paradox is that, when Europeans encountered Africa at the outset of the colonial era, they encountered a human population probably smaller than it had been since the Iron Age revolution 2,000 years before, reaching its nadir between 1900 and 1930. The same is true of livestock which were drastically reduced by the rinderpest pandemic of 1890–1900. As human and livestock populations crashed, wildlife and its habitats expanded, a situation which was perpetuated and exaggerated by colonial conservationist legislation.

The consequence of these events was that the western world gained a false impression of the 'natural' relationship between humans and their environments in Africa that has coloured western attitudes towards development and conservation in Africa ever since. As Graham (1973) has pointed out, the West found in Africa the Garden of Eden of its romantic imagination. The subsequent recovery and development of humans and livestock were therefore seen as unnatural, threatening and ecologically unsound. The international establishment has in the past come to apply a double standard with regard to conservation and development, applying more rigorous constraints to development to the Third World and Africa in particular, than to the developed countries. The picture has of course been complicated by the droughts and civil disturbances, both of which factors have led to local shortfalls in food production. Their effects are independent of human density, but those looking for evidenece of density-induced ecological collapse have found it in their effects. Such erroneous conclusions have tended to reinforce the western view that the problems of development in Africa are primarily the result of human population increase and that they can be solved by constraints to resource utilisation as indicated by a conservationist programme.

Strategies of the attainable

The recent trend in Africa has been towards a more flexible and liberal approach to conservation. This approach recognises the need to identify valid objectives for conservation, to reduce the conflicts between short-term individual interests and long-term communal interests, and to balance the costs and benefits equally between different sectors of the community, international, national and local.

The first requirement is to clarify the objectives of conservation. Most statements of conservation objectives, such as the World Conservation Strategy (IUCN, 1980), give no guidelines on how much conservation is enough; the more the better, they imply. The World Conservation Strategy objective of preserving diversity gives few guidelines on what levels of diversity are required. It does not satisfactorily address the questions of how to deal with evolutionary change, nor that certain organisms are harmful and undesirable. As it stands, it represents the impractical and counterproductive intention to freeze the biosphere in its present state. Clarke & Bell (1986b) conclude that the decision as to how much to conserve, and in what state, is essentially an arbitrary or aesthetic decision (Bell, 1983). This means that each country has to formulate a national conservation strategy which represents a selective application of the World Conservation Strategy. Such a strategy has to answer the following questions (Bell & Clarke, 1986b):

(i)   Which species of animal and plant does the country intend to conserve?
(ii)   What numbers of these species does it intend to conserve?
(iii)   Where does it intend to conserve them?
(iv)   How does the country intend to utilise them?

Such a strategy implies a policy that defines the relationship between man and his environment. The policy statement of the Department of National Parks and Wildlife, Malawi (Clarke, 1983), explicitly recognises the predominance of human interests:

Wildlife means all species of wild indigenous plants and animals. It includes undesirable as well as desirable species, and those that may be considered insignificant . . . the government recognises that wildlife . . . has positive and negative values in relation to human needs. The government's intention is to manage these resources in a professional and scientific manner for the benefit of man, in particular the people of Malawi . . . the government recognises three broad classes of management: conservation, utilisation and control . . . The government appreciates that, in practical terms, a large proportion of wildlife is either insignificant or incapable of being managed by the state . . . The species or individuals that are to be subject to state management are defined by legislation. Wildlife not subject to state management may be conserved, utilised or controlled by the public as it sees fit . . .

Similarly, the Parks and Wildlife Act of Zimbabwe (Act no. 14 of 1975 as amended in 1982) establishes a series of categories of wildlife (specially protected, protected, ordinary) and a series of categories of land (national park, botanical reserve, sanctuary, safari area, open land and private land) aimed at providing for different levels of protection and different types of use. This Act differs from most other African wildlife legislation in that it gives landowners a high level of control and use rights (if not actual ownership) of wildlife on their land. This has triggered the growth of a large and lucrative game ranching industry. A similar situation exists in South Africa.

Clarke (1983) and Clarke & Bell (1986a) have proposed a form of wildlife legislation in which each interaction between humans and wildlife is defined in terms of a three-dimensional matrix, the dimensions being: category of wildlife, category of land and category of interaction. We have also proposed (Bell & Clarke, 1986a) a national wildlife master plan demarcating conservation and development zones, in each of which the objectives are specified in terms of:

(i)   the permissible quantities of settlement, agriculture and livestock;
(ii) the permissible types of infrastructure development;
(iii) the permissible limits to change of physical and biological resources;
(iv) the permissible types and agencies of use of wildlife.

(The option of course exists for no limits to be specified.) Zoning systems of this type are coming into use in a number of countries, usually more or less informally, in the form of integrated land-use plans with conservation components, e.g. Luangwa, Zambia (Dalal-Clayton, 1984); Vwaza Marsh, Malawi (McShane, 1985); Pilanesberg, Bophuthatswana (Bophuthatswana National Parks Board, 1985); and Gambella, Ethiopia (WCO, 1985a).

As a starting point, it is important to remember that the two major sets of costs of conservation are directly interrelated; reducing one set of costs automatically reduces the other set. The first set of costs comprises costs born by interface residents and other users of wildlife resource in lost opportunity (of land, resources and direct benefits). The larger these costs, the greater the pressure for illegal use of wildlife resources, and the greater the cost to the government of containing that pressure by means of law enforcement and public relations, that is, the other major set of costs.

The first step, then, is to create a conservation policy that the key sectors of interface residents and other potential wildlife resources users can agree with or tolerate. Goals should not be set too high. I would like to offer the proposition that most of the World Conservation Strategy objectives could be met by allocation of five per cent of the land area of each country to national parks and equivalent reserves, with these zoned to allow managed consumptive utilisation (as advocated by Anderson, 1983, and others) where this is deemed desirable, and with educated management of natural resources outside conservation areas. If this goal is regarded as inadequate by most conservationists, it is because of the unstated, aesthetic objectives associated with the World Conservation Strategy.

Next we must consider the indirect costs of such a policy, that is, those that can be neutralised by the substitution of some equivalent benefit. A key aspect here is damage to human life, property and crops. Many species of large African animal are incompatible with most forms of rural development, for example elephant, hippopotamus, rhinoceros, buffalo, lion and crocodile, as well as some of the larger antelopes, primates and pigs. This has been a chronic problem in the integration of wildlife with other forms of land use. Solutions have traditionally involved extensive graded-use 'buffer zones' and control hunting (Martin & Taylor, 1983), both of which tend to be ineffective and economically inefficient (Bell, 1986d). A radical improvement has recently occurred, however, through the development of a new generation of electric fencing, which has now been used successfully, cheaply and flexibly to control large wild mammals in Malaysia, Malawi, Kenya and South Africa (Bell, 1986d). This development is expected to lead to considerable progress in integrated land use, allowing, for example, the protection of villages and cultivation within wildlife areas with the consequent realisation of the full benefits of agriculture and wildlife utilisation side by side, and the elimination of nuisance wildlife from areas zoned for agricultural or other developments.

The indirect costs in lost opportunity can be reduced in a number of ways. The standard approach is that revenues earned by protected wildlife or land (i.e. from tourism, professional hunting or culling) should be fed back to the community bearing the cost, in the form of a rent for the sequestered resources. An early example initiated in the 1940s was that of Nsefu Game Reserve, Zambia, where revenues from tourism were fed back to the chief in whose area it was established (Carr, 1979). The arrangements in Amboseli and the Mara areas, where tourist revenues are returned to the relevant group ranches and county councils, are similar (Western, 1976; Western & Henry, 1979; Lindsay, Chapter 7). Revenues from professional hunting from Vwaza Marsh Game Reserve, Malawi, are intended to be re-allocated to the District Development Committees (DDCs) (McShane, 1985). Similarly, revenues from reduction culling in the Sebungwe region, Zimbabwe, were allocated to DDCs under Operation Windfall, and are reported to have led to a reduction in illegal hunting in the area (Martin, 1986a).

These revenue allocation schemes are probably a step in the right direction, but, as Martin (1986a) and Lindsay (Chapter 7) have pointed out, they have been somewhat disappointing to all concerned. The main problems are twofold. Firstly, the fund allocations are not pinpointed accurately enough on affected sectors of society. As on the national scale, the district or county or chieftainship is too large a unit; the interface residents who carry the bulk of the costs, are not benefited by funds allocated to the DDC to build a school or a clinic 40 miles away or to provide transport for the DDC membership. The second, and in my view larger problem, is that in such schemes the recipients are essentially passive. They do not participate in decision-making, nor do they enjoy the direct aesthetic benefits associated with personal use of wildlife areas and resources. They are being treated as a nuisance that is being bribed to keep quiet.

A rather more radical proposal has been suggested by Bell (1982, 1986c) and Martin (1986b). This is the suggestion that interface residents should be allocated concessions to use wildlife resources in certain areas and that the conservation agencies should act as marketing agents for their products (see Parker, 1964, for an earlier proposal of a similar type). By acting as marketing agents, the conservation agency would obtain revenue for itself to strengthen its law enforcement capability, while the concessionaire himself would obtain a greater financial return than he does illegally. For example, illegal hunters in Malawi in 1981 were obtaining about $10 per kg for ivory while the world price was at least $50 per kg. If, in this situation, the conservation agency purchased the ivory from the hunter for, say, $30 per kg and resold it for $50 per kg, all parties would benefit, while the reward would be targeted at precisely that sector of society paying the costs of lost opportunity. The size and location of the quota would be determined by the agency and illegal offtake would be subtracted, so that the concessionaire would have a strong incentive to assist in law enforcement. Finally, and most importantly, the concessionaires would enjoy the important aesthetic and cultural benefits associated with utilisation and distribution of wildlife resources (Marks, 1976).

This brings us to the direct costs and benefits of conservation, those which are essentially ethical and aesthetic and which cannot be substituted by financial rewards or other compensations. Such direct aesthetic benefits are the primary motivation towards conservation at all levels, international, national and interface. Especially at national and interface levels, the recognition of these benefits dictates the payment of unexpectedly high and usually unrecognised costs in their interest (Bell, 1983, 1985). The indirect, utilitarian benefits attributed to conservation are for the most part rationalisations used to make up for the perceived inadequacy of the aesthetic motivation. This can clearly be demonstrated by rigorous accounting of most conservation situations (with some notable exceptions) where, in utilitarian and financial terms, conservation is negative rather than positive. The equations can only be made to make sense by admitting the existence of the invisible term associated with aesthetic motivations. In Malawi, for example, 11 per cent of the country's land area is allocated to conservation, most of it arable land; the government allocates over $0.5m annually to conservation, while the largest source of revenue, equivalent to about one third of this expenditure, is derived from ivory confiscated from poachers and shot on control, both of which sources the government intends to reduce by more effective management; tourism revenues are insignificant and wildlife-related tourism operates at a loss (Clarke, 1983; Carter, 1985). I argue that careful accounting would reveal the situation in most African countries to be similar. The recent annual report of Pilansberg National Park, Bophuthatswana (Bophuthatswana National Parks Board, 1985) contains just such a careful accounting and shows financial losses of over half a million rand per year, although it is the intention of this organisation to cover its costs in the future. Possible exceptions include South Africa, Zimbabwe, Botswana and Kenya.

The recognition of the importance attached by African societies to the direct, aesthetic significance of wildlife and conservation is of considerable importance to land-use strategies. Most importantly, it implies that conservationists are misdirected when they emphasise the indirect, utilitarian and economic aspects of conservation. By doing so, they risk appearing insincere or naïve and disparaging of African value systems. It implies that greater attention should be paid to the problem of local involvement in conservation-related activity. I refer here to the problem that conservation areas are widely seen as playgrounds for wealthy expatriates from which national residents are effectively excluded. For example, in Malawi, nationals account for 1.0 per cent of all fee-paying visits to national parks (Carter, 1985) although they make up 99.75 per cent of the resident population. This disproportion, I believe, is not due to lack of interest, but to the costs and difficulties of transport and accommodation for the average African national. This is indicated by the great success and popularity of education and public relations programmes aimed at providing access by nationals to conservation areas (Price, 1986; Sefu, 1986). It is basic to effective conservation planning to provide access by nationals, in the form of cheap accommodation and transport, to the commodity, that is the recreational experience of wildlife, for which the community has paid a considerable price (Bell & Clarke, 1986b). It is a mistake to believe that the only interest in wildlife is utilitarian and that it can be bought off with development schemes or cash.

The recognition of the aesthetic significance of conservation accounts for a number of apparently irrational attitudes common to conservationists, international or African, for example the widely held view that culling in national parks for reasons of habitat management and revenue generation is unethical. This view is the dominant official view in Africa north of the Zambezi and is found among the general public (Munthali & Banda, 1985) as well as conservation agency personnel (Sheldrick, 1973; Kombe, 1983; Bell, 1983). It accounts for the unpopularity of expatriate professional hunting commonly found among residents of the areas concerned (Lewis, 1982; McShane, 1985), even where the residents derive revenue and employment therefrom (as is not always the case, Malama, 1984). Here, one may suppose that the social and recreational benefits of hunting on one's own account outweigh the economic benefits of 'renting' the hunting rights to others.

Participation in the planning process

This brings us to the final issue, that of participation in the decision-making process. Land-use strategies are intended to identify attainable conservation objectives and to minimise conflicts of interest. However, as Thorsell (1984) and Bell & Clarke (1986b) have emphasised, the *process* of development and implementation of the plan is as important as its content. However well-intentioned, plans imposed from above are liable to generate social conflicts or to contain technical errors. To avoid these problems, input from all parties involved must be incorporated into land-use plans of this type. Thus another feature of the current trend is representation of all interested parties, e.g. Kenya, Amboseli (Western, 1976); Liberia, Sapo National Park (IUCN, unpublished data); and Ethiopia, Simen National Park (WCO, 1983) and Bale Mountains

National Park (WCO, 1985b). This is a very recent feature, although Zimbabwe made a start in 1975 with its local wildlife boards and owner's control of wildlife on private land. Zimbabwe has carried the concept much further with its CAMPFIRE proposal (Communal Area Management Plan for Indigenous Resources, Martin, 1986b), in which it is envisaged that residents in communal lands may form companies owning and controlling the use of all natural resources on a communal basis, within limits laid down by the government. A similar proposal is under consideration for part of Zambia's Luangwa valley (Larsen & Lungu, 1985).

We reach the conclusion, then, that land-use planning and conservation represent a microcosm of government. Can human nature be trusted to maintain equable access to resources either between sectors of the community or between generations in time? The case for strong central control rests on a negative answer, the belief that Africa is on the brink of man-induced ecological collapse. If these beliefs can be queried, or be shown to be incorrect at least in part, then there is room for conservation with a human face.

Acknowledgements

This chapter has benefited from discussion with Ian Parker, Jonah Western, Mike Norton-Griffiths and Jim Thorsell. Kathy Homewood made many helpful editorial suggestions. I would like to thank Mike Norton-Griffiths for permission to quote information collated by his company, Ecosystems Ltd, and Manuel Msikati, who typed the manuscript.

References

AERSG (1985). Minutes of a meeting of the IUCN/SSC African elephant and rhino specialist group. Held at Victoria Falls, Zimbabwe, 21–22 September, 1984.

ANDERSON, J.L. (1983). Sport hunting in National Parks: sacrilege or salvation? In *Management of Large Mammals in African Conservation Areas* ed. R.N. Owen-Smith, pp.27–80. Pretoria: Haum.

ANON (1980). *1980 United Nations list of National Parks and Equivalent Reserves*. Gland, Switzerland: IUCN.

BELL, R.H.V. (1982). The problem of traditional use of wildlife resources in Malawi. Paper read to the Conseille Internationale du Chasse, Monaco, June 1982, pp.1–18.

BELL, R.H.V. (1983). Decision-making in wildlife management with references to problems of overpopulation. In *Management of Large Mammals in African Conservation Areas*, ed. R.N. Owen-Smith, pp.145–72. Pretoria: Haum.

BELL, R.H.V. (1984). Law enforcement in Malawi conservation. *Newsletter of the African Elephant and Rhino Specialist Group*. no. 3, pp.7–8.

BELL, R.H.V. (1985). The ecologist in Africa: his role for the next two decades. *Bulletin of the Ecological Society of America*, **66** (1), 11–14.

BELL, R.H.V. (1986a). Problems in achieving conservation goals. In *Conservation and Wildlife Management in Africa*. ed. R.H.V. Bell & E. McShane-Caluzi, pp.31–42. Washington: US Peace Corps.

BELL, R.H.V. (1986b). Carrying capacity and off-take quotas. In *Conservation and Wildlife Management in Africa*. ed. R.H.V. Bell & E. McShane-Caluzi, pp.145–82. Washington: US Peace Corps.

BELL, R.H.V. (1986c). Soil–plant–herbivore interactions. In *Conservation and Wildlife Management in Africa*. ed. R.H.V. Bell & E. McShane-Caluzi, pp.107–30. Washington: US Peace Corps.

BELL, R.H.V. (1986d). The man–animal interface: an assessment of crop damage and wildlife control. In *Conservation and Wildlife Management in Africa*. ed. R.H.V. Bell & E. McShane-Caluzi, pp.387–416. Washington: US Peace Corps.

BELL, R.H.V. & CLARKE, J.E. (1986a). Funding and financial control. In *Conservation and Wildlife Management in Africa*. ed. R.H.V. Bell & E. McShane-Caluzi, pp.543–56. Washington: US Peace Corps.

BELL, R.H.V. & CLARKE, J.E. (1986b). Master-plans. In *Conservation and Wildlife Management in Africa*. ed. R.H.V. Bell & E. McShane-Caluzi, pp.501–28. Washington: US Peace Corps.

BOPHUTHATSWANA NATIONAL PARKS BOARD (1985). *Pilansberg National Park: Annual Report no.2, 1982–3, no.3, 1983–4*: Mafeking: Bophuthatswana National Parks Board.

BRADLEY MARTIN, E. (1980). *The international trade in rhinoceros products*. Gland, Switzerland: IUCN/WWF.

BRADLEY MARTIN, E. (1983). *Rhino exploitation*. Gland, Switzerland: IUCN/WWF.

BRADLEY MARTIN, E. & BRADLEY MARTIN, C. (1983). *Run Rhino Run*. London: Chatto & Windus.

CARR, N. (1979). *The Valley of the Elephants*. London: Collins.

CARTER, J.M. (1985). *Tourism Master Plan for the National Parks and Game Reserves in Malawi*. Lilongwe: Department of National Parks and Wildlife.

CAUGHLEY, G. (1977). What is this thing called carrying capacity? In *North American Elk: Ecology, Behaviour and Management*, ed. M.S. Boyce & L.D. Hayden-Wing, pp.2–8. Laramie: University of Wyoming.

CHARNEY, J.G., QUIRK, W.J., CHOW, S-H. & KORNFIELD, J. (1977). A A comparative study of the effects of albedo change on drought in semi-arid regions. *Journal of Atmospheric Science*. **34**, 1366–85.

CLARKE, J.E. (1972). One Man's View. *Black Lechwe Magazine*. **10**, 29–33.

CLARKE, J.E. (1981). A model wildlife program for developing countries. Unpublished Ph.D. thesis, University of Georgia.

CLARKE, J.E. (1983). *Principal Master Plan for National Parks and Wildlife Management*. Lilongwe: Department of National Parks and Wildlife.

CLARKE, J.E. & BELL, R.H.V. (1986a). Wildlife legislation. In *Conservation and Wildlife Management in Africa*, ed. R.H.V. Bell & E. McShane-Caluzi, pp.479–500. Washington: US Peace Corps.

CLARKE, J.E. & BELL, R.H.V. (1986b). Representation of biotic communities in protected areas: a Malawian case study. *Biological Conservation.* **35** (4), 293–312.

COLLAR, N. & STUART, S.M. (1984). *Threatened Birds of Africa. IUCN/ICBP Bird Red Data Book, Part 1.* Gland, Switzerland: IUCN/WWF.

CUMMING, D.H.M., MARTIN, R.B. & TAYLOR, R.D. (1984). Questionnaire survey on the management and conservation of elephant and rhino. In *The Status and Conservation of Africa's Elephants and Rhinos.* Proceedings of the joint meeting of IUCN/SSC African elephant and rhino specialist groups in Hwange Safari Lodge, Zimbabwe, 30 July to 7 August 1981, ed D.H.M. Cumming & P. Jackson, pp.46–62, Gland, Switzerland: IUCN.

✱ CURTIN, P., FEIERMAN, S., THOMPSON, L. & VANSINA, J. (1981). *African History,* London: Longman.

DALAL-CLAYTON, D.B. ed (1984). *An Integrated Approach to Landuse Management in the Luangwa Valley. Proceedings of the Lupande Development Workshop,* held at Nyamaluma Wildlife Camp, Lupande Game Management Area, 19–22 September 1983. Lusaka: Govt Printer.

DOUGLAS-HAMILTON, I. (1984). *Elephant Populations Since 1981.* Report to a meeting of the IUCN/SSC African elephant and rhino specialist group, held in Maun, Botswana, September 1984.

ECOSYSTEMS (1985). *Integrated Land Use Survey of Western Kenya.* Final Report of the Lake Basin Authority, Kisumu, Kenya. Kisumu: Lake Basin Authority.

EPSTEIN, H. (1971). *The Origins of the Domestic Animals of Africa.* 2 vols. New York: Africana Publishing Company.

√ FORD, J. (1971). *The Role of Trypanosomiasis in African Ecology.* Oxford: Oxford University Press.

GRAHAM, A.D. (1973). *The Gardeners of Eden.* London: George Allen & Unwin.

GRIMSDELL, J.J.R. & BELL, R.H.V. (1975). *Ecology of the Black Lechwe in the Bangweulu Basin of Zambia.* Black Lechwe Research Project Final Report. Lusaka: National Council for Scientific Research.

GROVE, A.T. (1968). *Africa.* Oxford: Oxford University Press.

GROVE, A.T. & WARREN, A. (1968). Quaternary landforms and climate on the south side of the Sahara. *Geographical Journal.* **134.** 194–208.

HANCOCK, G. (1985). *Ethiopia, the Challenge of Hunger.* London: Victor Gollancz.

HARTWIG, G.W. & PATTERSON, K.D. (1978). *Disease in African History.* Duke University Press.

HUNTER, N.D. (1979). The development of agriculture in Dedza (Malawi) with particular reference to the farmer's management practices and his natural resource base. Unpublished M.Sc. thesis, University of Exeter.

INGRAM, J. (1985). 'We need a sustained effort'. Interview with the Director of the World Food Programme. *Newsweek.* 28 October 1985, p.56.

IUCN (1976). *Proceedings of a Regional Meeting on the Creation of a Coordinated System of National Parks and Reserves in Eastern Africa.* Gland, Switzerland: IUCN.

IUCN (1978). *Red Data Book, vol. 1, Mammalia.* Gland, Switzerland: IUCN.

IUCN (1979a). *Red Data Book, vol. 2, Aves.* Gland, Switzerland: IUCN.

IUCN (1979b). *Red Data Book, Amphibia and Reptiles.* Gland, Switzerland: IUCN.

IUCN (1980). *World Conservation Strategy.* Gland, Switzerland: IUCN.

IUCN (1984). *Plants in danger: what do we know?* Gland, Switzerland: IUCN.

IUCN (1985). *Joint Statement of the Participants in the Review Workshop of the Afrotropical realm.* Held at Kasungu National Park, Malawi, June 1985. Gland, Switzerland: IUCN.

JACKMAN, M.E. & DAVIES, D.H. (1972). *Population Density Map of Northern Zambia.* Lusaka: National Council for Scientific Research.

KENYA LAND COMMISSION (1934). *Report of the Kenya Land Commission (Carter).* London: HMSO.

KERR, R.A. (1985). Fifteen years of African drought. *Science.* **227**, 1453–4.

KIDSON, J.W. (1977). African rainfall and its relation to upper air circulation. *Quarterly Review of the Royal Meteorological Society.* **103**, 441–56.

KLEIN, R.G. (1984). Mammalian extinctions and stone age people in Africa. In *Quaternary Extinctions.* ed. R.B. Martin & R.G. Klein. Tucson: University of Arizona Press.

KOMBE, A. (1983). Government and public reactions to culling in conservation areas in Malawi. In *Management of Large Mammals in African Conservation Areas,* ed. R.N. Owen-Smith, pp.24–8. Pretoria: Haum.

LAL, R. & GREENLAND, D.J. (1979). *Soil Physical Properties and Crop Production in the Tropics.* Chichester: Wiley.

LAMB, P.J. (1982). Persistence of sub-Saharan drought. *Nature,* **299**, 46–8.

LAMPREY, H.F. (1975). *The Distribution of Protected Areas in relation to the needs of biotic community conservation in Eastern Africa.* Gland, Switzerland: IUCN.

LARSEN, T. & LUNGU, F. (1985). *Preparation Report on the Luangwa Integrated Resource Development Project (LIRDP).* Report to NORAD. Oslo: NORAD.

Le HOUEROU, H.N. (1976). Rehabilitation of degraded arid land. In *Can Desert Encroachment be Stopped, Ecological Bulletin no.24,* ed. E. Rapp, H.N. Le Houerou & T. Lundholm. Stockholm: Secretariat for International Ecology.

Le HOUEROU, H.N. & SKOURI, M. (1980). Conclusion and recommendations. In *Browse in Africa, the Current State of Knowledge.* Papers presented at the International Symposium on Browse in Africa, Addis Ababa, 8–12 April 1980, and other submissions, ed. H.N. Le Houerou, pp.485–6. Addis Ababa: International Livestock Commission for Africa.

LEWIS, D.M. (1982). Lupande Research Project: summary report for June to November, 1982. Report to the National Parks and Wildlife Service, Lusaka, pp.1–16.

MALAMA, Chief G. (1984). Address at the opening of the Lupande Development Workshop. In *An Integrated Approach to Land Use Management in the Luangwa Valley, proceedings of the Lupande Development Workshop,* ed. D.B. Dala-Clayton, pp.8. Lusaka: Govt Printer.

MARKS, S. (1976). *Large mammals and a Brave People: subsistence hunters in Zambia.* Seattle: University of Washington Press.

MARTIN, R.B. (1986a). Wildlife utilisation. In *Conservation and Wildlife Management in Africa.* ed. R.H.V. Bell & E. McShane-Caluzi, pp.219–32.

MARTIN, R.B. (1986b). Communal Area Management Plan for Indigenous

Resources (Project CAMPFIRE). In *Conservation and Wildlife Management in Africa*. ed. R.H.V. Bell & E. McShane-Caluzi, pp.279–96. Washington: US Peace Corps.

MARTIN, R.B. (1986c). Establishment of ivory export quotas and associated control procedures. In *African Elephants*. ed R.B. Martin, J.R. Caldwell & J.G. Barzdo, pp.1–102, + 14 Appendices. Lausanne, Switzerland: Secretariat of the Convention on International Trade in Endangered Species of Wild Fauna and Flora.

MARTIN, R.B. & TAYLOR, R.D. (1983). Wildlife conservation in a regional land-use context: the Sebunge region of Zimbabwe. In *Management of Large Mammals in African Conservation Areas*, ed. R.N. Owen-Smith, pp.249–70. Pretoria: Haum.

McSHANE, T.D. (1985). *Vwaza Marsh Game Reserve: a baseline ecological survey*. Lilongwe: Department of National Parks and Wildlife.

MUNTHALI, S.M. & BANDA, H.M. (1985). Public opinion survey about the culling of Nyala (*Tragelaphus angasi*, Gray) and Warthog (*Phacochoerus aethiopicus*) in Lengwe National Park. Lilongwe: Department of National Parks and Wildlife.

MYERS, N. (1980). Kenya's baby boom. *New Scientist*, **87**, 848–50.

MYERS, N. (1984). Problems and opportunities in habitat conservation. In *Conservation of Threatened Natural Habitats*, ed. A.V. Hall, pp.1–15. Pretoria: Council for Scientific and Industrial Research.

NICHOLSON, S.E. (1979). The nature of rainfall fluctuations in subtropical West Africa. *Monthly Weather Review,* **108**, 473–87.

NICHOLSON, S.E. (1983). Subsaharan rainfall in the years 1976–80: evidence of continued drought. *Monthly Weather Review,* **111**, 1646–54.

NORTON-GRIFFITHS, M., HERLOCKER, D. & PENNYCUICK, L. (1978). The pattern of rainfall in the Serengeti ecosystem, Tanzania. *East African Wildlife Journal.* **13**, 347–74.

NYE, P.H. & GREENLAND, D.J. (1960). The *Soil Under Shifting Cultivation*. Technical Communication no.51. London: Commonwealth Bureau of Soils.

OSCARSSON, G. (1984). Regional aspects of development in the Luangwa Catchment. In *An Integrated Approach to Land Use Management in the Luangwa Valley, Proceedings of the Lupande Development Workshop*, ed. D.B. Dalal-Clayton, pp.56–62. Lusaka: Govt Printer.

OTTERMAN, L. (1974). Baring high albedo soils by overgrazing: a hypothesised desertification mechanism. *Science.* **186**, 531–53.

PANKHURST, R. (1966). The Great Ethiopian Famine of 1888–92: A new Assessment. *Journal of the History of Medicine*, **21** (2), 96–124.

PANKHURST, R. (1972). The History of famine and pestilence in Ethiopia prior to the founding of Gonder. *Journal of Ethiopian Studies*. **10** (2),

PARKER, I.S.C. (1964). The Galana Game Management Scheme. *Journal of Epizootic Disease of East Africa*, **12**, 21–31.

PARKER, I.S.C. & AMIN, M. (1983). *Ivory Crisis*. London: Chatto & Windus.

PRESCOTT-ALLEN, R. (1984). Threatened habitats: the challenge for humanity. In *Conservation of Threatened Natural Habitats*, ed. A.V. Hall, pp.16–45. Pretoria: Council for Scientific and Industrial Research.

PRICE, S. (1986). Conservation education. In *Conservation and Wildlife Man-*

agement in Africa. ed. R.H.V. Bell & E. McShane-Caluzi, pp.425–31. Washington: US Peace Corps.

RANESFORD, O. (1983). *Bid the Sickness Cease: Disease in the History of Black Africa*. London: John Murray.

RZOSKA, J., ed. (1976). *The Nile, biology of an ancient river.* The Hague: Junk Publishers.

SEFU, L.D. (1986). The role of the Environment Unit of the Department of National Parks and Wildlife, Malawi. In *Conservation and Wildlife Management in Africa*, ed. R.H.V. Bell & E. McShane-Caluzi, pp.431–40. Washington: US Peace Corps.

SHELDRICK, D. (1973). *The Tsavo Story*. London: Collins & Harvill Press.

SINCLAIR, A.R.E. & FRYXELL, J.M. (1985). The Sahel of Africa: ecology of a disaster. *Canadian Journal of Ecology*, **63**, 987–94.

SOULÉ, M.E. (1984). Conservation in the real world: real conservation or conservation-as-usual? In *Conservation of Threatened Natural Habitats*. ed. A.V. Hall, pp.46–65. Pretoria: Council for Scientific and Industrial Research.

THORSELL, J. (1984). Some observations on management planning for protected areas in East Africa. In *Proceedings of the 22nd Working Session, Commission on National Parks and Protected Areas.* Victoria Falls, Zimbabwe, 22–27 May 1983, pp.47–51. Gland, Switzerland: IUCN.

TIMBERLAKE, L. (1985). *Africa in Crisis: the causes, the cures of environmental bankruptcy*. London: Earthscan.

TRAPNELL, C.G. (1953). *The soils, vegetation and agriculture of north-eastern Rhodesia. Report of an Ecological Survey. Lusaka: Govt Printer.*

WADE, N. (1974), Sahelian drought: no victory for Western Aid. *Science*, **185**, 234–7.

WCO (1983). *Proceedings of a Workshop to discuss a management plan for the Simen National Park*. Addis Ababa: Wildlife Conservation Organisation.

WCO (1985a). *A Development Plan for Wildlife Conservation in Ethiopia*. Addis Ababa: Wildlife Conservation Organisation.

WCO (1985b). *Proceedings of a workshop to discuss a management plan for the Proposed Bale Mountains National Park*. Addis Ababa: Wildlife Conservation Organisation.

WESTERN, D. (1976). A new approach to Amboseli, *Parks*, **1**(2), 1–4.

WESTERN, D. & HENRY, W.R. (1979). Economics and conservation in Third World National Parks. *BioScience*, **29** (7), 414–8.

WORLD BANK (1984). *Toward Sustained Development in Sub-Saharan Africa: a joint programme for action*. Washington: World Bank.

YOUNG, A. (1976). *Tropical Soils and Soil Survey*. Cambridge: Cambridge University Press.

PART TWO

Wildlife, parks and pastoralists

Introduction

PAUL HOWELL

Pastoralists, using the broad definition of the term adopted by Sandford (1983), are very often regarded as a threat to the interests of wildlife conservation, either on grounds of their hunting as a subsidiary economic activity, or of the pressure their mode of livelihood imposes on the grasslands shared by wild herbivores, whose grazing needs and seasonal movements are so often identical with those of domestic stock. It is frequently their misfortune to occupy territories which are not only unstable and peculiarly susceptible to even minor climatic fluctuations, but are also the habitat of wildlife species that have already been exterminated in or driven from land used for cultivation by settled communities. Pastoral societies, ranging from the true nomad to transhumant communities whose populations make use of different and seasonally variable land types, have frequently come to be regarded as obstacles to the national development process and contemporary perceptions of the aims of 'modernisation'. In the post-colonial era 'exponents of sedentary civilisation have come to regard the word nomad as a term of abuse' (Abdel Ghafar, 1976). The reasons for this are many. Migratory life is perceived as incompatible with the introduction of essential social services, especially education and health. Pastoral systems are also often seen as wasteful of available land resources, regardless of the fact that such resources are usually marginal and incapable of viable exploitation by other means. Highly mobile societies present problems of administrative control, public security and the administration of justice, while they have often been regarded as outmoded reservoirs of separatist tribal consciousness, an obstacle to national awakening and incompatible with the aspirations of the modern state. These perceptions are not, as some would claim, always the legacy of colonialism; indeed in many ways and in many areas colonial policies tended to encourage the persistence of pastoralist lifestyles, which were at the time regarded with disfavour by the indigenous educated élite and subsequently, therefore, policies to be reversed.

Attitudes and policies are fortunately changing. The possibility that the migratory pastoralist may be less directly responsible for the degradation of the environment has begun to find credence, as the chapters that follow demonstrate. The objectives of development and conservation are beginning to be regarded not as irreconcilable, but part of one and the same process. The aim of mutually advantageous coexistence between man, domestic livestock and wild animals is entering the spectrum of policy and practice. The four chapters in this part of the volume address themselves to particular aspects of this debate and forcibly add to the changing perceptions of the conservationist's view.

Let us take Chapter 8 first, since it demonstrates, and vigorously attacks, the less acceptable face of conservation policy in which human interests are virtually ignored. Here the author turns our attention to the Mursi of southwest Ethiopia, and the question of their incorporation or exclusion from the Omo–Mago National Parks. Few readers concerned with dynamic and imaginative forms of development, of which conservation must be an integral component, will not share something of Turton's lingering sense of 'impotent rage' over the assumption that the exclusion of people is a prerequisite of successful park management. They will also share his concern that the examination of all aspects of human ecology is not recognised as an essential ingredient in the research that should precede the creation of wildlife reserves of all forms. The account provides a telling illustration of the need for the interdisciplinary approach if, as the author says, good development, primarily aimed at the betterment of human life, 'is synonymous with conservation and vice versa'.

Returning to Chapter 5, by Homewood & Rodgers, we are presented with a more theoretical approach, but to an aspect of pastoralism that is far from being only of hypothetical significance. It is one of the most important chapters in the book as a whole. The authors challenge the assumption that pastoralists, through overstocking and overgrazing, necessarily cause total and irreversible degradation of their environment, a notion often used to reinforce the argument that their rangelands, or parts of them, would be better devoted exclusively to wildlife. Homewood & Rodgers present a convincing case that there has been much confusion over the real meaning and effect of these processes; that the concept of overgrazing, for example, is often viewed in the context of a specific management objective when there are wide differences of perception here between the commercial rancher and the migratory subsistence herdsman. Moreover, while mismanaged pastoral practice can certainly lead to environmental degradation, the degree of damage may vary from minor, temporary, and rapidly recoverable forms of deterioration to irreversible destruction of the pastoral environment. These observations are illustrated by case studies of Baringo District in Kenya and the Ngorongoro Conservation Area in Tanzania, but they represent lines of research that would with great advantage be extended to other parts of the continent, and, indeed, beyond it.

In Chapter 6 Collett begins with an analysis of archaeological material which, despite its complexity, suggests that prehistoric pastoralists occupying what is now Maasailand only seriously exploited wildlife as an ingredient in their diet in times of economic crisis after reduction of their herds by drought and disease. This interpretation would repay examination in the light of later and more contemporary evidence of relationships between pastoralists and wild herbivores. There is some reason to believe, for example, that in the comparatively favourable ecological conditions prevailing between the 1920s and early 1960s, the Nilotic inhabitants of the Sudd region of the Sudan were for the most part indifferent to hunting as a food source except in times of real shortage (Evans-Pritchard, 1940; Howell, 1954; JIT, 1954). Recent surveys (Mefit-Babtie, 1983) suggest that, since the decimation of their herds caused by the exceptional river flooding of the 1960s combined with the catastrophic dislocations of civil war, hunting plays a more important part in their subsistence economy and that wild animals provide as much as 25 per cent of total meat consumption. The excavation of cattle camp sites in this region and the correlation of faunal assemblages with known hydrological, and hence ecological, events might in this connection be rewarding. Similar excavations might add a missing dimension to the story of Maasailand by adding quantitative evidence of Maasai hunting responses to massive reductions in their herds immediately after the rinderpest pandemic in the 1890s.

The second important theme explored by Collett stems from an historical analysis of European perceptions of the Maasai, an image which provided the motivation for their exclusion from certain parts of their former territory and simultaneously a convenient justification for the expropriation of land for European settler occupation. This image was of the Maasai as invaders of other peoples' territory, indolent, indomitable and intractable, who consistently failed to make the best use of the land they had seized and contributed nothing to the national economy. An early objective was not only the confinement of the Maasai to much less extensive tracts of country, but the encouragement of what was perceived as a more rewarding mode of livelihood, aimed at a greater release of meat for the market, the introduction of a cash economy, and where feasible a settled existence which would include crop production. The greater the Maasai resistance to these policies the more the image grew, compounded by the claim that the Maasai represented a threat to wildlife resources, not so much by hunting as by pressure on grasslands and hence the degradation of the habitat.

The validity of this historical analysis is not in question. The authors, however, argue that the persistence of this image has been an obstacle to a rational view of the potential of the Maasai as the best guardians of their own environment, including the wildlife. Wildlife populations of the Amboseli and Mara Parks are, after all, seasonally dependent on grasslands outside their boundaries and within the Maasai Reserve. This calls into question the effectiveness of the parks as a protective measure without the consent of the Maasai, who in effect continue to sustain wildlife as they did in the past, and thus contribute directly to the maintenance of a resource of great importance to the tourist industry and the country as a whole. If there were not this image of the Maasai, could they not, even if the parks were abolished, provide a model in Africa for the coexistence of man and wildlife? This is a notion that finds an echo in Turton's view of the Mursi as better conservationists than those who seek to impose conservation measures upon them.

Lindsay, in Chapter 7, is concerned with the same geographical area, but provides a detailed analysis of more recent events, changes in policy and local reactions to them. Despite the increasing attraction of wildlife as a major feature of Kenya's growing tourist industry, the approach adopted in Amboseli recognises that people who have traditional, some would say inalienable, rights of tenure in territories that lie within or adjacent to areas set aside for conservation should receive some measure of the revenue that wildlife generates in this way. By this means they would be encouraged to view wildlife populations as an integral component of their own exploitable resources, no less than their domestic stock. These principles might be applied with advantage to other parts of Africa, though if their application were to succeed anywhere it should be in Kenya with one of the most financially successful tourist industries in the continent. In fact there have been many pitfalls. For example, water supplies specifically provided in pursuance of this policy have often failed, sometimes at critical moments in the annual grazing cycle, for want of sustained financial support from the centre and lack of skills to service them. Annual contributions have not been consistently maintained, either through local government bodies or group ranches, and in any event it is debatable whether the benefits penetrate much beyond the 'opportunistic' minority. Adequate attention to the social responses to different options at the level of the herdsmen might have prevented some of the more unfavourable reactions, including incidentally the assassination of elephants and rhinoceroses as a novel form of political protest. There have been other repercussions. Ironically there has recently been an increasing tendency to turn to a settled form of livelihood on small scale irrigation schemes, just the kind of economic strategy the Maasai disdained and were for that reason criticised in the past. This recent contradiction to the image of the Maasai outlined by Collett has, paradoxically, increased rather than diminished the threat to wildlife. As Lindsay says, attempts have been made to introduce the concept and practice of conservation to a changing pastoral society without sufficient attention to the nature of that change.

Lindsay's discerning analysis of prolonged attempts to integrate parks and pastoralists with the best objectives of reconciling development and conservation, including local participation in the process, makes discouraging reading for those who see in this an imaginative approach to seemingly conflicting interests in the use of grasslands. Yet if some of the guidelines suggested by the author are followed there may be scope for the coexistence of developing pastoral economies and wildlife resources, and for the experience of Amboseli still to provide a model for application elsewhere.

References

ABDEL GHAFAR, M.A. (1976). *Some aspects of Pastoralist Nomadism in the Sudan*. Khartoum: Khartoum University Press.

EVANS-PRITCHARD, E.E. (1940). *The Nuer*. Oxford: Clarendon Press.

HOWELL, P.P. (1954). *A Manual of Nuer Law*. London: Oxford University Press.

JONGLEI INVESTIGATION TEAM [JIT] (1954). *The Equatorial Nile and its Effects in the Sudan*. Khartoum: Waterlow, for the Sudan Government.

MEFIT-BABTIE (1983). *Development Studies in the Jonglei Canal Area. Final Report*. Khartoum and Rome.

SANDFORD, S. (1983). *Management of Pastoral Development in the Third World*. Chichester: Wiley.

5

Pastoralism, conservation and the overgrazing controversy

KATHERINE HOMEWOOD AND W.A. RODGERS

One striking aspect of the scramble for resources in East Africa has been the interaction of pastoralism and conservation (Homewood & Rodgers, 1984b). The general outcome has been that large areas of pastoral range-lands have been expropriated for exclusive wildlife conservation use (Hjort, 1982; Little, 1984). This has commonly been justified on the *lay* argument that pastoralists overstock, overgraze and damage their range while wildlife are seen as existing in harmony with their surroundings. The same argument of environmental misuse and deterioration through pastoralist activities has been and continues to be used as a basis for a variety of land-use development policies. Conventional wisdom now equates pastoralist regimes with overgrazing, though there are differ-ences of opinion as to its underlying cause. Ecologists (exemplified by Lamprey, 1983) see the process as stemming from mismanagement inher-ent in traditional patterns of communal land tenure combined with indi-vidual herd ownership, along the lines of the Tragedy of the Commons (Hardin, 1968). Social scientists tend to attribute it to external constraints – such as compression due to the loss of rangelands to other forms of land use (Hjort, 1982), or the breakdown of traditional controls under outside influence (Bonte, 1976, quoted in Sandford 1983:12; Little, 1981). Although overstocking, overgrazing and desertification may be occur-ring, too often these processes are simply invoked without evidence to back up their existence; they have become self-reinforcing concepts, with counter examples not infrequently suppressed for political reasons (Sandford, 1983:15). Despite early reservations (e.g. Warren & Maizels, 1977) it is only recently that the universal applicability of the concepts of overgrazing and its endpoint, desertification, has been seriously ques-tioned (Horowitz, 1979; Sandford, 1983; Homewood & Rodgers 1984b).

Glantz (1983) discusses the confusion that has arisen over the wide range of meanings attached to the term desertification. This chapter outlines the way in which the apparently precise technical ecological concept of overgrazing now covers a whole range of different meanings, from the trivial to the serious. It looks first at conventional wisdom on

111

the subject and illustrates this with examples of ecological studies of vegetation and livestock parameters that are taken as incontrovertible support for environmental deterioration through overgrazing. It then investigates ideas of carrying capacity and stocking levels, the problem of divergent management aims and appropriate measures of productivity. Theoretical models of pasture dynamics illustrate the diversity of situations labelled as overgrazed, the different processes leading up to these situations and the likely differences in response to management intervention. Finally, two examples illustrate use of the overgrazing concept in development planning both past and present.

Conventional wisdom

So many documents, officials and even scientists repeat the assertion of pastoral responsibility for environmental degradation that the accusation has achieved the status of a fundamental truth, so self-evident a case that marshalling evidence on its behalf is superfluous if not in fact absurd, like trying to satisfy a skeptic that the earth is round . . .   *(Horowitz, 1979)*

This is still very much the case, as illustrated by the UN State of Knowledge report on Tropical Grazing Land Ecosystems (UNESCO/UNEP/ FAO, 1979), the latest major expert compendium on Tropical Savannas (Bourlière, 1983), and current World Bank policy planning documents (World Bank, 1984). These influential works, while invoking overgrazing, fail to define the process clearly or to produce evidence of its occurrence. The UN report, in 655 pages devoted to the description, functioning, evolution, human land-use patterns and regional case studies of tropical grazing land ecosystems, simply takes overgrazing as given in subsistence pastoralist systems (UNESCO/UNEP/FAO, 1979:500). Lamprey (1983) sketches the overall idea the term evokes (note the number of qualifying terms):

Whereas communities of indigenous herbivores are normally regulated in their numbers by density dependent limiting factors in their environment, the livestock populations of pastoralists are evidently less vulnerable to such limitations . . . Their numbers often give stocking rates considerably above the carrying capacity of the grazing lands . . . heavy grazing tends to reduce species diversity in plant communities and, if permitted to continue, may progress towards threshold levels beyond which recovery is unlikely or, in the event of subsequent protection, would be greatly delayed. As the process of degradation continues with the removal of vegetation, denudation exposes the soil surface to increased wind and water erosion, which commonly lead to the removal of the top soil layer. When this happens, the former plant communities are prevented from reestablishing themselves and a threshold of virtual irreversability may have been passed . . .   *(Lamprey 1983)*

Lamprey goes on to indicate a variety of possible successional outcomes (eroded dwarf shrubland replacing productive grassland; loose sand surfaces that, windblown, invade and damage adjacent productive areas), and adds in the destructive effects of pastoralist grass fires and tree felling. Every reference to overgrazing evokes this overall picture, typically without questioning which (if any) of its elements are in fact applicable to a specific situation, and to what extent those which do apply may be genuinely undesirable in the particular management context involved. Yet there is a world of difference between a shift in plant species composition and abundance, and an irreversible and spreading deterioration in productive capacity. Sandford (1983) points out that it is easy to demonstrate short-term changes in the former but virtually impossible to demonstrate the latter. This is because in the arid and semi-arid rangelands in question annual variation in productivity as a function of rainfall is usually greater than any short-term progressive decline due to degradation. Ecological studies are recent and short term, and it is hard to establish the relative importance of grazing regime versus other factors in historical accounts.

These problems are illustrated in a study by Kelly & Walker (1976) aiming to establish hard ecological data on the implications of different grazing regimes. Primary production was measured over a two-year period for a number of plots drawn from ungrazed, lightly, moderately and heavily grazed rangeland areas, more or less matched for rainfall and some soil features, with half of each site protected from grazing during the study. Heavily grazed zones showed a different species composition with fewer palatable sensitive perennial grasses, a greater proportion of less palatable perennials and sparser (but nutritious) annual grasses. These plots also showed lower ground cover and attendant differences in soil structure, rainwater infiltration and soil water availability. Lightly and moderately grazed plots showed the highest plant yields overall. The study recommended control of stocking levels based on this result. Despite the 'hard data' the implications are not necessarily as clear as they may seem. Production on even temporarily ungrazed study plots is not representative of production under continued grazing. It is interesting that the most productive plot in the first year of the trial produced least of all in the second year, while the most heavily grazed plots, producing least in the first year, showed a 400 per cent increase in yield in the wetter second year, bringing them within the range of values for the 'most productive' plots. Plots differed significantly in soil nitrates and phosphates, which are major constraints on production elsewhere in sub-Saharan Africa (Breman & de Wit, 1983). Crude protein figures were highest and crude fibre lowest for the most intensively grazed plots – that is, yields aside, they produced the more nutritious forage. Although the herbivores involved were primarily grazers they consumed 22–33 per cent available browse in the heavily used areas (cf. 3 per cent in the lightly and moderately used areas) without detriment to the woody vegetation. The results mask dramatic annual variation and cannot distinguish the relative importance of local and short-term rainfall, soil minerals and grazing regime. Although the differences between plots are interpreted as different points along a temporal succession of overgrazing, the study cannot actually demonstrate this, nor that the differences arise as part of an irreversible process. The results are interpreted as unequivocal support for the intermediate grazing regimes as the most productive, but this conclusion, though perhaps valid for grass production *per se*, is hardly justified in the broader sense without some knowledge of how many animals (and people) are in practice supported by the different regimes. Kelly and Walker's study illustrates the extent to which results are extrapolated as evidence either of temporal trends or of conditions over wider areas, and used as an unassisted basis for management decisions involving human subsistence. The easily demonstrated differences in species composition or simply standing crop are taken as signs of a longer term trend involving serious, potentially irreversible degradation and loss of productivity. The observed deviation from a western stock and range management expert's ideal is automatically seen as undesirable.

Interpretation of livestock records is as problematic as that of vegetation studies. Many livestock counts imply prolonged and continuing rapid growth hardly consistent in ecological terms with simultaneous accusations of serious overstocking and progressive environmental degradation. Sandford (1983:12–5) investigates this and questions both the accuracy of techniques used to count livestock and estimate densities and the concept and application of stocking levels. Fowler (1981) provides an example of the sort of livestock records that are available for investigating the possibility of overgrazing and progressive rangeland deterioration. He points out that overgrazing has been reported for over 50 years in Swaziland, though not universally agreed on. During most of that period and particularly since the last major drought/epidemic setback in 1964–6, the national herd and the average stocking densities have both increased steadily. Working from national census figures (counts but not age/sex breakdowns) Fowler presents evidence for declining calving and extraction rates and mounting death rates for the total herd since the mid 1960s. He concludes that despite continuing growth in total numbers these indices show deteriorating environmental productivity as a result of grazing pressure. This is a reasonable interpretation but there are other possibilities which are not considered. For example changing age and sex structures as the herd gradually recovered after drought and epidemic disasters in 1964–6 could produce comparable results. This would be expected, with proportions of calves and old animals returning to pre-die-off levels, as well as some accumulation of steers and male stock which would have been sold or slaughtered in time of need. Extraction or offtake rates are as much a function of people's need and willingness to sell as of successful herd performance, so it may be unwise to extrapolate from census figures in this way. The fact that average herd size has not changed but numbers of individual herds have increased suggest this last factor may be important in the Swazi data.

Carrying capacity

There are fundamental reasons why the apparently coherent successional picture presented by Lamprey (1983) may not be as logical as it seems. Perhaps the most basic flaw lies in the concept of carrying capacity as applied to arid and semi-arid rangelands. The idea of carrying capacity implies that the environment is capable of supporting a set number of grazing animals, and by implication a certain maximum sustainable yield for offtake. At stocking levels below carrying capacity there will be unused resources; above carrying capacity there will be environmental damage and eventually a die-off of the exploiting animals. The factors limiting carrying capacity in arid and semi-arid grazing lands are the availability of water and forage, both ultimately dependent on rainfall. However, the rainfall in these areas – and consequently primary production and water availability – is highly unpredictable and variable in space and time. Unlike more temperate climates it is not possible to maintain a satisfactory average stocking level which makes use of most of the available resources in most years without ever exceeding them. Current World Bank policy, while acknowledging this problem, maintains that carrying capacity is still a necessary concept in Sahelian and Sudanian zones and substitutes a worst-case minimum value (World Bank, 1984), which would entail under-utilisation in most years while avoiding environmental damage through overuse. By contrast Sandford (1982) suggests that neither average nor minimum carrying capacity values are necessarily appropriate in determining subsistence pastoralist stocking levels. Sandford (1982) models the outcome of conservative management with stable stocking levels versus opportunistic strategies that allow stock numbers to fluctuate with environmental conditions. He suggests that tracking environmental variation may in many cases be more efficient in terms of overall production for the subsistence pastoralist – a strategy that incorporates mobility, inevitable die-offs, and the capacity for both rapid recovery from disaster and exploitation of temporarily advantageous conditions. These ideas are applied independently by Caughley (1983) to the closely comparable issue of imposing controlled wildlife population levels by culling in National Park management.

Management aims and productivity measures

Inconsistencies in the concept of carrying capacity and overstocking go further than this. Different management goals entail different optimal stocking rates, and management goals which are in themselves economically valid and environmentally sustainable are easily misjudged by an outsider with alternative management intentions. There is a range of levels of sustainable yield, and the level which maximises one particular product may not be optimal in other ways. The western stock manager ranching animals for meat production sees as optimal a stocking rate which gives maximum growth rate per individual animal over the first few years of life. This allows rapid sale and turnover of a particular culturally desirable quality of meat fetching a high price. The subsistence pastoralist is more likely to see as optimal a stocking rate which supports a larger number of animals at lower rates of meat production per individual animal but a higher output in terms of the much wider range of desired products – milk, calves, subsistence and security for a large number of people. It is only very recently that comparisons of productivity of traditional and developed livestock systems have begun to take these differences of aim into account (Sandford, 1983: 123–7). The failure to appreciate these different goals has often led to the western livestock expert's instant assessment of pastoralist rangeland as overgrazed on the basis of low plant standing crop and species composition differences. Caughley (1983) stresses that failure to consider the related distinction between economic and ecological carrying capacities bedevils management decisions on wildlife cropping in National Parks.

Pasture models

Interpretation of vegetation parameters may be made easier by an understanding of the range of possible outcomes of different grazing regimes and the ways in which they are likely to be manifested. Noy-Meir (1975,

1978, 1982) uses graphical analyses to explore different patterns of pasture growth combined with different herbivore consumption responses. Despite the restrictions of their basic assumptions the models are fairly robust. They can be extrapolated to cover realistic situations and a limited number of outcomes can be predicted for a pasture under increasing herbivore pressure. To summarise, a pasture may respond as either a continuously or a discontinuously stable system. In both cases plant growth shows an initial increase in response to grazing up to a maximum productivity for both plant and animal populations. A continuously stable system then shows a progressive steady decline with ever heavier grazing. By contrast a discontinuously stable system continues at a high level of productivity up to a critical threshold of grazing pressure, at which it crashes dramatically to a new, much lower level. Noy–Meir reviews evidence to suggest that in general improved or commercially managed pasture systems correspond to the discontinuously stable type. In a discontinuously stable system range condition cannot be inferred from animal production, which will remain high on the very threshold of collapse of the whole system.

The ultimate survival of a pasture system under progressively heavier grazing is dependent on the presence of an ungrazeable plant reserve which is not removed whatever the herbivore pressure. 'Grazeability' is a composite of palatability, accessibility of growth form and efficiency of the grazer. The reserve may be present as green biomass or as the underground storage organs of perennial grasses and forbs which permit survival and new growth in consecutive years. Walker & Noy-Meir (1982) see trees and woody shrubs as having secure, ungrazeable reserves under any herbivore utilisation conditions, creeping perennial grasses (e.g. *Cynodon*) and relatively unpalatable tussocks (e.g. *Eleusine*) as intermediate, and erect, palatable perennial grasses as having the least protected reserves. 'Pasture improvement' techniques, producing pastures that conform to a commercial management ideal with selective elimination of less palatable or less 'grazeable' species (see below), maintenance of high standing crop and protection against disturbance, all tend to predispose towards the possibility of a crash. Under continued heavy grazing (which draws on the reserve for continued growth but does not allow its replenishment) palatable perennial grasses may be replaced by woody vegetation. The latter is competitively superior in terms of not only ungrazeable reserve but also soil moisture utilisation, though the important effects of fire, seed predation and seedling browsing on the recruitment of woody species may override any advantage or even prevent establishment.

Finally, the outcome of overgrazing will also depend on the response of herbivore numbers (and therefore grazing pressure) to resource availability. In the latter case the time lag is an important factor. The most rapid response is migration (not considered by Noy-Meir, but obviously a major pastoral management strategy). Reproduction or mortality involve a longer lag and may therefore cause oscillations between high plant/low animal biomass and low plant/high animal biomass states. Such oscillations, depending on their interaction with the earlier features discussed, may or may not drive the system to extinction. Any density dependent limitation of herbivore numbers (man, disease, predation) increases the stability of the system.

In outlining several possible outcomes these Noy-Meir models are a useful illustrator of the complexity of the overgrazing concept and the pitfalls both of diagnosing the condition and of attempting management intervention. Any of the following cases is likely to be labelled overgrazed:

(i)   A system with a subsistence stocking rate higher than the commercial, resulting in lower rates of production per animal but a higher overall output of subsistence products per unit area.

(ii)   A system where stocking rates are higher than optimum for both commercial and subsistence management, where all measures of productive output are low and continue to show a steady decline with increasing grazing pressure. Poor stock condition is an indicator of poor range condition; removal of stock and consequent relaxation of grazing pressure leads to a smooth return to higher productivity by any management criterion.

(iii)   A 'crashed' system which has been pushed over its critical threshold bringing about the collapse of both plant and herbivore populations. In this case it requires more than just removal of stock to get the system to 'jump' back to its former high productivity. These are the cases rightly labelled seriously or even irreversibly degraded.

(iv)   The low plant/high animal biomass phase of a continuously fluctuating system in which the lag in herbivore population response to resource availability produces recurrent oscillations. Poor stock condition is followed by their emigration or die off, which leads to plant recovery.

Case (i) is undesirable from the viewpoint of the commercial beef rancher but desirable (as well as environmentally sustainable) to a subsistence pastoralist population. In the last three cases the pasture will survive and can recover, given an ungrazeable reserve in the herb layer;

extinction ensues if there is none. It is important to note that where a system is just below the critical grazing pressure and is liable to crash it is unlikely to be recognised as overgrazed. Cases (ii) and (iii) are probably undesirable to all livestock managers, though Birley (1982) suggested that Sukumaland range may be deliberately overgrazed as in Case (ii) to preclude range conditions which would allow the spread of disease-bearing tick populations. Case (iv), though apparently alarmingly unstable, may afford higher returns to the pastoralist than the same system under stable, conservative low stocking levels (Sandford, 1982). It may be the commonly observed situation in semi-arid rangeland, with oscillations being partly imposed by variation in environmental factors other than grazing pressure. The negative feedbacks inherent in such a system tend to restore equilibrium, while attempts to stabilise – e.g. by controlling herbivore numbers – may have the opposite effect (Caughley, 1983).

Savannas are characterised by low stability (with frequent major changes due to flood, fire, heavy grazing, major fluctuations in herbivore numbers, etc.) but are highly resilient with a strong tendency to return to a central equilibrium despite disturbance (Noy-Meir, 1982; Walker & *Resilience* Noy-Meir, 1982). This resilience is attributed to such features as higher reproductive rates of savanna plants under stress conditions; increased growth rates of vegetation at low biomass; spatial heterogeneity which encourages herbivore migration and provides habitat refuges and recolonisation sources; underground reserves; dormancy mechanisms, and the 'predator switching' flexibility of the herbivore community exploiting the multispecies plant biomass. Attempts to protect savanna against disturbance or to reduce heterogeneity may damage this resilience. For example, protection against fire renders the range vulnerable to much more severe eventual fire damage through a buildup of dry matter; creation of new waterpoints to allow more even grazing pressure may lead to locally concentrated damage; pasture improvement methods producing dominance of highly grazeable species, and reducing or even eliminating the less palatable, predispose the system to crash. Rotational grazing methods applied to pasture which responds as a discontinuously stable system are potentially dangerous, as periods with no herbivore utilisation (i.e. no useful production) alternate with intensive grazing periods during which the whole system may crash. Using both theoretical models and empirical observation Noy-Meir and his co-workers cast doubt on the necessity for and wisdom of commonly advocated range management measures. Caughley (1983) puts an identical case in terms of the response of herbivore populations (rather than plant species) to culling schemes.

To summarise, there is considerable confusion as to what is meant by overstocking, overgrazing, and environmental damage resulting from these processes. The principle of stocking levels relies on an underlying concept of stable carrying capacity which is of limited use in areas where primary productivity fluctuates widely from year to year. The concept of overgrazing is first of all only valid with respect to a specified management aim: what is overgrazed pasture from the viewpoint of a commercial beef rancher may be good grazing in the view of subsistence pastoralists. Secondly, the term overgrazing implies some degree of environmental damage, but this may range from the trivial to the serious. For example at one end of the range a very temporary low grass cover may be observed in any bad dry season and is rapidly reversed with the onset of adequate rain. A longer term change in species composition will affect productivity and nutritional value of grazing in ways which could be interpreted as good or bad according to management aim. At the other extreme a serious loss of ground cover with erosion may mean a long-term, effectively irreversible decline in primary productivity available to domestic stock. Finally, theoretical models show there is potentially enormous variability in the processes leading up to these conditions, and in the likely future dynamics of such systems, particularly in response to intervention. This is not to maintain that pastoralist mismanagement and consequent environmental damage never occur, but to suggest the need for a more clearly defined approach to the problem in general, and in particular for methods which will allow objective evaluation of individual cases. Despite the confusion over these terms, and not least the confusion between value judgements based on subjective ideals of livestock management and those based on objective criteria of land-use potential, the concepts of overstocking and overgrazing are widely used to guide planning and policy decisions. This chapter goes on to look at two case studies that illustrate some of these general points.

Baringo District, Kenya

Baringo District incorporates a cross-section of the Rift Valley with high plateaux, steep scarps, salt flats and an inland drainage lake. This topography, combined with the semi-arid climate and naturally sparse vegetation ground cover, predispose to high erosion rates and it is generally felt that human activity and particularly overstocking have accelerated the process at all levels. Soil, water and vegetation conservation efforts have been a major concern in Baringo since the 1930s (Anderson, 1984). Past campaigns have been aimed at restricting goat rearing (Maher,

1945), and despite recent re-evaluation of the vital importance of goats (e.g. Little, 1982), presidential statements in 1983 still reflected the strong government and planning prejudice against them even for areas dependent on small stock like the Tugen Hills. Conditions in other parts of the area are also seen as the result of primarily pastoralist-induced degradation. For example, the Njemps Flats bordering Lake Baringo are seen as owing their sparse and short-lived ground cover, dominated by unpalatable annual herbs, to Il Chamus overgrazing. The highly productive *Cynodon* and *Echinochloa* swamp grasslands associated with permanent rivers draining into the south end of Lake Baringo are seen as being in imminent danger of destruction through grazing pressure.

The history of livestock rearing in the area hints at long-term environmental trends and their ecological causes. Anderson (1981) has traced the history of the Il Chamus over the last 200 years from primarily hunting, gathering and cultivating activities in the eighteenth century to progressively more intensive irrigation-based agriculture in the nineteenth century supplying trading caravans with surplus grain. Despite their links with pastoralist groups the Il Chamus did not become major stockowners until the turn of the century, when their proximity to and relations with British administration facilitated their accumulation of stock. Anderson suggests that by 1914 their stock holdings were sufficient to warrant establishing an initiation *manyatta* along Maasai lines. In 1917 a river course change virtually destroyed the already declining irrigation system and the now important role of livestock precluded major labour investments required to rebuild the irrigation system. Anderson (1984) documents the first observations on land degradation in Baringo in 1928, with official concern about overstocking expressed in 1929. From 1930 on Baringo is repeatedly identified as having a major land-use problem, with erosion surveys rating it among the worst in the Colony.

Baringo District has reached an 'overgrazing endpoint' where most of the grass and the topsoil has already gone over large stretches of country and the ground is blanketed with thornbush, largely useless to man and beast alike, which cannot be eradicated . . . Land in a 35–40″ rainfall area once capable of supporting a stock unit to 4–5 acres is now scarcely capable of carrying a stock unit to 20 acres . . . In the drier part of the district, with a 20–25″ rainfall, land once capable of supporting a stock unit to 10 acres is now scarcely capable of supporting one to 30–40 . . . Baringo is a case where the human population in an attempt to maintain enough stock for their needs have already to a large extent destroyed their own habitat.   (*Brown, 1963, quoted in Ruthenberg, 1980*).

Since the 1930s various rehabilitation schemes have been planned and sometimes implemented in Baringo District. Anderson (1984) interprets this sequence of growing sensitivity to overstocking and environmental problems in relation to ecological, political and economic factors. A general run of dry years 1926–36 in East Africa; the impact at this time of the Dust Bowl of North America on the training of generations of agricultural officers worldwide; the Depression, the growth of the African population and the resulting exacerbated competition between white settlers and African producers for both land and markets, all contributed. The dry period between the 1920s and 1930s has been succeeded by a series of droughts each accompanied by a dramatic stock die-off. The most recent involved overall herd reductions of at least 50 per cent in 1979–80 (Little, 1981) and 60–80 per cent in 1983–4 (Homewood & Lewis, 1987).

What are the ecological 'hard facts' behind the perceived trend? Local informants report that there has been a shift from annual grasses (*Eragrostis*) to less palatable or even toxic annual herbs (*Portulaca* and *Tribulus*) on the Njemps Flats since the turn of the century (P.D. Little, personal communication). The palatable grasses are still present in small amounts and exclosure or controlled grazing trials both past and present (1937–8: Anderson, 1984; Baringo Pilot Semi-Arid Area Project (BPSAAP) – Lewis, 1982) show that they spread back. It seems likely that their dominance is indeed an inverse function of grazing pressure but that there is little question of irreversible degradation. As in the theoretical case (case iv) stock die-offs are followed by the re-emergence of palatable grasses, stock build up by their decline to levels that represent an ungrazeable reserve. It is unlikely that the Njemps Flats have ever been productive grazing on a par with the swamp and lakeside grasslands as the edaphic conditions are so very different (Homewood & Hurst, 1986). The *Cynodon* and *Echinochloa* swamp grazing areas themselves comprise classic ungrazeable reserves. The creeping habit of *Cynodon* makes it virtually impossible for cattle to graze out. The Baringo drought of 1983–4 illustrated this with stock starving to death on a close cropped, green, growing, effectively undamaged swamp sward (Homewood & Lewis, unpublished data). Physical difficulties of grazing underwater and while swimming preclude total removal of the *Echinochloa* growth. The swamp can be 'overgrazed' in terms of its provision of forage to the stock using it but is unlikely to suffer in terms of its speed of recovery and its long-term potential.

What effect has environmental concern had on management policy and subsistence conditions for local pastoralists? The current environmental rehabilitation and development scheme (BPSAAP) acknowledges the role of climate and topography in local environmental problems but points out that little can be done about these, while stock densities can at least in principle be manipulated (Lewis, 1982). The practice is more elusive. During the 1970s Kenya implemented a series of group ranch schemes designed to improve range management and stock production through controlling stock densities and grazing pressures. In general these have failed for ecological as well as socio-economic reasons. While a group ranch adjudication programme was begun in Baringo along government policy lines it has not been pursued with any enthusiasm by either herdowners or planners, all of whom suspect its inability to solve livestock production problems. Instead, BPSAAP emphasises soil and water conservation and management. The programme relies on long-term trial and demonstration to show a sequence of improved condition of animals grazed on improved range at controlled densities, with high auction prices and easy marketing of such stock to illustrate the pay off. This programme (and the intended demonstration of its advantages) has been disrupted by two severe droughts and stock die-offs (Little, 1981; Homewood & Lewis, 1987), as well as by the deterioration of reseeded plots due to undergrazing (Lewis, 1982).

Despite anxiety about swamp grazing resources it seems unlikely that controlled grazing schemes could be imposed there (Homewood & Hurst, 1986). Traditional mechanisms for controlling grazing access have been eroded by socio-economic changes (Little, 1982). The common practice of taking on non-Il Chamus absentee herdowners' stock to graze there for a fee is growing, though the caretaker must seek permission from the location Chief. For all its disadvantages (P.D. Little, 1985, personal communication), it provides a source of cash and subsistence products to poorer Il Chamus.

The general assumption that livestock have damaged and are further endangering a fragile area persists. Fifty years of environmental concern have done little to alter either this idea or local conditions. In perspective, the history of the area is more suggestive of a series of oscillations in stock numbers and vegetation conditions precipitated by the major unpredictable climatic fluctuations governing this semi-arid area, rather than a long-term trend of anthropogenic environmental deterioration.

Ngorongoro Conservation Area

The example of Ngorongoro Conservation Area (NCA) is very different. NCA is a joint wildlife conservation/pastoralist land-use area in northern Tanzania, adjacent to the Serengeti Plains and part of the ecological unit exploited by the Serengeti wildlife population migrations. The current administration plans to expel the 19,000 pastoralists and their livestock because of environmental degradation and their impact on conservation values. Detailed studies of pastoralist ecology in the area have been published elsewhere (Arhem, Homewood & Rodgers, 1981; Homewood & Rodgers, 1984a, b; Homewood, Rodgers & Arhem, 1987; Rodgers & Homewood, 1986). The main points are:

(i)   Pastoralists, livestock and wildlife have coexisted in the area for over 2,000 years; pastoralist grazing and burning activities have helped to shape the area's present highly valued landscape.

(ii)   Livestock numbers monitored for over 20 years have fluctuated but show no overall trend of increase.

(iii) Wildlife populations have undergone a dramatic increase over the same period, making the idea of adverse competitive impact of livestock dubious if not untenable.

(iv)   Disease interactions between cattle and wildlife populations favour the latter.

(v)   There is no evidence to bear out suggested changes in vegetation composition whether in pastoralist-occupied areas or in areas from which pastoralist stock have been excluded for 10 years or more.

(vi)   The NCA shows negligible erosion. Rates are lower than for all surrounding areas despite the greater geomorphological and topographic predisposition of the area to erosion.

Despite these facts (and a political history of voluntarily accepted exclusion from the Serengeti in return for restricted rights in NCA) the suspicion of pastoralist damage is so strong that their expulsion remains a more or less foregone conclusion. One probable outcome is the very deterioration of NCA conservation values the management policy purports to avoid (Homewood & Rodgers 1984a, b; Rodgers & Homewood, 1986; Homewood, Rodgers & Arhem, 1987).

Discussion and conclusions

The two case studies illustrate some of the general points raised by the review of the overgrazing concept. Firstly, they show the extent to which the concept is used in management. In both Baringo and NCA successive policies have been justified on the basis of pastoralist overgrazing. In the case of Baringo 50 years of environmental concern, rehabilitation attempts and development schemes have had rather little impact due to a number of factors including changing administrations, recurrent droughts and perhaps a lack of strong vested interests. In NCA, policies based on the assumption of overgrazing and backed by a strong international conservation lobby are likely to have a very major impact on the subsistence of a large number of resident pastoralists.

Secondly, the case studies show the degree of confusion that the term overgrazing masks. In both Baringo and NCA the term is applied throughout, despite major ecological diversity within each area. In Baringo the Tugen Hills and Plateau are seen as 'overgrazed' because they have sparse, mainly thornbush vegetation, with high runoff and soil erosion rates – all due primarily to climate and geomorphology. The Njemps Flats are 'overgrazed' because they have a sparse vegetation cover (again the inevitable result of edaphic conditions) and the proportion of grass cover varies with fluctuating stock densities and grazing pressure. The productive swamp grasslands are 'overgrazed' not because there is any problem of environmental degradation (whether through pastoral use or natural agents) but because at the peak of drought conditions the sward is temporarily grazed down to a level whereby cattle can no longer benefit. The impact on the pasture itself is transient and negligible. These different conditions, the different processes producing them and their very different implications for future productivity trends should hardly be pooled under the same misnomer. Similarly in NCA the term is applied to the cool high-altitude tussock grasslands of the Crater Highlands and to the hot arid lowland short grass plains around Gol (with little justification in the former case and apparently none in the latter – Homewood & Rodgers, 1984b).

Thirdly, successive administrations in both cases have considered set stocking levels that overlook the considerable local, annual and seasonal variation perhaps better exploited by traditional pastoralist opportunism. The BPSAAP range management trial stocking densities (BPSAAP, 1983) are based on a view of economic (i.e. commercial) rather than ecological (subsistence) carrying capacities, though the latter may be more appropriate to local herdowners. Finally, in neither case are the repeated assertions of overgrazing borne out by satisfactory evidence of long-term trends of degradation or declining productivity, but this has not prevented potentially far-reaching management interventions – particularly in NCA.

The major difference between the two cases is the powerful international wildlife conservation lobby operating in NCA and effectively absent from Baringo. Anderson's 1984 analysis suggests that in past years competition between African and European producers under a colonial administration might have provided a strong (however unconscious) incentive to discredit pastoralist management in areas other than those of wildlife interest. Elsewhere in sub-Saharan Africa pastoralist peoples continue to lose considerable areas of rangeland to other forms of land-use on the grounds of alleged actual or potential misuse and to alternative commercial livestock production or agricultural enterprises as well as to conservation use. A current programme in Somalia plans intensified livestock production through elimination of tsetse from riverine areas currently used on a seasonal basis by migrating pastoralist stock (Somali Democratic Republic, 1984). The environmental impact studies set up have, ironically, come to focus on potential pastoralist-induced degrada-tion of the riverine environment (rather than, for example, the serious threats to conservation of spreading cultivation with ensuing complete habitat modification; commercial livestock production with its intoler-ance of 'unproductive' plant and animal species; and the impact of toxic chemicals during tsetse elimination and control). There are many other examples. This discussion does not seek to establish that there is no pastoralist-induced damage to rangelands, or to maintain that where such damage may occur it is necessarily superficial, short-term and rever-sible. It does, however, show the need for care in applying the overgrazing concept and point to the need for objective methods, both ecological and socio-economic, in investigating individual cases.

Acknowledgements

The University of London Central Research Fund and the Hayter Fund provided financial support for the field work that gave rise to this chapter. We are grateful to the Maasai of Ngorongoro and the Conservation Authority staff for their interest and support. The herdowners and gov-ernment officials of Baringo as well as the staff of Baringo Pilot Semi-Arid Area Project were generous with their assistance and the Lewis family gave us unlimited help and hospitality.

References

ANDERSON, D.M. (1981). Some thoughts on the nineteenth century history of the Il Chamus of Baringo District. Research Paper no. 149, Institute of African Studies, University of Nairobi.

ANDERSON, D.M. (1984). Depression, Dust Bowl, Demography and Drought: the Colonial State and Soil Conservation in East Africa in the 1930s. *African Affairs*, **83** (332), 321–43.

ARHEM, K., HOMEWOOD, K. & RODGERS, W.A. (1981). *A pastoral food system: Ngorongoro Maasai in Tanzania*. BRALUP Research Report no. 70, University of Dar-es-Salaam.

BIRLEY, M. (1982). Resource management in Sukumaland, Tanzania. *Africa*, **52** (2), 1–30.

BOURLIERE, F. ed.(1983). *Ecosystems of the World 13, Tropical Savannas*. Amsterdam: Elsevier.

BPSAAP [BARINGO PILOT SEMI-ARID AREA PROJECT] (1983). *Quarterly reports for 1983*, Nairobi: Ministry of Agriculture.

BREMAN, H. & de WIT, C. (1983). Rangeland productivity and exploitation in the Sahel. *Science*, **221** (4618), 1341–7.

CAUGHLEY, G. (1983). Dynamics of large mammals and their relevance to culling. In *Management of Large Mammals in African Conservation Areas*, ed. R. Norman-Smith, pp. 115–26. Pretoria: Haum.

FOWLER, M. (1981). Overgrazing in Swaziland? A review of the technical efficiency of the Swaziland herd. Pastoral Network Paper 12d. London: Overseas Development Institute.

GLANTZ, M. (1983). Desertification: a review of the concept. *Desertification Control Bulletin*, **9**, 15–22.

HARDIN, G. (1968). The tragedy of the commons. *Science*, **162**, 1243–8.

HJORT, A. (1982). A critique of 'ecological' models of land use. *Nomadic Peoples*, **10**, 11–27.

HOMEWOOD, K. & HURST, A. (1986). Comparative ecology of pastoral livestock in Baringo, Kenya. Pastoral Network Paper 21. London: Overseas Development Institute.

HOMEWOOD, K. & LEWIS, J.G. (1987). Impact of drought on pastoral livestock in Baringo District, Kenya, 1983–5. *Journal of Applied Ecology*. (In press.)

HOMEWOOD, K. & RODGERS, W.A. (1984a). *Pastoralist ecology in Ngorongoro Conservation Area, Tanzania*. Pastoral Development Network Paper 17d. London: Overseas Development Institute.

HOMEWOOD, K. & RODGERS, W.A. (1984b). Pastoralism and conservation. *Human Ecology*, **12** (4), 431–41.

HOMEWOOD, K., RODGERS, W.A. & ARHEM, K. (1987). Ecology of pastoralism in Ngorongoro Conservation Area, Tanzania. *Journal of Agricultural Science*. **108**, 47–72.

HOROWITZ, M. (1979). *The sociology of pastoralism and African livestock projects*. USAID Program Evaluation Discussion Paper no. 6.

KELLY, R. & WALKER, B. (1976). The effects of different forms of land use on the ecology of a semi-arid region in south-western Rhodesia. *Journal of Ecology*, **64**, 553–76.

LAMPREY, H. (1983). Pastoralism yesterday and today: the overgrazing problem. In *Ecosystems of the World 13, Tropical Savannas*, ed. F. Bourlière, pp. 643–66. Amsterdam: Elsevier.

LEWIS, J.G. (1982). Baringo Semi-Arid Area Project. Paper presented to the meeting on Human Settlement Planning for Arid and Semi-Arid Areas, Nairobi.

LITTLE, P.D. (1981). *A sociological report on the Il Chamus of Baringo District, Kenya*. Consultant Report to Baringo Semi-Arid Area Project. Nairobi: Ministry of Agriculture.

LITTLE, P.D. (1982). Risk aversion, economic diversification and goat production: some comments on the role of goats in African pastoral production systems. *Proceedings of the 3rd International Conference on Goat Production and Disease*. Tucson, Arizona.

LITTLE, P.D. (1984). Critical socio-economic variables in African pastoral livestock development: towards a comparative framework. In *Livestock Development in subsaharan Africa*, ed. J. Simpson & P. Evangelou, ch.13. Boulder, Colorado: Westview Press.

LITTLE, P.D. (1985). Absentee herdowners and part-time pastoralists: the political economy of resource use in Northern Kenya. *Human Ecology*, **13** (2), 131–51.

MAHER, C. (1945). The goat: friend or foe? *East African Agricultural Journal*, **11**, 115–21.

NOY-MEIR, I. (1975). Stability of grazing systems: an application of predator-prey graphs. *Journal of Ecology*, **63**, 459–81.

NOY-MEIR, I. (1978). Grazing and production in seasonal pastures: analysis of a simple model. *Journal of Applied Ecology*, **15**, 809–35.

NOY-MEIR, I. (1982). Stability of plant–herbivore models and possible applications to savanna. *Ecological Studies*, **42**, 591–609.

RODGERS, W.A. & HOMEWOOD, K. (1986). Cattle dynamics in a pastoral community in Ngorongoro, Tanzania, during the 1982–83 drought. *Agricultural Systems*. **22**(1), 35–51.

RUTHENBERG, H. (1980). *Farming Systems in the Tropics*. 3rd edn. Oxford: Oxford University Press.

SANDFORD, S. (1982). Pastoral strategies and desertification: opportunism and conservatism in dry lands. In *Desertification and Development: dryland ecology in social perspective*, ed. B. Spooner & H. Mann. London: Academic Press.

SANDFORD, S. (1983). *Management of Pastoral Development in the Third World*. Chichester: Wiley.

SOMALI DEMOCRATIC REPUBLIC (1984). *Report of the National Tsetse and Trypanosomiasis Control Project on species of woody plants and vertebrates in riverine and coastal forest habitats of southern Somalia*. Overseas Development Administration/Ecology & Conservation Unit, University College, London/Tropical Development & Research Institute Consultancy Report.

UNESCO/UNEP/FAO (1979). *Tropical Grazing Land Ecosystems: A State of Knowledge Report*. Paris: Natural Resources Research Series.

WALKER, B. & NOY-MEIR, I. (1982). Aspects of the stability and resilience of savanna ecosystems. *Ecological Studies*, **42**, 556–90.

WARREN, A. & MAIZELS, J. (1977). Ecological Change and Desertification. In *Desertification: its causes and consequences*, ed. A. Warren, pp. 169–261. Oxford: Pergamon Press.

WORLD BANK (1984). *Desertification and the Sahelian and Sudanian zones in West Africa*. Internal Document: West African Projects Department, Washington.

6

Pastoralists and wildlife: image and reality in Kenya Maasailand

DAVID COLLETT

The transformation of the pastoral and nomadic societies of East Africa has long been perceived as one of the more problematic aspects of the development process. This has given rise to an extensive literature focusing on the 'development' of pastoral areas (Monod, 1975; Galaty & Salzman, 1981; Galaty, Aronson, Salzman & Chouinard, 1981; Salzman, 1982). A number of specialised journals (e.g. *Nomadic Peoples; Production Pastorale et Société*) and informal communication networks (e.g. the Overseas Development Institute's Pastoral Development Network) continue the debate on questions of pastoral 'development'. However, in East Africa the development of pastoral areas is not simply a matter of integrating the pastoralists into the national economy, because this land can be put to a second use: the creation of reserves and parks for wildlife. This aspect of the development of pastoral areas has received less academic attention despite the fact that National Parks and Game Reserves, with their associated tourist industry, have a very obvious impact on pastoral communities (Western, 1982; Turton, 1984, Chapter 8). The alienation of grazing land for the exclusive use of wildlife and tourists has a very direct impact upon pastoralist communities, giving rise to questions about 'people versus animals' in the formulation of African wildlife policy. National Parks and Game Reserves are never justified solely in terms of the economics of tourism: both the conservationists and national governments support the creation and maintenance of these areas by moral arguments based on the need to conserve wildlife and the intangible benefits that conservation confers on humanity (Huxley, 1961; Government of Kenya, 1974).

The disparate justifications set out in support of National Park and Game Reserve policies may seem obvious enough in the debates over the desirability of conserving species, or of encouraging a lucrative tourist industry, but it is important to acknowledge the fact that present policies represent the continued imposition of an essentially European view of how pastoral areas should be 'managed'. Under colonial government, wildlife policy in the pastoral areas was closely bound up with the broader

129

aims of the 'development' process. In this respect, colonial images of
pastoral societies were not without prejudice; they were influenced by
dominant European perceptions of how land should best be utilised,
and by European attitudes towards wildlife and its 'natural environment'.
These images not only shaped colonial policies in the pastoral areas,
but were subsequently inherited and largely accepted by the independent
states of East Africa in the 1960s. There is a need, therefore, to examine
the historical context of present wildlife policies, and to consider whether
the inherited images of pastoralist society and its attitude towards wildlife
are realistic.

This chapter applies such an approach to the experience in Kenya
Maasailand. The Maasai have long been considered an administrative
and development problem (Sandford, 1919; Jacobs, 1963), and provide
an almost paradigmatic case for examining the relationship between
pastoralists, wildlife and tourism in the development of pastoral areas
in East Africa. While there is a wealth of literature on the Maasai,
beginning with the accounts of the early explorers (Krapf, 1860; Fischer,
1884; Thomson, 1887), the period covered is too short to provide any
meaningful answer to the question of whether pastoralism poses a threat
to wildlife. We shall therefore use archaeological data to shed light on
the long-term ecological relationship between people, stock and wildlife.
Historical accounts of the colonial era are used as the basis for a detailed
study of the evolution of the colonial image of the Maasai, demonstrating
the linkages between these views of Maasai society and the wider goals
of colonial administration. Finally, the combination of archaeological
and historical data provides the basis for assessing the compatibility of
wildlife and pastoralism and the impact of official policy on conservation
in Maasailand.

Archaeology and 'the pastoralist threat to wildlife', *c.*750 BP – *c.*1880.

Archaeological research in Maasailand, principally in the Central Rift
Valley, has revealed that pastoralism has a long history in this area. A
recent re-examination of the radiocarbon chronology indicates that the
earliest acceptable evidence for domesticates comes from the Lake
Turkana area and dates to about 4,000 BP (Collett & Robertshaw, 1983a).
In this case, the domestic stock (caprines) is associated with pottery
(Nderit 'ware') which belongs within the Olmalenge Tradition (Barth-
elme, n.d.; Collett & Robertshaw, 1983b). A number of sites in the
Central Rift Valley (L.S.B. Leakey, 1931; M.D. Leakey, 1945; Bower,
1973; Bower, Nelson, Waibel & Wandibba, 1977) and the Athi Plains

(Gramly, 1975; Ambrose, 1983) belong within the Olmalenge Tradition which, although it is poorly dated, shows evidence for diversification of ceramic styles, implying a fairly long history (Collett & Robertshaw, 1983b). Unfortunately very little is known about this, the earliest ceramic tradition in East Africa associated with pastoralism, and therefore this tradition will not be further considered.

Stratigraphic evidence indicates that the Olmalenge Tradition is replaced by the Oldishi Tradition in the southern part of the Rift Valley and on the Athi Plains (Bower & Nelson, 1978; S.H. Ambrose, personal communication). The Oldishi Tradition shows evidence for internal differentiation of ceramic styles in both space and time (Collett & Robertshaw, 1983b). The earliest occurrence of this tradition is at Narosura where it is dated to about 2,600 BP (Odner, 1972) and it continues until at least 1,700 BP and probably beyond (Collett & Robertshaw, 1983a). The third ceramic tradition associated with domesticates is the Elementeitan Tradition, which is partly contemporary with the Oldishi Tradition but which is found on the Mau Escarpment and to the west of the Central Rift Valley (Bower *et al.*, 1977; Nelson, 1980; Marshall & Robertshaw, 1982; Collett & Robertshaw, 1983b). This tradition probably begins around 2,500 BP, continuing until at least 1,100 BP, when it is represented by a late phase at Deloraine Farm (Collett & Robertshaw, 1983a; Ambrose, Collett, Marshall, & Mudida, 1987). This tradition seems to be ancestral to the ubiquitous twisted-cord roulette decorated pottery found over most of the Central Rift, to the west of the Central Rift and on the Athi Plains, dating between about 450 BP and the present (Blackburn 1973).

This survey of the culture-history of Maasailand indicates the complexity of the prehistory of the area (Fig. 6.1), but this taxonomic approach, based on ceramic similarity, does not incorporate some sites where there is evidence for a diverse range of ceramics, e.g. Prolonged Drift (Gifford, Isaac & Nelson, 1980) and Naivasha Railway Rockshelter (Onyango-Abuje, 1977a). These sites are probably contemporary with Oldishi and Elementeitan Traditions and form a third, indeterminate, tradition.

A comparative analysis of faunal assemblages can be made from the detailed descriptions so far published for three Oldishi Tradition sites (Narosura – Gramly, 1972a; Lemek North East – Marshall & Robertshaw, 1982; Crescent Island – Onyango-Abuje, 1977a, b), two Elementeitan/ twisted-cord roulette Tradition sites (Deloraine farm – Gramly, 1972b; Hyrax Hill – Onyango-Abuje, 1977a), and two indeterminate sites (Prolonged Drift – Gifford *et al.*, 1980; Naivasha Railway Rockshelter – Onyango-Abuje, 1977a). There are also a number of statements about

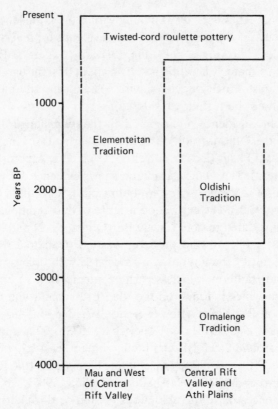

Fig. 6.1. Outline of the archaeological sequence in Kenya Maasailand.

the composition of faunal assemblages from other sites belonging to the Oldishi and Elementeitan Traditions (Bower *et al.*, 1977; Marshall & Robertshaw, 1982). An examination of the species composition of these faunal reports shows a tremendous variation in the number of wild species at each site (Table 6.1). Some of these species, such as rodents, are probably accidental inclusions and are associated with the occupation of the site (Onyango-Abuje, 1977a). Others may have been hunted but not used for food, for example the carnivores, while some of the larger mammals, e.g. the hippopotamus and the rhinoceros, were probably scavenged rather than hunted. Thus, the fauna on the site do not necessarily reflect human predation on wild animals.

If carnivores, rodents and pachyderms are excluded from consideration then it is possible to examine variation between sites in those species which were most probably hunted. If the numbers of individuals belonging to wild and domestic species are compared then domesticates make

Table 6.1 *Species composition and species contribution to the diet from pastoral Neolithic sites*

	Prolonged Drift			Naivasha Railway Rockshelter			Crescent Island			Narosura			Lemek North East			Deloraine Farm			Hyrax Hill (Iron Age)		
	MNI[a]	Wt[b]	%Wt	MNI	Wt	%Wt	MNI	Wt	%Wt	MNI	Wt	%Wt	MNI	Wt	%Wt	MNI	Wt	%Wt	MNI	Wt	%Wt
Domesticates																					
Bos taurus – adult	22	3674	25.7	2	334	27.0	15	2505	51.0	47	7849	75.5	3	501	52.0	21	3507	93.6	8	1336	81.9
– immature										5	500	4.8				4	200	5.3			
Ovis/Capra – adult	5	110	0.7	4	84	6.8	6	126	2.6	71	1491	14.3	22	462	48.0	2	42	1.1	8	168	10.3
– immature										4	48	0.5									
Perissodactyla																					
Rhinocerotidae																					
Diceros bicornis	1[c]	—	—																		
Ceratotherium simum										1[c]	—	—									
Equidae																					
Equus burchelli	16	2672	18.7	1	167	13.5	2	334	6.8	2	334	3.2									
Artiodactyla																					
Hippopotamidae																					
Hippopotamus amphibius							2[c]		—												
Suidae																					
Phacochoerus aethiopicus	1	51	0.3	1	51	4.1	1	51	1.0	1	51	0.5									
Potamochoerus porcus							1	45	0.9												
Giraffidae																					
Giraffa sp.	1[d]	788	5.5				1[d]	788	16.0												
Bovidae																					
Taurotragus oryx	4	1696	11.9				1	424	8.6												
Tragelaphus scriptus							1	36	0.8												
Kobus defassa																			1	127	7.8
Alcelaphus buselaphus	18	1746	12.2	4	388	31.3	2	194	3.9												
Connochaetes taurinus	17	2159	15.1				1	127	2.6	1	127	1.2									
Aepyceros melampus	7	294	2.1	1	42	3.4	1	42	0.9												
Gazella granti	11	451	3.2	4	164	13.2	1	15	0.3												
Gazella thomsoni	15	225	1.6				1	8	0.2												
Sylvicapra grimmia							1	3	0.1												
Raphicerus campestris																					
Rhynchotragus kirkii																					
Syncerus caffer	2	424	3.0	1	9	0.7	1	212	4.3												
Wild meat weights	77.5	10506	73.5	66.7	821	66.2	44.7	2282	46.4	3.8	512	4.9	—	—	—	—	—	—	5.9	127	7.8
Domestic meat weights	22.5	3784	26.5	33.3	418	33.8	55.3	2631	53.6	96.2	9888	95.1	100.0	963	100.0	100.0	3749	100.0	94.1	1504	92.2
Total meat weights	100.0	14290	100.0	100.0	1239	100.0	100.0	4913	100.0	100.0	10400	100.0	100.0	963	100.0	100.0	3749	100.0	100.0	1631	100.0

[a] MNI = minimum number of individuals.
[b] Weights are in kilograms.
[c] These have been excluded from the meat wt. counts as they are likely to be the result of scavenging.
[d] These are larger than *G. camelopardalis* (Gifford *et al.*, 1980).

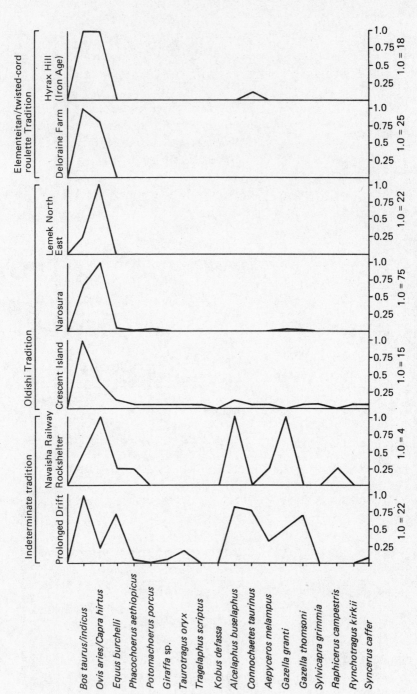

Fig. 6.2. Faunal assemblages from pastoral neolithic sites.

up 80 per cent or more of the faunal assemblage at four of the sites: Narosura, Lemek North East, Deloraine Farm and Hyrax Hill (Fig. 6.2). Two unanalysed faunal assemblages also fit into this group – the material from an Elementeitan site, Ngamuriak (Marshall & Robertshaw, 1982), and the fauna from the Oldishi Tradition horizon of Lukenya Hill GvJm 44 (Bower *et al.*, 1977). At two of the sites, Prolonged Drift and Naivasha Railway Rockshelter, wild fauna account for more than half of the assemblage, while the proportions of wild and domestic fauna are roughly equal at Crescent Island. However, a simple comparison of the proportion of the minimum numbers of individuals belonging to wild and domestic species is not necessarily very informative because animals have a wide size range, so that a giraffe and a goat cannot be treated as equivalents. One way to deal with this problem is to use the carcase weight for each species, multiplied by the minimum number of individuals present for that species, to obtain an estimate of the contribution to the meat component of the diet. Species weights were obtained from Dorst & Dandelot (1972) and from Epstein (1971), with the carcase weight being estimated as two-thirds of the body weight. This value was used because some of the viscera would probably be eaten and the use of gutted and beheaded carcase weights (Voigt, 1983), which are about half the live animal weight, would probably underestimate the meat provided by an animal. However, the use of these values does not appreciably alter the contribution of wild and domestic species to the diet (Table 6.1).

If a comparison is made between the traditions then both of the Elementeitan/twisted-cord roulette Tradition sites, Deloraine Farm and Hyrax Hill, show a negligible contribution from wild animals to the diet. The same is probably true for Ngamuriak. Two Oldishi Tradition sites, Narosura and Lemek North East, fit this pattern, as does the Oldishi Tradition level fauna from Lukenya Hill GvJm 44. The two indeterminate tradition sites, Prolonged Drift and Naivasha Railway Rockshelter, show a very different pattern. Not only do wild species form the bulk of the diet, but the minimum numbers of individuals for some wild species are as large as the numbers of cattle or sheep/goats (Fig. 6.2).

The sites examined so far indicate that prehistoric pastoral societies in East Africa can be divided into two groups which have a very different relationship to wildlife: (i) Oldishi and Elementeitan/twisted-cord roulette Tradition communities which appear to have concentrated on livestock and only occasionally killed or scavenged wildlife, and (ii) the indeterminate tradition communities with only a few domestic stock and a heavy dependence on wildlife. Unfortunately, one Oldishi Tradition site, Crescent Island, does not appear to conform to either group in terms of the faunal composition. The minimum numbers of individuals attributable to wild and domestic fauna are fairly even (Table 6.1) but, unlike the Prolonged Drift and Naivasha Railway Rockshelter assemblages, only one or two individuals of each species are present in the faunal assemblage (Fig. 6.2). However, an examination of the weight of meat contributed to the diet by each wild species shows a different pattern. In this case, two individuals belonging to wild species, the giraffe (*Giraffa* sp.) and the eland (*Taurotragus oryx*) contribute over half of the total weight of wild fauna meat in the assemblage (Table 6.1). The disproportionate contribution by these two individuals suggests that the principal focus of this community was their livestock and that the hunting or scavenging of wildlife was not as important. This would mean that Crescent Island probably conforms to the pattern observed on other Oldishi Tradition sites.

The presence of two distinctive types of faunal assemblage, which were probably contemporary, needs some form of explanation. Palaeoenvironmental studies indicate that climatic conditions during the period under discussion (2,600 BP–present) have remained more or less constant (Richardson, 1966; Coetzee, 1967; Richardson & Richardson, 1972). However, one of the features of the present climate in East Africa is periodic droughts. These are known to be associated with stock losses (Helland, 1980) and the same was probably true in the past. If some pastoralists lose all or a large proportion of their stock, then they have to rebuild their herds; the indeterminate tradition sites probably represent communities trying to rebuild herds, while the Oldishi Tradition and Elementeitan/twisted-cord roulette Tradition sites represent 'successful' pastoral communities. This, in turn, suggests that the exploitation of wild fauna by prehistoric communities in Maasailand represents a crisis resource, something that is turned to only when stock is lost. Such a strategy is unlikely to have produced any large-scale threat to wildlife, a thesis supported by the fact that all the species of wild fauna from these sites occurred in Maasailand at the time of European contact, despite more than 2,500 years of exploitation of the area by pastoralists. Although the archaeological data show that 'successful' prehistoric pastoralists largely ignored the exploitation of wildlife, the faunal remains do not enable one to infer whether the pastoralists concentrated on meat or milk production. However, at the time of European contact with the Maasai pastoralists who inhabited the Central Rift Valley and adjacent areas, it is clear that the primary emphasis was on milk production (Thomson, 1887).

The creation of an image: the Maasai and the British, c.1880–1960

The first European traveller to give a detailed account of the Maasai, Joseph Thomson (1887), reported that wildlife in Maasailand was not hunted by the Maasai and accordingly showed a remarkable lack of fear. Thus, wildlife was generally defined as a 'non-resource' by the Maasai, and was largely ignored. However, the Dorobo, who had no cattle, did hunt (Thomson, 1887), and this conforms to the pattern that has been proposed for the prehistoric period. But by the time of Thomson's journey across Maasailand the fearsome reputation acquired by the Maasai had already come to dominate the European view of their society. This reputation was largely based on hearsay, but was enhanced by the murder of Fischer, the first European to enter Maasailand, in 1883. While certain aspects of Thomson's description of the Maasai presented an image of a seemingly barbaric, lawless and lustful society, he was also careful to explain the social context of the *moran*, the importance of trade with neighbouring peoples and the consumption of agricultural produce acquired by that trade, and was even equivocal about the military might of the Maasai (Thomson, 1887).

Thomson's reasonably balanced account of the Maasai did not survive the advent of British administration in East Africa, swiftly giving way to an ethnocentrically 'British' image of both the Maasai and Maasailand. Lugard, in his polemic in support of the British annexation of the East African Protectorate and Uganda, initiated what was to become the orthodox view:

The Masai country has at present the disadvantage that its inhabitants are purely pastoral, and hence there is no food or cultivation in the country, though the soil is rich and the country fairly watered. The warlike instincts of the Masai, moreover, render them at present an obstacle to peaceful development, and a terror to the more industrious and agricultural tribes around them.
(*Lugard, 1893, Vol.1:417*)

Lugard emphasises two aspects of Maasai society, the warlike *moran* and the lack of cultivation, and draws false inferences from them. His statements about food are of particular importance because they form the basis of the most prevalent stereotype of the Maasai. Of course, starvation among the Maasai in the 1890s (Lugard, 1893, vol.2) was not caused simply by their failure to cultivate, but was rather as a result of the decimation of their herds by rinderpest and by drought (Waller, 1976). However, Lugard's comment on the fertility of the country introduces the notion that the land was not being fully utilised by the Maasai, a point that ultimately helped to justify the annexation of Maasai lands for European settlement. Lugard's emphasis on the warlike nature of the Maasai is also used to justify British annexation, at least by implication, because the British could enforce peace and protect the 'defenceless' agricultural tribes from the 'predatory' Maasai.

Subsequent works written by colonial administrators reinforced this image. Hinde & Hinde (1901) and Hollis (1905) portray the Maasai as pure pastoralists, subsisting entirely on milk, meat and blood from their flocks and herds. They present this as an ideal condition from the recent past, when the Maasai had huge herds, and while they acknowledge the eating of agricultural produce by the Maasai, they see this as a temporary result of the privations of the 1890s. The notion that the Maasai were *pure* pastoralists eliminated the need to understand how a 'predatory' group could simultaneously terrorise and trade with neighbouring peoples. Thus, the Maasai were seen as a proud and aloof people who did not have a 'normal', non-predatory, relationship with any of their neighbours. The European image of the Maasai at this time also incorporated their relationship with wildlife. On this point authors were in agreement with Thomson, that the Maasai were not hunters of game, although there were some animals they would kill and eat, notably buffalo, eland and kudu (Hinde & Hinde, 1901; Johnston, 1902; Hollis, 1905). But even this was no attribute in the eyes of Europeans who were themselves, more often than not, hunters and sportsmen (see MacKenzie, Chapter 2). In this respect, as in so many others, the Maasai showed a disdain for the values and standards of European society.

Of course, this evolving European stereotype of the Maasai was not created *in vacuo*; it formed part of a justification for British annexation, colonisation and administration in East Africa. This has significance precisely because of its relation to administrative goals. Lugard makes this clear:

The advent of British administration, and the prevention of raiding and cattle-lifting, would eventually compel this predatory tribe to settle down, and the natural advantages of their country would thus be utilised.

(*Lugard, 1893, vol.1:417*)

The administrative goal for the Maasai was to be sedenterisation and the conversion of the pastoralists into agriculturalists. The consequences of failure to accept such a transition were bluntly spelt out: the Maasai either 'alters his habits or ceases to exist' (Hollis, 1905). At its most basic, this view equated nomadic and semi-nomadic pastoralism with a primitive and undeveloped form of social order, contrasted with the fostering of modern civilisation and progress represented by settled agriculture. Maasai reluctance to take up agriculture was therefore seen as an indication of backwardness. There was no place in this assessment for any notion of pastoralism as a more viable form of production in the context of savanna ecology.

This hoped-for transformation of Maasai society was only part of the encompassing European vision which involved the remodelling of nature in East Africa. The vision was most clearly annunciated by Eliot (1905:4):

Nations and races derive their characteristics largely from their surroundings, but, on the other hand, man reclaims, disciplines and trains nature. The surface of Europe, Asia and North America has submitted to this influence and discipline, but it still has to be applied to large parts of South America and Africa. Marshes must be drained, forests skilfully thinned, rivers be taught to run in ordered course and not to afflict the land with drought or flood at their caprice . . .

This is a vision of capricious and chaotic nature domesticated into order, analogous to the proposed transformation of the nomadic, predatory, pastoral Maasai into settled peaceful agriculturalists. The first step in this process of domesticating nature was the construction of the Uganda Railway, which was swiftly followed by the arrival of European colonists to farm tracts of land alongside the line-of-rail (Eliot, 1905; Sorrenson, 1968). It was at this time that the administrative stereotype of the Maasai became particularly powerful, and was invoked to justify the policy of settlement. Maasai grazing areas around Lakes Naivasha and Nakuru, and on the Mau Escarpment were considered suitable for European settlement. Characterising the Maasai as having 'hitherto done no good in the world that anyone knows of', of having 'lived by robbery and devastation', and having 'made no use themselves of what they have taken from others' (Eliot, 1905:143), the implications of the stereotype were clear: the predatory Maasai have stolen land from others, and by failing to cultivate it they have made no use of their ill-gotten gains, and we are justified in taking this land and giving it to Europeans who will use it properly. Therefore, the power of the administrative stereotype lies initially in the way in which it can be used to justify the policy of land alienation.

The advent of colonialism in Maasailand was marked by two stages of land alienation. In 1905 the Maasai were moved into two reserves, one to the south of the railway, and one on the Laikipia Plateau to the north. This situation lasted only until 1911, when the Northern Reserve was also taken for European farmland, and the Maasai were moved into an enlarged Southern Reserve (Cranworth, 1919; Sorrenson, 1968). This began the process of 'packaging' land in colonial Kenya, setting down boundaries to separate European from African and cultivated land from 'wilderness', and legislating for the maintenance of differing forms of land-use in each area. This immediately transformed part of the Maasai grazing lands into 'ordered' farmlands, and had a direct impact upon wildlife as well as the Maasai. The creation of National Parks and Game Reserves was part of this redefinition of space and land use introduced by colonial administration. Describing this pattern of settlement and 'development' of the land, Cranworth noted that wildlife presented a threat both to areas of ploughed crop-land and to the rearing of livestock by European settlers:

> . . . there are at the present time certain animals, such as the eland and buffalo, which are under taint of suspicion of bringing in their train tsetse-fly or other obnoxious parasites, and therefore are inimical to stock raising. Should this suspicion develop into a certainty, these species must disappear from all settled lands . . .   (*Cranworth, 1919:391*)

Such comments implied the superiority of European livestock production over African pastoralism, while also expressing the necessity of expelling wildlife from the domesticated environment of the farmlands. Cranworth therefore recognised that the transformation of the environment along the lines of the European farmer presented an enormous threat to wildlife, noting that while representatives of every genus and species could be preserved, it would be impossible to 'preserve the natural conditions and type of country under and over which the game flourished' (Cranworth, 1919:391). As the frontier of European farming extended, so did the threat to wildlife.

Of course, the activities of European hunters had posed a considerable threat to wildlife in East Africa since the latter part of the nineteenth century, with the slaughter of a prodigious quantity of game (cf. Cranworth, 1919; Meinertzhagen, 1957; MacKenzie, Chapter 2). Under colonial administration, it was hoped that hunting could be controlled and turned to the advantage of the state by the creation of a number of Game Reserves which would generate income for the administration (Johnston, 1902). In the early 1900s the Maasai Reserves were declared as Game Reserves, on the grounds that they were not required for European settlement and were occupied by a people (the Maasai) 'who do not kill game' (Eliot, 1905:278–9). The Northern Reserve was quickly sacrificed under the pressure for European farmland, but the Southern Maasai Reserve was maintained as a Game Reserve. However, the happy coincidence that the game reserve was inhabited by people who did not kill game, was not seen as a universal insurance for the continued existence of wildlife. Here again, an administrative stereotype of the Maasai was invoked to suggest that Maasai pastoral production and the survival of wildlife were incompatible:

[the Maasai] have but one thought, and that is cattle and sheep, but as surely as the game interferes with the grazing for their enormous herds of cattle and sheep, so surely will the game be banished. (*Cranworth, 1919:326–7*).

Behind this argument lay the assumption that the Maasai accumulation of livestock was uneconomic and irrational, and that by advancing their own prosperity without contributing to the development and progress of Kenya Colony, they would ultimately threaten the remaining wildlife and jeopardise the revenue-raising potentials of the Game Reserve. Putting forward a surprisingly 'modern' argument combining a moral duty to conserve wildlife, the benefit and gratification that wildlife can confer on humanity, and the potential for revenue to be raised from the management of game reserves, Cranworth therefore provided yet further justification for restricting Maasai use of their own lands (Cranworth, 1919:396–7).

The notion that the Maasai were not contributing adequately to the colonial economy, like all other images of the Maasai, was largely manufactured. The Maasai were regular suppliers of meat to Nairobi butchers, and in considerable quantity, and were not adverse to trading stock with Europeans, *at a fair price* (Waller, 1975). The view that they were not contributing to the national economy was merely an elaboration of the earlier image of the Maasai as a people who did not trade. Of course, the Maasai were far from model subjects under British administration, the early moves from their grazing lands having awoken a sense of opposition and suspicion towards the colonisers. Their rejection of many of the apparent benefits of colonialism, as much as anything else, confirmed their image in European eyes. Colonial views of 'developing' the Maasai therefore continued to focus on the need to alter their lifestyle by settlement and the encouragement of cultivation. Only with such a transformation could they make a full contribution to the development of the Colony, and reciprocate the 'gift' of colonialism.

By 1932, when the Kenya Land Commission was taking evidence on the land needs of all Kenya's peoples, cultivation in Maasailand had begun, but this was being undertaken by Kikuyu squatters and not by the Maasai. This movement was frequently based on Maasai-Kikuyu intermarriage, and in some cases Maasai had actively encouraged Kikuyu settlement, possibly as a means of reconstructing pastoral-agricultural exchange networks which were not hampered by administrative controls on livestock and population movements. This penetration of the Kikuyu into Maasailand raised questions about the security of land tenure, because the Kikuyu had no legal right to settle in an area which had been granted to the Maasai for their exclusive use (Kenya Land Commission, 1934a, b). However, the Commission saw peaceful Kikuyu penetration as advantageous, arguing that the creation of Kikuyu agricultural settlements was a benefit and example to the Maasai, and that vast areas of land which were not being utilised would now be cultivated. This judgement, once again made on the grounds of an image of the Maasai as people who could not properly utilise their lands, effectively gave the administration the right to alienate further tracts of Maasailand without the consent of the Maasai, this time for the use of Kikuyu cultivators (Kenya Land Commission, 1934a).

Criticism of Maasai land use was deepened during the later 1930s and the 1940s by fears that overstocking and overgrazing of pastoral rangelands was contributing to increased environmental degradation (Anderson, Chapter 12). It was widely held that the Maasai, along with other pastoralists in East Africa, suffered from a 'cattle-complex', which led them to stress the quantity rather than the quality of their livestock (Herskovits, 1926; Kenya Land Commission, 1934a). This was supported by the image of the Maasai as a miser, not interested in trading or selling his stock but merely concerned to accumulate more. Failure to implement a compulsory destocking campaign among the Kamba in 1938, in the face of an organised political protest, discouraged the administration from adopting a similar approach in Maasailand (Tignor, 1972). Instead, a solution was sought through the more gradual process of education and official propaganda aimed at encouraging the regular marketing of livestock, and the greater integration of the Maasai into the cash economy. In fact, anxiety over degradation of Maasai pastures at this time was more imaginary than real, being influenced by political pressure from European settlers for stricter colonial control of the African livestock economy and by the emergence of a wider consciousness among settlers and administrators of the potential evils of soil erosion.

Throughout the 1950s the question of Maasai land use, in the form of criticism of what was seen as overstocking and overgrazing, remained prominent in the succession of government development initiatives mounted in Maasailand. The orthodox view held that the Maasai, suffering from their cattle-complex, habitually overstocked their lands, to the detriment of the quality of the stock and the local environment (ALDEV, 1962). Notions of Maasai poor land husbandry were based upon European attitudes towards livestock production and rangeland management (see Homewood & Rodgers, Chapter 5), which continued to provide the justification for attempting to transform Maasai society. The tone of the Narok District Development Plan of 1955 indicates the extent to which the colonial administration had failed in its efforts to transform Maasai society:

In their attitude to progress the Masai are utterly supine. Their distrust of government and of the European, which to them are the same, has led them into the false belief that if they hold fast to that which is theirs by tradition, they may discount at will all that passes beyond their borders. The Masai have been subject to few of the economic and religious forces which have compelled the acceptance by other tribes of western influences: they are rich, and economic competition has not been a spur to their survival or ambition. Their staunch refusal to accept innovation, and Government's lack of insistence on it, has placed the Administration in the role of Curator of a nomad museum.[1]

The Maasai rejection of the 'gift' offered by the colonial administration of culture and progress, through sedenterisation and cultivation, had been complete.

While the administration recognised the failure of previous policies, they did not give up the attempt to transform the Maasai and Maasailand. Under the ALDEV schemes of the 1950s, emphasis turned to reforming the Maasai *through* the pastoral economy, firstly by the establishment of ranching schemes set up on the basis of supplying water. This was a revitalisation of ideas that had been proposed in the 1930s (Perham, 1976:127–8), with the aim of encouraging the integration of the Maasai into the national economy by providing services, in this case water, which they wanted and would be prepared to pay for (ALDEV, 1962). This would, it was hoped, encourage them to sell cattle to pay for the services provided, while the designation of a 'ranch' linked to the water supply would foster a sense of property, and ultimately lead to greater sedenterisation. Thus, the aim was the same, though the means of achieving it had been modified. However, it was realised that the successful operation of the Maasai ranching scheme would threaten Maasailand's wildlife. As was noted in the Narok Development Plan of 1955, the vast herds of wildlife in the vicinity of the Loita Plains 'make annual depredations on pasture that will be imperatively required by the Masai when grazing control (ranching) is established'.[2] The answer to this problem was to create Game Reserves which were exclusively dedicated to wildlife and the tourists, the providers of income for the Colony (see Lindsay, Chapter 7).

Once again, Maasai grazing had been identified by the administration as a threat to wildlife. Colonial government in Maasailand came to an end as it had begun, proposing land alienations from the Maasai grazing area. This policy, along with the attitude which justified it, was echoed in Huxley's report for UNESCO in 1961 on the status of wildlife in East Africa. Citing the scientific evidence produced by an ecologist, Huxley argued that the Serengeti Park 'and its marvellous fauna were being gravely threatened, ... largely by the rapidly increasing Masai', whose cattle were 'ruining the grazing and water-supplies on the migration route along its edge' (Huxley, 1961). But careful scrutiny of Huxley's report suggests that the scientific evidence for the separation of domestic stock from wildlife may have been more imaginary than real. This is clearly illustrated by his discussion of game on the Athi Plains, where he quotes Meinertzhagen's (1957) census of 1905; the effect is diminished by the fact that the most common species, by a factor of more than four, is *Bos indicus*, otherwise known as Maasai cattle. This can hardly be taken as evidence for a wild animal population being destroyed by pastoralists, especially given the existence of pastoralism in the area for at least the preceding 2,500 years.

Discussion

The flourishing history of the growth of National Parks and Game Reserves in Maasailand since independence, stimulated by a rapid increase in wildlife tourism, illustrates the extent to which the colonial image of the Maasai has continued to influence government policies towards wildlife conservation (Lindsay, Chapter 7). Government policies have been modified in so far as they have sought to make the alienation of further lands more acceptable to the Maasai by offering greater participation in decision-making and providing alternative resources for the pastoralists, as Lindsay (Chapter 7) and Western (1982) have described in the case of Amboseli. But the principle of setting aside separate blocks of land for the sole use of wildlife remains an essential element of conservation thinking. There is archaeological and historical evidence to show that prior to European colonisation pastoralists tended not to exploit wildlife except during periods of stock loss. Thus, there is no evidence to indicate that pastoralism is inimical to wildlife. It was precisely the lack of any threat to wildlife from the Maasai that Eliot (1905) noted when describing the Kenyan game reserve policy in the early 1900s. By the 1970s, this situation had been transformed to a point where the Maasai were systematically slaughtering rhinoceros in Amboseli as a protest against land alienation for wildlife preservation (Western, 1982).

The roots of this transformation lie in the image of the Maasai created by early colonial administrators, an image that erroneously portrayed the Maasai as predators terrorising neighbouring groups; nomads who lived off the milk, meat and blood of their animals; people who were only interested in accumulating stock, and would not trade. This image was used to justify the alienation of Maasai territory because, not only had they 'stolen the land from others', but having stolen it they did not even utilise it. The early land alienations had a profound effect upon subsequent Maasai attitudes, as an administrator noted in 1955:

[The Maasai] hold that they were fleeced of Laikipia, and they are determined that they shall not be so treated a second time. Therefore, in every government proposal that might affect the status quo, they discern an attempt to endanger their rights: and every time that government acquiesces to their objectives, they are encouraged in their twin falsehoods of European perfidy and Maasai superiority in having detected it.[3]

The point is demonstrated in the insistence of the Amboseli Maasai on access to the Ol Tukai swamps, even though alternative water sources had been provided away from the Amboseli Park (Western, 1982; Lindsay, Chapter 7). In Amboseli, access to the swamp has proved to be important because of the inadequacy of the alternative water supplies, a failure which has generated further Maasai resentment. Of course, the inadequacy of the water supplies provided has largely been a consequence of the Maasai rejection of the aim of sedenterisation which formed a component of administrative development goals. Sedenterisation is also associated with the concept of the exclusive ownership of property as a resource (see Little & Brokensha, Chapter 9). As early as 1919, Cranworth had suggested that as Maasai stock increased, then competition for grazing would force the Maasai to drive wildlife away. In the 1955 Narok Development Plan sedenterisation was associated with range management and this was seen as a threat to wildlife, and therefore used to justify further measures for the conservation of wildlife. Thus, the development goal for the Maasai, sedenterisation, involves a fundamental transformation which may ultimately threaten wildlife, in a similar way that European colonisation transformed the 'White Highlands' and led to the destruction of wildlife in the Naivasha–Nakuru Basin, on Laikipia and the Uasin Gishu Plateau.

While both the economics of tourism and the desire to preserve wildlife have played a part in the development of National Parks and Game Reserves in Maasailand, it is the covert power of the administrative image of the Maasai that has provided the most sustained justification for these policies. It is precisely the continuity and power of this stereotype that is likely to be ignored in political analyses of wildlife conservation, where the image remains embedded and its role in the formulation of and response to policy may be missed. If range management and sedenterisation are accepted by the Maasai, then the fears expressed by the British administrators for wildlife may become a reality. Perhaps the only active conservation policy in Maasailand has been the consistent Maasai rejection of the transformation and development implicit in the colonial and post-colonial 'gift' of administration. The experience of Amboseli could also be used to question the value of land alienation for Parks in the Maasai areas. The mere fact that the wildlife populations of Mara and Amboseli are dependent on access to grazing in the Maasai areas, means that the Parks, on their own, are not an effective conservation strategy. The acceptance by the Maasai of wildlife in their grazing areas is therefore central to the maintenance of tourism in Kenya. In this way they make an enormous contribution to Kenya and its development simply by being Maasai and not sedentary ranchers. But perhaps the Maasai could confer the ultimate gift on humanity if the Parks were abolished: they could provide a model of man coexisting with wildlife. It is the destruction of this alternative image, the Maasai as pastoralists who are able to coexist with wildlife in a way that pastoralists have done in this area for at least 2,500 years, that is the ultimate irony of conservation policy in Kenya Maasailand today.

Notes

1.   'Narok District Development Plan, 1955', Kenya National Archives [KNA] DC/NRK 1/3/2.
2.   'Narok District Development Plan, 1955', KNA DC/NRK 1/3/2.
3.   'Narok District Development Plan, 1955', KNA DC/NRK 1/3/2.

References

ALDEV (1962). *African Land Development in Kenya 1946–62*. Nairobi: English Press.
AMBROSE, S.H. (1983). Archaeology and linguistic reconstructions of history in East Africa. In *The Archaeological and Linguistic Reconstruction of African History*, ed. C. Ehret and M. Posnansky, pp. 104–57. Los Angeles: University of California Press.
AMBROSE, S.H., COLLETT, D., MARSHALL, F., & MUDIDA, N. (1987). Excavations at Deloraine Farm, Rongai, *Azania*, **19**. (In press.)
BARTHELME, J. (n.d.). Late Pleistocene-Holocene Prehistory to the North-East of Lake Turkana, Kenya. Unpublished Ph.D. thesis, University of California, Berkeley.
BLACKBURN, R.H. (1973). Okiek ceramics: evidence for central Kenya prehistory. *Azania*, **9**, 139–58.
BOWER, J. (1973). Seronera: excavations at a stone bowl site in the Serengeti National Park, Tanzania. *Azania*, **8**, 71–104.
BOWER, J. & NELSON, C.M. (1978). Early pottery and pastoral cultures of the Central Rift Valley, Kenya. *Man*, **13**, 554–66.
BOWER, J., NELSON, C.M., WAIBEL, A.F., & WANDIBBA, S. (1977). The University of Massachusetts' Late Stone Age/Pastoral 'Neolithic' comparative study in Central Kenya: an overview. *Azania*, **12**, 119–46.
COETZEE, J.A. (1967). Pollen analytical studies in eastern and southern Africa. In *Paleoecology of Africa, 3*. ed. E.M. van Zinderen Bakker.

COLLETT, D. & ROBERTSHAW, P. (1983a). Problems in the interpretation of radiocarbon dates: the Pastoral Neolithic of East Africa. *African Archaeological Review*, **1**, 57-74.

COLLETT, D. & ROBERTSHAW, P. (1983b). Pottery traditions of early pastoral communities in Kenya. *Azania*, **18**, 107–25.

CRANWORTH, Lord (1919). *Profit and Sport in East Africa*. London: Macmillan.

DORST, J. & DANDELOT, P. (1972). *A Field Guide to the Larger Mammals of Africa*. London: Collins.

ELIOT, C. (1905). *The East African Protectorate*. London: Edward Arnold.

EPSTEIN, H. (1971). *The Origins of the Domestic Animals of Africa*. 2 vols. New York: Africana Publishing Company.

FISCHER, G.A. (1884). Report of a journey in the Masai country. *Proceedings of the Royal Geographical Society*, **6**, 76–83.

GALATY, J.G. & SALZMAN, P.C., ed. (1981). *Change and Development in Nomadic and Pastoral Societies*. Leiden: Brill.

GALATY, J.G., ARONSON, D., SALZMAN, P.C. & CHOUINARD, A., ed. (1981). *The Future of Pastoral Peoples*. Ottawa: International Development Research Centre.

GIFFORD, D., ISAAC, G.Ll. & NELSON, C.M. (1980). Evidence for predation and pastoralism at Prolonged Drift: a Pastoral Neolithic site in Kenya. *Azania*, **15**, 57–108.

GOVERNMENT OF KENYA (1974). *Development Plan, 1974–8*. Nairobi: Govt Printer.

GRAMLY, R.M. (1972a). Report on the teeth from Narosura. *Azania*, 7, 87–91.

GRAMLY, R.M. (1972b). A note on the teeth from the Deloraine site. *Azania*, 7, 166–7.

GRAMLY, R.M. (1975). Pastoralists and hunters: recent prehistory in Southern Kenya and Northern Tanzania. Unpublished Ph.D. thesis, Harvard University.

HELLAND, J. (1980). *Five Essays on the Study of Pastoralists and Development of Pastoralism*. Bergen: Social Antropologisk Institut.

HERSKOVITS, M.J. (1926). The cattle complex in East Africa. *American Anthropologist*, **28**, 230–72.

HINDE, S.L. and HINDE, J. (1901). *The Last of The Masai*. London: Heinemann.

HOLLIS, A.C. (1905). *The Masai: Their Language and Folklore*. Oxford: Clarendon Press.

HUXLEY, J. (1961). *The Conservation of Wildlife and Natural Habitats in Central and East Africa*. Paris: UNESCO.

JACOBS, A.H. (1963). *The Pastoral Masai of Kenya. A Report of Anthropological Field Research*, London: Ministry of Overseas Development.

JOHNSTON, H.H. (1902). *The Uganda Protectorate*, 2 vols. London: Edward Arnold.

KENYA LAND COMMISSION. (1934a). *Report of the Kenya Land Commission (Carter)*. London: HMSO.

KENYA LAND COMMISSION. (1934b). *Kenya Land Commission (Carter): Evidence and memoranda*. 3 vols. London: HMSO.

KRAPF, J.L. (1860). *Travels, Researches and Missionary Labours during Eighteen Years in Eastern Africa*. London: Trubner.

LEAKEY, L.S.B. (1931). *The Stone Age Cultures of Kenya Colony.* Cambridge: Cambridge Unversity Press.

LEAKEY, M.D. (1945). Report on the excavations at Hyrax Hill, Nakuru, Kenya Colony. *Transactions of the Royal Society of South Africa*, **30**, 271–409.

LUGARD, F.D. (1893). *The Rise of our East African Empire: Early efforts in Nyasaland and Uganda,* 2 vols. London: Blackwood.

MARSHALL, F. & ROBERTSHAW, P. (1982). Preliminary report on archaeological research in the Loita–Mara region, S.W. Kenya. *Azania*, **17**, 173–80.

MEINERTZHAGEN, R. (1957). *Kenya Diary, 1902–6.* London: Oliver & Boyd.

MONOD, T. ed. (1975). *Pastoralism in Tropical Africa.* Oxford: Oxford University Press.

NELSON, C.M. (1980). The Elementeitan lithic industry. In *Proceedings of the Eighth Pan-African Congress of Prehistory and Quaternary Studies.*

ODNER, K. (1972). Excavations at Narosura, a stone bowl site in the southern Kenya highlands. *Azania*, **7**, 25–92.

ONYANGO-ABUJE, J.C. (1977a). A Contribution to the study of the Neolithic in East Africa with particular reference to the Nakuru–Naivasha Basins. Unpublished Ph.D. thesis, University of California, Berkeley.

ONYANGO-ABUJE, J.C. (1977b). Crescent Island, a preliminary report on excavations at an East African Neolithic site. *Azania*, **12**, 147–59.

PERHAM, M. (1976). *East African Journey: Kenya and Tanganyika, 1929–30.* London: Faber & Faber.

RICHARDSON, J.L. (1966). Changes in the level of Lake Naivasha, Kenya, during post-glacial times. *Nature*, **209**, 290–1.

RICHARDSON, J.L. & RICHARDSON, A.E. (1972). The history of an East African Rift Lake and its climatic implications. *Ecological Monographs*, **42**, 499–534.

SALZMAN, P.C. ed. (1982). *Contemporary Nomadic and Pastoral peoples: Africa and Latin America.* Williamsburg: College of William and Mary.

SANDFORD, G.R. (1919). *An Administrative and Political History of the Masai Reserve.* London: Waterlow & Sons.

SORRENSON, M.P.K. (1968). *The Origins of European Settlement in Kenya.* Nairobi: Oxford University Press.

THOMSON, J. (1887). *Through Masai Land: A Journey of Exploration among the Snowclad Volcanic Mountains and Strange Tribes of Eastern Equatorial Africa.* London: Sampson Low.

TIGNOR, R.L. (1972). Kamba political protest: the destocking controversy of 1938. *International Journal of African Historical Studies*, **5**, 629–39.

TURTON, D. (1984). Mursi Response to Drought: the lessons for relief and rehabilitation. *Production Pastorale et Société*, **15**, 9–18.

VOIGT, E.A. (1983). *Mapungubwe: An Archaeozoological Interpretation of an Iron Age Community.* Johannesburg: Transvaal Museum Monograph 1.

WALLER, R.D. (1975). Uneconomic growth: the Maasai livestock economy, 1918–39. Paper presented at the Conference on 'The Political Economy of Kenya Colony', Trinity College, Cambridge.

WALLER, R.D. (1976). The British and the Maasai, 1895–1905: The origins of an alliance. *Journal of African History*, **17**, 529–54.

WESTERN, D. (1982). Amboseli. *Swara*, **5** (4), 8–14.

7

Integrating parks and pastoralists: some lessons from Amboseli

W.K. LINDSAY

Introduction

Many of the regions with abundant and diverse wildlife communities remaining in East Africa are occupied by pastoralists. While livestock-herding people have coexisted with wildlife for thousands of years (Collett, Chapter 6), the potential for conflict over land use has increased in recent decades, following the intervention of modern governments in pastoralist lifestyles (Sandford, 1983). Some biologists and conservationists have concluded that pastoralists now compete severely with wildlife for food, water and living space (Huxley, 1961; Simon, 1962; Lamprey, 1983). They advocate the reduction of perceived conflicts by the exclusion of livestock and settlement from contested areas. Certain wildlife populations have been protected in this way in the short term, but this enforced exclusion can create hardships for local herdsmen (Turton, Chapter 8) and new conflicts with conservation interests (Myers, 1972). In recognition of the potential antagonism between the goals of nature preservation and the right of indigenous people to land tenure and use, some conservationists have proposed that the human neighbours of nature protection areas should receive direct, compensatory benefits from the reserves (Myers, 1972; IUCN, 1980; Cumming, 1981). The aim of this policy is to return to a sustainable coexistence between people and wildlife.

In the Amboseli area of southern Kenya, efforts to resolve conflicts between Maasai pastoralists and wildlife have been made by conservationists and government authorities since the 1950s. In 1977, a new programme was initiated to involve the Maasai in direct benefits from a National Park which was created in their critical grazing lands (Western & Thresher, 1973). It was predicted that the Maasai of Amboseli would come to view the wildlife and their habitats as a local resource, subject to the same concerned husbandry as their cattle. Successful results have been reported, and the Amboseli Park programme has been proposed as a general model for the integration of conservation and development (Western, 1982). By 1984, however, it was apparent that early successes

149

were limited by novel or re-emerging problems which were unexpected
or were inherent in the design of the programme.

This chapter analyses the problems encountered in Amboseli with a
brief summary of their historical background and a more detailed description of the recent developments. The discussion centres on the specific
circumstances of Amboseli, but should apply more generally to the problem of reconciling nature conservation with indigenous peoples' land
tenure and use.

Ecological background of Amboseli

The area referred to as Amboseli – 'Empusel' or 'salty dust' in the Maasai
language (Mol, 1978) – is the closed basin of a former Pleistocene
lakebed, in the midst of the bushlands of Kajiado District in southern
Kenya (Fig. 7.1). The lake basin of some 600 km^2 is now dry and supports
a diverse, shifting mosaic of woodlands and saline/alkaline grasslands
(Western, 1973). The only permanent sources of water in this semi-arid
region are a series of springs emerging in the Amboseli basin from the
watershed of Mount Kilimanjaro, 30 km to the south in Tanzania. The
combination of springs and swamps with the complex pattern of soils
and vegetation has allowed a variety of wild animals to inhabit the
relatively small area. The faunal diversity of Amboseli was recorded by
European explorers in the late nineteenth century (Thomson, 1887) and
has been noted by naturalists and wildlife conservationists since then
(Johnson, 1935; Simon, 1962).

The large mammal community is dominated by migratory herbivores
which alternate seasonally between the arid bushlands and swamp mar-
gins. Migrants, such as wildebeests, zebras and elephants, scatter in wet
seasons across the bushland pastures, concentrating in the basin woodlands and swamps each dry season as water availability becomes limiting
(Western, 1975). Domestic livestock constitute a major portion of the
migrant community, and the Maasai herd their cattle and small stock in
parallel with the seasonal movements of the wild herbivores. Maasai
have occupied the Amboseli area in this manner for several hundred
years (Jacobs, 1975), and they were preceded by other pastoralists and
hunter/gatherers (Foley, 1981). The Amboseli Maasai are members of
the Ilkisongo section.

The focus for potential competition between Maasai and wildlife is
over the use of the Amboseli basin habitats for dry season grazing.
Livestock have comprised up to 60 per cent of the large mammal biomass

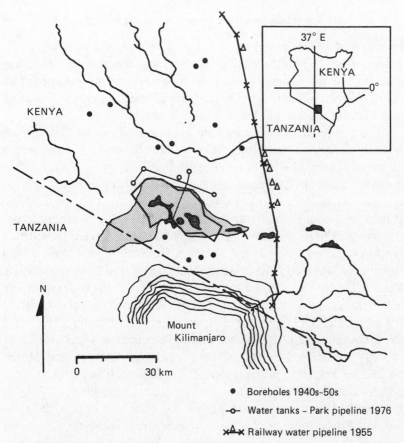

Fig. 7.1. Amboseli and its environs. The Amboseli basin (light shading) and National Park boundaries (heavy line) are shown. Swamps (dark shading) and seasonal rivers are noted, as are man-made water sources: boreholes constructed in the 1940s and 1950s (closed circles), water tanks of the Park pipeline completed in 1976 (open circles), and the railway water pipeline (solid line with crosses, water points are triangles) built in 1955.

in the basin in dry seasons (Western, 1975) and, in their association with people, may have had some competitive advantages over wild herbivores. However, stock numbers were also limited by relatively rapid disease transmission and by their ability to forage and travel to water within a daytime, herded grazing regime. In recent years, water development and modern veterinary techniques such as dips and inoculations have reduced some of the ecological restrictions on livestock populations (Prole, 1967; Western, 1973; Lamprey, 1983).

Early conservation programmes 1899–1977

From colonial times to the present day, three protagonists – the central government, the wildlife conservationists, and the Maasai – have had separate but interacting interests in Amboseli and its environs. This interaction was influenced by the changing political, economic and social conditions in the country throughout this period.

At the onset of colonisation, the Maasai occupied an area of East African rangeland stretching from Mount Kenya to north-central Tanzania (Jacobs, 1975). In an effort to pacify the Maasai and to clear preferred land for European settlers, the British government in 1904 created the Northern and Southern Masai Reserves in the Laikipia Plateau and an area of southern Kenya. By 1911, the Northern Masai Reserve had been abolished and its resident Maasai were moved to a northwestern extension of the Southern Reserve. A year later, a final 'agreement' was made, requiring the Maasai to stay within a single Masai Reserve area of some 38,000 km^2 (Fig. 7.2) and effectively denying them access to many productive rangelands. Additional regulations were passed prohibiting large-scale cattle movements and trading. They were left to continue their 'traditional' land-use practices, but these were now strongly constrained by the colonial legislation. The 'Maasai Moves' created an enduring mistrust among the Maasai towards the central government (Jacobs, 1975). Disease epidemics and famine in the 1890s had resulted in tremendous losses of livestock and human life (Fosbrooke, 1948). These factors, as well as internal social divisions, may have made the Maasai easier to contain politically, but also made them ever more intent to retain tenure over their remaining water and grazing resources.

From the early days of the East Africa and Uganda Protectorates, concern was expressed for the need to control the hunting of wild animals by both Europeans and Africans (Johnston, 1902). In 1899, the British Government established a Game Reserve in the south of Kenya between Nairobi and the border of German East Africa. It was regazetted in 1906 with adjusted boundaries (Fig. 7.2), which roughly corresponded to the Southern Masai Reserve of that time (Cranworth, 1912). Within the Southern Game Reserve, all hunting of wild animals was prohibited, but many authorities apparently felt that the Maasai could continue to coexist with the wildlife populations. The two types of Reserve were seen as serving the same purpose: the preservation of a primitive Africa where 'native and game alike have wandered happily and freely since the Flood' (Cranworth, 1912:310).

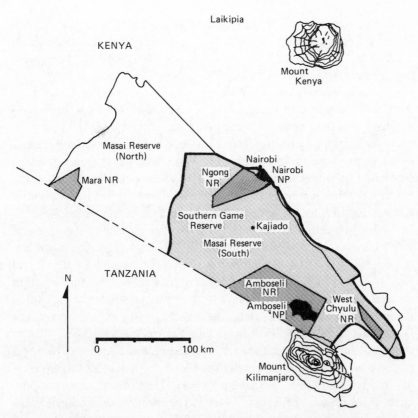

Fig. 7.2. Masai Reserve and wildlife conservation administrative boundaries around the Amboseli area, from 1906 to the present (after Cranworth (1912), Kenya Government (1958) and WPU (1981)). The Masai Reserve (1912) is bounded by the thin solid line. The Southern Game Reserve (1906) is indicated by the thick solid line and light shading. The four National Reserves (1958) are shown with medium shading. Nairobi National Park (1948) and Amboseli National Park (1977) are indicated with dark shading.

By the 1940s to 1950s, however, government interventions may have begun to alter this 'natural balance'. After the Second World War, the colonial authorities adopted policies aimed at sedenterising the Maasai and increasing the productivity and national participation of their livestock economy. Dams and boreholes were constructed under the African Land Development (ALDEV) Programme in the 1940s and 1950s in the bushlands surrounding Amboseli and watering points were tapped from a railway water pipeline completed in 1955 (Fig. 7.1), although local elders were rarely consulted (ALDEV, 1962). Livestock numbers appeared to increase rapidly in subsequent decades (Western, 1973,

1982) and when Maasai herdsmen concentrated their cattle in Amboseli in late dry seasons, they were reported to supplant wild herbivores from pasture areas and degrade habitats through livestock overgrazing and bush-cutting for fencing (Cowie, 1956; Simon, 1962). Although systematic evidence was lacking, many conservationists believed that wildlife in Amboseli faced new and severe ecological competition from the Maasai livestock and their herders (Kenya Wild Life Society, 1957).

Under combined pressure from European hunters who wanted access to the 'game' populations and from naturalists who wanted more effective protection of wilderness areas, the colonial government abolished the Southern Game Reserve in 1952. Three smaller National Reserves took its place, with a fourth added in the Mara area of the Masai Reserve. In 1948, the Amboseli National Reserve was gazetted as an area of 3,260 km^2 surrounding the Amboseli basin (Fig. 7.2). Administrative responsibility for the National Reserves was granted to the Royal National Parks of Kenya, an independent trusteeship with funding from government and private donors. Hunting was prohibited within these Reserves, but licenced shooting was administered by the government's Game Department in the surrounding Controlled Areas. The Maasai were still allowed to herd livestock in and around the Amboseli National Reserve, as the central government's official policy was 'not to interfere with indigenous peoples or stand in the way of legitimate human development' (Government of Kenya, 1946:6). However, many National Parks staff apparently expected that central Amboseli would soon be given full Park status, to the exclusion of Maasai livestock (Cowie, 1951).

The Reserve wardens began limited development of the central Amboseli basin, and as visits by foreign and resident Europeans grew more frequent, the colonial government faced increasing pressure to protect Amboseli wildlife. These cries became particularly vocal in the local and international press after a drought in 1955 forced the Maasai to concentrate in the central basin habitats (see above). In the late 1950s, Parks and central government authorities attempted to shift livestock concentrations away from the centre of the Amboseli basin by constructing watering points in peripheral areas and controlling livestock grazing patterns (Kenya Game Department, 1956). An enlightened forum for negotiation with some of the local Maasai elders was established by the Park wardens at that time (Lovatt Smith, 1986). As with ALDEV, however, few pastoralists were consulted at broader levels of land-use planning. A National Game Policy Committee (Government of Kenya, 1958) recommended that the existing water supply be expanded with a major pipeline system, that livestock numbers be limited around the main swamp areas, and that central Amboseli be made an official Game Reserve with control over wildlife and livestock. Most of these recommendations were not followed, as the government of the day was apparently not convinced that the benefits of preserving an 'untouched' Amboseli were worth the financial and political costs (Huxley, 1961).

By the early 1960s, revenues from tourists' entrance fees had increased to substantial levels. A small portion of this income had been allotted to the Kajiado African District Council, the Maasai native representative body responsible for the area including Amboseli, to encourage their acceptance of the Reserve. The District Council also received hunting fees from the Controlled Areas surrounding Amboseli. In 1961, full control of the Reserve was removed from the National Parks Trustees, much to their consternation (Cowie, 1963), and granted to the Council as a pre-independence conciliatory move by the British government. The Council administration was expected to conserve the area as both a local and a national economic resource and to be more acceptable to the residents of Amboseli. Thus, a financial motivation was added to nature conservation for the separation of livestock and wildlife in Amboseli, and this motivation assumed ever greater importance for emerging politicians in the Council as well as for the central government.

Rental and tax income from new tourist lodges and entrance fees grew rapidly in the years following independence (Western, 1982). Within central Amboseli, a section of about 80 km^2 was officially declared a livestock-free area after intensive negotiation between the Olkejuado County Council (as the Kajiado District Council was now called) and the local herdsmen. However, the Council, based in Kajiado town over 100 km from Amboseli, represented only another level of bureaucratic authority to the Maasai, who received no direct revenue from the Reserve. The latter increased their use of the central basin, suspecting that the 'livestock-free' areas would be continually expanded if not occupied by cattle (Kenya Game Department, 1964).

In addition, Maasai warriors began killing wildlife such as rhinoceroses and elephants as a protest against the threatened loss of their dry season grazing lands. A number of these animals may have been killed in self-defence during encounters at waterholes, which became increasingly frequent as cattle herds multiplied. More recently, there has been collaboration with poachers in response to the growing international trade in ivory and horn (Douglas-Hamilton, 1979; Bradley Martin, 1980). However, a large proportion of the spearings was apparently 'political', rather than commercial, in nature (Western, 1982). Paradoxically, government action in the interests of conservation and financial returns seems to have aggravated the uneasy relations with the Maasai to trigger this destructive form of social protest. The County Council was unable or unwilling to curtail these activities.

By the late 1960s, as income from wildlife-orientated tourism in the Reserve continued to increase, the position of the central government grew closer to that of the conservationists, who actively lobbied for the protection of central Amboseli in a National Park. At the same time, the indigenous Maasai demanded formal ownership of all the land in the region. In 1970, a Presidential Decree declared the government intention to set aside a large portion of the Amboseli basin as a Park, contingent upon a satisfactory agreement with the local residents. The lines of confrontation were drawn between conservationists and government authorities on one side, and the resident pastoralists on the other.

Recent conservation plans: the 1977 Park agreement

Against this background of conflict, an ecological study by Western (1973) reaffirmed that the Maasai formed an integrated, if changing, component of the ecosystem structure (see above), and that many of the observed habitat changes could be explained by climatic fluctuations rather than by overgrazing or wood cutting. An economic analysis, part of a proposed management plan by Western and Thresher (1973), suggested that the best use of the Amboseli area would be a combination of tourism and commercial livestock ranching, since the Maasai appeared to be entering the cash economy through employment and livestock sales. The report also stressed the importance of Amboseli in the National Park system of Kenya, and recommended that ecological processes should be preserved and that human disturbance should be kept to a minimum. These goals were echoed in a government statement of conservation policy (Government of Kenya, 1975).

On the basis of these recommendations, a 488 km^2 portion of the Amboseli basin was gazetted as a National Park in 1974 while negotiations continued with the Maasai. The Park was to be administered by the National Parks Trustees, with development and running costs provided by them and the bulk of entry fees returning to their Nairobi headquarters. The County Council would retain control of 160 ha in the centre of the Park and continue to receive rental from lodges located there as well as a portion of the Park entry fees.

Some 2,000 people with 26,000 livestock used the Amboseli basin each dry season (Western & Thresher, 1973). In a nationwide programme of land adjudication, these local Maasai became joint owners of the surrounding bushlands in a number of group ranches organised roughly along clan/subsection lines and traditional grazing areas. Recognising that earlier conservation plans had failed to provide the Amboseli Maasai with sufficient compensation, the Park plan proposed that the group ranches receive the following benefits from the National Park in their midst:

(i) Guarantee of adequate water supplies outside the proposed Park area, through maintenance of existing boreholes, and through the construction of a pipeline to carry water from a major spring in the basin to outlying water tanks (Fig. 7.1). National Park staff were to assume responsibility for operating the pipeline and boreholes, with funds from the Ministry of Water Development and the County Council.

(ii) Compensation for the 'opportunity costs' of tolerating wildlife grazing on their group ranch lands. This 'wildlife utilisation fee' was to equal the theoretical market value of cattle which could have been raised instead of the equivalent biomass of wild herbivores which migrate across the group ranches. It was calculated to start at £25,000 per annum and to increase with a projected growth in the wildlife populations after the Maasai vacated the basin grasslands.

(iii) Direct economic benefits to the Maasai group ranches through the development of wildlife viewing circuits and tourist campsites, and through trophy hunting and possibly cropping on the group ranch lands. Under existing tourism trends, it was predicted that additional tourist lodges would be developed on the ranch lands within three and six years in the best and worst cases respectively. The 'wildlife utilisation fees' paid by the central government could then be replaced by earnings from rental fees charged to the new lodges, as well as from the other sources of direct income.

(iv) Additional direct benefits in the form of services such as a school, dispensary, and community centre which would be included in a new Park headquarters at the edge of the Park.

These plans were subjected to extensive negotiations between group ranch representatives, the County Council, and the central government. The process resulted in compromises over the Park boundaries, which finally encompassed an area of 390 km^2 around the basin springs (Figs. 7.1, 7.2). A development project jointly funded by the World Bank and the Kenya Government began upgrading Park facilities in Amboseli, as prescribed by the Wildlife Act of 1976 and later by the government's Wildlife Planning Unit (Kenya Wildlife Planning Unit, 1981). The Wildlife

Act also dissolved the Parks Trustees and placed National Parks under direct government control in combination with the Game Department. The overall policy was to integrate the Park with surrounding livestock grazing lands so that the effective area for wildlife was much larger than the central protected areas, while the local herdsmen enjoyed improved living standards and developed a vested interest in the Park. In addition, the various levels of government were to continue receiving substantial revenues from the Park. The final agreement was implemented in June 1977, as the Maasai agreed to vacate the Park land in return for the benefits described.

Outcome of the 1977 Park policies

Has the National Park programme in Amboseli achieved its conservation and development objectives? Western (1982) describes a number of positive results with few qualifications. The local group ranches received wildlife compensation fees from the central government for five years and were able to build a school and a cattle dip. They developed sources of direct income in the sale of gravel and wood to the Park and lodges, in a campground which they operate, and fees from tented camp concessions to private companies. A committee composed of a few elders and full-time employees of the group ranch immediately surrounding the Park has met with the Warden and resolved a number of Park management issues such as the location of the campsites and the use of Park grasslands by livestock. The new Park headquarters has been constructed and will eventually provide a dispensary for Maasai on the southern side of the Park. But has the programme as a whole been successful in integrating land use between the Park and the pastoralists, and resolving the long-standing conflicts?

Benefits to the Maasai and land-use integration

The water supply. The pipeline and borehole system worked well for the first few years, which was also a period of higher than average rainfall. However, by 1980 the system was operating poorly for both technical and administrative reasons. The pipeline to the northern bushlands was unable to pump enough water to the outermost areas; its initial design was inadequate and modifications are apparently under way (Western, 1982). Its operation required high recurrent expenditure on maintenance and diesel fuel and directly reflected fluctuations in government spending. Since 1981–2, national economic priorities apparently changed, possibly in response to the pressures of an international recession and external loan requirements. Borehole operation was complicated as two separate government Ministries (Water Development; Tourism and Wildlife) and the County Council were required to supply funds and manpower. Funding allocation to the water system from the National Treasury through Ministry channels had to receive approval from Parliament, which made it subject to political pressures from other parts of the country. For some or all of these reasons, the artificial water supply was interrupted during critical dry periods. The Maasai herdsmen had little option but to return to their traditional sources of water and grazing, the springs and the adjacent grasslands within the Park.

Wildlife utilisation fees. Although regular from 1977 to 1981, payments were irregular or lacking during subsequent years. The reasons for this failure in financial support may have been similar to those faced by the water system. As the wildlife utilisation fee was their major source of income, the Maasai received little financial benefit from the Park after 1981. During a drought in 1984, the Amboseli Maasai lost substantial numbers of livestock (WKL, personal observation) and Park authorities were unable to offer material or logistical assistance.

Direct income from Park tourism. This remained limited to wood and gravel sales and campsite fees, perhaps as much as £8,000 per annum. In 1977, in an effort to control poaching, the government imposed a national ban on all hunting of wildlife and has not yet removed it. The income from trophy hunting licence fees has not been available to the group ranch during this time. No new lodges or viewing circuits have been constructed on the group ranch (Olalarashi) most affected by the Park and its wildlife, and thus the potentially large rental fees have also been absent. It was a source of resentment among the Maasai that while alternative income sources have been slow to develop, Park entry fees have not been shared with the group ranches. The retention of a portion of Park fees for local use had been proposed in the original recommendations, but with amalgamation of National Parks and Game Department under central government authority, this considerable revenue has gone directly to the National Treasury.

Conservation objectives

Since the National Park plan came into effect, the populations of many Amboseli wildlife species have apparently grown in size (Western, 1982). The numbers of wildebeests and zebras have risen, possibly as a result of decreased grazing competition from livestock in the basin habitats.

Rhinoceros numbers have almost doubled and the elephant population has increased by about 30 per cent in the central Park areas. However, between 1983 and 1985, three rhinoceroses and over 20 elephants were speared (WKL, personal observation; C. Moss, unpublished records) by Maasai warriors.

It had been suggested that poaching was reduced when the Maasai developed a growing appreciation of the wildlife on their lands, as they received increasing benefits from the Park (Western, 1982). Indeed, the group ranch elders frequently helped park authorities in identifying poachers, whether they were local warriors or outsiders, in the optimistic years immediately following the Park agreement. With the failure of many of the terms of the agreement, there has been less of this cooperation, and a degree of poaching has resumed. However, the detection of a 'conservation ethic' among the Amboseli Maasai in the period 1977–82 may have been confounded by changes within their social structure. As with many pastoralists, Maasai society is organised in age-grades (Fosbrooke, 1948). Most of the hunting of wildlife is done by the active, 'junior' warriors, and elders may have only limited authority over this activity. When an age-set graduates from 'junior' to 'senior' warriorhood, its members settle into a more sedate lifestyle which includes marriage and the accumulation of cattle. Typically a new age-set of junior warriors is recruited before the previous one retires, but there can be considerable geographical and temporal variation in this pattern (Fosbrooke, 1948). In 1978, the incumbent age-set of junior warriors in Amboseli passed to senior rank, and initiation of the subsequent age-set was apparently delayed until 1983–4 (K. Olesei, personal communication). Thus, the harmonious relations between Park and Maasai occurred when there were few active warriors in the Amboseli area with the opportunity to hunt, and the resumption of elephant and rhinoceros spearings coincided with the appearance of the new warriors. While this analysis does not necessarily refute the 'conservation ethic' hypothesis, it does show how the reaction of a local populace to a conservation plan can be masked by social dynamics in the area.

In 1983–4, a small area of irrigated agriculture was greatly expanded around the Namalog swamp system immediately to the east of the Park. Agricultural land use inevitably encounters conflict with primates and larger wild herbivores (elephants, buffaloes, other bovid antelopes); the primary management options are expensive fencing or removal of the wildlife (Woodley, 1965, Anon, 1981). This development is likely to have a large impact on the wildlife community of Amboseli. The farmers of this land are members of two of the Maasai group ranches (Olalarashi and Kimana) involved in the Park agreement. They have shown a growing desire to diversify their subsistence lifestyle, a trend which may have accelerated during recent drought conditions. They have also demonstrated a lack of faith in the promise of sustainable benefit from the Park. Meanwhile, the expansion of cultivated land in close proximity to the Park could dramatically reduce its value as a conservation area, and create new conflicts between people and wild animals.

In summary, the Maasai living around Amboseli had little incentive to remain out of the Park, and strong reasons to return, just a few years after the 1977 agreement was made. Direct benefits from the Park have been limited and interrupted, and the lack of improvement in economic status has left the Maasai at least as susceptible to the effects of periodic drought as they had been in previous years. Some wildlife populations have increased in size, but for elephants and rhinoceroses, the relief from competition and hunting has been only temporary. Agricultural expansion adjacent to the Park has introduced new divisions between the interests of the local populace and of wildlife conservation. With the disruption of the Park agreement, any incipient appreciation by the Maasai of the Park and its wildlife as an integrated component of a developing pastoralist lifestyle may have suffered a damaging blow.

Lessons for the future

The National Park plan in Amboseli, as recommended by Western & Thresher (1973), extended earlier policies of wildlife conservation with new proposals for direct benefits to the Maasai and decreased spatial competition between livestock and wildlife. The subsequent agreement increased the involvement of local herdsmen in the development planning process in comparison with earlier management actions. But all the programmes to date, including the Amboseli Park plan, have ultimately failed to provide the Maasai community with continuous appreciable benefit in return for compromises in their use of land. Largely as a consequence, progress towards the goals of wildlife conservation has also been disrupted. This lack of success may be explained by unexpected changes in the economics of tourism and inherent problems in the design of the programme itself. These problems and possible alternative approaches are discussed below.

The Park plan required financial returns from tourism to replace central government funding, but the tourist economy in Amboseli failed to behave as expected. Despite predictions of exponential growth from the early 1970s, the number of tourists visiting Kenya levelled off shortly thereafter. It has not grown until recently (1985), for a variety of political and economic reasons (Eltringham, 1984; Sindiyo & Pertet, 1984). While tourism may be a more stable source of income than cash crop agriculture or extraction-based industries (Myers, 1972), it is influenced by different factors: political stability and security in the host countries, economic conditions in the source and host countries, and the psychology of tourists (Pullan, 1983; Eltringham, 1984). The shortfall in tourism growth may have been impossible for economic planners to predict, but such an outcome could have been included in the original plan as one of the possible scenarios. The lack of investment in new lodges in Amboseli may also be due to aesthetics and limited siting opportunities, and the short-term nature of most tourist visits to Amboseli in relation to nation-wide patterns.

Amboseli currently receives 90,000–100,000 visitors each year; in Kenya it ranks with Nairobi National Park and the Mara Reserve in annual tourist volume (Kenya Wildlife Planning Unit, 1981), and Kenya has one of the most successful tourism industries in Africa (Pullan, 1983). If a conservation plan based on tourism were to work anywhere, it should have succeeded in Amboseli. A corollary is that what works in a park like Amboseli might not succeed where tourist potential is lower. In many places, including Amboseli, conservation programmes depending largely on tourism may suffer in the long term and may require additional commitment by governments or international organisations (Pullan, 1983; Sindiyo & Pertet, 1984).

In its design, the Park programme was based almost entirely on a single factor, the input of money for the water supply system and for the large annual payments to the group ranches. When the supply of external funds was interrupted, the fragility of the arrangement became apparent. However, even if funds had been continuously available, there may have been social problems with the money-based plans. Western & Thresher's (1973) economic analysis demonstrated that, viewed from above, the Park development was a better financial option than livestock ranching alone. But while this argument may have been convincing to national economists and planners, it was not clear whether the majority, or simply an opportunistic minority, of the Maasai population surrounding Amboseli was socially prepared to value money as a substitute for potential livestock.

Surveys of the attitudes of the local populace towards different development options and an assessment of their satisfaction with the Park programme were lacking. Equally, there was no extension work included to encourage the pastoralists in their appreciation of benefit from the Park, although a programme of survey and extension is currently in progress in an area near Amboseli (D. Berger, personal communication). The resumption of elephant and rhinoceros spearing may be viewed as a return to political protest in the absence of communication within the established system.

Responsibility and accountability for the pipeline and compensation system were centralised, and satisfactory solutions to problems were difficult to achieve at the local level. Acting within these limitations, the Park Wardens showed considerable initiative in negotiating short-term arrangements on livestock movements and other management issues with the group ranch members, but more fundamental solutions remained elusive. While local funding sources failed to develop (as above), there were no financial guarantees in place to support the Park system. The success of the programme depended critically on continuous support from the higher government levels, which often failed to materialise.

At the level of individual herdsmen, the group ranch in its present form may be an ineffective transition from a 'traditional', to a 'modern' land tenure system (see Little & Brokensha, Chapter 9). There is currently pressure building for subdivision of the Olalarashi group ranch into individually owned plots, especially in the Namalog agricultural area (D. Olashimbai, personal communication). A number of Maasai apparently feel alienated from the group ranch committee. These events may signal an erosion of group ranch authority and could reduce the ability of the group ranch to represent the local community at higher government levels. The exclusion of livestock from the Amboseli basin and development of the new water pipeline outside has altered previous grazing and tenure patterns (Peacock, de Leeuw, & King, 1982) and places additional pressure on the group ranch. A review of the current system may be necessary to suggest new approaches for the control of communal grazing resources among the Amboseli Maasai.

Additional ecological and sociological studies would be useful for generating options for future planning in Amboseli. The nature of change in Maasai society and its relations with the environment, the potential for competition or sharing of resources by wildlife and domestic stock, and the influence of external pressures on the system, remain largely unquantified (see Collett, Chapter 6; Homewood & Rodgers, Chapter 5). Such studies would aid decision-making on the exclusion from or access to Amboseli basin habitats by Maasai livestock.

The problems encountered in Amboseli illustrate some of the pitfalls attending the combination of pastoral development and wildlife conser-

vation. Western & Thresher's (1973) innovative Park development plan
recognised that the two should be integrated, and that good development
includes and promotes good conservation. But perhaps the chief draw-
back to all the programmes in Amboseli was that they approached the
issue by attempting to graft conservation onto a changing pastoralist
society, without addressing the nature of the change itself. Many difficulties have been encountered in the field of pastoral development, as
recent discussions have illustrated (Galaty *et al.*, 1981; Sandford, 1983).
These include problems with water development, sedenterisation, land
tenure, veterinary services and husbandry practices, marketing systems,
and the role of different levels of government. The consequences of most
interventions have been simple failures in the best cases, or the disruption
of ecological systems and of pastoralist social organisation and equity
in the worst. It is perhaps not surprising that similar problems have been
seen in Amboseli. Constructive suggestions for pastoral development
are slowly emerging (Sandford, 1983), with new approaches to development incorporating and extending existing 'traditional' land use systems
in environmentally sound practices (see Little & Brokensha, Chapter 9).

Within the context of national government priorities, further development in Amboseli could be decentralised in operation, and should consider local attitudes and aspirations, social dynamics and ecological
realities. The Park plan assumed that the Amboseli Maasai were becoming increasingly incorporated into the national market economy, beyond
the level of subsistence trading. This may be the case for a few entre-
preneurial individuals who have accumulated considerable wealth. However, the average Amboseli herdsman may be at least a generation away
from modern commercial ranching and, as many authorities suggest,
development activity might advisedly treat other aspects of life than
simply the monetary. A coordinated approach to local development and
land-use planning could involve personnel from the areas of public health
and social services, education/extension, veterinary services, livestock
marketing and production, and resource (including wildlife) conservation
from government Ministries or Institutes, or from international organisations (especially if the latter provide funds). The National Park headquarters could provide a venue for discussion of development options
and conflicts as they arise.

The water supply system could be less expensive and more reliable
in operation; alternative energy sources or the linkup to a gravity-fed
pipeline some 20 km to the northeast (Fig. 7.1) have been suggested
though not implemented. Maasai could be encouraged and trained to
operate the borehole and pipeline system themselves, thus making the

availability of their critical water resources more directly accountable. If tourism is to contribute to the operation of such a programme, then sufficient funds from Park entry fees should be retained locally to cover basic operating expenses until dependable alternate income sources are developed. There is a need for an unambiguous declaration of government priorities in the fields of pastoralist development and nature conservation, and an indication of the degree of commitment to these separate, but complementary goals. Redefinition and land-use zoning of the existing National Park and surrounding group ranches might be considered.

The history of conservation and development in Amboseli suggests that a broad approach must be taken both for the conservation of nature in semi-arid regions and for the well-being of the pastoralist inhabitants. While it is premature to view Amboseli as a model for nature conservation in Africa, the potential may still exist for the development of new programmes which will allow the coexistence of both wildlife and developing pastoralism.

Acknowledgements

My period of stay in Amboseli was made possible by grants from the New York Zoological Society and the East African Wild Life Society, and by a Postgraduate Scholarship from the Natural Sciences and Engineering Research Council of Canada. My ideas on the subject of conservation and development in Amboseli evolved through discussions with Peter Hetz, Jonathan Leboo, Phyllis Lee, Kirasoi Olesei, and David Western. I received helpful comments on the manuscript from Tim Caro, Phyllis Lee, Cynthia Moss, Martyn Murray, John Scherlis, and an anonymous reviewer.

References

ALDEV (1962). *African Land Development in Kenya 1946–62*. Nairobi: English Press.
ANON (1981). Keeping elephants out. *Oryx*, **16**, 9.
BRADLEY MARTIN, E. (1980). Selling rhinos to extinction. *Oryx*, **15**, 332–3.
COWIE, M. (1951). *Annual Report 1946–50*. Nairobi: Royal National Parks of Kenya.
COWIE, M. (1956). *Annual Report 1955*. Nairobi: Royal National Parks of Kenya.
COWIE, M. (1963). *Annual Report 1961–2*. Nairobi: Royal National Parks of Kenya.

CRANWORTH, B.F.G. (1912). *A Colony in the Making*. London: Macmillan.

CUMMING, D.H.M. (1981). The management of elephant and other large mammals in Zimbabwe. In *Problems in Management of Locally Abundant Wild Animals*, ed. P.A. Jewell & S. Holt, pp. 91–118. New York: Academic Press.

DOUGLAS-HAMILTON, I. (1979). *The African Elephant Action Plan*. Nairobi: IUCN/WWF/NYZS Elephant Survey and Conservation Programme.

ELTRINGHAM, S.K. (1984). *Wildlife Resources and Economic Development*. Chichester: Wiley.

FOLEY, R. (1981). Off-site archaeology and human adaptation in eastern Africa. *BAR International Series*, **97**, 1–265.

FOSBROOKE, H.A. (1948). An administrative survey of the Masai social system. *Tanganyika Notes and Records*, **26**, 1–50.

GALATY, J.G., ARONSON, D., SALZMAN, P.C. & CHOUINARD, A., ed. (1981) *The Future of Pastoral Peoples*. Ottawa: International Development Research Centre.

GOVERNMENT OF KENYA (1946). *Second Interim Report of the Game Policy Committee*. Nairobi: Govt Printer.

GOVERNMENT OF KENYA (1958). *Report of the Game Policy Committee*. Sessional Paper no. 7 of 1957/8. Nairobi: Govt Printer.

GOVERNMENT OF KENYA (1975). *Statement on future wildlife management policy in Kenya*. Sessional Paper no. 3 of 1975. Nairobi: Govt Printer.

HUXLEY, J.S. (1961). *The Conservation of Wild Life and Natural Habitats in Central and East Africa*. Paris: UNESCO.

IUCN (1980). *World Conservation Strategy*. Gland, Switzerland: International Union for the Conservation of Nature and Natural Resources.

JACOBS, A.H. (1975). Maasai pastoralism in historical perspective. In *Pastoralism in Tropical Africa*, ed. T. Monod, pp. 406–25. London: Oxford University Press.

JOHNSON, M. (1935). *Over African Jungles*. New York: Harcourt Brace.

JOHNSTON, H.H. (1902). *The Uganda Protectorate*. London: Edward Arnold.

KENYA GAME DEPARTMENT (1956). *Annual Report 1954–5*. Nairobi: Govt Printer.

KENYA GAME DEPARTMENT (1964). *Annual report 1963*. Nairobi: Govt Printer.

KENYA WILDLIFE PLANNING UNIT (1981). *Amboseli National Park Management Plan*. Nairobi: Wildlife Planning Unit, Ministry of Environment & Natural Resources.

KENYA WILD LIFE SOCIETY [KWLS] (1957). *First Annual Report 1956*. Nairobi: Kenya Wild Life Society.

LAMPREY, H.F. (1983). Pastoralism yesterday and today: the overgrazing problem. In *Ecosystems of the World, 13 Tropical Savannas*. ed. F. Bourlière, pp. 643–66. Amsterdam: Elsevier.

LOVATT SMITH, D. (1986). *Amboseli. Nothing Short of a Miracle*. Nairobi: East African Publishing House.

MOL, F. (1978). *Maa. A Dictionary of the Maasai Language and Folklore*. Nairobi: Marketing & Publishing Ltd.

MYERS, N. (1972). National Parks in savanna Africa. *Science*, **178**, 1255–63.

PEACOCK, C.P., de LEEUW, P.N. & KING, J.M. (1982). *Herd Movement in the Mbirikani Area*. Nairobi: International Livestock Centre for Africa.

PROLE, J.H.B. (1967). Pastoral land use. In *Nairobi: City and Region*, ed. W.T.W. Morgan, pp. 90–7. Nairobi: Oxford University Press.

PULLAN, R.A. (1983). Do national parks have a future in Africa? *Leisure Studies*, **2**, 1–18.

SANDFORD, S. (1983). *Management of Pastoral Development in the Third World*. Chichester: Wiley.

SIMON, N. (1962). *Between the Sunlight and the Thunder*. London: Collins.

SINDIYO, D.M. & PERTET, F.N. (1984). Tourism and its impact on wildlife conservation in Kenya. *Swara*, **7**, 13–7.

THOMSON, J. (1887). *Through Masailand*. London: Sampson, Low, Marston, Searle & Rivington.

WESTERN, D. (1973). The structure, dynamics and changes of the Amboseli ecosystem. Unpublished Ph.D. thesis, University of Nairobi.

WESTERN, D. (1975). Water availability and its influence on the structure and dynamics of a savannah large mammal community. *East African Wildlife Journal*, **13**, 265–86.

WESTERN, D. (1982). Amboseli National Park: enlisting landowners to conserve migratory wildlife. *Ambio*, **11**, 302–8.

WESTERN, D. & THRESHER, P. (1973). *Development Plans for Amboseli*. Washington: International Bank for Reconstruction and Development.

WOODLEY, F.W. (1965). Game defense barriers. *East African Wildlife Journal*, **3**, 89–94.

8

The Mursi and National Park development in the Lower Omo Valley

DAVID TURTON

Let me begin with two anecdotes. In 1970 I met a foreign advisor to the Ethiopian Wildlife Conservation Department at the Department's Head-quarters in Addis Ababa. On the wall of his office was a map of the Lower Omo Valley, showing the boundaries of two designated National Parks, the Omo National Park and the Mago National Park (see Fig. 8.1). Between the two parks was a narrow wedge of territory which had been labelled 'Tama Wildlife Reserve'. ('Tama' is one of several names for the Mursi, among whom I was then carrying out my first period of anthropological fieldwork.) I asked the advisor if he was aware that there were 5,000 or so Mursi living between the Omo and Mago rivers and that, if they were excluded from the proposed parks, their subsistence system would collapse. At first he claimed that the area was uninhabited: he had flown over it many times and had seen no 'villages'. And then, after I had persuaded him that the Mursi did indeed exist, he merely brushed this information aside with the observation that the game war-dens would need to employ a good deal of local labour!

During the 1970s the Mursi experienced their worst drought and famine in living memory. This led, at the end of the decade, to a migration from the drought-prone Omo Lowlands to higher land in the Mago valley where a more reliable rainfall offered better prospects for cultivation. When I visited these migrants, in August 1983, their latest harvest had been very poor and they were so short of food that parties of people were spending days on end in the bush, living on buffalo meat and honey. On 8 September a man, a woman and her two children (one unweaned and the other about seven) were arrested by game guards from the Mago National Park because they were carrying between them about a kilogram of dried buffalo meat. They were taken to Jinka, the local administrative centre, in the back of a lorry, the man being tied with rope to prevent his escape. In Jinka he was made to parade round the market square with the meat suspended from his neck, after which he and the woman and children were taken off to prison. They were released after two

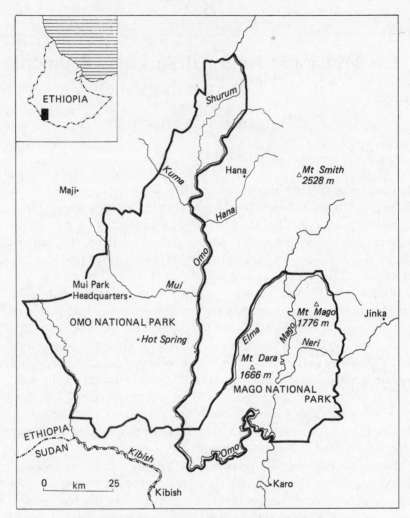

Fig. 8.1. Omo and Mago National Parks.

nights through the intervention of the administrator immediately responsible for the Mursi who happened (as I did) to be in Jinka at the time
and who understood well the severe food shortage they were facing.

Incidents like these filled me at the time with impotent rage against
the Wildlife Conservation Department and all its works. Could any set
of objectives, I wondered, which led to results as grotesque as these,
be defensible? But, of course, a more reasoned response is required:
one which accepts that the aims and aspirations of the wildlife authorities
and their advisors are as legitimate, in their own way, as those of the
Mursi, and which makes some constructive suggestions as to how these

apparently conflicting interests may be reconciled. This chapter is an attempt to find such a reasoned response, although it will be clear that I have not entirely exorcised my 'impotent rage'. I shall first describe briefly the activities of the Wildlife Conservation Department in the Lower Omo Valley since the late 1960s, when the first steps were taken to develop it as a conservation area. Secondly, I shall describe the actual and potential impact of these activities on the Mursi. Here I shall be playing the role of advocate for the Mursi, laying out the kind of information which, one would hope, might lead to some modification of conservation policies to take account of their rights and interests. Although this is a role which anthropologists frequently find themselves playing on behalf of 'their people' (and for which they are frequently criticised by planners and administrators), it is one which is imposed upon them not by their academic discipline but by simple fellow-feeling for a group of people whose hospitality they have depended on and whose knowledge and values they have learnt to respect. In the third part of the chapter I shall take a more detached and specifically anthropological view, treating the confrontation between conservation objectives and those of the local population as, at base, a conflict of cultural values – a conflict of taken-for-granted assumptions about the relationship between human society and the external world of nature and wild animals. Here I shall be playing the role of cultural translator, interpreting for members of my own culture another cultural point of view in the hope, thereby, of bringing into prominence cultural assumptions of our own which we normally do not question simply because we are unaware of them. Finally, I shall summarise what appear to me to be the lessons of this case for conservation policies and practice.

Wildlife conservation in the Lower Omo Valley

Compared with certain other African countries, with longer colonial histories, Ethiopia was a late starter in the business of wildlife conservation. In 1962, spurred on no doubt by the success of neighbouring Kenya in establishing a tourist industry based on wildlife safaris, Ethiopia requested the help of UNESCO in formulating a wildlife conservation policy. A mission headed by Sir Julian Huxley visited Ethiopia in 1963 and in the following year a two-man team, consisting of Major Ian Grimwood and the late Mr Leslie Brown carried out a survey with the specific objective of recommending areas suitable for national parks. They identified three such areas – the Simen Mountains, the Awash Valley and the Lower Omo Valley. In each case the rationale was somewhat different. A crucial purpose of the proposed Simien Park was the preservation of an endangered species – the Walia ibex, which is found nowhere else. The Awash Valley was not outstandingly rich in wildlife but it was close enough to Addis Ababa (about 200 km to the east), and accessible enough, for its development as a tourist attraction to be a feasible short-term prospect. The Lower Omo Valley was seen as a 'wilderness area' with the potential to rival the leading national parks of East Africa but the isolation of which would make this a long-term project (Stephenson, & Mizuno, 1978: 1, 39).

The Headquarters of the Omo Park were established on the River Mui, about 30 km west of the Omo, in 1966, the first game warden being Mr George Brown (brother of Leslie) who had been a District Commissioner in pre-independence Kenya. Two years later, when I arrived in the Omo Valley for the first time, the basic infrastructure of the park was well established. There were neat rows of thatched houses for the game guards, a substantial prefabricated bungalow for the game warden, an all-weather motorable track to an airstrip a few miles distant from the headquarters and a dry season motorable track to the Omo–Mui junction. Here there was a small outpost, manned by four game guards who were relieved at weekly intervals. These were impressive achievements, in view of the fact that all supplies had to be transported by air from Addis Ababa and that the Mui airstrip was frequently and unpredictably out of use because of rain.

George Brown left the service of the Wildlife Conservation Department in 1970 and thereafter a state of decline seems to have settled over the Mui headquarters. The Omo outpost was closed and the level of patrolling by the game guards fell. Logistical problems continued to dominate the administration of the park and these became particularly severe in the late 1970s with the closing of Ethiopian Airlines' scheduled flights to Mui. Supplies now had to be brought by road from Addis to Jinka and then down the Mago Valley to the Omo where they were ferried across to be met on the west bank by lorries from Mui. The route through the Mago Valley is frequently impassable in the wet season and it became commonplace for the staff at Mui to be short of basic rations for months at a time. It is hardly surprising, then, that use of the park by tourists has been negligible, although between 1974 and 1977 two to three hundred foreign visitors a year were accommodated at a tented camp set up at Mui by a Swedish safari operator, C.G. Forsmark. Apart from this, tourism has been confined to annual trips down the Omo, organised by an American company (Sobek), for 20 or so people at a time, using inflatable craft (Stephenson & Mizuno, 1978: 40).

Despite this slow and difficult start, the Wildlife Conservation Department-ment has pushed ahead with ambitious plans for the expansion of its activities in the Lower Omo Valley. The Brown–Grimwood mission had recommended that the area east of the Omo be surveyed with a view to such expansion and in 1969 a British ecologist, Melvin Bolton, visited the Mago Valley in the course of a survey of Ethiopian wildlife resources, funded by the then Overseas Development Ministry of the British Government. I have not seen his report but he gave a glowing account of the potential of the Mago Valley as a national park in a book published a few years later.

It was at once obvious that, as game country, Mago was something out of the ordinary in Ethiopia . . . Nowhere in Ethiopia had I encountered such a variety of big game in so small an area . . . Throughout the Valley one could find animals of the open plains such as Grant's gazelle, oryx and zebras, within a stone's throw of cover-loving animals such as buffalo, bushbuck and waterbuck . . . It did not need much imagination to see a system of carefully laid out motor tracks leading with studied informality to viewing platforms at selected vantage points
(*Bolton, 1976: 135*).

By 1970, as I discovered during my meeting with the foreign advisor described at the beginning of this chapter, the boundary of a proposed Mago National Park already existed on paper, although it was to be another ten years before the first practical steps were taken towards realising Bolton's vision.

Between 1976 and 1978 a Japanese 'Park Planning Team', based at Mui, carried out surveys of flora and fauna west of the Omo and in 1978 what I believe remains the most comprehensive report to date on conservation in the Lower Omo Valley was submitted to the Wildlife Conservation Department by J. Stephenson and A. Mizuno. Based on aerial surveys both east and west of the Omo, the report's principal conclusion was that a single 'greater' Omo–Mago National Park should be set up, instead of the two parks separated by a wildlife reserve which had hitherto been envisaged. A permanent headquarters, with a resident game warden, was set up in the Mago Valley in 1979–80 and priority was then given to establishing an east–west road-link from here to Mui, crossing the Mago and Omo rivers. There is now a bridge across the Mago and a ferry has been constructed on the Omo at its junction with the Mui. A permanent outpost has been re-established here, but on the east bank of the Omo. With the continuing absence of a scheduled flight to Mui, what little tourist activity there has been in the Lower Omo Valley over the past five years has been confined (apart from the annual river trips) to what is generally known now as 'the Mago Park', since this can be reached by road with relative ease from Addis, via Arba Minch and Jinka. The trip remains arduous, however, and there is no doubt that the main attraction of this area for tourists is its 'wilderness' character.

The efforts of the Wildlife Conservation Department's staff in the Omo Valley have been largely devoted to establishing what remains, after nearly twenty years, a fairly rudimentary administrative structure. From conversations I have had with them, however, it is clear that, in their own eyes, the chief long-term problem is the presence of a human population, consisting almost entirely of Mursi, wholly within the 'greater' Omo Park. The present area of Mursi occupation and use is bounded to the west and south by the Omo and to the east by the Omo–Mago watershed. Its northern boundary may be imagined as an east–west line, intersecting the Omo about 10 km north of its junction with the Mui. (North of this line live the Bodi, who number about 3,000 and speak a different language from the Mursi but whose economy and cultural values are broadly similar.) Over the past six years, migrants from northern Mursiland have spontaneously occupied the Mago Valley, cultivating on both banks of the river, northeast of Mount Mago. Because of the high tsetse challenge in this area, the migrants, who numbered about 1,000 in 1985, are coming to rely wholly on cultivation, despite their traditionally strong cultural commitment to cattle herding (Turton & Turton, 1984).

Resettlement of the Mursi is presented by Stephenson and Mizuno (1978: 49) as a fundamental prerequisite of successful national park development in the Lower Omo Valley. Although there seems no immediate prospect of such action being taken, I was told by the local *awraja* (district) administrator, in 1985, that an area had been set aside for this purpose. In order to assess the argument for resettlement it is necessary to know something of Mursi subsistence and ecology – a topic which the conservation authorities and their advisors seem to have made very little effort to understand. It is remarkable, for example, that the Stephenson–Mizuno report, excellent as it is in many other ways, virtually ignores the *human* ecology of an environment which has so obviously been moulded by human activity. In the next section I describe the subsistence activities of the Mursi, assess the actual and potential impact on these of national park development and consider the case for human resettlement as a precondition of successful conservation.

The impact of wildlife conservation on the Mursi

The economy of the Mursi rests upon the integration of three main subsistence activities: flood-retreat cultivation on both banks of the Omo, rain-fed cultivation along the seasonal westward flowing tributaries of the Omo's east bank and cattle herding in the wooded grassland that rises gradually to the Omo–Mago watershed. Each one of these is insufficient in itself, or even in combination with one of the other two, to provide for long-term survival. Because of unpredictable rainfall, diversification is the key to economic success in this environment.

Preparation for planting along the banks of the Omo begins, as the flood recedes, in September, and the main sorghum crop is ready for harvesting in December or January. Some maize, beans and cowpeas are also planted. Since there are no 'swamps' or 'flats' such as are found further down stream and which provide more cultivable land than the local population is able to make use of (Tornay, 1981; Almagor, 1972), every available pocket of inundated land is cultivated, on both banks. The size of these plots belies the vital contribution they make to subsistence. The importance of flood-retreat cultivation for the Mursi lies in its reliability, which derives from two factors. Firstly, the flood level depends not on the erratic local rainfall but on the heavy rains which fall over the highland catchment area of the Omo between June and September and, secondly, the same plots can be cultivated year after year, since their fertility is annually renewed by the deposition of flood-silts.

Rain-fed cultivation takes place in clearings along the eastern margin of the belt of bushland thicket that flanks the east bank of the Omo to a maximum width of about 10 km. Lack of adequate records makes it difficult to give a reliable figure for mean annual rainfall in this part of the Omo Valley. Butzer's data (1971) would suggest a figure of around 500 mm, while Stephenson & Mizuno estimate 550–600 mm for Mui and 600–700 mm for the wooded grassland between the Omo and Mago (1978: 11). The figure itself is not important, however, since it is rainfall reliability that matters for successful cultivation. There are two rainfall maxima, one in March/April, the primary maximum, and the other in October/November. It is the March/April rain that the Mursi depend on for their main rain-fed crop and it may vary greatly from one year to the next in timing, location and intensity. Ideally, planting takes place in March, following the first two or three days of heavy rain, the principal crop being sorghum, as at the Omo. Given enough (but not too much) rain at this time, the crop will be ready for harvesting in ten to twelve weeks. But if the rain is late, falling in mid to late April, or if the first few days of rain are followed by two or three weeks of dry weather, the crop may be ruined. If one adds to this the large variety of pests and diseases to which sorghum is subject (cf. Bacon, 1948: 312–5), it is evident that no Mursi family could afford to rely solely on rain-fed cultivation but must combine this with flood-retreat cultivation at the Omo.

The actual, as opposed to potential, impact of wildlife conservation on the agricultural activities of Mursi has not been great. Immediately following the establishment of the Mui headquarters there was undoubtedly some diminution of flood-retreat cultivation on the west bank of the Omo particularly in the vicinity of the Mui junction. But with the closing of the Omo outpost in 1970 and the consequent absence of regular patrolling between Mui and the Omo, the Mursi were able to resume full use of these areas. The setting up of a new game outpost, opposite the Omo–Mui junction, and the associated construction of a ferry, may, however, have imposed some restrictions on Mursi cultivation over the past two or three years. Rain-fed cultivation in the Mui Valley has also been affected, although I am not sure how extensive this was before the Omo Park was established. I believe that the Mursi have always carried out most of their rain-fed cultivation along the westward flowing tributaries of the Omo's east bank and this activity has not been affected by the National Park.

Despite their heavy reliance on cultivation, the cultural values of the Mursi are overwhelmingly centred around cattle and this has led to their being viewed by the administrative and wildlife authorities as 'pastoral nomads', a description which could hardly be further from the truth. They have only about one head of cattle per head of human population, which means that they would need at least ten times their present cattle wealth to subsist entirely on pastoral products (Brown, 1971; Dahl & Hjort, 1976) and that they must depend on cultivation for at least 75 per cent of their subsistence needs. Pastoralism obviously makes an important contribution, in the shape of milk, blood and meat, to the remaining 25 per cent of subsistence needs but it is not only for this reason that it must be regarded as of equal importance to flood-retreat and rain-fed cultivation in the Mursi economy. The particular economic importance of cattle to the Mursi is that they are a highly mobile form of capital which can be converted into grain through market exchange in times of famine. The role of cattle as famine insurance was clearly demonstrated by the response of the Mursi to the drought of the early 1970s, the worst in living memory. I was told that those who survived this period best were those who had cattle to exchange for grain in the highlands and that some men, having few or no cattle to make use of in this way, took back by force animals they had paid in bridewealth, thereby divorcing themselves in the process (Turton, 1977, 1980).

Cattle herding is confined to the wooded grassland east of the Omo, between the eastern edge of the bushbelt and the Omo–Mago watershed. The Omo itself is unsuitable for cattle because of the high tsetse challenge and lack of grazing but the open grass plain west of the Omo was used by the Mursi for cattle herding before the National Park Headquarters were established at Mui. Indeed I was told that the very spot chosen for the Headquarters was regularly used for both cultivation and grazing, since it is the best source of permanent water for miles around. Another important pastoral asset found on the west bank is the hot mineral springs just south of Mui. The Mursi formerly took their herds across the Omo to graze in the vicinity of these springs for several weeks at the height of the dry season, in December and January, and indeed were still doing so during my first period of fieldwork (1968–70). This practice has now either stopped or become much less regular. A far more serious threat to the pastoral activities of the Mursi is posed by the Mago Park, the western boundary of which encloses virtually all their best dry season grazing in the Elma Valley. If they were to be excluded from this area they would have virtually no pastoral resources left – which is ironic in view of the fact that one of the chief virtues claimed for the Mago Park by those who proposed its present boundary was its supposed lack of human habitation.

It is, presumably, the hunting activities of the Mursi that the conservation authorities have, in the short term, been most eager to control. Hunting, mainly of buffalo, is a seasonal standby during the hungry months before the June/July harvest and may also be heavily relied upon in more extreme conditions. Since the Mursi are well armed with ex-Italian-army long rifles and carbines, it may well be imagined that this subsistence hunting represents a serious threat to the buffalo and other species of wildlife. There is, however, no particular prestige or ritual importance attached to hunting and no particular desire, other than in times of hunger, for game meat. Nor do the Mursi have the 'sporting' approach to hunting, in which the excitement of the chase is an end in itself. Other animals, however, are killed either exclusively or (in the case of the elephant) primarily for their non-edible products: giraffe tail hair (used for threading necklaces), elephant tusks, rhinoceros horns and leopard skins. Apart from giraffe tail hair, the value of all these products to the Mursi derives from the existence of an insatiable external demand, which they are happy to exploit but the reason for which they find it difficult to understand. (One theory that was tried out on me during my first visit was that Europeans construct their houses out of ivory.) Perhaps the most important use to which these products are put is in obtaining fire-arms and ammunition from highland traders. Money and cattle may also be obtained in this way and there is no doubt that, especially in times of such severe hardship as the Mursi have experienced over the past fifteen years, these are very strong incentives.

The presence of game guards at Mui and in the Mago Valley has, at the very least, added a further factor of risk and uncertainty to an already fairly problematic activity. Buffalo were still being hunted in the Mui Valley as recently as 1982, but there must have been a great deal more subsistence hunting in the vicinity of Mui itself before the Park Headquarters were established there. As was shown by my second opening anecdote, hunting in the Mago Valley has also become more problematic, although the chances of being arrested must remain fairly low. Indeed I have not heard of any Mursi being caught red-handed at a buffalo or any other animal kill. As for non-edible game products, the *exchange* of these in the highlands does appear to have become a more risky business in recent years, no doubt because of pressure brought to bear on the administrative authorities by the Wildlife Conservation Department.

The overall impact of national park development on the economy of the Mursi is impossible to estimate precisely, but there can be no doubt (i) that this impact has, up to now, been less than the conservation authorities would have liked; (ii) that the effective implementation of their existing plans would be incompatible with continuing Mursi occupation of their present territory; and (iii) that what impact there has been over the past twenty years has made the Mursi marginally more vulnerable to ecological crisis. It is a commonplace that famine is rarely the result of a straightforward natural disaster, such as drought. Drought, it is often pointed out, is the occasion rather than the cause of famine, pushing communities over a precipice to which they have been nudged dangerously close by other influences – local, national and even global – from their human environment. The activities of the Wildlife Conservation Department have been one such influence on the Mursi: by making their economy less diversified, they have reduced its capacity to respond successfully to ecological uncertainty. These activities must therefore be included among the factors which have helped to make the last fifteen years the worst period of drought and famine in the Lower Omo Valley in living memory. And of course, if the integrity of the Omo and Mago Park boundaries had been successfully maintained against human occupation and use, there would simply have been no Mursi economy left. Are we then to conclude that resettlement of the Mursi is the only logical, and indeed humane, answer to this apparent conflict of interest?

This is certainly the view put forward by Stephenson and Mizuno, although they do not present the case in such stark terms:

The case for a single, large, viable national park in the place of two with a wildlife reserve in between is indisputable. Taking a long term view, the Omo and Mago will lose their value as national parks if vested human interests are permitted to exist between them. For one thing, some of the wild animals, chiefly elephant, lion and zebra will interfere to an increasing extent with the rights of the people of the Tama wedge and conversely the people will interfere to an increasing degree with the wildlife of the Tama and the two neighbouring national parks. Riverine belts of forest would be cut down, a feature that would interfere with the natural life on the opposite bank.   (*1978: 41*).

It is clear from this passage that Stephenson and Mizuno have a far from adequate knowledge of Mursi subsistence and ecology. They also greatly underestimate the size of the Mursi population, suggesting a total of 1,750 individuals, divided between the east bank of the Omo (750) and the wooded grassland of the so-called 'Tama wedge' (1,000). In fact, of course, flood-retreat cultivation on both banks of the Omo is an integral part of the economy of the entire population, the size of which is more in the region of 5,000. Nor do they seem aware of the use made by the Mursi of the area east of what they call the Tama River (called Elma by the Mursi) for dry season grazing. Unaware of these factors, their argument for the absorption of the 'Tama wedge' into a 'greater' Omo National Park rests on the assumption that human activity in the vicinity of two separate parks would 'interfere' with conservation policies within them. I say 'assumption' because the nature of this interference is not precisely specified as indeed it could not have been on the basis of such an imperfect knowledge of the size and ecology of the human population. Their argument could have been made much stronger if they had been aware of the full extent of Mursi dependence on both agricultural and pastoral resources, that would be denied to them if they were successfully excluded from the Omo and Mago Parks. The argument would, however, have proceeded from a different and politically and morally unpalatable premise: namely, that since national park development, as presently envisaged, would render the economy of the Mursi totally unviable, the logical step is to remove the Mursi altogether from what remains of their territory.

If the conservation authorities and their advisers are unwilling to recognise the extent to which the Mursi *already* make use of land lying within the national park boundaries, this must be because of their some-what paradoxical belief that the Lower Omo Valley is a 'wilderness', relatively unaffected as yet by human activity. According to Stephenson & Mizuno it is Ethiopia's 'most unspoiled wilderness' which has 'retained its primeval character from ages past' (1978: 1–2). The title of Bolton's book, referred to earlier, *Ethiopian Wildlands*, is indicative of the same view. This is paradoxical because, as any ecologist should surely recognise, virtually every square inch of this country bears the imprint of human activity. The open grass plain west of the Omo and the wooded grassland to the east are the products of centuries of burning and of grazing by domestic stock, while the bushland thicket flanking the Omo has been produced by clearing for cultivation. The Lower Omo Valley 'wears man's smudge and shares man's smell' (G.M. Hopkins, 'God's Grandeur') just as surely, though not with such dire environmental consequences, as the Lower Thames Valley. The fact that this country appears to the European eye as a wilderness is a remarkable tribute to the successful 'conservation policies' of its human inhabitants. The Mursi, in other words, are better conservationists than we are.

Where does this lead the argument for resettlement? Stephenson and Mizuno again:

As has been pointed out, the human pressures on the area selected to be a national park are now minimal. This will not be for long, as land hunger in the highlands is becoming so acute that regional administrations are now searching the low-lands for resettlement areas for large numbers of their people . . .

This indicates all too clearly the necessity to resettle adequately the inhabitants now in the selected park area at the earliest possible moment. Once this has been done the integrity of the boundaries must be rigidly preserved. It is further emphasised that the onus of resettlement of the people falls fairly and squarely on the Administration and not on the Wildlife Conservation Department.

(1978: 49)

The argument here seems to be that the Mursi should be removed from their territory, not because they themselves represent a threat to wildlife conservation (which was the argument presented in the passage quoted earlier), but because their removal (presumably to the already over-crowded highlands) would make it easier to withstand political pressure for an alternative form of land use in the Omo Valley. Another argument that might have been used here is that it cannot reasonably be expected, nor should it be wished, that the Mursi will remain unaffected by modern veterinary or health services which, by increasing the human and cattle population, could set in train processes of environmental degradation.

Such arguments, by taking for granted an irreconcilable conflict between conservation and development, reveal a narrow, defeatist and fundamentally pessimistic approach to conservation policy. For, having realised that the real threat to the natural environment of the Omo Valley comes from forces ultimately emanating from the developed world, the response is to throw up a supposedly impenetrable barrier around as much of the area as possible, leaving these forces to wreak their inevitable havoc outside. What is clearly needed is to make development compatible with conservation, in the broadest sense of both terms (cf. Arhem, 1985).

We have thus reached a point in the argument where our own cultural assumptions about the relationship between human society and the external world of nature need to be scrutinised. One – perhaps the only – way to do this is to attempt to understand a different view of this relationship, held by members of another culture. It is to this specifically anthropological task that I now turn, seeing the conflict of interests between the Wildlife Conservation Department and the Mursi as, at base, a clash of cultural values.

The domesticated and the wild: two views of the relationship between human society and the external world of nature

One phrase is used by the Mursi more than any other when they talk about the aims and activities of the National Park staff: 'They tell us to herd the buffaloes like cattle'. To give the Mursi term which I have here translated by 'herd' (*ibwe*) its full range of meaning, one would have to add such equivalents as 'look after', 'protect', 'care for' and 'manage'. It is therefore properly applied to domestic animals and, above all, to cattle (the Mursi also keep some goats and fewer sheep). If, however, we are to understand how the Mursi see their relationship to cattle, we would do better to think of attitudes in our own society to pets rather than to farm animals. Cattle, for the Mursi, are almost part of human society. Both men and women are named after them; they are, through bridewealth, the crucial means of establishing family units and they are as dependent on human beings for their survival as human beings are dependent on them. Evans-Pritchard's description of the intimate relationship between Nuer and their cattle may be applied equally to the Mursi:

Nuer wash their hands and faces in the urine of cattle, especially when cows urinate during milking, drink their milk and blood, and sleep on their hides by the side of their smouldering dung. They cover their bodies, dress their hair, and clean their teeth with the ashes of cattle dung, and eat their food with spoons made from their horns. When the cattle return in the evening they tether each beast to its peg with cords made from the skins of their dead companions and sit in the windscreens to contempate them and to watch them being milked.

(*Evans-Pritchard, 1940: 136–7*)

Perhaps the most distinctive mark of the special status of cattle in Mursi culture is that they are not killed simply for utilitarian ends. They are eaten when they die but they are not killed to be eaten. This would be to treat them as buffaloes which, given the supreme cultural importance to them of cattle, is the epitome of un-Mursi behaviour.

The world of wild animals, therefore, derives its meaning and significance for the Mursi from the special relationship that exists between human beings and cattle. Wild animals are, for the Mursi, everything that cattle are not. Here it is significant to note that there is no general term in Mursi equivalent to the English 'wild animals'. There are, of course, terms for particular species but the category as a whole is referred to by a phrase meaning 'things of the bush', *aha dusoin*. *Aha* is a residual concept which is applied to any indeterminate, undefined, vaguely apprehended and usually inanimate collection of objects. The fact that wild *animals*, of which the Mursi have a profoundly detailed empirical knowledge, are referred to in this way suggests a determination to keep them, as it were, at arm's length from human society and from human concern and interest. They kill them to obtain economically useful products and, when necessary, to protect their cattle, but otherwise their disposition is, as Evans-Pritchard again writes of the Nuer, 'to live and let live' (1956: 267).

From the Mursi point of view, then, the protection of wild animals is an idea which obliterates the distinction between two fundamentally opposed categories, the domestic and the wild, and the significance of this distinction cannot be fully appreciated by treating it as a replica of our own. For the Mursi, to protect wild animals is to treat them as cattle and this means bringing them into human society, thereby destroying the category 'things of the bush' altogether. Since it is the contrast between these two categories which gives each its meaning, if there are no 'things of the bush' there are also no cattle and if there are no cattle, there is no Mursi culture. I make this point merely to show how different the Mursi view of the relationship between human society and the external world of nature is from that which lies behind the Western ethos of conservation. The resulting paradox – that the Mursi are nevertheless better conservationists than we are – is explained by the fact that the same view of nature which lies behind the Western drive to conserve it also lies behind the Western drive to exploit it. For conservation and exploitation are both ways of dominating nature, of bringing it under human control. Whereas the Mursi see themselves as living *in* nature, we see ourselves as living over and above it. We see it as our right and obligation to bend nature to our will, to 'show it who's boss', whether by economic exploitation or scientific investigation. The conservation movement is a response to the worst and most destructive effects of this view of the relationship between human society and nature, but it is a response which is nevertheless, and inevitably, fully in accordance with that same view. We have, in other words, two ways of relating to nature: we plunder it or tame it, but either way we exercise our control over it.

If the Mursi view of their relationship to nature is summed up in their bemused response to the injunction 'to herd the buffaloes like cattle', ours is epitomised by the famous mountaineering justification for climbing Everest: 'because it is there'. The elegance of this response, and the reason why it became so quickly a household phrase, lies not only in its conciseness but also in its appeal to an irreducible cultural premise beyond which we experience no urge to reason further. The total absence of this premise in Mursi culture was brought home to me when, during my first period of fieldwork among them, I decided to climb the 1,666 m summit of the range of hills which forms the watershed between the Omo and Mago rivers. These hills, called Dara by the Mursi, dominate the skyline wherever one happens to be in Mursi country and it seemed perfectly 'natural' to me to wish to stand on their highest point, although I had no practical or scientific reason for doing so. Requiring the services of a Mursi guide, however, and realising the difficulty of explaining to him that I wished to climb Dara 'because it was there', I explained myself by saying that I wished to collect a specimen of a medicinal plant which only grew on the Dara range. After walking for two days, we reached a point just below the summit and my companion pointed out to me several of the plants in question. He was obviously very surprised when, having collected my specimen, I announced that I was going to continue the few steps further to the summit and I was equally surprised that he, having come so far, merely sat down and waited for me to return.

Was I, on this occasion, playing the role of scientist, explorer or tourist? At the time I would have probably plumped for the second, but all three roles gain their impetus from, and find their justification in, the same Western view of the relationship between human society and the external world of nature. They are all, in their different ways, representative of the conservation movement but, while conservationists are happy to see themselves as scientists and perhaps also, on occasion, as explorers, they are, in their own eyes, never tourists. The tourist is, at best, a mixed blessing, a necessary evil, to the conservationist: a powerful incentive for foreign exchange hungry governments to develop national parks, but a dangerously unreliable one, given the sensitivity of the tourist industry to the winds of economic change in the developed countries. And then, of course, there is the capacity of tourists to love a National Park to death, which makes them a positive enemy of conservation, particularly in so-called 'wilderness' areas. But in wishing, however impractically, to keep tourists out of, or at least greatly restrict their access to, such areas, are not conservationists *themselves* acting as tourists? Bolton's mixed feelings about the future transformation (which he no doubt recommended) of the 'wildland' of the Mago Valley into a national park strongly suggest that they are.

It would all need careful planning. Setting up the area for visitors would itself have an unavoidable impact. For those who value such things (and the solitude seekers are always the first to lose out) the feeling of remoteness would disappear for a start.   (*Bolton, 1976: 135*)

Surely one can recognise here, in the disdain felt by the 'solitude seeker' for the mere 'visitor' the same disdain that tourists notoriously feel for each other? The reason why conservationists dislike tourists, and the reason why they cannot, however much they try, do without them, is that they *are* tourists. Indeed, so are we all, for, as MacCannell plausibly argues, '"the tourist" is one of the best models available for modern-man-in-general' (1976: 1). It is not without a certain perverse justice, therefore, that tourists should be treated as scapegoats for the global environmental havoc caused by an affluent, leisured, middle-class lifestyle in which all of us aspire to share.

Conclusion

Conservation should not be treated as something apart from, and still less opposed to, development, as though the one gave priority to animals and the other to people. It should not be a matter of *reconciling* conservation with development, as though these were activities with different objectives, based upon fundamentally opposed views of the natural world, but of recognising that good development, seen as an activity that is primarily aimed at the betterment of human life, *is* conservation, and vice versa. Two conclusions, neither of them in the least original, follow from this.

(1) In the long term, successful conservation depends more on modifying our own economic behaviour, which can only be done by rethinking the assumptions that lie behind it, than on defending the integrity of national park boundaries in Africa.

Most of the destructive environmental effects of human activity are direct consequences of our drive for affluence and growth and our commitment to the economic system which requires both . . . Nothing much can be achieved by fighting to save this forest or that species if in the long term we do not change from an economic system that demands ever-increasing production and consumption of non-necessities.

(Trainer, 1985: 6)

Conservation must begin at home: it is a problem of the developed world which will not be solved by exporting it to the underdeveloped. (2) In the short term, conservation should be seen as an integral part of development planning (cf. Arhem, 1984, 1985), which means putting the local people first. There is a pragmatic as well as a moral argument for this, since it is the *human* inhabitants of such an area as the Lower Omo Valley who constitute its chief asset. The following incident, which occurred during a visit to the Omo National Park headquarters at Mui in 1981, and which was another cause of 'impotent rage' at the time, brings out the tragic irony of a conservation policy that sees human life as a more expendable resource than animal life.

I was sitting in the Warden's Office one morning, looking out through the open doorway at a group of four or five men who were standing, thin and bedraggled, in a drizzle of rain, exchanging a kind of tragicomic banter with the game guards. They were Chai, a people who speak the same language as the Mursi but who live west of the Omo and south of Maji. The Chai have probably suffered even more during the recent years of drought than the Mursi. These men were about to leave Mui after spending a few days living on food given to them by the game guards. One of them, who looked the weakest, said, only half jokingly, that if he were not given food for the journey he would be a corpse before he arrived home. Above the inside of the doorway that framed this little group, forming a kind of caption to the picture, were these words in large black letters: 'Wildlife is our national asset'. (Turton, 1985: 344).

Acknowledgements

I am grateful to Mr George Brown, the first Game Warden of the Omo National Park, for his advice, help and hospitality during my first period of fieldwork amongst the Mursi (1968–70). For fieldwork funding I am grateful to the Social Science Research Council (now the Economic and Social Research Council) of the United Kingdom (1968–70, 1973–4 and 1983) and the Area Studies Committee of the University of Manchester (1982). The paper was read to a seminar at the African Studies Centre, University of Cambridge, in a series entitled 'Reconciling Conservation and Development'. In revising it for publication, I have been greatly helped by the discussion which took place on that occasion.

References

ALMAGOR, U. (1972). *Pastoral Partners*. Manchester: Manchester University Press.

ARHEM, K. (1984). Two sides of development: Maasai pastoralism and wildlife conservation in Ngorongoro, Tanzania. *Ethnos*, **14** (3–4), 186–210.

ARHEM, K. (1985). *Pastoral Man in the Garden of Eden: the Maasai of the Ngorongoro Conservation Area, Tanzania*. Uppsala Research Reports in Cultural Anthropology. Uppsala: University of Uppsala.

BACON, G.H. (1948). Crops of the Sudan. In *Agriculture in the Sudan*, ed. J.D. Tothill, pp. 302–400. London: Oxford University Press.

BOLTON, M. (1976). *Ethiopian Wildlands*. London: Collins.

BROWN, L.H. (1971). The biology of pastoral Man as a factor in conservation. *Biological Conservation*, **2** (3), 93–100.

BUTZER, K. (1971). *Recent History of an Ethiopian Delta: The Omo River and the Level of Lake Rudolf*. Chicago: Department of Geography, University of Chicago.

DAHL, G. & HJORT, A. (1976). *Having Herds: Pastoral Herd Growth and Household Economy*. Stockholm: Department of Social Anthropology, University of Stockholm.

EVANS-PRITCHARD, E.E. (1940). *The Nuer*. Oxford: Oxford University Press.

EVANS-PRITCHARD, E.E. (1956). *Nuer Religion*. Oxford: Oxford University Press.

MacCANNELL, D. (1976). *The Tourist: A New Theory of the Leisure Class*. London: Macmillan.

STEPHENSON, J. & MIZUNO, A. (1978). Recommendations on the conservation of wildlife in the Omo–Tama–Mago rift valley of Ethiopia. Report submitted to the Wildlife Conservation Department of the Provisional Military Government of Ethiopia, Addis Ababa.

TORNAY, S. (1981). The Nyangatom: an outline of their ecology and social organisation. In *Peoples and Cultures of the Ethio–Sudan Borderlands*, ed. M.L. Bender. East Lansing: African Studies Center, Michigan State University.

TRAINER, F.E. (1985). *Abandon Affluence*. London: Zed Books.

TURTON, D. (1977). Response to drought: the Mursi of South West Ethiopia. In *Human Ecology in the Tropics*, ed. J.P. Garlick & R.W.J. Keay. London: Taylor & Francis. Reprinted in *Disasters* (1979), **1** (4), 275–87.

TURTON, D. (1980). The economics of Mursi bridewealth: a comparative perspective. In *The Meaning of Marriage Payments*, ed. J. Comaroff. New York: Academic Press.

TURTON, D. (1985). Mursi response to drought: some lessons for relief and rehabilitation. *African Affairs*, **84** (336), 331–46.

TURTON, D. & TURTON, P. (1984). Spontaneous resettlement after drought: an Ethiopian example. *Disasters*, **8** (3), 178–89.

PART THREE

Conservation priorities
and rural communities

Introduction

JOHN McCRACKEN

One of the most constant features of conservation in Africa over the last century has been the increasing externalisation of control over environmental resources. Up to the 1880s, management of ecological systems was still retained largely by rural communities, some of them using the mechanism of state power in order to achieve their objectives, others employing more informal means of control. With the establishment of colonial rule, however, the process began, at first sporadically and ineffectually and, from the 1940s, on a larger and more dynamic scale, by which the central government, drawing on a reservoir of metropolitan-based technical expertise, intervened in the shaping of African environments. For a brief period in the aftermath of independence the more irksome controls placed on African cultivators were frequently relaxed. But by the 1970s, growing concern at the mounting environmental crisis led to a renewal of state intervention, much of it inspired, financed and directed by agencies external to Africa. Attempts were made to reincorporate farmers and herders within the decision-making process but, as Little and Brokensha (Chapter 9) show, they were normally incomplete and left producers uncertain and concerned as to who was ultimately responsible for regulating the use of natural resources.

The four chapters contained in this Part move beyond a simple description of the process of externalisation to emphasise a variety of issues integral to that process. The first of these is the importance of indigenous African views of conservation and environmental management. Until recently, conservation as a means of providing long-term protection of the natural environment was often assumed to be an essentially 'modern' concern, introduced to Africa by expatriate experts and unrelated to the perspectives of African producers who were believed to be interested only in the short-term exploitation of natural resources. The growth in knowledge of African economic and social systems, however, has led to the recognition that many pre-colonial communities had developed institutions, often religious in character, designed to enforce environmen-

tal restraint. The description given by Little and Brokensha of the
strategies used by pastoralists in East Africa in managing range resources
can be supplemented from a different angle by the account provided by
J.M. Schoffeleers (1978) of the ecological function of Central African
cults as 'Guardians of the Land'.

It would be wrong to idealise these attempts at ecological control.
Territorial cults were not expressions of some universal public will: rather
they reflected the shifting balance of political power. Pre-colonial
societies were no more infallible than their successors in averting ecological collapse. The decline of the northern Ngoni kingdom west of Lake
Malawi from the mid-nineteenth century is an instructive example of
the undermining of an African state through a process of environmental
decay (Vail, 1981). It is also true, as Little and Brokensha note, that
the practices employed in pre-colonial times in managing the environment may work less well in the new conditions of the twentieth century.
Demographic pressure, when combined with changes in the distribution
of political power and the expansion of the market, can result in a
weakening of indigenous control systems so complete as to render them
powerless. All the same, the evidence suggests that where the interests,
institutions and expertise of rural communities are ignored in the planning and implementation of conservation schemes, the likelihood of
failure is high. For more than fifty years, so Millington demonstrates
(Chapter 11), conservation schemes in Sierra Leone were based on the
assumption that shifting cultivation of upland rice was a cause of environmental degradation. Only recently have technical experts become aware
of the intrinsic virtues of the system.

One of the points that emerges most forcefully from these chapters
is the important but deeply ambiguous role played by foresters in English-
speaking Africa in the shaping of conservation priorities. Drawing on a
coherent body of ideas developed in India in the course of the nineteenth
century, and elaborated upon at the Imperial Institute of Forestry at
Oxford and at the handful of British universities specialising in the
subject, foresters led the way, in many parts of Africa, in identifying
environmental degradation and in presenting measures to combat it. As
members of a close-knit, professional community, sharing the same basic
conservationist assumptions, they rarely doubted that where human and
environmental interests clashed the public good would be best served
through the protection of forest and water resources, even if this meant
the displacement of local communities. Individually often sensitive, as
a group they exuded professional conviction. It comes as no surprise
that in the Lembus Forest of Kenya, described by Anderson (Chapter

12), the main threat to the rights of African pastoralists and cultivators came not from the settler-owned concessionary company but rather from the Forestry Department.

Yet while Anderson's chapter demonstrates the single-minded concern of forestry departments all over Africa for the preservation of natural resources, it also reveals how ineffective they could be in getting their proposals implemented. As he stresses, conservation priorities cannot be divorced from the political context in which they operate. Had African forestry departments possessed the commercial basis of their Indian counterpart, it is likely that governments would have listened more sympathetically to their recommendations. In the event, they all too often functioned as the poor cousins of agricultural departments whose interests in turn were frequently subordinated to those of district administrations. Anderson's chapter is an essay in impotence; an example of how a technical agency could be repeatedly frustrated by demands for commercial profits on the one hand and for the preservation of social order on the other.

It is this emphasis on the political dimension of conservation that gives unity to the chapters under discussion. A particularly valuable feature of Millington's essay is that he is able to demonstrate that fluctuations in environmental awareness and the evolution of conservation policies followed the same broad pattern in Sierra Leone as they did in eastern and southern Africa. Yet if the ideas and prescriptions on offer in East and West Africa were similar, the practice was certainly not. In eastern and southern Africa, conservationist concern was translated into energetic action in the late 1940s and early 1950s. The state intervened on a wide front in the countryside with the aim of halting erosion and restructuring African farming systems. In Sierra Leone, by contrast, few conservation schemes were implemented and the 1950s, according to Millington, 'were generally characterised by a rather *laissez-faire* attitude to environmental protection'. No doubt that contrast reflected environmental differences between the two areas; but it also mirrored political differences involving variations in the pattern of power relations in different parts of the continent.

A similar conclusion can be drawn from Hughes' account (Chapter 10) of the problems of firewood provision currently facing a development scheme on the Lower Tana River in Kenya. Planning officers had no difficulty in predicting that the rapid increase of the population living in the irrigation schemes area would give rise to greater demands for fuelwood. However, their proposals to construct additional plantations had still not been implemented by the time that the first settlers arrived, with the result that fuelwood needs have had increasingly to be met from the vulnerable floodplain forest. As Hughes notes, the impact of the scheme could have been predicted more clearly with better preliminary research. But the most basic lessons appear to be the general ones: that technical considerations cannot be divorced from political ones and that conservation is one more field in which the removal of the decision-making process from the local community into the wider arena of international expertise can be a mixed blessing for those it is intended to benefit.

References

SCHOFFELEERS, J.M., ed. (1978). *Guardians of the Land: Essays on Central African Territorial Cults.* Gwelo, Zimbabwe: Mambo Press.

VAIL, L. (1981). The making of the 'Dead North': a study of Ngoni rule in northern Malawi, *c.* 1855–1907. In *Before and After Shaka: Papers in Ngoni History*, ed. J.B. Peires. Grahamstown: Rhodes University.

9

Local institutions, tenure and resource management in East Africa[1]

PETER D. LITTLE AND DAVID W. BROKENSHA

Introduction

Considerable attention has been given recently to the role of local institutions and communities in the management of Africa's natural resources (Odell, 1982; Sandford, 1983; Doughlin, Doan & Uphoff, 1984). Much of the research has focused on the part that tenure rules play in resource use and conservation, and has resulted in a highly charged debate dividing, on the one hand, advocates of private property and radically new forms of resource management and, on the other hand, supporters of indigenous tenure systems (often based on some form of collective allocation) and institutions. The empirical evidence to support either side has been flimsy at best, and ahistorical in most cases. Thus, for example, what is proffered as 'proof' of institutional inefficiencies among East African herders – for instance, 'overgrazing' – is more often a result of historical circumstances that limited the pastoralists' land base, than it is of land mismanagement (Little, 1984).

Here, we examine the role of local institutions and communities in the management of rangelands and forests in East Africa, which until recently were managed on a common property basis, often either neighbourhood- or clan-based.[2] Particular attention is given to those variables that are likely to make local resource management systems ineffective. As will be shown, change in tenure patterns is only one of many factors that have implications for natural resource use, and that in specific cases it becomes difficult to disaggregate the causal effects of tenure from other, perhaps even more significant variables. These include: changes in the level of decision-making; wealth differentiation (and the related factor of poverty); commercial market linkages; and demographic pressure.[3] Case materials drawn from the authors' research in Kenya are presented within an historical framework, particular attention being given to the continuities and discontinuities in resource management policy from the colonial to post-colonial eras. While 'yet another' presentation of case study materials will not resolve theoretical issues, it can help clarify the relationship between ecology and changes in tenure and management practices.

The chapter consists of four parts: (i) the elaboration of a conceptual framework; (ii) a case study on range management; (iii) a case study on forest management; and (iv) a discussion summary. In each of the case studies, a similar set of issues is addressed. Where appropriate, materials from elsewhere in East and southern Africa are presented.

A conceptual framework

Most communities in East Africa had mechanisms – either formal or informal – for managing such critical natural resources as range and forests (Brokensha, Riley & Castro, 1983; Sandford, 1983; Little, 1984), although conservation of resources may not have been the primary goal. However, changes have occurred, both in the colonial and independence eras, that make it difficult to test hypotheses about the effectiveness of these indigenous institutions and practices. The question is not whether or not such practices and institutions ever existed; rather it is the degree to which they have adjusted or not adjusted to changing parameters. In this section, we discuss the elements of a framework for examining natural resource use. Here we are not concerned with the general characteristics of common property systems (see Ciriacy-Wantrup & Bishop, 1975; Oakerson, 1984), but only in those factors that, when changed, are likely to affect the nature of local resource management.

Levels of decision-making

Shifts in the locus of resource-related decision-making have considerable implications for local resource use. In the Sudan, for example, the state took control of range regulation from local authorities in the late 1960s (Haaland, 1980), while in Botswana local grazing and water management systems have been supplanted by District Land Boards, which currently regulate access to these resources (Gulbrandsen, 1980). The general pattern is for the transfer of decision-making from local communities to state-controlled institutions and organisations; even though vestiges of the indigenous management system may survive, they seldom have critical significance. Yet the usurpation of decision-making power by governments has been incomplete in most African states, creating for farmers and herders what Runge (1981) calls a problem of 'assurance'. In this situation producers lack confidence in the capacity of either state or local institutions to regulate resource use, creating considerable ambiguities over who has legal access to range, water and forests.

Wealth distribution

Economic differentiation is severe in many rural communities of East Africa. Where wealth distribution is especially polarised and poverty widespread, many impoverished families find it difficult to mobilise labour and other inputs for conservation purposes. Those areas that are characterised by impoverishment, where people may be landless and/or stockless, are likely to experience environmental problems, since short-term cash needs will outweigh conservation investments among the poor. Charcoal burners and forest squatters are examples of impoverished groups whose actions cause environmental degradation. As will be shown below, different classes of producers have different production strategies and uses for the environment, which make problematic collective efforts at resource management. The ecological problems often associated with poverty can be found both in areas where production is organised on private lands and where it is practised on common lands.

Market linkages

The emergence of market value for range and forest products is likely to change local resource use. First, increased commercialisation attracts outside entrepreneurs who are likely to have a different set of interests and, in general, may be less concerned with resource conservation than the local community. Second, these individuals are often from groups with powerful linkages to the state and may, in some cases, be supported by state-enforced legislation. Thus, even where local regulations on natural resources exist, these outsiders are able to operate outside indigenous controls and, when necessary, they can evoke their ties to more powerful groups. Finally, where the market value of the resource increases there are likely to be pressures from both outside interests and local élites for the privatisation of lands and other resources.

Demographic pressure

The demise of community-based resource management systems is often linked to population growth. As demographic pressure (and associated land shortage) increases, it is argued, pressures toward privatisation accelerate. While this is generally true, it is difficult to separate population from those other variables indicated above, such as market linkages and state encroachment. Especially, the resource degradation associated with overpopulation may be a *result* of the loss and/or privatisation of lands around communal areas. A good example of this in Kenya's colonial period was the European farm settlement surrounding the south Tugen communal lands in Baringo District, which monopolised critical dry-season grazing and water sources. The alienation of these lands created the stock/human crowding problems in the south of the District (Anderson, 1982).

Population pressure is a factor that makes common property management vulnerable. The resource shortages associated with high population densities create competition and tensions that local institutions and mechanisms may not be able to resolve. Where population pressure is especially great, the deferment of communal dry-season grazing, for example, may be problematic. Pressures toward privatisation of trees will also increase.

The characteristics indicated above provide a framework for examining local resource management in the context of social change. Simplistic causal statements about the breakdown in local resource management and associated ecological problems are inappropriate. Equally misleading is the isolation of land tenure as the critical variable, while ignoring labour availability, social differentiation, and other important factors.

Indigenous systems of range management

Understanding of indigenous systems of range management remains rudimentary, although such knowledge is crucial to the design of effective range management programmes. The number of unsuccessful attempts at intervening in pastoral management systems is well documented both for the colonial (Sobania, 1979) and post-colonial periods (Migot-Adholla & Little, 1981). The African Land Development (ALDEV) schemes in Kenya (1946–62) are excellent examples of grazing programmes that were imposed without any prior knowledge of the local management system, or without consulting the local people. As Fumagalli (1978:57) notes for the Leroghi Grazing Scheme of the ALDEV period, 'the Samburu elders were never consulted, never given active voice, and all their remonstrations, protests and complaints were systematically ignored'. Like the forestry and soil conservation programmes of the colonial period, policies toward the range were concerned with the protection and conservation of the natural resource, not with the development of the resource users.

While there have been several excellent field studies of pastoral sys-

tems of East Africa, few have systematically examined the organisation
of grazing and the tenure systems that affect it. Critical details of rules
determining access to grazing and water, as well as of institutions for
regulation, are lacking. Nor are micro-level data readily available on
how these grazing regulations relate to the 'where' and 'when' of pastoral
livestock movements; that is, the areas livestock move to and the months
when such movements occur. The examples used in this section are drawn
from the Maa-speaking areas of East Africa, particularly the Maasai and
the Il Chamus (Njemps) areas of Kenya. The Il Chamus material was
collected by one of us (Little) in 1980–1 and 1984, while the Maasai
examples are based on the reports of Peacock *et al.* (1982), Pasha (1983),
de Souza (1984) and de Souza & de Leeuw (1984).

The historical context

Colonial policies drastically affected the territorial boundaries of the
Maa-speaking peoples. Prime range and agricultural lands of Uasin
Gishu, Laikipia, and other Maasai areas of the Rift Valley were approp-
riated for European settlement. Early colonial administrators sought to
pacify the pastoral regions and, in some cases, they directly intervened
in the resource management system to achieve this. For example, the
Provincial Commissioner of the Northern Frontier District was given
powers to define grazing and water boundaries for the different ethnic
groups in an attempt to avoid armed conflict and raids on livestock
(Migot-Adholla & Little, 1981).

One of the earliest attempts to deal with 'perceived' problems of
resource management (i.e., as perceived by colonial authorities) was
through compulsory destocking. Beginning in the 1930s several destocking programmes were initiated – including among the Il Chamus – in an
attempt to reduce grazing pressure. Most were abandoned because of
the negative, and sometimes violent, response on the part of local herders.

In the 1940s and 1950s the colonial perception of the range problem
shifted from that of overpopulation to that of land mismanagement.
Under the ALDEV programme (1946–62) efforts were made to rehabili-
tate the severely degraded areas, such as Baringo, and to introduce –
and often forcefully implement – new resource management techniques
(e.g. rotational grazing). While the ALDEV programme generated useful
information on technical approaches to semi-arid/arid land-use problems, it further alienated pastoralists from the state because of its style
of intervention (ALDEV, 1962).

With independence and the ensuing political dominance of agriculturalists, cultivating groups were given greater freedom of movement. They often settled in dry-season grazing areas, such as around Ngong and Loitokitok in Kajiado District, and in the Mau Escarpment of Narok District. Without access to traditional highland and swamp grazing areas, pastoral groups had to concentrate their animals on already depleted lowland ranges. This often resulted in severe livestock losses during droughts.

The Maasai management system

While historical factors make problematic any discussion of 'traditional' management systems among the Maasai, there is evidence that in some areas these systems have existed relatively intact until recently. The Maasai of Kajiado District have several different strategies for managing range resources. Jacobs (1980:287) indicates some of these as such:

elaborate grazing sequences (including irregular rotation as well as simple alter-ation) based on systematic reconnaissance of, and movement to, grazing flushes in order to create standing hay in the dry-season reserves; regular use of donkeys to carry water for immature livestock and human consumption, both to expand the grazing area and to permit camps to stay away from their dry season reserves as long as possible; detailed knowledge about the nutritional value to livestock of a wide range of grasses, herbs, and seeds, and use of these at the appropriate stage of their growth . . . and regular social rebuke and avoidance of families or camps that fail to adhere to good management practices in their locality.

In addition to these practices, the Maasai have a system of reserved grazing with an elaborate local terminology to describe it. For example, in the Meruishi area of Kajiado District, there are 13 reserved grazing areas (called *olopololi*) of which two are managed by single producers, while the others are managed by more than one herdowner (de Souza & de Leeuw, 1984). The *olopololi* is located near a homestead (or collection of homesteads) and was traditionally reserved for calf grazing. These areas can range between 100 ha and 800 ha, and in the case of Meruishi they account for approximately 20 per cent of available range. During the dry season, producers must seek permission from the homestead heads associated with a particular reserved area before they can move animals across it.

In recent times, adult cattle and small stock have begun to utilise the *olopololi*, which, as noted above, were traditionally reserved for calves. Within the *olopololi*, the grazing is sub-divided and certain stock species are restricted to grazing only on certain parts of the *olopololi*. For example, kids, lambs and young suckling calves are kept in one subsection of the *olopololi*; while adult cattle, mature small stock, and non-suckling calves each have their own areas. It is noted that 'according to Maasai informants the basic objective in the management of reserved grazing areas is that grazing resources are used in a manner to ensure conservation and annual regeneration' (de Souza & de Leeuw, 1984:9).

There are also neighbourhood-based controls on grazing. Residential neighbourhoods have associated with them two types of dry-season reserves: *dokoya unkishu* (to be used in early to mid dry season) and *enkaroni* (to be used in late dry season as a final reserve). As Peacock *et al.* point out, 'collective action may be taken against any person herding prematurely in the reserved area, whether they are from the controlling neighbourhood or from elsewhere' (1982:4). Elders decide upon the date of opening for each of these reserves, and they also ensure that permanent settlements are not allowed in these areas.

Several factors have changed both the practice of *olopololi* and the reserved dry-season grazing system. With the adjudication of group ranches in Kajiado District, the responsibility for resource control has moved from the homestead and neighbourhood to the ranching committees. 'It is unclear to both group ranch committee members and non-members, what role, if any, the recently formed group ranch committee has either in the old system, or in creating a new system of grazing resource control' (Peacock *et al.*, 1982:29). The ambiguity has allowed some individuals to carve off large areas of the range, by establishing *olopololi* and then using this as the basis for claims to land ownership. The 'owners' of some of these areas are leasing pasture rights to neighbouring individual ranchers to allow them to fatten steers (de Souza, 1984:14–5). In the Poka area of Kajiado District, this practice is most widespread, and in this area individual claims to *olopololi* are to be used as a basis for subdivision on an individual ownership basis (Pasha, 1983:8).

The practice of reserving areas for dry-season use is also complicated by the initiation of group ranches and the development of water sources. In the Mbirikani area several permanent homesteads, including one with a wooden stockade yard, were constructed in reserved areas (Peacock *et al.*, 1982:29). There are recent indications, however, that at least certain members of the Mbirikani ranching committee are concerned about the lack of grazing control. Residential areas and dry season grazing areas are being demarcated, and those homesteads residing in grazing zones are being told to move. While this proposal has been initiated by a minority of committee members, it has been endorsed by the committee chairman and action taken to regulate settlements and the use of dry-season grazing. In some cases, 'temporarily unoccupied bomas sited outside the residential areas were burned, and one resident who refused to move was arrested by police' (Peacock *et al.*, 1982:31). It is still unclear whether this solution will be acceptable to the majority of members, and whether or not it will effectively replace the earlier system. What is apparent, however, is that privatisation, the increased value of range lands and the introduction of ranching committees has affected local conservation techniques.

The Il Chamus management system

The management of common grazing resources is less complex among the Il Chamus, who control a much smaller area and are not as rich in livestock as the Maasai. Because of the limited mobility of the Il Chamus, and the dry-season use of predominantly two grazing resources – the swamps and the hills at the base of the Laikipia Escarpment – regulation is facilitated. Grazing controls (called *olokeri*) were predominantly on a neighbourhood basis, with each neighbourhood, or a coalition of two or three neighbourhoods, having a council of elders (*lamaal*) to enforce them. Members of the *il murran* generation (18–30 years of age) were responsible for enforcing grazing restrictions. They looked after the swamps in the wet season to ensure that stock did not trespass, and during the dry season kept non-neighbourhood (except where local permission had been granted) as well as non-Il Chamus animals out of the area. Individuals who violated the regulations were fined a small number of sheep or goats.

Reasons for the breakdown of the *olokeri* system are several. They include:

(i)   the decline in the political power of elders *vis-à-vis* the government chiefs in the area, which results in the usurpation of local decision-making power;

(ii)   increased inequalities in the past 15 years that make it difficult to reach collective decisions, as well as to discourage non-pastoral production strategies by the poor, including the cultivation of rainfed farms in range areas;

(iii) the involvement of *il murran* in non-pastoral activities, such as wage employment, agriculture and formal education, which means that many are no longer residing in their home neighbourhoods, nor are they available for herding;

(iv)   the loss of dry season areas in the hills to outside agropastoralists, which forces the Il Chamus to crowd their animals on available grazing resources and makes it difficult to reserve pastures.

The changes indicated above make the area prone to resource mismanagement and to outside exploitation by non-Il Chamus. Without grazing
restrictions, which new leaders have not been willing to reinstate, traders,
townsmen (residing in Marigat), and ranchers residing nearby are able
to graze their animals in certain areas, often with the support of local
élites (Little, 1985). They are able to take advantage of the wealth differentiation by hiring stockless Il Chamus to herd their stock. The principle of exclusion, an important characteristic of common property systems, is blurred since it has become unclear as to who has legal access
to the range.

The contemporary grazing system in Il Chamus is not without controls.
It is still managed on a communal basis, and has not yet reached the
level of an open access or 'free for all' system. Those herding families
who reside in the area and who depend heavily on pastoral production
for their livelihood are aware of the current problems. Most would like
to see a form of grazing regulation reinstated, but under the control of
the local communities, not the state. They are also aware of the current
ambiguity over land ownership, which has allowed outside groups (particularly neighbouring agropastoralists) to encroach. The receptiveness
among herders to the introduction of group ranches is related to the
uncertainty over territorial claims caused by encroachment. Because the
group ranch provides legal recognition of land, the Il Chamus favour
them as a means of establishing formal boundaries, thus reintroducing
the notion of exclusiveness (cf. Galaty, 1980).

Indigenous management of forest resources

The historical context

The Mbeere, who occupy a savanna area east of Mount Kenya, reaching
down to the Tana River, had developed an extensive knowledge of the
local woody vegetation, which supplied many products – including fruits,
material for housing, fodder, fuelwood, medicines and fibres. Similar to
the experience of the pastoral groups discussed above, the implementation of colonial policies affected their resource management system.
Beginning in the 1920s, several natural resource regulations were introduced, which forced the Mbeere to follow certain new resource practices
and forbade them to practise others. To give an idea of the scope of the
new regulations (which were nearly all passed by the Embu Native Local
Council), here is a summary of the new rules, most of which relate to
agriculture rather than forestry:

Do	Do not
build soil conservation terraces;	cultivate on hillsides and
plant famine reserve crops	near streams;
(cassava, sweet potatoes);	burn grass (except by permit);
plant trees;	cut down certain species of
set aside forest reserves.	trees, or trees less than a
	specified size.

Not all regulations were consistently enforced, and most were very unpopular, being regarded as unwarranted intrusions into what had been seen as a satisfactory local system of natural resource management. In some cases, it is clear that this was not true; for example, Colin Maher's report on soil erosion in Embu District (1938) convincingly argues that soil erosion was widespread and threatening, and he confirms his findings with striking photographic evidence of the deterioration. There is no doubt that (i) soil erosion was a major problem, especially in Evorore Location, and (ii) some immediate measures were essential to prevent further loss of soil in this already marginal area. What was controversial, however, was the series of measures proposed – and introduced. The compulsory building of terraces was especially disliked, and elderly men told many stories of bullying or corrupt agricultural instructors who enforced the new regulations in arbitrary ways.

In the case of forest reserves, three were established in Mbeere in the late 1930s and early 1940s, and despite local protests, the people were excluded from these reserves. This was elsewhere a cause of much resentment: the Kikuyu, for example, complained bitterly about not being allowed into Mount Kenya Forest, even to collect honey or medicines. Later, permits were sold for specific purposes, enabling local people to enter the forest to collect fallwood for fuel, or other minor forest products. Because the Mbeere reserves were relatively small areas, only a few were affected, notably those who were accustomed to collecting honey, gathering medicinal plants, or hunting in the forests. These people were now excluded from the reserves.

During the colonial period, African forestry departments, reflecting western notions of conservation and resource management, shared some common aims and values. Among the hallmarks of African forestry departments were the following:

(i)   There was an emphasis on commercial forestry, on growing timber that could be sold either within the country (primarily for mines and industries) or for export.

(ii)   There was a corresponding emphasis on exotic species, conifers and *Eucalyptus* spp. being among the most popular.

(iii) Conversely, there was little interest in indigenous species, which were for the most part completely ignored.

(iv) There was also little enthusiasm for the impressive ethnobotany of local peoples, which was beginning to be documented in the colonial era. Instead, local people were usually regarded as ignorant about forestry and conservation and, in fact, as spoilers of the environment.

(v) Most forestry officials were dedicated to setting aside certain proportions (e.g. six per cent) of the total land area for forest reserves, which usually included both national and local reserves.

(vi) Foresters were regarded by local people as a sort of auxiliary police, since one of their main functions was to keep people out of reserves, and to prosecute them for infringement of regulations.

Apart from the establishment of forest reserves, few other interferences were made in the land-use system of the Mbeere, whose semi-arid lands had no attraction for European farmers. Right at the end of the colonial period plans were started to develop Meka Sisal Estate, with several thousand hectares being set aside in a sparsely populated area of Mavuria Location. The estate was actually started in 1964, just after independence, and by the time of first production world prices for sisal had fallen drastically, so the estate was never commercially successful.

Several features are familiar in colonial management of natural resources. These include: the emphasis on markets; the neglect of subsistence and domestic products; the contemptuous dismissal of indigenous knowledge; and the policing function of the forestry personnel. Similar to the pastoral programmes of the colonial period, there was virtually no understanding of the local management system nor any attempt to seek local involvement.

The management system

Throughout the colonial period it was officially assumed that land in 'the native reserves' was under communal control. But in Mbeere, as happened elsewhere in Kenya, some individuals had acquired individual holdings. These were not registered with the government until much later, but were obtained by negotiation with the elders of the *muhiriga* (lineage). For example, one man who lived near the British–American Tobacco Centre, at Ena, was a pioneer in planting trees, starting in 1951. To ensure that he and his sons would not lose the benefit of his foresight, he persuaded the elders to recognise his right to his own land. Most other people had a customary right to cultivate the same land each year, or to make new fields, when necessary, in an area not occupied by another. In those days, conflicts over land were rare, except for the small fertile part of Mbeere nearest to Mount Kenya, which was beginning to attract settlers from the more arid lowlands at the end of the colonial period.

Because it seemed that there was adequate land for all, and because the population seemed small in relation to land, it was even relatively easy for a stranger (who was usually an Akamba) to acquire rights to cultivate land as a *mu-hoi*, or tenant. Some tenants went through customary rituals to become lineage members, which supposedly allowed them full rights in land. But when individual titles began to be issued in the 1970s, the claims of many of these strangers were not recognised.

Apart from relatively small areas of land that were cultivated, or grazed regularly, or were near homesteads, land was regarded as *weru*, or wilderness, where all were free to go to hunt, and to collect honey, thatching-grass, fuelwood or any of the other forest products on which Mbeere material culture was based. The 'traditional' land tenure system, then, was flexible and vague, in that boundaries between clans were usually not clearly known, as there had not been a need for clarity when land was abundant. This vagueness gave rise to numerous conflicts and bitter litigation when individual land titles were introduced.

A few trees, especially the large hardwoods and valuable building trees (e.g. *mukau, Melia volkensii*) were regarded as clan or even individual trees. But with these exceptions, all trees were considered as common property to which all Mbeere had access. There is little evidence of any systematic, widespread management of the forest resource, which did not appear to be needed in earlier years because scarcities were few. There is also little evidence of deliberate conservation practices, although several inadvertent mechanisms served a conservation purpose. For example, it was usual to leave riverine vegetation undisturbed; this provided good protection for the rivers and streams, and also helped prevent soil erosion. In addition, hillside cultivation was rare, possibly because it was easier to cultivate flat lands, which were readily available in the pre-colonial period. Finally, the Mbeere had many sacred groves, more than 100 being listed by an early colonial official. These were areas ranging from a quarter of a hectare to three hectares in size, where the cutting of any tree was forbidden, and which were used for ritual sacrifice. A few of these groves survived as late as the 1970s, providing excellent sites for examining the vegetation of a century ago, as several species of trees were rare, or not seen at all outside the groves.

There was, until recently, little tree-planting, with the exception of a few fruit (especially mango), shade and ornamental trees near the homestead; and it was relatively few homesteads who practised even this limited form of tree-planting. Trees were seen as an abundant and accessible resource, but this attitude changed drastically during the last ten years.

Recent changes

One immediate effect of independence was a weakening of soil conservation measures, which were generally so disliked, and which had been so closely identified with the worst aspects of colonial rule. In Mbeere, it was not until the late 1970s that the agricultural extension service again embarked on widespread soil conservation measures, very similar in aims to those used in the colonial period. This time, gentle persuasion rather than compulsion was used, with marked success. Once again, farmers are being discouraged from cultivating on steep slopes, and they are being encouraged and helped to construct terraces, and to plant trees.

There has also been a general encroachment, in many parts of Kenya, into forest reserves, not only by subsistence producers but also by tea growers, and people seeking construction timber and other forest products. Sometimes authorities have found it politically expedient to turn a blind eye to such illegal incursions into forest reserves.

We stated above, in our conceptual framework, that it is difficult to distinguish the important characteristics of common management systems from each other. Although this is true for Mbeere, it is possible to list and comment on the most important factors.

First is the overriding factor of demographic pressure, especially as comparatively little area is really suitable for rainfed cultivation. This has led to increased competition for the small fertile areas in the north-western parts. The increase in population cannot be understood except in conjunction with other factors, notably land adjudication. Most of Mbeere has by now been individually registered and most farmers have been given title to land. There are, however, land disputes that have not yet been finally settled.

We summarise the salient points of this major change, full accounts being available elsewhere (see Brokensha & Glazier, 1973). Government effectively left land allocation decisions to the clans, which had to:

(i)   determine their own boundaries *vis-à-vis* other clans, some of which might have land in several discrete units;

(ii)   decide who was eligible: for example, were women, children, strangers, and urban-based workers (migrants) to be given land? Each clan decided on its own, and for a period of a few years the clan elders possessed more power than they had before or since. There was a widespread suspicion that decisions were influenced by bribes, and the land division has left a legacy of bitterness (Brokensha & Njeru, 1977).

At this time, the Embu County Council had the power to reserve some land for common use. It would have been possible even to reserve all the sacred groves as common lands, but such was the pressure by individuals and clans, that no common lands were established. Within the space of a few years, there was a remarkable transition in land tenure, and all common land disappeared. People complained that it was difficult or even impossible to use another's land for any purpose, unless one had obtained permission or, in some cases, even made a payment. These are the possible uses, in increasing order of difficulty, of others' land: walking across land; collecting medicinal herbs, fallwood and building timber; grazing livestock; placing honey hives; planting crops; and planting trees.

Once land became a marketable commodity, rich outsiders from land-hungry areas, such as Embu Division, bought up large tracts of land in the more fertile areas. Some of them used tractors or irrigation, and there was a rapid growth in inequity. For example, in one sub-location in 1977, five per cent of the population owned 24 per cent of total land, while the poorest 53 per cent controlled only 20 per cent of land.

Mention has been made of market links, which were important in relation to charcoal. Until the early 1970s, there had been a small charcoal industry for use by local blacksmiths and by a few people like school-teachers and owners of local tea shops, who used it for cooking. Since then, there have been drastic changes, spurred on partly by the rural roads that were built under the Special Rural Development Programme. Intended to facilitate the marketing of cotton and other export crops, the roads were a significant factor in the increase of charcoal production. Charcoal became a major cash crop, especially for poor families at times of food shortage, and such times occurred frequently in Mbeere. The charcoal was destined both for the towns and for export to the Gulf nations. The export trade has been largely stopped, but the urban markets maintain a high demand, despite a stream of bans, price regulations and trader licensing.

One last factor is the loss of land as a result of the construction of dams (Kindaruma, Kamburu, Gitaaru, and Masinga) along the Tana River. Each dam inundated parts of Mbeere, resulting in a further loss of land, much of it valuable to local people as it provided honey and other savanna woodland products.

Discussion

The two case studies illustrate some of the changes in resource management practices in Kenya that have occurred in the present century. These
transitions should be seen in the broader context of social and agrarian
change, which has increasingly differentiated producers; restricted their
access to critical natural resources; created markets for land, trees and
range products; strained domestic labour supplies; and weakened local
institutions for managing natural resources. While land tenure becomes
a variable to examine in resource management, it may prove less significant than these other factors which deal more with the process and actual
management practices, than with jural rules. As the Mbeere data
demonstrate, tree management by individuals was taking place prior to
legal changes in the land tenure system.

In spite of the recent changes, many remnants of the indigenous management systems still exist in the Maasai, Il Chamus and Mbeere areas;
and producers of these regions maintain a sophisticated knowledge of
the environment. As was the case with many colonial programmes, however, many donor-funded natural resource programmes fail to build upon,
or even to acknowledge, local practices and knowledge. Yet these projects
usually require producers to invest their own labour (and, in some cases,
capital) in conservation activities that may be less viable than existing
practices and that may be implemented with no real local participation
in decision-making. Given the current political and social context of
resource use in East Africa, we are not arguing for a return to indigenous
systems of resource management. We do suggest, however, that these
systems be examined, and that some of the current paradigms of natural
resource use be subjected to more rigorous empirical and analytical tests
before radically new forms of management are introduced.

Notes

1.   This chapter was written under the auspices of the Clark University/Insti-
tute for Development Anthropology Cooperative Agreement on Settlement and Resource System Analysis. This Cooperative Agreement is
funded by the Office of Rural Development, Bureau for Science and
Technology, Agency for International Development, USA. The field data
on the Il Chamus, Baringo District was collected by Peter Little, with
financial support provided by the Social Science Research Council, the
American Council of Learned Societies, and Indiana University. Much
of the forestry section is based on research done by Brokensha and his
colleague, Bernard Riley, in Mbeere Division, Embu District, Kenya.

This work was funded by grants from the National Science Foundation, USA.

2. The characteristics of common property systems have been subject to considerable review recently. For a current anthropological perspective on the topic, see Peters (1985).

3. This conceptual framework is derived, in part, from Oakerson's (1984) model of common property management.

References

ALDEV (1962). *African Land Development in Kenya 1946–62*. Nairobi: English Press.

ANDERSON, D.M. (1982). Herder, settler and colonial rule: A history of the peoples of the Baringo Plains, *c*. 1890–1940. Unpublished Ph.D. thesis, University of Cambridge.

BROKENSHA, D. & GLAZIER, J. (1973). Land reform among the Mbeere of Central Kenya. *Africa*, **43**, 182–206.

BROKENSHA, D. & NJERU, E. (1977). Some consequences of land adjudication in Mbeere Division, Embu. Working Paper no. 320, Institute for Development Studies, University of Nairobi, Kenya.

BROKENSHA, D., RILEY, B. & CASTRO, A. (1983). *Fuelwood use in Rural Kenya: Impacts of Deforestation*. Binghamton, New York: Institute for Development Anthropology.

CIRIACY-WANTRUP, S.V. & BISHOP, C. (1975). 'Common property' as a concept in natural resource policy. *Natural Resources Journal*, **15**, 713–27.

de SOUZA, M. (1984). Reserved grazing areas in Meruishi Group-Ranch: a response to sedentarization. Nairobi: International Livestock Centre for Africa.

de SOUZA, M. & de LEEUW, P.N. (1984). Smallstock use of reserved grazing areas on Meruishi Group-Ranch. Nairobi: International Livestock Centre for Africa.

DOUGHLIN, D., DOAN, P. & UPHOFF, N. (1984). *Local Institutional Development and Natural Resource Management*. Special Series on Local Institutional Development no. 2. Ithaca, New York: Cornell University Press.

FUMAGALLI, C.T. (1978). An evaluation of development projects among East African pastoralists. *African Studies Review*, **21**, (3), 49–63.

GALATY, J. (1980). The Maasai Group Ranch: politics and development in an African pastoral society. In *When Nomads Settle*, ed. P. Salzman, pp. 157–72. New York: J.F. Bergin.

GULBRANDSEN, D. (1980). *Agro-Pastoral Production and Communal Land-use: a socio-economic study of the Bangwaketse*. Gaberone: Ministry of Agriculture.

HAALAND, G. (1980). Social organisation and ecological pressure in Southern Darfur. In *Problems of Savanna Development*, ed. G. Haaland, pp. 54–105. Occasional Paper no. 19. Bergen, Norway: Department of Social Anthropology, Bergen University.

JACOBS, A. (1980). Pastoral Maasai and tropical rural development. In *Agricultural Development in Tropical Africa*, ed. R. Bates & M. Lofchie, pp. 275–301. New York: Praeger.

LITTLE, P.D. (1984). Land and pastoralists. *Cultural Survival Quarterly*, **8** (1), 46–7.

LITTLE, P.D. (1985). Absentee herdowners and part-time pastoralists: the political economy of resource use in Northern Kenya. *Human Ecology*, **13** (2), 131–51.

MAHER, C. (1938). Soil erosion and land utilization in Embu. Nairobi: Ministry of Agriculture.

MIGOT-ADHOLLA, S.E. & LITTLE, P.D. (1981). Evolution of policy toward the development of pastoral areas in Kenya. In *The Future of Pastoral Peoples*, ed. J. Galaty, D. Aronson, D. Salzman and A. Chouinard, pp. 144–56. Ottawa: International Development Research Centre.

OAKERSON, R.J. (1984). A model for the analysis of common property problems. Paper prepared for the Common Property Steering Committee, National Research Council, Washington DC.

ᴶODELL, M.J. (1982). Local institutions and management of communal resources: lessons from Africa and Asia. Pastoral Network Paper 14e. London: Overseas Development Institute.

PASHA, I.K. (1983). Reserved grazing: a Maasai traditional concept. Nairobi: International Livestock Centre for Africa.

PEACOCK, C.P., de LEEUW, P.N. & KING, J.M. (1982). *Herd movement in the Mbirikani area*. Nairobi: International Livestock Centre for Africa.

PETERS, P. (1985). Embedded systems and rooted models: the grazing lands of Botswana and the 'Commons' debate. Discussion Paper no. 203, Harvard Institute for International Development, Harvard University.

RUNGE, C.F. (1981). Common property externalities: isolation, assurance, and resource depletion in a traditional grazing context. *American Journal of Agricultural Economics*, **63**, 595–606.

⌒SANDFORD, S. (1983). *Management of Pastoral Development in the Third World*. Chichester: Wiley.

SOBANIA, N. (1979). *Historical Background to the Mt. Kulal Region of Kenya*. IPAL Technical Report no. A-2. Nairobi: UNESCO.

10

Conflicting uses for forest resources in the Lower Tana River basin of Kenya

FRANCINE HUGHES

Introduction

Forest resources are in increasing demand in most developing countries. About 90 per cent of people in these countries depend on firewood as their chief source of energy (Eckholm, 1975). Africa has the largest per person per annum consumption of firewood with an average of $1.18m^3$ per person in the least developed countries (UN, 1981). In most of these countries the demand for fuelwood is outstripping local supplies and whilst studies on fuelwood use have been carried out in some places, very little is known about natural forest productivity, so that it is extremely difficult to put values on supply and demand ratios.

Concern over fuelwood supplies in Kenya was voiced in the late 1960s and the 1970s, especially over the impact of diminishing forest cover on soil erosion, and in 1975 the Kenyan Government banned charcoal exports. Subsequently the Ministry of Energy in conjunction with the Beijer Institute has been trying to assess demands and supply. A number of studies in Kenya provide information on levels and patterns of fire-wood use and some consider alternative energy supplies, e.g. Brokensha & Riley (1978), Hosier (1981), Kamweti (1981), Shakow, Weiner & O'Keefe (1981), Hughes (1982) and most recently Barnes, Ensminger & O'Keefe (1984). On average it has been found that 1.4–2.4 m^3 per person per annum of wood is used, based on household surveys (Hosier, 1981). Openshaw (1981) particularly considers alternative energy sources including biogas plants, solar and wind energy and various fossil fuels, and concludes that the only practical energy source is wood. This means increasing tree planting on a local scale with local involvement in rural areas, and increasing investment in forest plantations for industry and urban areas. There has been an increase in the number of studies carried out on patterns of fuelwood use, but in many ways they provide us with little new information if they do not relate use to availability. Whilst studies of fuelwood use have tended to be carried out by social anthropologists and socio-economists, studies of timber production have

211

been carried out by foresters in plantations and by no-one in natural woodlands and forests. The gap in knowledge between fuelwood demand and supply is a serious one, since it makes sustainable management of existing supplies and prediction of future plantation needs over and above natural supplies very difficult. It is a gap which is created partly by the difficulty of collecting data on natural wood production and standing volumes of wood, and partly by the fact that most studies follow one line of research instead of being interdisciplinary in nature.

The most comprehensive study of natural wood supplies in Kenya has been carried out by Western & Ssemakula (1981) in conjunction with the Kenya Rangeland Ecological Monitoring Unit (KREMU). They estimate wood supplies using aerial survey techniques and conclude that woodstocks and production, under prevailing patterns of land-use, provide the bulk of Kenya's present energy needs, mainly through domestic consumption. In their report they point out that 87 per cent of Kenya's land surface can be classified as rangeland and supports 600m tons of wood. However, they estimate that sustainable production amounts to only 14m tons. Access to much of the woodstocks in these rangelands is difficult and expensive so that wood harvesting is concentrated around agricultural areas. Although in the short term woodstocks appear to be increasing as agricultural areas expand into rangelands, Western & Ssemakula (1981) predict a sharp decline in wood availability by 1990 with tree cover nationwide being reduced by half over the next ten to thirty years. They urge the planning and planting of woodlots in areas in or adjacent to arable lands and also the gathering of information on natural wood availability.

This chapter presents the results of a study carried out in the floodplain forest of the Lower Tana River of Kenya. It attempts to relate use of the forest resources to its availability and to predict how long wood supplies can last in the area.

Developments in the Tana River basin

The Tana River rises on Mount Kenya and the Aberdare Mountains and flows into the Indian Ocean north of Malindi (Fig. 10.1). In its lower course it is a highly meandering river with a floodplain that can extend to around six kilometres in width. In this lower stretch it supports a narrow band of floodplain forest in an otherwise semi-arid area. It holds the greatest agricultural potential in terms of existing and improvable land in Kenya, as it is the only river capable of supporting large-scale

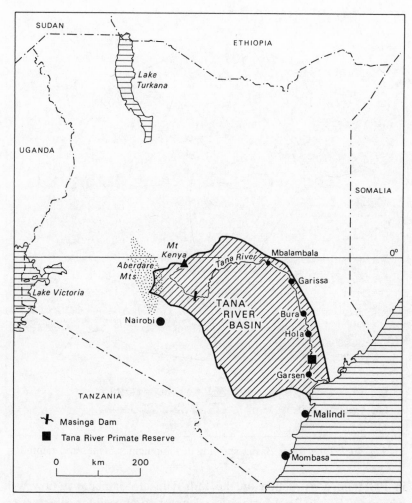

Fig. 10.1. Map of Kenya showing the Tana River Basin and the location of some of the development schemes within it.

irrigation schemes. It has been estimated that 2 per cent of the basin is irrigable, mainly in the lower basin, and that this is over half the national irrigation potential (Tana River Development Authority, 1980). There is a considerable programme of dam-building in the upper basin, prompted by water and hydroelectric power demands, mainly from Nairobi. The first three dams that were built on the Upper Tana received much criticism for their lack of social, environmental and economic assessment before project construction (Odingo, 1979). The fourth and largest completed to date, the Masinga Dam (The Upper Reservoir Scheme) was closed

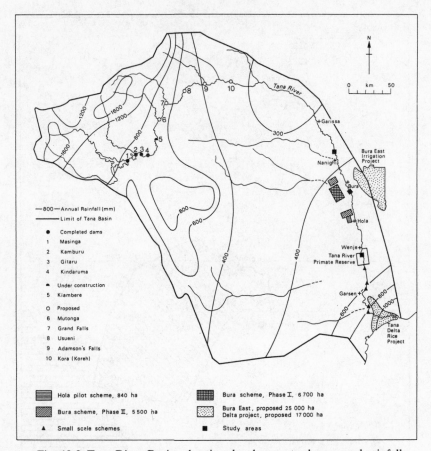

Fig. 10.2. Tana River Basin: showing development schemes and rainfall.

in 1981 and construction on the fifth dam at Kiambere is now well advanced (Fig. 10.2). A further five dams are proposed for construction over the next two decades including one as far downstream as Kora Rapids.

In the lower reaches of the Tana a large-scale irrigation scheme is being built near Bura, called the Bura Irrigation Settlement Project (Bura irrigation scheme). Further downstream, towards the delta, various small-scale irrigation schemes (about 100 ha each) in some village sites have been constructed and pre-feasibility studies have been carried out for an irrigated rice scheme in the delta (Fig. 10.2). The upper reservoir scheme and the other dams and the lower basin irrigation schemes have been funded independently of each other, with different combinations of aid donors supporting each scheme.

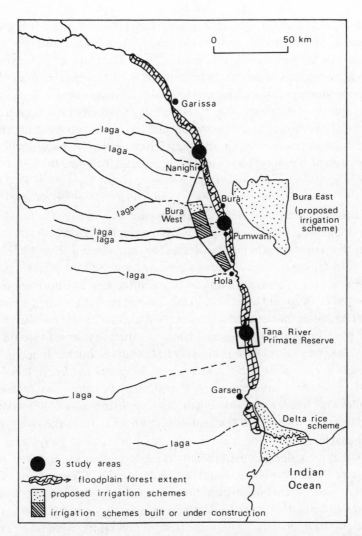

Fig. 10.3. The Lower Tana Basin showing floodplain forest extent, irrigation schemes and the study areas used for measuring the volumes of wood in various forest types.

The Lower Tana

Construction of the Bura irrigation scheme in the Lower Tana was begun in 1978 alongside the floodplain forest (Fig. 10.3). This forest is mainly evergreen and extends for approximately one kilometre on either side of the river, but is present for about 300 km of river length upstream from the delta and covers approximately 50,000–60,000 ha. It is a relic of forests that were once more widespread, though when and how widespread is still under debate (Hamilton, 1982). The plant species diversity increases towards the coast where there is also higher rainfall. It is possible that some species have extended their range into the Tana forest from the coastal forests. The forest has high conservation importance since it is a very specialised ecosystem and has species endemic to certain East African rivers, notably the Tana River poplar (*Populus ilicifolia*). The forest also supports some endemic primates including the Tana River Mangabey (*Cercocebus galeritus galeritus*) and the Tana River Red Colobus (*Colobus badius rufomitratus*), which are classified as 'critically endangered' and 'rare' respectively by the IUCN (1978). These are afforded some protection in the Tana River Primate Reserve, downstream from the irrigation scheme, between Hola and Garsen (Fig. 10.3).

The irrigation scheme at Bura essentially consists of the pilot irrigation scheme at Hola, covering 850 ha and the main scheme at Bura comprising an initial 6,700ha and later, should the funding be forthcoming, a further 5,500 ha, all on the west bank (Fig. 10.2). An initial 25,000 ha of irrigated land were proposed for the east bank but the low success rate on the first 6,700 ha at Bura West is unlikely to encourage further funding. The schemes on the west bank stretch along 80 km of the floodplain (Fig. 10.4), and affect approximately 15,000 local Pokomo and Malekote people who live on the floodplain, and approximately 6,400 pastoral Orma people who live in the semi-arid bush away from the river.

The scheme is being built in the semi-arid areas away from the immediate floodplain environment, using irrigation water taken from the Tana River near Nanighi and distributed to the different parts of the scheme via a 50 km long distributary canal (Fig. 10.4), which is fed using pumps to bring the water from the river level to the canal level. Many problems have occurred with these pumps, and efforts were being made in 1984 to obtain funding for construction of a barrage above Nanighi which could maintain water levels at a certain height in order to gravity-feed water into the irrigation canal. This barrage was initially planned to gravity-feed both Bura West and Bura East and is not at all economically viable for feeding water to Bura West alone. Nevertheless, plans for its construction are being pursued. The initial 6,700 ha currently under construction will accommodate 5,150 tenant farmers plus their families, and it is estimated that approximately 60,000 people will eventually live on or in association with this first part of the scheme, trebling the local population. The scheme will have several impacts on the flood-

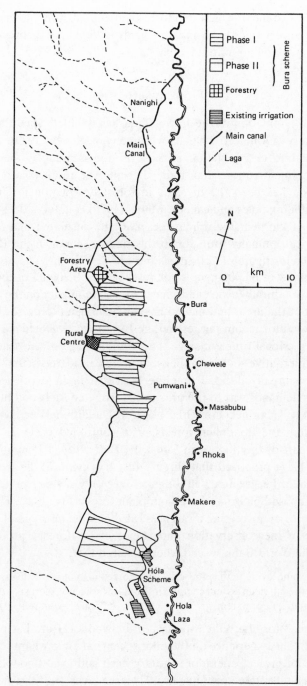

Fig. 10.4. Bura Irrigation Scheme in the Lower Tana.

plain forest, some of which are more direct and quantifiable than others. The most direct and severe impact is likely to be that of fuelwood cutting by the new population in the area.

Forest resource use

The local population of the Lower Tana has doubled since the turn of the century (Ormerod, 1896; Government of Kenya, 1979), although the local rate of population increase is not as great as the national average, which is more than four per cent. The result of an increased population has been the increase in forest destruction for fuelwood, house-building poles and canoes. Marsh (1976) counted a density of 2.4 canoes per km near the primate reserve and calculated that 31.7 trees must be cut annually to maintain this fleet. A count in the Bura area gave a similar figure of 2.4 canoes per km.

The influx of 60,000 people for just the first 6,700 ha of the scheme at Bura is naturally expected to have a massive impact on the fuelwood supplies of the area, and indeed has already begun to do so. Provision of fuelwood for tenant farmers on the Bura Irrigation Scheme has been seen as a critical problem since the planning stage of the scheme, and several alternative sources of fuelwood were considered in the late 1970s. It was eventually decided that the least-cost method of meeting the project's demands was to use gravity-fed irrigated fuelwood plantations adjacent to the project area (Fig. 10.4), with additional dead wood being taken from the floodplain forests on a controlled basis. In order to protect part of the floodplain forest the Bura Project Planning Report [PPR] (1977) proposed that three forest blocks of 70, 85 and 90 km^2 each should be gazetted, although in fact only a small percentage of these proposed blocks include floodplain forest (Fig. 10.5). This was in response to an increasing awareness, at the planning stage of the Bura scheme, of the conservation importance of the forests, an awareness which the World Bank voiced when it stated that:

it has become evident that the only way to retain biological diversity and to preserve the full richness and complexity of these indigenous forests is to preserve an entire forest ecosystem.   *(IBRD, 1977:p76, Annexe 9, Appendix 1)*

The need for alternative sources of fuelwood at Bura has been highlighted by the experience on the pilot scheme at Hola where, during the 26 years of project operation, the dry bush and local floodplain forest have been devastated over increasingly large areas, the 'phryganasphere' of Warren & Maizels (1977). At present, fuelwood is collected from

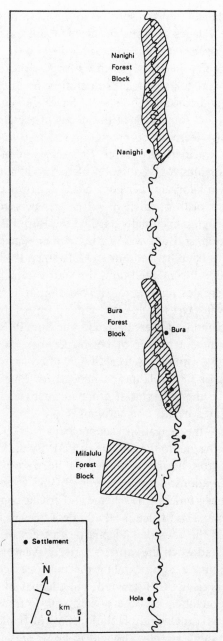

Fig. 10.5. Proposed gazetted forest blocks.

considerable distances and transported to the town of Hola by bicycle. In many scheme villages at Hola, the women still walk to collect their wood but spend over half a day each time they do so.

The exact area that needs to be under irrigated forestry is clearly a function of demand for wood and plantation productivity. Ideally, a survey of fuel wood consumption should have been carried out on the Hola scheme to give some idea of the needs of the Bura scheme and, therefore, to assist decisions on plantation size at Bura. The Bura PPR (1977) bases its calculations on the figures given in a World Bank report, which estimates Kenyan figures of fuelwood consumption to be approximately two kilograms per person per day (using an average specific gravity factor of 0.75, this is 0.991 m^3 per person per year (Bura PPR 1977)). The figure eventually used by the Bura PPR (1977) for the irrigated plantation at Bura was 0.7 m^3 per person per year. Forest species trials have been carried out at Hola since 1965, but almost no usable results were documented until the start of a new set of trials in 1979, to choose species suitable for the plantations at Bura and to give some idea of how fast trees could grow under different irrigation regimes. Thus, when the plantations were designed, the Bura PPR (1977) assumed an average mean increment of 15 m^3 per ha per year, which was reckoned to be a conservative estimate. A total of 4,500 ha was eventually arrived at as the size of irrigated plantation needed for Phase 1 of the Bura scheme, alongside the 6,700 ha of cropped area (cf. Fig. 10.4, which shows a smaller area in the scheme plans).

Construction of the irrigation scheme began in 1978 and the first tenant farmers moved onto the scheme in 1981. By the time they arrived to plant the first crop, no tree seedlings had been sown in the areas put aside for the plantations, despite it being obvious to the scheme managers, the aid agencies funding the scheme and private companies involved in scheme design and construction, that unless trees were planted at the very beginning of the construction phase, no trees would be ready to harvest for firewood when the farmers arrived. An attempt to alleviate the problem was made by stockpiling the bush cleared from irrigated areas for villagers to use as fuelwood, but this has by no means been adequate. By September 1984 there were still no trees planted in the area designated as a fuelwood plantation (World Bank, personal communication) and there are now thought to be severe limitations on the amount of water available for irrigating any plantation, because of consistent pump failure at the Nanighi pump station which brings water to the main distributary channel.

The lack of success in implementing a forestry plantation has proved a massive threat to the floodplain forest. This threat is compounded by the fact that a large work-force of several thousand people has been in residence at Bura since construction began in 1978. No provision was made for firewood for these people. Furthermore, a large shanty town has developed informally around the scheme and materials for building its houses have been taken from the forest near Bura, since no suitable plants grow in the dry bush for providing straight poles for house construction. In the manner typical of large-scale development projects, a number of informal arrangements were made between people attracted to the shanty town and employees of the National Irrigation Board (which used to manage the scheme), so that lorries and drivers from the National Irrigation Board were used to transport house-building materials from the forest to the scheme, whilst local Pokomo and Malekote people were persuaded to cut and pile these materials in the forest in readiness. Houses officially constructed in the new irrigation scheme villages, on the other hand, have deliberately been built using mangrove poles from the Kenyan coast, both in order *not* to deplete local forest resources and because of their greater durability. The construction of informal housing in the shanty town, and the presence of the construction crews, have therefore had a quite unforeseen and unplanned-for impact on forest resources.

In view of all these considerations, an attempt was made to quantify the impact that the influx of people into the area is having and will have on the floodplain forest through fuelwood collection, since this extracts the most wood and is in constant demand, and to compare this with current levels of use by the local people. Attention was also focused on the species most frequently collected for fuelwood.

Fuelwood use and wood availability

Two separate studies were carried out, to establish levels of fuelwood use on the irrigation schemes at Hola and Bura and in floodplain villages, and to measure volumes of wood available in the forest and where possible, natural growth rates in the forest.

The results of the fuelwood survey have been published elsewhere (Hughes, 1984) and are briefly summarised here. The most notable feature of the results is the great difference in fuelwood consumption between all irrigation scheme villages and villages in the floodplain forest. On average, consumption in floodplain villages is 3.7 kg wood per person per day whilst irrigation scheme villages have an average consumption value of 1.8 kg wood per person per day.

As noted by Bialy (1979) in Sri Lanka, consumption of wood in the Lower Tana does not vary greatly between households, despite variable family sizes. Thus, wood consumption per household is a more useful figure to use, and stands at an average of 9.6 kg per household per day in irrigation scheme villages, compared with 21.6 kg per household per day in floodplain villages. The discrepancies in fuelwood use between irrigation scheme villages and those on the floodplain were found to be related to availability of wood, since women on the irrigation schemes had to walk from two to five kilometres in the dry bush to collect wood, the round trip taking up to five hours, whilst women on the floodplain walked 200–800 m along shaded forest trails. At present most women at the Bura scheme collect their wood in the dry bush away from the floodplain forest, since it is still a convenient source of wood. However, with time, they will have to walk farther for wood, and the floodplain forest area may become a more attractive source of wood as it already has done for those irrigation scheme villages sited near the floodplain.

As well as giving figures for scheme village and riverine village wood consumption per household, the survey revealed that some households on the Bura irrigation scheme had begun to use charcoal rather than wood, especially if the woman of the family had managed to get a job, for example as a cleaner or a typist on the scheme. In this case, charcoal was bought from the shanty town, which in turn was supplied by the riverine people. The women of the local riverine peoples were quick to appreciate the ready market for charcoal at Bura, especially for the non-tenant farming sector and at the time of survey had begun to fell *Acacia elatior* trees and to convert them to charcoal for sale at Bura. Despite being less efficient in terms of total energy yield (Earl, 1975), charcoal is a more desirable form of fuel for administrative staff at Bura.

The survey of species preferred for wood collection showed a strong preference by riverine women for *Acacia elatior, Cordia gharaf, Lecaniodiscus fraxinfolius* and some *Terminalia brevipes. Lecaniodiscus fraxinfolius* is used as a kindling wood, whilst the others are dense woods and are used for keeping a fire going slowly. It was interesting to note the cooperation between women living on the floodplain and women from other areas in Kenya who had been brought to the irrigation scheme. The former formed mixed wood-collecting groups with the latter to instruct them on which species to use, since many species in the Lower Tana were foreign to women from other parts of Kenya.

The study of forest wood volume initially classified the floodplain forest vegetation into different types, based on species assemblages and the soils in which each vegetation type grew, as well as their position in the floodplain. The classification is given in Table 10.1 and consists of five mature forest types and two pioneer vegetation types. Within each vegetation type the standing volume of all shrubs above one metre in height and all trees were measured in a series of 25 m × 25 m vegetation sample plots and calculated using the equation

$$v = gh/2$$

where v = total above-ground volume including branchwood
g = basal area of main stem at breast height
h = tree height

(after Dawkins, 1970 in Synott, 1979)

Table 10.1. *Initial floodplain forest classification based on tall trees*

Forest type	Characterististic species and location
Active levee evergreen	On sandy levees with several characteristic species including *Ficus sycomorus* and *Sterculia appendiculata* in the overstorey
Inactive levee evergreen (transitional)	As above but on cut-off meanders and with shrub species in the undergrowth more typical of dry floodplain areas
Acacia	Dominated by *Acacia elatior*, away from river's edge on dry floodplain
Clay evergreen	In clayey wet floodplain areas away from the river's edge. Dominated by *Diospyros mespiliformis* and *Garcinia livingstonei*
Populus or poplar	Dominated by *Populus ilicifolia*. Usually on sandy banks at the back of point-bars
Point-bar (pioneer)	Low shrubs on sandy point-bars, most common species include young *Populus ilicifolia* and *Pluchea dioscoridis*
Oxbows (Pioneer)	Clay or sand oxbow infill often colonised by *Terminalia brevipes* and/or *Spirostachys venenifera*

Disturbed areas, due to either former human occupation or frequent disturbance by the changing river course are often colonised by *Hyphaene coriacea, Pluchea dioscoridis* and *Spirostachys venenifera*. It is not usually easy to determine the origin of these scrub areas and they have been omitted from the classification.

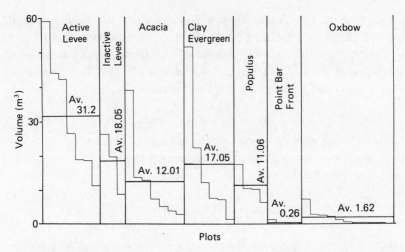

Fig. 10.6. Volumes of standing wood in plots in the different vegetation types of the floodplain.

The results are given in Fig. 10.6. It would appear that *Acacia* forests in particular, plus inactive levee forests and oxbow vegetation, are most at risk from fuelwood collection, since these vegetation types contain one or more of the preferred fuelwood species mentioned above.

Impacts of fuelwood collection

It appears from the various discussions above that two major forms of wood cutting are carried out in the floodplain forests for fuel:

(i) Felling of whole trees and conversion of these into charcoal for sale at Bura.

(ii) Direct collection of wood by floodplain tribeswomen and by some tenant farmer families from the irrigation scheme at Bura.

The first of these is not quantifiable, since no figures were obtained on how many women were converting wood to charcoal, and anyway, distribution of this activity was restricted to areas near access roads. However, it can safely be assumed that the trend will continue at an accelerating pace as more people come to Bura. The second form of fuelwood cutting, as has been shown above, can be quantified. The average figure of 1.8 kg of wood used per person per day on the irrigation schemes at Hola and Bura is equivalent to 6.13 m^3 solid volume of wood used by an average family of seven per annum (calculated using the specific gravity conversion factor of 0.75). A similar calculation for floodplain families gives a value of 11.3 m^3 per annum wood consumed by the average family, almost twice as much.

From Fig. 10.6 it is obvious that the mature forest types have much greater volumes of standing wood than the pioneer vegetation types of the oxbows and point-bars. The greatest volume is found in the active levee evergreen forest, whilst the inactive levee evergreen forest shows a general decrease in volume as levee species die-off and *Acacia* forest species come to dominate (Hughes, 1985). When these volumes are compared with fuelwood use, the following statistics can be extracted. Two families from the irrigation schemes used the equivalent of one 25 m × 25 m plot of *Acacia* forest per year (i.e. approximately 12 m³ solid volume of wood). Therefore 32 irrigation scheme families would use one hectare of *Acacia* forest per year. Since 5,510 families are expected in the first part of Bura West (Phase 1), they could use approximately 160 ha of *Acacia* forest per year or 1.6 km². In the primate reserve, *Acacia* forest occupies approximately 700 ha, an area equivalent to which could be devastated by the families on Phase 1 alone of the Bura scheme in only 4.5 years. When it is considered that the primate reserve spans 31 km of river length, it can be seen that it would not take long for large sections of the floodplain forest to be devastated, especially as the calculations do not take account of the non-tenant farmer families. In an area of floodplain forest near Bura which has been mapped (see Hughes, 1985) and which extended for approximately 12 km of river length, 842 ha of *Acacia* forest were found to exist, a quantity which would be felled in just over five years. Naturally, at present, a great number of people on the irrigation scheme at Bura collect wood from the dry bush area, but when this ready supply of wood runs out the wholesale destruction of parts of the forest can be expected, a trend which has already begun at Hola.

A study was carried out of the growth rates of trees and shrubs in oxbows whose date of cut-off could be determined from aerial photographs. In an oxbow near Nanighi the average wood volume is 0.182 m³ per 25 m × 25 m vegetation plot after approximately ten years of growth. The average irrigation scheme family, which uses 6.13 m³ wood per annum, therefore uses slightly more than the equivalent of 2 ha of ten-year-old oxbow growth per annum. Again, continuous use of oxbow species for fuelwood will rapidly reduce oxbow vegetation, which is, in any case, very limited in extent (less than ten per cent of the floodplain forest area).

Approximately 15,000 local Pokomo and Malekote people farm the banks of the Tana in the vicinity of the proposed scheme. Although they number less than one third of the number of people on the irrigation scheme, it was calculated above that they use twice as much wood per household, and in their case all wood collection is from riverine areas.

Local population increase, therefore, is also having the effect of rapidly destroying some forest types, especially in the vicinity of village sites. That this destruction is occurring is supported by the measured values of 15.9 per cent forest destruction between 1960 and 1974 (Marsh, 1976) and 31 per cent between 1960 and 1975 (Allaway, 1979) for different parts of the Tana River Primate Reserve. Their differing values are apparently due to varying forest definitions.

Clearly the situation is serious for the forests of the lower Tana. Loss through canoe building and house building has occurred over many decades through local peoples' use and is particularly severe in active levee and clay evergreen forests, whilst losses through fuelwood collection are particularly great in *Acacia*, oxbow and inactive levee vegetation types. These losses are greatly accelerating, and will continue to do so for the various reasons outlined above associated with the Bura irrigation scheme. The threat posed by the scheme is considerable and unless the planned plantations on the scheme are made operational rapidly, then wholesale forest destruction will occur with loss of both local ways of life and critical wildlife habitat.

Conclusions

This study in the Lower Tana River basin has described how the Bura irrigation scheme has greatly increased the fuelwood demand in the Lower Tana because of totally inadequate provision of wood for the scheme. Poor allocation of funding by aid agencies and lack of coordination between Kenyan Government departments are the principal causes of this situation. Prior to irrigation scheme construction, a rapidly growing local population on the floodplain was already causing marked depletion of forest areas through clearance for agriculture, canoe-building and cutting for house-building poles and firewood. Only the Tana River Primate Reserve has had any level of protection from these activities. This local problem of overuse of forest resources is common all over Kenya but has been greatly magnified by irrigation scheme construction. A study of fuelwood use in both irrigation scheme villages and in floodplain villages has been compared with wood availability in the forest.

The results show that wood depletion in most major forest areas will occur over the next five years. The irrigated rice scheme that has recently been started in the delta of the Tana River should learn from the situation at Bura that the first priority is to provide fuelwood, probably through irrigated plantations, if further destruction of forest resources is to be avoided. The Tana River floodplain forest is an unusual ecosystem and provides a home for endemic primates that have already been greatly reduced in number over the last decade (Marsh, 1985). It also provides a livelihood for approximately 32,500 people who live on the floodplain (Government of Kenya, 1979). The impact of the scheme at Bura could have been predicted with a combination of ecological and firewood use studies. Such studies are best carried out by women researchers to enable good cooperation with the local women, since they are always the ones who are involved in fuelwood collection. This information might have provided an impetus to fund and plan the firewood plantations at an early stage, and is recommended as an integral part of feasibility studies for other development projects.

References

ALLAWAY, J.D. (1979). Elephants and their interactions with people in the Tana river region of Kenya. Unpublished Ph.D. thesis, Cornell University.

BARNES, C., ENSMINGER, J. & O'KEEFE, P., ed. (1984). *Wood, Energy and Households: perspectives on rural Kenya*. Energy, Environment and Development in Africa 6. Stockholm: Beijer Institute and Scandanavian Institute of African Studies.

BIALY, J. (1979). Firewood use in a Sri Lankan village: a preliminary survey. Occasional Papers on Appropriate Technology, School of Engineering Science, University of Edinburgh.

BROKENSHA, D. & RILEY, B. (1978). Forest, foraging, fences and fuel in a marginal area of Kenya. Paper prepared for USAID Africa Bureau, Firewood Workshop, Washington.

BURA PROJECT PLANNING REPORT [PPR] (1977). *Bura Irrigation Settlement Project Planning Report*. Nairobi: Sir M. MacDonald & Partners/Hunting Technical Services/National Irrigation Board, Kenya.

EARL, D.E. (1975). *Forest Energy and Economic Development*. Oxford: Clarendon Press.

ECKHOLM, E. (1975). *The Other Energy Crisis: firewood*. Worldwatch Paper 1. Washington: Worldwatch Institute.

GOVERNMENT OF KENYA (1979). *Compendium to vol.1. 1979 Population Census*. Central Bureau of Statistics, Ministry of Economic Planning and Development. Nairobi: Govt printer.

HAMILTON, A.C. (1982). *Environmental History of East Africa*. London: Academic Press.

HOSIER, R.H. (1981). *Surveys of Domestic Energy Consumption in Kenya: a summary*. Nairobi: Beijer Institute and Ministry of Energy, Kenya.

HUGHES, F.M.R. (1982). Provision of fuelwood for irrigation schemes: the case of Bura Irrigation Settlement Project, Kenya. In *Problems of the Management of Irrigated lands in Areas of Traditional and Modern Cultivation*, ed. H.G. Mensching. IGU Working Group 1, Cairo.

HUGHES, F.M.R. (1984). Fuelwood: a forgotten dimension of irrigation planning. In *Irrigation in Tropical Africa*, ed. W.M. Adams & A.T. Grove, Cambridge African Monographs 3. Cambridge: African Studies Centre.

HUGHES, F.M.R. (1985). The Tana River Floodplain Forest, Kenya: Ecology and impact upon development. Unpublished Ph.D. thesis, University of Cambridge.

IBRD (1977). Bura Irrigation Settlement Project Appraisal Report. Washington: International Bank for Reconstruction and Development.

IUCN (1978). *Red Data Book, vol.1 mammalia*. Gland, Switzerland: IUCN.

KAMWETI, D.M. (1981). An overview: fuelwood and charcoal/tree planting for energy in Kenya. Paper presented at the UN conference on 'New and Renewable Sources of Energy', Nairobi.

MARSH, C.M. (1976). *A Management Plan for the Tana River Game Reserve*. New York: New York Zoological Society & University of Bristol.

MARSH, C.M. (1985). *A Resurvey of Tana River Primates*. Report for the Institute of Primate Research, Kenya and the Dept of Wildlife Conservation and Management, Kenya. Nairobi.

ODINGO, R.S. ed. (1979). An African Dam: ecological survey of the Kamburu/ Gtaru hydro-electric dam area, Kenya. *Ecological Bulletins*, **29** Stockholm: Swedish Natural Science Research Council.

OPENSHAW, K. (1981). Woodfuel and Energy Crisis: problems and possible solutions. Paper presented at the UN conference on 'New and Renewable Sources of Energy', Nairobi.

ORMEROD, Rev R.M. (1896). The Rev. Ormerod's Journeys on the Tana River. *Geographical Journal*, **7**, 283–90.

SHAKOW, D., WEINER, D. & O'KEEFE, P. (1981). Energy and Development: the case of Kenya. *Ambio*, **10**, 206–10.

SYNOTT, T.J. (1979). *A manual for permanent plot procedures for tropical rain forests*. Tropical Forestry Paper 14, Commonwealth Forestry Institute, Oxford.

TANA RIVER DEVELOPMENT AUTHORITY [TRDA] (1980). *The Tana Irrigation and Reservoir Scheme*. Nairobi: Govt of Kenya.

UNITED NATIONS (1981). *Report of the Technical panel on fuelwood and charcoal to the UN conference on 'New and Renewable Resources of Energy'*. Nairobi: UN.

WARREN, A. & MAIZELS, J.K. (1977). Ecological change and desertification. In *Desertification: its causes and consequences*. ed. A. Warren, 169–261. Oxford: Pergamon Press.

WESTERN, D. & SSEMAKULA, J. (1981). *A survey of natural wood supplies in Kenya and an assessment of the ecological impact of its usage*. KREMU Technical Report Series no.55. Nairobi: KREMU.

11

Environmental degradation, soil conservation and agricultural policies in Sierra Leone, 1895–1984

ANDREW MILLINGTON

Awareness of the need to prevent environmental degradation and to institute soil conservation measures formed an important element in colonial forestry and agricultural policies throughout the African continent. Recent studies of colonial agricultural policies in East and southern Africa have noted that political considerations, as well as influences from outside the colonies, were significant factors in the implementation of soil conservation programmes, particularly in the colonies of white settlement (Berry & Townshend, 1971; Robinson, 1978, 1981; Stocking, 1983; Anderson, 1984; Beinart, 1984). However, it has not yet been demonstrated whether the generalisations drawn from these studies are applicable to the trade-orientated, West African colonies. This study analyses the relationship between agriculture and soil conservation policies, and environmental degradation during the past century in Sierra Leone (see Millington, 1987a). The period has been divided into three phases, the first beginning with the establishment of the Sierra Leone Protectorate in 1895, the second running from 1939 until independence in 1961, and the third dealing with the years since independence.

Environmental degradation, 1895–1939

The first detailed statements on environmental degradation in Sierra Leone during this period are to be found in the extensive forest surveys conducted in 1909 and 1911. These concentrated on water resources (Unwin, 1909) and soil degradation (Lane-Poole, 1911) respectively, but both concurred in attributing large-scale deforestation to 'wasteful' and 'reckless' shifting cultivation. Severely degraded areas were noted in many of the mountainous regions in the south and east of the protectorate, in the areas of intense nineteenth-century wood cutting (Unwin, 1909), and along the railway line as far as Moyamba (Lane-Poole, 1911), (see Fig. 11.1). A later report (Government of Sierra Leone [hereafter GOSL], 1938) identified serious erosion on ginger farms in the hills and

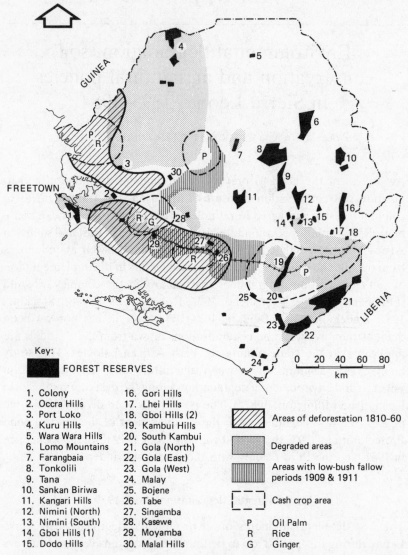

Key:

▓ FOREST RESERVES

1. Colony	16. Gori Hills
2. Occra Hills	17. Lhei Hills
3. Port Loko	18. Gboi Hills (2)
4. Kuru Hills	19. Kambui Hills
5. Wara Wara Hills	20. South Kambui
6. Lomo Mountains	21. Gola (North)
7. Farangbaia	22. Gola (East)
8. Tonkolili	23. Gola (West)
9. Tana	24. Malay
10. Sankan Biriwa	25. Bojene
11. Kangari Hills	26. Tabe
12. Nimini (North)	27. Singamba
13. Nimini (South)	28. Kasewe
14. Gboi Hills (1)	29. Moyamba
15. Dodo Hills	30. Malal Hills

▨ Areas of deforestation 1810–60

▒ Degraded areas

▥ Areas with low-bush fallow periods 1909 & 1911

⌐ ⌐ Cash crop area

P   Oil Palm
R   Rice
G   Ginger

Fig. 11.1. Deforestation and cash cropping, 1910–11; and Forest Reserves established since 1911.

under short fallow casava cultivation on sandy soils. The lack of an adequate water supply was also noted as an effect of bush degradation in the Freetown Peninsula, although afforestation was felt to have effectively controlled erosion in some parts of the peninsula as early as 1911 (Sierra Leone Forestry Department, 1911).

Agricultural policy and soil conservation, 1895–1939

The formation of the Sierra Leone Forestry Department in 1911 was a direct result of the 1909 and 1911 surveys. Forestry Ordinances were legislated in 1911 and 1912, and by 1913, after protracted negotiations with District Commissioners, thirteen reserves had been proposed (Table 11.1). Despite the problems of farming high up in the mountains of the proposed Kambui, Kangari, Nimini and Loma Reserves (Sierra Leone Forestry Department 1914), the undercapitalisation of planting programmes (Sierra Leone Forestry Department, 1916), the difficulty of obtaining land for fuelwood plantations along the railway, and persistent labour shortages for planting and for forest patrols (Sierra Leone Forestry Department, 1916, 1919), the surveying, demarcation and planting of these reserves continued until 1924. Between 1911 and 1924, 246.7 sq mi. of forest were reserved and a further 114.85 sq mi. demarcated (Sierra Leone Lands & Forests Department, 1924).

It is clear that the Forestry Department's policy of afforestation had three main aims between 1911 and 1923:

Table 11.1. *Forest reserves proposed in 1913*

Reserve	Area (Acres)	Purpose
Peninsula (Colony)	73.5	
Kangari	60	
Kambui	60	Conservation of existing forest
Nimini	100	
Loma	100	
Gola I & II	300	
Kangahun	4	
Boia (Bauya)	4	Timber for Freetown and export
Rokell River	4	
Scarcies	4	
Freetown	10	Fuelwood from mangrove swamp
Bonthe	?	forests
Kasewe	30	Gum copal production

Source: Correspondence, 18 March 1913, CO 267/165.

(i)   most importantly, to check environmental degradation (in terms
        of deforestation, soil degradation and the hydrological regimes)
        due to shifting cultivation;
(ii)   the role of forests in controlling water supplies was seen as an
        important benefit accruing from afforestation (Sierra Leone Fores-
        try Department, 1919).
(iii)   the economic potential of forests was recognised, particularly line-
        of-rail plantations for timber and gum copal tapping (Sierra Leone
        Protectorate Agriculture Development Branch, 1906).

The foresters saw shifting cultivation as a critical problem. In 1917 it
was noted that deforestation rates in Sierra Leone were greater than in
southern Nigeria and the Gold Coast. It was the view of both the Forestry
Department and the Governor that this was due to the increasing Protectorate population. It was felt that the most judicious solution to the
latter problem would be to allow increased food crop production after
forest clearance, although they were aware that major climatic modifications due to forest clearance by burning would ensue. Consequently,
forest conservation 'at all costs' and the adoption of intensive permanent
cultivation were the policies mooted. However, these policies were tempered by advice from the Agriculture Department, which indicated that
local farmers were very unlikely to readily adopt such far-reaching reforms
in their husbandry practices.[1] Instead, the cultivation of crops such as
rubber, cocoa, citrus, coffee, coconuts and swamp rice, which could be
grown with manure and without impoverishing the soil, was suggested.
While the Conservator of Forests accepted these points in principle, he
stressed that the effective introduction of large-scale afforestation would
need the political force of rigorous government ordinances.[2] An afforestation target of 30 per cent of the land area (8,100 sq mi.) was projected,
a similar proportion to the Gold Coast and India. The costs of afforestation were estimated at £5 per acre, and it was suggested that the total
sum of £25,920,000 could be spread over five or six years.[3]

The programme finally adopted by the Forestry Department in 1918
had seven clear guidelines:[4]

(i)   to conserve existing forest and stop encroachment;
(ii)   to introduce markets for forest products that did not involve
        deforestation;
(iii)   to restrict burning as far as possible;
(iv)   to reafforest abandoned land;
(v)   to continue the search for suitable rotations;
(vi)   not to encourage the cultivation of cocoa and rubber unless mar-

kets could be found and competition with other colonial products could be avoided;

(vii) not to oust native food crops by the introduction of industrial crops.

The Sierra Leone Agricultural Department was more equivocal in its policies during this period. Cash crop production dominated the early activities of the Agriculture Department, but in 1907 attention was turned to upland rice cultivation. In 1909 it was suggested that Sierra Leone was suitable for large-scale rice production, and this was swiftly acted upon with Indian upland rice variety trials in 1911 (Sierra Leone Agricultural Department, 1912) and swamp rice trials (from other colonies) in 1914. However, this work was only geared toward information gathering and no rice farming policy had yet evolved (Sierra Leone Agricultural Department, 1914). In the discussions that took place in 1917 on the question of the upland rice cultivation system, it is clear that there had emerged points of disagreement between the Director of Agriculture (Douglas Scotland), the Governor, and the Colonial Office. The relationship between shifting cultivation and environmental destruction had caused the colonial authorities in Freetown and London to investigate the possibilities of eliminating burning. But this suggestion was dismissed by the Director of Agriculture, Scotland, who considered that 'putting a stop to bush fires is tantamount in any tropical country to the stoppage of all agriculture'.[5]

As Director of Agriculture, Douglas Scotland was something of a 'Jekyll and Hyde' character. On the one hand he appeared to be strongly in favour of advanced agricultural techniques, as can be seen in his research on maize introduction and rotational cropping, his encouragement of swamp rice cultivation and fruit tree plantations, and the disastrous introduction of long-staple cotton (Richards, 1985). On the other hand, his correspondence with the Governor in 1917 showed a respect for, and understanding of, tropical farmers, and a certain amount of exasperation with colonial agricultural policies. These views are well illustrated in a report to the Governor in which he noted the important role of fire in bush clearance in Malaya by farmers and planters. In a subsequent letter he was critical of the Forestry Department in its clash with local chiefs over afforestation in the Panguma District, and reiterated his respect for local chieftancy control over farming matters, citing that increased rice yields in Safroko Limba Chiefdom were due to locally administered bush fire prohibition ordinances. Scotland's position was therefore a difficult one; whilst recognising native cultivation systems as environmentally unsound he did not allow himself the excessive criticisms voiced by the foresters and by other agriculturalists.

Therefore, while the Forestry Department had by 1920 formulated a clear long-term policy on afforestation and the restriction of shifting cultivation, the Agriculture Department remained uncertain of its position on native farming systems and soil conservation.

Tensions between the conflicting policies of the two Departments were exacerbated in 1922, when they were amalgamated to create the new Lands and Forests Department. However, by this time the cost of afforestation on the scale suggested by the Forestry Department had been rejected on economic grounds by Governor Wilkinson and consequently the afforestation lobby in the Lands and Forests Department found themselves in a weak position. Although the policy differences within the new Department led to the reforming of separate Forestry and Agricultural Departments in 1929, the foresters subsequently remained in a secondary role. With the foresters left to reiterate their central argument for the creation of forest reserves to preserve 'the few remaining areas of high-forest from destruction at the hands of the ubiquitous rice-farmer' (Sierra Leone Lands & Forests Department 1924), the policies of the agriculturalists came to dominate. Two important agricultural policies emerged in the early 1920s: firstly, the introduction and improvement of cash crops, particularly cocoa, coconut and cotton, and secondly, increased swamp rice production (Sierra Leone Lands & Forests Department, 1924).

The possibilities of increased swamp rice cultivation had been suggested as early as 1909 (GOSL, 1909), but it was not until 1922 that an Indian agriculturalist, A.C. Pillai, was brought to Sierra Leone to advise on swamp rice cultivation. Much to the surprise of colonial officials, he was unable to advise the experienced Temme rice farmers, whose cultivation methods he found to be advanced and whose yields exceeded those found in India (the latter finding being attributed to the higher natural fertility of the Sierra Leonean swamps, Sierra Leone Agricultural Department, 1922). From 1923 onwards the area of swamp rice cultivation was actively extended. In 1923 160 bushels of Sierra Leonean swamp rice seed from the Scarcies Estuary were planted in the Southern Province, and the Lands and Forests Department issued two extension pamphlets on swamp rice cultivation (Sierra Leone Lands & Forests Department, 1923, 1925). By 1926 250 acres had been cleared and 27 swamp rice demonstration farms had been created along the Turner's Peninsula.

The reason for the adoption of a policy of swamp rice development is interesting. Once swamp rice was regularly produced the Agricultural Department justified its introduction by pointing out that shortfalls in household rice supplies prior to harvest had been eliminated. Yet this had not figured as a prominent argument prior to the intensification of swamp cultivation. An alternative interpretation adopted by Millington (1987a) and Richards (1985), suggests that swamp rice cultivation was initiated as a covert conservation policy to move shifting cultivators from the uplands to the swamps. The main trigger in adopting a swamp rice policy was the political expediency of rapidly increasing rice production after the disastrous harvests of 1918. The political ramifications of the poor 1918 harvest were exacerbated by Lebanese traders hoarding rice, leading to popular riots in 1919 (Spitzer, 1975; Richards, 1985). Further impetus was given to this policy in 1935, when diamond mining began in the Kono District. Young male labour was attracted to the mines, depleting the upland rice-farming labour pool. This created a situation of decreased agricultural productivity simultaneously with increased rice demand, consequently increasing the urgency of swamp rice development.

By the mid-1930s the Agricultural Department was committed to its policy on rice cultivation:

The improvement and spread of swamp rice cultivation [will occur] to such an extent that not only will the needs of the people be supplied in a bad year but [that] there will be surpluses for export in ordinary years.

(Sierra Leone Agricultural Department, 1936)

By this time swamp rice cultivation and research were progressing swiftly. In 1930 a rice research station had been established, in 1937 the RAF conducted an aerial survey of swamp distribution and in 1939 the Protectorate Mining Benefits Fund (PMBF) contributed £500 towards swamp clearance.

Environmental degradation, 1939–61

Reports on environmental degradation in Sierra Leone were non-existent during the Second World War but after the war attention focused on soil degradation in the mountainous areas with high population pressure and in grazed savanna and edaphic grasslands. Farming had encroached into the forest reserves of the Freetown Peninsula and the Kambui Hills in the late 1930s (GOSL, 1938). Grass burning was recognised as a problem on the Guinea border, where pastoralists burnt grass in the late dry season to encourage new growth with the first rains. This was environmentally unsound as the highly erosive first rains fell on bare, burnt soils resulting in severe erosion.

The national awareness of soil degradation was high at this time and

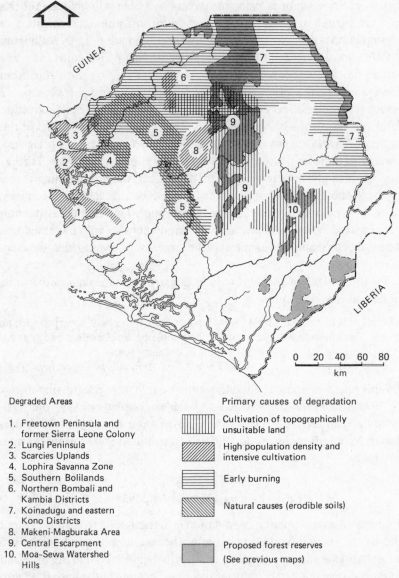

Degraded Areas

1. Freetown Peninsula and
   former Sierra Leone Colony
2. Lungi Peninsula
3. Scarcies Uplands
4. Lophira Savanna Zone
5. Southern Bolilands
6. Northern Bombali and
   Kambia Districts
7. Koinadugu and eastern
   Kono Districts
8. Makeni-Magburaka Area
9. Central Escarpment
10. Moa-Sewa Watershed
    Hills

Primary causes of degradation

Cultivation of topographically
unsuitable land

High population density and
intensive cultivation

Early burning

Natural causes (erodible soils)

Proposed forest reserves
(See previous maps)

Fig. 11.2. Sierra Leone: Land use and Soil Conservation Survey, 1950 (after
Waldock, et al., 1951).

in 1950 a land-use and soil conservation survey was commissioned (Waldock, Capstick & Browning, 1951). The major results were the identifi-
cation and mapping of degraded areas and the examination of the major
causes of soil degradation. Ten degraded areas were identified (Fig. 11.2).
Three of these areas had been recognised prior to the survey – the

Freetown Peninsula, the Moa–Sewa Watershed Hills, and the savanna area in Koinadugu and Kono Districts. In the other seven areas, the emergence of soil degradation was attributed to four primary causes: farming on topographically unsuitable land (mainly dissected mountains); intensive farming due to high population densities and nearby markets; early dry-season grass burning; and unspecified natural causes, which on the basis of recent research (Millington, 1985) are related to erodible soils. Specific aspects of the upland farming system were seen as major causal factors (Waldock *et al.*, 1951). Of greatest importance were bush fallow periods of less than five years, particularly in the north and in hill areas where grass fallows had replaced bush fallows; two- and three-year cropping leading to serious erosion under second and third year cassava, *fundi* and groundnuts; and mound cultivation and down-contour ridging on cassava and sweet potato farms. Despite this, Waldock *et al.* (1951) concluded that shifting cultivation was the most appropriate upland farming system available to maintain fertility, but only under specific environmental conditions.

Agricultural policy and soil conservation, 1939–61

Although many agricultural policies were by this time related to swamp rice production, concern over soil conservation was indicated by the formation of the Standing Committee on Soil Erosion, the introduction of anti-erosion methods at Njala Agricultural College, and the establishment of integrated swamp and upland demonstration farms (Sierra Leone Agricultural Department, 1940, 1941). The major conservation effort immediately after the Second World War was the creation of soil conservation areas (SCAs) by tribal ordinance. In 1944 farming was restricted to the lower slopes of the Kambui Hills and lowland grass burning was controlled in Nongowa Chiefdom (Sierra Leone Agricultural Department 1945). Further SCAs were established between 1946 and 1948 (Fig. 11.3). All but Nongowa focused on grass-burning management, yet only four were established in the Guinea border region where this problem had initially been identified.

Research into permanent upland cultivation systems; particularly examining fallow quality improvement, the introduction of quick-growing tree species and leguminous cover crops, and intercropping, was revived at this time. The results dispelled some of the illusions about fertility and yields under shifting cultivation (Millington, 1987; Richards, 1985) and prompted the Agricultural Department to revise its earlier thoughts on shifting cultivation, coming to the realisation that:

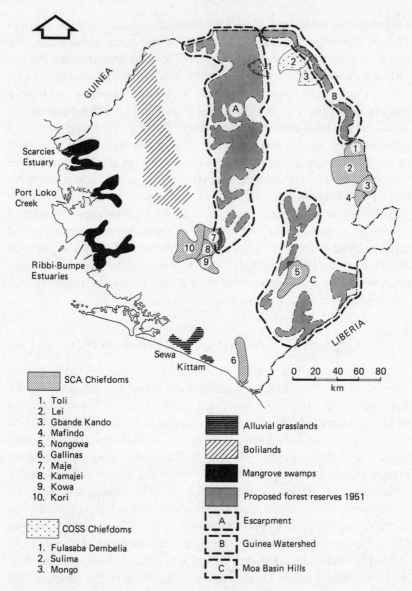

Fig. 11.3. Sierra Leone: conservation initiatives, 1944–62.

. . . it may be less a device of barbarism than a concession to the characteristics of a soil which needs long periods of recovery and regeneration.

(Sierra Leone Agricultural Department, 1948)

This renewed emphasis on upland cultivation can be seen as an outgrowth of the revived populist arguments concerning West African agriculture stimulated by the reports of the West African Commission in 1948 (Richards, 1985).

If it can be said that the major post-war research effort was focused on the uplands, then it must also be said that the major policy developments were in swamp rice cultivation. The Second World War saw a further loss of agricultural labour and an increased rice demand exacerbated by an influx of soldiers to Freetown. In response, the PMBF increased loans for mangrove swamp clearance. An Irrigation and Drainage Branch of the Department of Agriculture was established in 1941–2, and in 1943 a 'Grow More Swamp Rice Campaign' was initiated. By 1945, 13,550 acres of mangrove swamp and 10,480 acres of inland valley swamp had been cleared for rice cultivation, mostly subsidised by the PMBF and funds provided under the Colonial Development and Welfare Act (Sierra Leone Agricultural Department, 1948). Swamp clearance continued after the war, particularly in Bonthe and Moyamba Districts, as many of the paid workers did not return to the agricultural sector, and presumably because the government felt that swamp rice might provide a future export crop. Yet by 1948 yields in some swamp areas had declined by 31 per cent, due to soil acidity and toxicity problems.

By 1950 the general agricultural situation had declined from one of relatively high activity in the immediate post-war years to a moribund state of affairs, and the 1950s were generally characterised by a rather *laissez-faire* attitude to environmental protection. The deceleration of activity during this period was due to a series of policy shifts epitomised by the Plan for the Economic Development of Sierra Leone (Childs, 1949). The *laissez-faire* attitude is exemplified by the failure to take up the recommendations of the 1951 survey (Waldock *et al.*, 1951), which proposed two major soil conservation strategies: an afforestation programme (Fig. 11.3) and rationalised bush fallow cultivation, along the lines of Taungya system in the Belgian Congo. These were given little recognition by the government. Afforestation was not implemented, probably due to the politically weak Forest Department and the large amounts of land and capital involved, while it is doubtful if the proposed modifications to the shifting cultivation system were socio-economically viable.

During the 1950s the *laissez-faire* attitude toward conservation continued alongside the well-established mechanised swamp rice and upland cash crop cultivation policies. The only new conservation policy adopted was the Cattle Owners Settlement Scheme (COSS) in northeast Sierra Leone. In 1952 the possibility of settling the nomadic Fula pastoralists was examined in the light of French Guinean experiences and a year

Table 11.2. *Evolution of the cattle owners settlement scheme 1953–62*

Year	Settlements registered	Settlements occupied
1953	17	14
1954	36	14
1955	37	33
1956	49	29
1957	63	57
1958[a]	110	86
1959	110	89
1960	109	86
1961	132	93
1962	134	86

[a] Until 1958 only two chiefdoms were included in the scheme, Fulasaba Dembelia and Sulima; after 1958 Mongo was also included.

Source: GOSL (1954–63).

later 17 settlements were demarcated. Stocking rates were set at one cow and follower per 2.8 ha, with a maximum of 100 cattle per settlement. Settlement boundaries were surveyed and marked, small earth dams were built to supply water for dry-season grazing maintenance and wet-season crop irrigation, and ox-ploughs were made available. Rental levels were fixed and the rent was divided between the landowner, tribal authority and Koinadugu District Council. Cattle owners had sole right to keep cattle on the land but during the dry season, when no crops were being grown, extensive grazing was allowed. Three chiefdoms, Fulasaba Dembelia, Sulima and Mongo were ultimately included in the scheme (Fig. 11.3) (UNDP/FAO, 1971), which expanded steadily throughout the 1950s (Table 11.2).

Environmental degradation, 1961–84

The newly independent Sierra Leone Government paid little attention to the state of the environment until the publication of the first National Development Plan 1974/5–1978/9 (1st NDP) (GOSL, 1974). The main areas of concern in the 1st NDP were the upland rice farms in heavy rainfall areas. Whilst there was general agreement amongst local ministerial staff and expatriate agriculturalists that soil degradation was a growing problem, it was recognised that the lack of a comprehensive environmental data base was hindering attempts to stimulate productive, environmentally sound agricultural development. Subsequently a reconnaissance survey of Sierra Leonean land resources was made between 1975 and 1980 (FAO, 1979). The findings were presented as land systems and crop suitability maps. It is difficult to obtain erosion assessments from the maps and consequently the FAO commissioned a short, but as yet unpublished, national soil erosion risk assessment in 1981. Soil erosion risks were simultaneously assessed by Millington (1985).

Agricultural policy and soil conservation, 1961–84

The immediate post-independence era saw a dramatic change of emphasis in government agricultural policy, from a research and advisory role to direct state involvement in agricultural production, particularly by the Sierra Leone Produce Marketing Board and the Rice Corporation. These projects were, on the whole, poorly planned and presented, were badly located and the quality of staff was generally poor; consequently crop yields were very low. Not surprisingly they attracted little external funding and direct state involvement in crop production was curtailed by the Military Government in 1967 (Spencer, 1981). Other developments in the period up to 1967 concentrated mainly on small agricultural modernisation schemes. The only large-scale agricultural policy to survive the transition to independence was the COSS. However, although many of the 124 settlements still exist, the scheme broke down during the early years of independence due to a series of misunderstandings by the pre-independence and early post-independence governments. This breakdown can be attributed to undercapitalisation, inadequate technical and veterinary services, unfavourable rental agreements, inadequate infrastructural improvement or maintenance by landowners and a lack of confidence in the supervisory personnel (UNDP/FAO, 1971). Unfortunately soil degradation was exacerbated in the settlements as a result of overstocking, due partly to the initially incorrect stocking rates and partly to a lack of planned herd expansion.

After the six year state involvement in production, the government retreated to small-scale producer encouragement policies. Important differences exist between the small-scale producer policies of the colonial era and those of the post-1968 era. The greatest contrast is that these latter policies have adopted an integrated approach (Spencer, 1981; Binns, 1982) in which great emphasis is placed on input supply provision and extension operations. Subsidised swamp rice development schemes, funded by the Diamond Corporation and the Ministry of Agriculture between 1967 and 1972, fall into this category. However, these schemes were poorly organised, had poor input delivery systems and were hampered by corruption. They were replaced by externally funded Integrated Agricultural Development Projects (IADPs) with greater credit facilities for farm inputs and better extension officer:farmer ratios.

Generally, the agricultural policies of the first thirteen years of independence have lacked coordination. None of these early projects were directly concerned with soil conservation, and the *laissez-faire* attitude towards soil conservation characteristic of the late colonial administration was continued. The 1st NDP has provided the only government policy statements relating to soil conservation since independence. It recognised the vital role of land resources in agricultural development:

Sierra Leone has reached a stage in its development where the rational utilisation of its land resources is essential for the accelerated growth of agricultural production.   *(GOSL, 1974)*

and as had already been shown, the formation of the Land Resources Survey Project was a direct result of it. Land conservation was mentioned as one of the eight objectives of agricultural policy but, as Spencer (1981) points out, the highest priorities were accorded to policy objectives of income distribution, generation and security.

Agricultural production and the contribution of the agricultural sector to the GDP were projected to increase during the period of the plan by public external and internal investment, almost half of which was directed to the relatively underdeveloped Northern Province. Swamp rice production featured strongly in the planned agricultural development of IADPs. Funding for these projects initially came from the IDA, while other bilateral and multilateral agencies were heavily committed to funding other aspects of the renewed push towards swamp rice cultivation. This large influx of funding covered the previously undercapitalised areas of research and extension work that had hitherto hampered the expansion of swamp rice cultivation.

Soil conservation programmes have not been a significant feature of the IADPs, even though in the subsequent phases of these projects the agricultural emphasis has shifted towards a more balanced and rational use of both uplands and swamps. The Eastern and Northern IADPs, which were established prior to the publication of the FAO land resource assessments in 1979, could argue that soil erosion risks could not be evaluated due to the lack of baseline data. Yet despite the availability of these data since 1979, other projects, with the exception of the Magbosi IADP (Millington, 1982a), have not assessed erosion risks or formulated soil conservation programmes. It must be concluded that, whilst agricultural personnel in Sierra Leone realise the magnitude of the erosion problem (GOSL, 1974), the political and economic arguments have not been strong enough to convince the Ministry of Agriculture and Forestry that the adoption of an effective national soil conservation programme is a prerequisite to sustained agricultural production.

Discussion and analysis

Various soil conservation strategies have been evident in Sierra Leonean agricultural and forestry policy during the last century. Very few of these policies have promoted the implementation of particular mechanical or biological strategies: rather, they have placed spatial and temporal restrictions on agriculture. Furthermore, covert soil conservation motives have been implicit in the long-term shift from upland rice cultivation to swamp rice cultivation.

The majority of specific soil conservation planning has been spatially-restrictive in zoning cultivated and non-cultivated areas, on either an altitudinal or an areal basis. Why were these policies undertaken? Firstly, although the uplands were referred to as degraded environments, they have always been important cash crop production zones. After the formation of the Protectorate, competition for upland areas between cash cropping and shifting cultivation first became a problem. Successful restriction of shifting cultivation would have therefore released uplands for cash cropping, particularly oil palm production. Although the conservation ethic was used as the primary argument in agricultural planning, the greatest benefits from a successful conservation intervention would have accrued to the cash crop economy. A major problem with spatially-restrictive conservation planning has been the reluctance of people to move, especially where the incentives to relocate farms are not perceived as beneficial, making such decisions both ecologically and socially marginal. The promotion of earlier grass burning, which can be classified as a temporally-restrictive conservation policy, was more successful than many other measures. However, it was a secondary affect of this policy, the production of better quality dry-season grazing, which was of greater benefit to the pastoralists and consequently led to the successful adoption of the policy.

General problems relating to conservation policy formulation and adoption in Sierra Leone can also be identified. Firstly, conservation policies have been characterised by apathetic attitudes towards implementation. This is manifest in the constantly changing policies which are difficult for farmers with limited resources to adapt to. Once a farmer adopts a particular conservation strategy it is difficult to change it a few years later. This argument assumes greater potency where significant time-lags between planting and income generation exist, such as in tree-crop cultivation. Additionally, an element of mistrust must surely be generated in these circumstances. Secondly, the level of policy implementation has been controlled by spatial funding biases and general undercapitalisation. This was partly due to the policy of making the Colony and Protectorate self-financing, which meant that the colonial state had little money available for conservation works. The best funded conservation measures have been the loan schemes for swamp clearance and land preparation. Other schemes were poorly financed, usually only at district or chiefdom level. A third problem concerns agricultural personnel and poor extension facilities. This is partly due to the low status afforded to agricultural work but also to poor pay and lack of adequate training and support facilities. Conservation planning can only be effectively implemented by an adequately trained, well-supported extension corps. A fourth factor affecting policy implementation is conservation education. Field trials and demonstrations have been used on a number of occasions to demonstrate conservation measures to farmers. Yet general levels of agricultural education, particularly in rural schools, are inadequate, inappropriate and need to be upgraded.

The most recent assessments of soil erosion (Millington, 1985) show that erosion hazards are generally high in Sierra Leone. Therefore it can reasonably be argued that these soil conservation policies have been relatively unsuccessful and, furthermore, despite the repetitious declamation against traditional shifting cultivation since 1909, it still remains the dominant food production system. Soil degradation in the early twentieth century was seen as a consequence of the widely practised traditional shifting cultivation of rain-fed upland rice. Recognition of the intrinsic value of the shifting cultivation systems was extremely rare during the colonial era. In the light of recent work (Millington, 1984; Richards, 1985) this can be seen as a major error which has continually dogged the effectiveness of conservation policies in Sierra Leone. The lack of criticism of shifting cultivation that continued until the late 1940s stifled attempts to conduct agricultural research into it. After this the government partially accepted that swamp rice cultivation had not stopped upland shifting cultivation and research was reinitiated in upland cultivation. Upland cultivation research has continued until the present time but, until the late 1960s, was grossly undercapitalised and concentrated on agricultural modernisation. A parallel research theme since the late 1970s has been examination of the local upland cultivation system as a basis for agricultural development in Sierra Leone. Recent studies (Millington, 1982b, 1984) have examined the formulation and adoption of indigenous soil conservation techniques in the absence of effective government soil conservation policies. Field trials have shown that these techniques are well adapted to both the socio-economic and environmental constraints facing small-scale agriculture in Sierra Leone.

The conclusions that can be drawn from this analysis of the response of government soil conservation policy to economic development focus on two questions: First, have government conservation policies been effective in reducing soil degradation or have they exacerbated the problems? Second, have soil conservation policies been assigned a primary role in Sierra Leonean agricultural policy? Successive surveys since 1909 have shown that soil degradation is a serious threat to sustained agricultural production in Sierra Leone: whether the situation is declining is far more difficult to establish. One obstacle in examining long-term trends in soil degradation rates has been that all of the surveys have been based on qualitative observations. A second is that as our knowledge of soil erosion processes has expanded, our awareness of the spatial distribution of soil erosion has also increased and, therefore, different surveys show different erosion patterns. The latest assessment (Millington, 1985) shows generally high erosion severity in the northern half of the country, an observation which concurs with those made earlier by Waldock *et al.* (1951). Undoubtedly, soil erosion *is* an important problem in Sierra Leone.

The key to answering the first question lies in examining government responses to the results of these surveys. The 1909-11, 1951 and 1979 surveys were preceded by increased environmental awareness (Millington, 1986). Between 1895 and 1909 this was motivated by a need to assess the economic potential of the Protectorate. This was done through forestry policies, as was the case in many East African colonies, and based on Indian experience in the nineteenth century. Similar motivation led to the formation of the Land Resources Survey in the late 1970s. However, the period prior to the 1951 survey was different in that before, and immediately after, the Second World War there was growing awareness of the severity of the erosion problems in Sierra Leone. This was partly generated by American experiences during the dust bowl of the preceding decade. There were also problems facing the post-war Colonial administration in meeting food demand. This survey can therefore be seen as a joint response to the need for increased food production and environmental concerns. What of the periods after these surveys? After the early forest surveys the responses were rapid. A Forestry Department was established and a short-lived afforestation programme implemented:

the responses of the Agriculture Department were, not surprisingly, muted. The recommendations of the 1951 survey were not implemented. It can be argued, then, that neither of these surveys generated effective long-term soil conservation programmes. However, not all conservation measures were implemented after national surveys (e.g. the establishment of SCAs between 1945 and 1948), although all have been formulated during periods of increased environmental awareness (Millington, 1986).

It is possible, then, to identify three phases of increased environmental awareness in Sierra Leone during which soil conservation policies were formulated.

(i)   *c.*1900 to 1920–5, reaching a peak between 1910 and 1915;
(ii) *c.*1937 to 1960, interrupted by the Second World War and reaching a peak between 1945–51;
(iii) *c.*1975 to the present.

Each of these phases was heralded and concluded by important political events. The first period began soon after the Protectorate had been formed and concluded when the Agriculture and Forestry Departments were amalgamated. The second period is more complex, but much of the activity is attributable to a generally increased level of concern in the Colonial agricultural administration with soil degradation, prompted by the American Dust Bowl. These initiatives lost momentum in the late 1940s and new initiatives prompted by the Childs Plan initiated conservation efforts which culminated around about Independence. The third period was initiated after the 1st NDP and the growing recognition of the role of soil resources during and after the Sahelian Drought of the early 1970s.

In conclusion then, soil conservation policies have not really exacerbated soil erosion in Sierra Leone, but due to their ineffectiveness have done little to ameliorate its effects. All of the policies used in Sierra Leone can be categorised as top–down approaches in which government policy has been implicit in conservation strategy formulation and policies have been ineffective due to the reasons outlined previously. However, part of the problem also lies in the lack of understanding of rain-fed rice cultivation. The recent emphasis placed on this by researchers in Sierra Leone has shown that bottom–up approaches, based on improved traditional farming techniques, have a greater chance of successful implementation than government policy directives (Millington, 1984; Richards, 1985). Soil conservation policies have been minor objectives within broader agricultural policies in Sierra Leone over the past century. Without a fundamental commitment to soil conservation as an integral component of future agricultural policy, the probability of effective long-term conservation strategies being implemented is negligible.

Notes

1 Correspondence from D. Prain to Royal Botanic Gardens, Kew, 10 December 1917.
2 Correspondence from Conservator of Forests to Colonial Secretary, FD 30/1918.
3 These figures were agreed in a series of letters between the Conservator of Forests and the Colonial Secretary FD38 of 14 April 1918, 26 April 1918 and FD37/1918 of 22 May 1918.
4 Correspondence from Colonial Secretary to Conservator of Forests. Ag 45/1917 of 18 February 1918.
5 This correspondence is in the form of letters. Letters from Governor to the Colonial Office on 9 August 1917 (which includes letters from Mr D.W. Scotland to the Governor and Ministerial Paper FD 31/1916, no. 22 of 15 January 1917); 10 August 1917 (including a report from the Director of Agriculture); 10 October 1917 and letters from Mr D.W. Scotland to the Governor on 9 August 1917 and subsequent correspondence.

References

ANDERSON, D.M. (1984). Depression, Dust Bowl, Demography and Drought: the Colonial State and Soil Conservation in East Africa during the 1930s. *African Affairs*. **83** (332): 321–43.

BEINART, W. (1984). Soil erosion, conservationism, and ideas about development in Southern Africa. *Journal of Southern African Studies*. **11** (2): 52–83.

BERRY, L. & TOWNSHEND, J. (1971). Soil conservation policies in the semi-arid region of Tanzania: an historical perspective. *Geografiska Annaler*, **54A**, 241–53.

BINNS, J.A. (1982). Agricultural change in Sierra Leone. *Geography*, **67**, 113–25.

CHILDS, H. (1949). *A Plan For The Economic Development of Sierra Leone*. Freetown: Govt Printer.

FAO (1979). *Land in Sierra Leone: A reconnaissance survey and evaluation for agriculture*. Technical Report 1, FAO/UNDP LRSP. Freetown: FAO.

GOVERNMENT OF SIERRA LEONE [GOSL] (1909). *Reports of Forest Authority of Sierra Leone at British Empire Forestry Conference*. Sessional Paper 7, Freetown: Govt Printer.

GOVERNMENT OF SIERRA LEONE [GOSL] (1938). *Agricultural Possibilities of the Colony Peninsula*. Sessional Paper 8, Freetown: Govt Printer.

GOVERNMENT OF SIERRA LEONE [GOSL] (1974). *National Development Plan 1974/5–1978/9*. Central Planning Unit, Ministry of Development & Economic Planning. Freetown: Govt Printer.

LANE-POOLE, C.E. (1911). *Report on the Forests of Sierra Leone*. Freetown: Govt Printer.

MILLINGTON, A.C. (1982a). *Soil erosion hazard and farmer conservation strategies in the Magbosi IADP*. Report to the Project Monitoring and Evaluation Services Unit, Freetown, Sierra Leone.

MILLINGTON, A.C. (1982b). Soil conservation techniques for the Humid Tropics. *Appropriate Technology*, **9**, 17–8.

MILLINGTON, A.C. (1984). Indigenous soil conservation studies in Sierra Leone. In *Challenges in African Hydrology*, International Association of Hydrologists Publication 144, 529–38.

MILLINGTON, A.C. (1985). Soil erosion and agricultural land-use in Sierra Leone. Unpublished D.Phil. thesis, University of Sussex.

MILLINGTON, A.C. (1986). Conservation consciousness: How the pendulum has swung in Sierra Leone. In *Sierra Leone Studies at Birmingham, Proceedings of the 4th Sierra Leone Studies Symposium*, ed. P.K. Mitchell & A. Jones.

MILLINGTON, A.C. (1987). *Environmental Degradation, Soil Conservation and Agricultural Policies in Sierra Leone, c.1500–1985*. University of Sussex: Dept of Geography Research Papers.

RICHARDS, P. (1985). *Indigenous Agricultural Revolution*. London: Hutchinson.

ROBINSON, D.A. (1978). *Soil Erosion and Soil Conservation in Zambia: A Geographical Appraisal*. Occasional Study 9, Zambia Geographical Association, Lusaka.

ROBINSON, D.A. (1981). A critical review of soil conservation policies and their implementation in Zambia, 1940–74. University of Sussex: Dept of Geography Research Papers.

SIERRA LEONE AGRICULTURAL DEPARTMENT (1912–48). *Annual Reports*. Freetown: Govt Printer.

SIERRA LEONE FORESTRY DEPARTMENT (1911–9). *Annual Reports*. Freetown: Govt Printer.

SIERRA LEONE LANDS & FORESTS DEPARTMENT (1923–5). *Annual Reports*. Freetown: Govt Printer.

SIERRA LEONE PROTECTORATE AGRICULTURE DEVELOPMENT BRANCH (1906). *Annual Report*. Freetown: Govt Printer.

SPENCER, D.S.C. (1981). Rice policy in Sierra Leone. In *Rice in West Africa*, ed. S.R. Pearson, J.D. Styker & C.P. Humphreys, 175–200. Stanford: Stanford University Press.

SPITZER, L. (1975). *The Creoles of Sierra Leone: responses to colonialism 1870–1945*. Ile-Ife, Nigeria: University of Ife Press.

STOCKING, M. (1983). Farming and environmental degradation in Zambia: the human dimension. *Applied Geography*, **3**, 63–77.

UNDP/FAO (1971). *Integrated Development of the Agricultural Sector, Sierra Leone: The Livestock Industry*. ESE:SF/SIL 3, Technical Report 5. Freetown: UNDP/FAO.

UNWIN, A.H. (1909). *Report on the Forests and Forest Problems in Sierra Leone*. Freetown: Govt Printer.

WALDOCK, E.A., CAPSTICK, E.S. & BROWNING, A.J. (1951). *Soil Conservation and Land Use in Sierra Leone*. Sessional Paper 1 of 1951. Freetown: Govt Printer.

12

Managing the forest: the conservation history of Lembus, Kenya, 1904–63

DAVID ANDERSON

In colonial Africa, as elsewhere, conservation has invariably been linked to the dynamics of political life. The colonial state in Africa set down the parameters within which conservation policies were defined. Attitudes to the African environment evolved as the colonial period progressed, and conservation accordingly took on new forms and new roles. Although historians have been able to mark out 'conservation eras', to monitor the rise of public awareness of particular issues, and to chart the emergence of technical expertise in the general field of conservation management, they have also stressed the conflicts of interest present at every phase of the evolution of conservation policies (Powell, 1976; McCracken, 1982; Anderson, 1984; Beinart, 1984; Ofcansky, 1984; Helms & Flader, 1985; Anderson & Millington, 1987). This chapter takes up these themes in an examination of the colonial history of conservation in the Lembus Forest of Kenya.

Lembus was awarded to a commercial company for the development of a timber industry while the British conquest of the region was still incomplete. It was one of the largest and most favourable land concessions made to Europeans in Kenya. The subsequent administration of this concession, and the political battles that ensued for control over the management of Lembus, are the central concern of this chapter. The political struggle that emerged was three-sided, between Africans who wished to continue to utilise the resources of the forest, the commercial company who wished to exploit the forest without interference, and the colonial Forest Department, who sought to control and conserve the forest in order to maintain a financial return while also sustaining the forest resource. Events in Lembus serve to illustrate the manner in which political considerations weighed heavily upon government attitudes towards land use and conservation. Contradictions between private and public interests were clearly exposed in the problems of managing the Lembus Forest, and exacerbated by the need to reconcile the often conflicting aims of commerce and conservation.

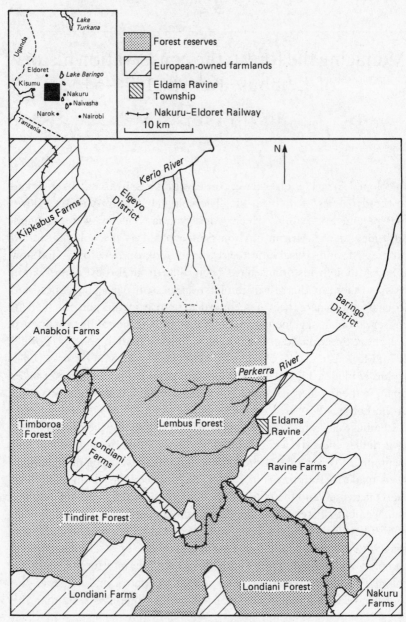

Fig. 12.1. Lembus Forest.

The Lembus Forest

The Lembus Forest covers an area of approximately 130 sq.ml. (see Figure 12.1). It is made up variously of valuable economic forest land, some scrub and bush areas, and a large number of glades. The glades, varying from 30 to 300 acres in size, offer valuable upland grazing to herders inhabiting the surrounding lowlands. Large areas of the forest-proper are dense, consisting mainly of Podo and Cedar woods, with considerable quantities of bamboo on the higher parts. Although earlier estimates had been consistently more optimistic (Johnston, 1902; Eliot, 1905), surveys completed in the 1950s revealed that around 55 per cent of Lembus then comprised economic forest, which might be reserved and exploited as such.[1] Aside from commercial aspects, the management of the ecosystem of Lembus has far-reaching importance for adjoining areas, the forest lying across the watershed dividing the river systems of the Rift Valley and western Kenya. The Perkerra River, which feeds Lake Baringo, rises in Lembus, as do several important tributaries of the Kerio River (Hutchins, 1909; Hughes, 1949; Kenya, 1950; ALDEV, 1962).

From the human aspect, a number of different groups have made use of the forest in the recent past. Uasin Gishu Maasai, Nandi, Elgeyo and Tugen peoples have each made seasonal or irregular use of the forest resources, gathering forest produce for themselves, using the forest glades to graze their animals, and clearing and cultivating areas of scrub-land on the forest fringes. Various Africans have taken up residence in the forest including a small number of Dorobo (Blackburn, 1974). To them all the forest has had considerable strategic importance, and all were in some senses dependent upon access to it (Matson, 1972; Anderson, 1982; Waller, 1985). The forest was not, then, a 'tribal' land during the colonial period (or previously). Rather, it was a zone of ethnic indeterminance, over which no single group exercised exclusive control. As we shall see, the demands of colonial administration helped to bring this situation to an end, with the Tugen of Baringo District asserting their dominance over the forest.

Commerce and conservation

The forests of the Mau, Nandi Plateau, and the slopes of Mt Elgon contain hundreds of thousands of magnificent conifers – juniper and yew. The timber of the juniper is to all intents and purposes like cedar-wood. The mere thinning of these woods which is necessary for their improvement, and which might be carried out concurrently with the establishment of European settlements, would provide millions of cubic feet of timber, which would find a ready market on the east coast of Africa.   *(Johnston, 1902: 291–2)*

Sir Harry Johnston's description of the potentials of forestry was typical of the optimism that brought European settlers to East Africa in the early years of this century. Seldom substantiated by anything more than the passing glance of the traveller's eye, large tracts of East Africa were heralded as being rich in the resources that, with some initial investment, could support a new white settler colony. Among the greatest supporters of this view of the future was the High Commissioner for East Africa from 1900 to 1904, Sir Charles Eliot. Aware that investment on a large scale would be necessary to establish the new colony on a sound footing, Eliot used his position to encourage 'men of capital', by offering land concessions on highly favourable terms (Sorrenson, 1968). Among the early proposals this attracted was one for the establishment of a timber industry in the Lembus Forest. Responding enthusiastically to this proposition, Eliot pressed quickly ahead with the negotiations of a concessionary lease, without seeking advice from within his own Forest Department. By the time of Eliot's resignation in 1904, the government found itself committed to the granting of a substantial forestry concession to a small group of businessmen, with Canadian and South African connections, headed by Ewart Grogan.[2]

In his haste to secure forestry investment in the colony, Eliot had placed substantial powers in the hands of the concessionaires, largely ignoring the requirements of the Forest Department and giving government very little control over the working of the concession. The Forest Department now foresaw huge difficulties in administering any programme of reafforestation in Lembus under the terms of the lease, and bemoaned the loss of revenue that would attend the working of the concession at the extremely low royalties stipulated. From 1904 to 1916 the Forest Department conducted protracted negotiations with Major Grogan, the concessionaire, in a belated attempt to recoup the situation. Grogan naturally wished to retain the powers granted in the original agreement, and shrewdly maintained his position. The government found itself in an unpleasant predicament. While keen to encourage investment in the development of a timber industry, the government found that the forest concession lay at the centre of a tangled web of land dealings involving Grogan, none of which seemed to accrue any great benefit to the government or the colony. The most worrying of these was Grogan's claim to 100 acres of valuable wharfage at Kilindini Harbour, Mombasa, which had been secured by Grogan as part of the forest concession.

While Grogan traded one proposal against another, and the Forest Department pressed for a foreclosure of the lease, the government, aware of consequences broader than the considerations of the Forest Department, sought to find the best political accommodation.[3]

When the renegotiated lease was finally signed in March 1916, the considerations of good forestry practice were indeed sacrificed to bring a settlement that would encourage investment in the timber industry. Grogan won exceedingly favourable terms for his concession, not substantially altered from the original lease, giving him considerable advantages over other sawmillers in East Africa and leaving his operations in Lembus largely beyond the control of the Forest Department.[4]

The Conservator of Forests was appalled by the freedom given to the concessionaire under the terms finally agreed.[5] The reasons for his outrage were partly commercial and partly conservationist. Colonial forestry in Kenya, as throughout British Africa, was initially modelled on the example of India (Unwin, 1920; Stebbing, 1937). During the second half of the nineteenth century Indian forestry had been established on a sound commercial base, raising revenue for government while also being able to finance extensive programmes of reafforestation (Stebbing, 1922). Forestry in India paid for itself, and from this position of strength gained support in government circles for a conservationist strategy that would ensure continued revenue surpluses. In short, commercial viability facilitated conservation. Indian-trained foresters were recruited to the African colonies in the hope of achieving the same result, but it became apparent that the lower yield of merchantable timber in the majority of African forests made it impossible to generate sustained revenue surpluses. Unable to realise their revenue raising potential, and in need of subsidy in order to mount programmes of reafforestation and preservation, Forest Departments came to be seen as a drain on the limited financial resources of the colonial state in Africa (Stebbing, 1941; Brasnett, 1942; Ofcansky, 1984). In these circumstances, the Lembus concession was particularly galling to the Kenya Forest Department. Not only was the Department being denied income because of the ludicrously low rates of royalties fixed under the lease, but the preservation work of the Department was being hampered by the manner in which Grogan's agents and contractors were exploiting the forest (Nicholson, 1931). To understand the attitude of the foresters we need to examine more closely the financial arrangements under the Lembus forest lease, and the working of the lease by the concessionaire.

An important feature of the early negotiations over the Lembus concession was the agreement that the normal royalties payable to government on all merchantable timber extracted from the forest would be set at a reduced rate. Therefore, despite the protests of the Conservator of Forests, the final agreement of 1916 set royalty payments at only two rupees per 100 cubic feet of timber, with an additional sum payable on each acre clear-felled. These rates were less than half those payable by sawmillers working other Kenyan forests. After 1919, when sawmilling concessions were granted only by competitive tender, the disparity between the terms operating in the Lembus concession and elsewhere in the colony became even more marked. In 1928, Grogan's sawmillers were paying only six cents per cubic foot of timber, while sawmillers elsewhere in Kenya paid 50 cents per cubic foot. Furthermore, Grogan's agents Equator Sawmills Ltd (ESM) paid a fixed annual licence fee of KShs 12,000/- (initially 6,000 rupees), against which royalty payments were offset. Timber to the royalty value of KShs 12,000/- had therefore to be felled before the Department saw any revenue on the timber extracted from the concession.[6] By the mid-1920s ESM were extracting more timber than all other Kenyan sawmillers put together, yet were paying considerably less for the privilege (Kenya Forest Department, 1919–28).

Forest Department antagonism towards ESM was deepened further by the suspicion that the company was infringing the already generous terms of its licence. The commercial working of the Lembus concession had begun prior to the First World War, but due to shortages of finance and staff, it was not until 1921 that the Forest Department began to monitor the activities of ESM (Kenya Forest Department, 1913–21). Even at this stage the only detailed map of the forest was held by Major Grogan, having been drafted by a surveyor in his employment in 1905. This gave the concessionaire a much clearer knowledge of the potential of the forest than had the Forest Department.[7] The unwillingness of ESM to furnish the Department with working plans for Lembus raised the suspicions of the Conservator of Forests, and by 1923 he had uncovered evidence of irregularities in ESM's calculation of royalties due and of areas clear-felled. Certainly, ESM were stretching the terms of the lease to their absolute limit in order to delay royalty payment and, seemingly, to avoid the supervision of the Forest Department. On their own admission, the policy of the company was 'to pick the eyes out of the forest', rather than to clear-fell.[8] Consequently, when the Department sought to reafforest areas that they believed ESM to have clear-felled, they invariably discovered that trees had been left standing. By claiming that these areas were not in fact clear-felled ESM avoided making any payment, while also preventing the Forest Department from getting on with its programme of reafforestation (under a clause that gave the company rights to re-enter any areas *not* clear-felled for a further 20 years after their original working).[9]

The Forest Department relentlessly pursued ESM over these practices throughout the 1920s, while pressing for the Attorney-General to declare foreclosure on the concession, in view of the company's infringements of the lease. As a result of this pressure, ESM were compelled to submit monthly returns on their activities in the forest, to settle outstanding royalties, and to hand over a number of clear-felled areas to the Department for replanting. But, while it was widely acknowledged by the late 1920s that the forest concession had been a serious error, the government was not prepared to challenge Major Grogan by attempting to terminate the agreement.[10] Further opportunities to terminate the lease occurred during the 1930s, as economic recession descended upon the timber trade and upon Kenya (Kenya Forest Department, 1930–34). Although the advantages of low royalties allowed the Lembus concessionaires to weather the depression better than their competitors, from 1933 financial difficulties prevented them from making full payment of the annual licence fee.[11] Non-payment of the licence fee was a specific clause under which government had power to terminate the lease, but wider political concerns again prevailed over the demands of the Forest Department: in the circumstances of the depression, the Kenya government was more intent on persuading businesses to remain in the colony than on seeking ways of expelling them. The Forest Department had succeeded in asserting a degree of control over the management of Lembus, yet one of Kenya's potentially richest forests continued to add only negligibly to the revenues of the Department (see Table 12.1).

While the commercial arrangements in the Lembus remained of grave concern to the Forest Department, the broader prospects for forest conservation improved considerably during the 1930s. Inspired by a variety of motives, public opinion in the colony became more conscious of the need for government to take an active role in implementing conservation measures (Anderson, 1984). With greater public attention focused upon questions of land use and environmental degradation, the Forest Department immediately benefited from the emphasis given to the importance of forest cover in relation to fears about soil erosion. Lively public debate on matters of conservation, much of it conducted through the newly formed Arbor Society, improved the image and status of the Forest Department, so that by the end of the 1930s opinion was very much in favour of stronger policies for forest protection (Ward, 1937; Anderson, 1982, 1984; Murray, 1982). These concerns were reflected in the promi-

Table 12.1 *Equator Sawmills Ltd: timber milled and royalty payments, 1912–36*

	Timber milled (cu.ft.)	Royalty payment (incl. licence fee)[a]
1912	56,450	6,000 rupee
1913	52,758	6,000 rupee
1914	143,166	6,000 rupee
1915	282,703	6,000 rupee
1916	151,175	6,000 rupee
1917	99,020	6,000 rupee
1918	90,701	6,000 rupee
1919	188,262	6,000 rupee
1920	176,926	6,000 florin
1921	222,186	13,313 sh
1922	462,249	14,103 sh
1923	47,590 [b]	12,000 sh
1924	121,111	12,000 sh
1925	223,260	14,467 sh
1926	397,148	25,150 sh
1927	582,102	36,163 sh
1928	475,279	30,363 sh
1929	548,723	33,594 sh
1930	498,239	30,500 sh
1931	167,809	12,000 sh
1932	83,324	12,000 sh
1933	111,600	12,000 sh
1934	109,357	12,000 sh
1935	?	12,000 sh
1936	?	12,000 sh

[a] From 1912 to 1920 the licence fee was 6,000 rupees p.a. In 1920 it was 6,000 florins, and from 1921 onwards it was 12,000 shillings p.a.
[b] The mills were shut down for part of 1923 because of a collapse in the timber market.
Source: Kenya National Archives, various Forest Department and Attorney-General files for the period 1902–39.

nent role played by the Forest Department in the rural development plans implemented after 1945, many of which were organised on the basis of catchment areas. One such scheme was centred on the Lembus Forest, at the head of the Perkerra River catchment. Protection of Lembus, and of the other forests around it, was accordingly given the highest priority in planning the future pattern of African land use and husbandry throughout the entire catchment. This gave the Forest Department the political authority after 1945 to exercise much greater control over commercial activities in Lembus (Kenya, 1950; ALDEV, 1962).

Table 12.2 *Kenya Forest Department: war-time revenue, 1938–45*

	Revenue (£)	Expenditure (£)	Surplus (£)
1938	41,550	31,323	10,227
1939	43,702	31,051	12,651
1940	57,170	30,800	26,370
1941	75,136	29,473	45,663
1942	119,020	36,608	82,412
1943	140,492	45,646	94,846
1944	142,079	60,920	81,159
1945	156,314	74,363	81,951

Source: Kenya Forest Department Annual Reports, 1938–47.

The enhanced status of the Forest Department was also bolstered in hard financial terms by the boom in timber trading during the Second World War. Timber production in the colony climbed from 19,750 Hoppus tons in 1938 to 116,500 Hoppus tons in 1945, and in the Lembus Forest alone a further six mills came into operation. Although this brief period of rampant exploitation left 'chaotic conditions' in many forests, the revenue gained by the Department was substantial (see Table 12.2) (Kenya Forest Department, 1945–7). Concern over forest conservation worked to strengthen the financial position of the Department at this time with the establishment of a Forestry Sinking Fund, an initiative unique to Kenya. Taking the surplus revenue raised for 1940 as the base line, all annual revenues raised by the Department above the 1940 figure were placed in the Sinking Fund, to be used to replenish and develop the forests exploited during the wartime boom. By the end of the war the Sinking Fund stood at over £300,000 (Gardner, 1942; Graham, 1945; Kenya Forest Department, 1945–7). The Forest Department was in a financially and politically healthy position for the first time, largely due to the emergence of broader concerns over environmental protection (Logie, 1962).

It might be said, then, that this marked the victory of the conservationist aims of the Forest Department over the commercial aims of the timber company. However, the important relationship between the successful commercial exploitation of the forest resource during the war and the subsequent implementation of improved forestry protection measures must be stressed. There was no necessary contradiction between commerce and conservation, so long as the foresters were able to utilise the former to achieve the latter. From the Forest Department's viewpoint, the Lembus Forest concession was undesirable because it made this difficult. After 1945 the operation of the lease continued, and although the controls enforced by the Department were improved they were still by no means complete. The reassertion of forest conservation in Lembus had only been made possible by a growing political will in government to protect the environment. But the conservation policies enforced as part of the post-war development effort in Kenya were not always greeted enthusiastically by the Africans on whose lives they impinged. As far as many Africans were concerned, conservation for the public good meant only the restriction of their private rights; rights to graze their animals, to cultivate, and to cut timber and fuelwood. Africans making use of the forest resources of Lembus were particularly energetic in defending those rights and it is this aspect of the conservation history of Lembus that we will now consider.

Conservation and African rights

The question of 'native rights' in Lembus had been raised during the early negotiations between the government and Major Grogan. The government was concerned to ensure that Africans living within the area of the concession would be permitted to continue to utilise the forest for their livelihood. As Major Grogan was of the opinion that the forest was 'virtually uninhabited', other than by a small number of Dorobo families, he raised no objection to a clause being included in the terms of the lease protecting the rights of these few 'traditional' forest dwellers (Kenya Land Commission, 1934).[12] However, during the final stages of the re-negotiation of the lease – June 1913 to March 1916 – dispute arose over the precise extent of such rights. A compromise was eventually agreed, that the Governor should, in the near future, 'be required to endeavour to ascertain and define the nature and extent of free grazing rights and other such customary rights as may have been exercised in the [forest] prior to the dates of the concession'.[13] This clause was not immediately acted upon, but once Grogan's agents began to work the forest more intensively it became apparent that the numbers of Africans occupying Lembus were much greater than had been supposed. While the timber contractors and the Forest Department shared the view that these were 'unauthorised persons' who should be removed from the forest, the District Administration at Eldama Ravine insisted that little could be done until a formal definition of native rights in the forest was proclaimed by the Governor.[14]

In December 1923, after a census of the forest had been conducted, Governor Coryndon issued his definition of native rights in Lembus.

This document, known as the Coryndon Definition, laid down eleven specific rights, including the rights to construct dwellings, to graze animals, to cultivate, and to gather forest produce. These rights were granted to all those Africans who were able to satisfy the administration that they had enjoyed rights within the forest 'according to native law and custom', prior to the initial signing of the lease. Appended to the Coryndon Definition was a full list of all African 'Right-Holders', as they now became known. The list was viewed with horror by both Major Grogan and the Forest Department, for it identified no fewer than 485 Tugen and 11 Dorobo right-holding families, and further stipulated that such rights were to be passed down to the descendants of each right-holder named. With the children of listed right-holders already numbering 650, and around 40 per cent of the adult males listed either unmarried or married but as yet without children, it was clear that the future management of the forest was going to be problematic.[15]

The Coryndon Definition remained a bone of contention throughout the colonial period. To the Africans of Lembus it was a charter of undeniable rights to be exercised in perpetuity; an absolute guarantee of their security in the forest. To the sawmillers and to the foresters it represented a serious hindrance to the economic and ecological management of the forest. The scene for political confrontation was set, with both the timber company and the Forest Department, though with differing motives, seeking to exploit other clauses in the lease to place firmer controls upon the right-holders and ultimately to press for new legislation that would override the terms of the Definition. There was also discontent among the Africans living on lands surrounding Lembus regarding the implications of the Definition, for by securing the rights of those families listed in the Coryndon Definition the Governor had effectively closed the forest to all others. From being a zone of ethnic indeterminance, the forest had become, *de jure*, the rightful home of a clearly defined section of the Tugen. Many other Tugen and Elgeyo who made periodic use of the forest, but were not listed as right-holders, now found themselves legally excluded from the forest.

This effective exclusion of the occasional and irregular users of the forest – mainly other Tugen and Elgeyo inhabiting lands adjacent to Lembus – came at a time when three related factors combined to make access to the resources of the forest increasingly important. Firstly, during the mid-1920s the administration completed the final demarcation of the Native Reserves, the parcels of land within which it hoped to confine each African group. African populations either remained resident in their designated Native Reserve, or took temporary labour contracts on European farms. These moves towards the establishment of boundaries and the control of the movement of Africans and their livestock across those boundaries served to accentuate the role of the forest as a place of refuge (Murray, 1982). Africans wishing to move livestock around from one area to another, and particularly those with labour contracts seeking to smuggle extra cattle onto European farmlands, did so under cover of the forests. Strategically placed at the heart of the White Highlands between several European farming areas, and coupled with the advantages of concealment and good grazing, the Lembus Forest became a particularly important entrepôt for Africans and their livestock. Secondly, between 1925 and 1936 a series of droughts affected the Baringo Plains, to the east of Lembus, and over the same period locust invasions damaged grazing in parts of the Elgeyo Reserve to the north of Lembus, and in southern Baringo (Anderson, 1984). Herders hard pressed for grazing in these areas made greater use of the forest glades, particularly during the dry seasons, and there is evidence that stockowners commonly 'loaned' animals to friends and relatives among the Lembus rightholders. At times of drought the forest was a crucial resource to pastoralists on the neighbouring plains (Anderson, 1982). Thirdly, in 1929 the colonial administration in Baringo initiated a programme for the reconditioning of pasture on the plains to the east of Lembus. This was prompted by anxieties over land degradation, believed to be caused by the overstocking of the area. The success of the reconditioning programme depended upon the restriction of the number of animals allowed back into reconditioned areas once the reseeding of pasture was complete. To accomplish this cattle counts had to be conducted, and attempts made to encourage the Tugen to accept the necessity of destocking. The Tugen herders naturally distrusted a process that seemed effectively to result in the enforced reduction of their livestock holdings. Their response was pragmatic. While their spokesmen accepted the pronouncements of the administration, each Tugen herder was busy depositing as many livestock as he could around his kinsmen in those locations as yet unaffected by reconditioning (Anderson, 1982). The Lembus Forest, with its population of right-holders, was the perfect destination for livestock displaced from southern Baringo by reconditioning schemes and the threat of destocking.

At a time when government policy was aimed at removing Africans from the forests, the legal residents of Lembus were therefore a striking anomaly. With right-holders legitimately entitled to graze cattle in the forest, it was difficult for the administration to detect the presence of cattle belonging to non-right-holders. Suspicion that the forest was heavily used in this way by non-right-holders was confirmed by occasional police raids, one such raid on Torongo Glade in 1929 uncovering more than 400 head of cattle herded illegally in the forest.[16]

All of this placed the Lembus right-holders in something of a predicament, for while the Coryndon Definition protected their status it also threatened the viability of the regional economy. The forest economy was based upon the cultivation of cereals within the forest, and the dynamics of movement between the forest glades and the surrounding lowland grazing areas. Forest grazing and forest cereals were critical dry-season reserves for the peoples over the surrounding region. Short-term (i.e. seasonal) and longer-term fluctuations in the utilisation of the forest could therefore be considerable, with forest resources being under greatest pressure during prolonged periods of drought. These were the conditions prevailing in the years following the Coryndon Definition, the enforcement of which implicitly demanded the breaking of economic linkages between the forest and its neighbouring areas. While the right-holders were happy to accept the guarantee of their security, they could not isolate themselves from the local economy. The influx of people and livestock into the forest throughout the 1930s were stimulated both by the importance of the forest within the regional economy, and by the privileged status enjoyed by the right-holders. The predicament this held for the right-holders was exposed towards the end of the 1930s, as the Forest Department mounted wider programmes for reafforestation and forest preservation.[17]

By the early 1930s regular complaints from ESM of shortages of grazing for their working oxen, and reports from the Forest Officer that the acreage under cultivation was steadily increasing, indicated that the Africans of Lembus were exploiting the Coryndon Definition to the full.[18] The efforts of the Forest Department to remedy this situation stirred the Tugen of Lembus into political action. Initially, Forest Officers simply tried to close parts of the forest to African grazing and cultivation, but the District Administration pointed out that this infringed the rights set out in the Coryndon Definition.[19] By 1938, strengthened by the growing conservation lobby in the colony, the Forest Department challenged the legality of the Definition by framing rules under the Forest Ordinance that gave them the power to restrict the numbers of animals in particular forest glades, control which areas could be cleared for cultivation, and remove people and livestock from areas where reafforestation programmes were to go ahead.[20] These measures were similar to regulations then being applied in other parts of Kenya in connection with soil conservation and grazing control, but once again the District Administration stepped in to uphold the special status of the Lembus right-holders. By this time theTugen of Lembus were well aware of the significance of the Coryndon Definition, and the administration were accordingly concerned that any attempt to curtail forest rights in Lembus would have serious political repercussions. These differences of opinion between the Forest Department and the District Administration were immediately apparent to the Tugen, who found that orders and advice from one wing of government were contradicted and countermanded by another. Skilfully playing one side against the other, the leaders of the Lembus Tugen were able to exploit the politics of conservation in the forest. Facing opposition from the District Administration, and hostility from the Tugen, the Forest Department was unable to implement its conservation programme in Lembus.[21]

This postponement was prolonged by the Second World War, during which non-right-holders enjoyed a further period of unhampered access to the forest. By 1946 the Lembus Tugen had taken advantage of the interregnum in administrative decision-making brought about by the war to organise themselves against the threat posed by the Forest Department. Two main issues had galvanised the right-holders towards a more organised defence of their position. The first concerned the failure of the Forest Department to provide shops, schools, medical dispensaries and other services within the forest, facilities for which the Lembus residents paid a supplementary tax. Because of the unwillingness of the Department to provide these services in the area worked under the concession, by the mid-1940s the right-holders still lacked *any* of the services that their taxes were supposed to pay for, and that were by then common in other African locations. This failure was deeply resented by the right-holders. The second issue concerned the arrangements to be made for Lembus on the termination of the forest lease in 1959. The right-holders were determined to avoid full control of the forest passing to the Forest Department, whose activities they now viewed as entirely hostile to their own interests. Also, the right-holders wished to ensure that their rights would be recognised beyond the expiry of the lease. These issues formed the basis of a campaign now initiated by the right-holders for the excision of the Lembus Forest from the forest reserve, to become part of Baringo District.[22]

To assert firmly their claim to Lembus, the Tugen right-holders embarked upon this campaign by exercising their rights in the forest to the full. Between 1945 and 1948 the 'alarming' increase in the level of cultivation in Lembus prompted the Forest Department to threatenTugen cultivators with prosecution under the 1941 Forest Ordinance. District Commissioner Simpson, again upholding the Coryndon Definition, thought this inadvisable. Commenting upon past arrangements made on an *ad hoc* basis by the Forest Department to prevent the right-holders from cultivating parts of the forest required for reafforestation, he noted that,

> . . . none of these arrangements has had the force of legal sanction behind them . . . Thus, to prosecute without being assured of a conviction and with acquittal resulting would, I am certain, open the eyes of the Tugen to the fact that they have been fooled for years, and that until rules are framed and made law, they can exercise their 'rights' indiscriminately to the detriment of the forest and to the loss of power behind administrative order.[23]

The Tugen right-holders were already aware that the government were hamstrung by the terms of the Coryndon Definition. In August 1948, Simpson again wrote warningly to the Forest Department: 'In view of the fact that the Tugen in the Lembus Forest intend to make a political issue of its future, it is essential that we proceed now strictly according to the law'.[24] But which law, the Forest Ordinance or the Coryndon Definition?

At this time the Forest Department came to play a more prominent role in the planning of rural development in Kenya, but ironically, just as forest preservation became central to government development plans, events in Lembus conspired to make the implementation of forest policies virtually impossible. From 1948 to 1951 the Tugen campaign gained momentum, culminating in May 1951 with the Lembus locational Council sending a petition on the matter directly to the Secretary of State. By this time the Lembus question had become embroiled in nationalist politics, with representatives of the leading African political party, the Kenya African Union (KAU), visiting the forest to speak at public meetings. The prospect of action by the Forest Department to enforce husbandry rules in Lembus 'stirring up the KAU' and contributing to serious unrest now seemed very real.[25] A census of the forest, completed in August 1951, did nothing to alleviate the administration's sense of impending doom: there were now no fewer than 920 legitimate right-holders and their families, 300 of whom actually resided outside the forest but still determinedly exercised their rights in Lembus. These people therefore exploited their status as right-holders to cultivate lands within the forest as well as lands in the neighbouring Native Reserve.[26]

With political tension mounting in Kenya throughout 1952 as the Mau Mau crisis unfolded, the administration were pushed into direct consultations with the Lembus Tugen in the hope of finding a political settlement. A 'Working Committee', with four African members was set up in August 1952 to solve the problems of the right-holders, but this came too late to salvage the Forest Department's conservation strategy for Lembus. The following month J. M. ole Tameno, an African Member of the Kenya Legislative Council, wrote formally to the Chief Native Commissioner, declaring his fear of 'genuine unrest' in Lembus, and accusing the government of giving 'twisting answers' to the Tugen to avoid telling the truth about their rights and about plans for the future of the forest. On 5 November 1952, only a fortnight following the Declaration of Emergency in Kenya, Tameno tabled a question in the Legislative Council on unrest in Lembus.[27] The political point was timely, for a recent ruling by the Solicitor-General, that the right-holders should be regarded as tenants-at-will, had given the Forest Department the necessary powers to override the Coryndon Definition and evict the Tugen from Lembus. However, the government were now very concerned to avoid confrontation in Lembus, and the legal victory of the Forest Department was lost amid the political realities of the situation. 'Whatever the legal position may now be', wrote the District Officer in 1952, 'even if we could evict these people, we have nowhere to put them'.[28]

With the legal solution they had so long struggled to achieve now denied them by the government's unwillingness to provoke further political unrest in Lembus, the Forest Department turned to ecological arguments. Backed by the African Land Development Board, the Forest Department insisted that to give way on husbandry rules in Lembus placed the whole development effort in the Perkerra catchment in jeopardy. By exercising their individual rights, the inhabitants of Lembus were accentuating erosion and degradation throughout the catchment.[29] This stand for strong conservation management in Lembus won the Forest Department many supporters, but only served to delay the now inevitable decision to find a practical and workable political solution to the Lembus problem. Although the forest was seriously overcrowded, and the lands to the east in Baringo were badly overgrazed, it was clear that none of the right-holders would meekly accept eviction from the forest. Political expediency prevailed over ecological considerations.

At a meeting of all sections of the administration involved in Lembus, held in March 1956, the Forest Department was finally forced to face the harsh political reality. The meeting accepted the Tugen's historical claim to Lembus, emphasising that current political aspects were 'most important' in evaluating the situation. Thus, the Tugen had successfully 'tribalised' the Lembus Forest. It was therefore agreed that control of the forest should revert to the Baringo African District Council upon the termination of the Grogan concession in 1959, as 'any other course of action would meet with the bitterest opposition from the whole tribe and might well require a levy force to impose government orders upon the people'. In other words, it was felt that Forest Department husbandry rules could only be applied by coercion. More generally, it was recognised that to destock the forest glades and to control excessive cultivation and deforestation, would be 'well nigh impossible' without accommodating the wishes of the people. The victory of the right-holders was complete.[30]

Conclusion

Although the granting of the Grogan concession shaped the history of Lembus in a unique way, the subsequent experience of the Kenya Forest Department in their attempts to manage the forest offers a striking illustration of the conflicts between indigenous forest users, commercial forestry, and the aims of forest conservation. Lacking the necessary influence in political decision-making before the late 1940s, the requirements of the Forest Department were overlooked firstly in the granting of the forest lease, and then in the definition of native rights within the forest. While these decisions made the management of the forest difficult, it was the growth of the African political opposition to the implementation of broader colonial regulations governing land use that marked the final defeat for the Forest Department's policies in Lembus. The determination of the colonial government to transform African husbandry after 1945 was stimulated and justified by the aims of conservation (Cliffe, 1972; Anderson, 1984; Throup, 1985). With the deeply rooted history of conflict over the rights of Africans in the forest, it is hardly surprising that Lembus should have become the focal point of political opposition to colonial conservation policies. In many respects the political victory of the Tugen in defending their rights in Lembus should be applauded, but it should also be noted that conservation was, by default, a casualty of this struggle. Conservation measures advocated by colonial governments were often stigmatised in the eyes of Africans, creating a resistance to the enforcement of land husbandry rules that the governments of independent Africa have found it difficult to overcome. The failures of colonial conservation have sometimes left a powerful and undesirable legacy.

Notes

1   G.S. Cowley, 'Memorandum on Agricultural Aspects of the main Forest-free areas of the Lembus Forest', Kenya National Archives (KNA) PC/ NKU/2/1/31.

2   Eliot to Grant, 8 February 1904; Hill to Eliot, 25 April 1904; Linton (Conservator of Forests), 'Lease for Timber Cutting at Ravine', May 1904;

Grogan to Eliot, 2 June 1904; and 'Original Licence for Lembus Forest Concession', 15 July 1904, all in KNA AG 4/2313.

3   Crown Advocate, 'Memo, on the Lingham and Grogan Timber concession', 11 October 1910, and other correspondence in KNA AG 4/2313.

4   Acting Conservator of Forests to Attorney-General, 3 November 1920, 'Copy of Forest Lease, 1 March 1916', and related correspondence KNA AG 4/2313.

5   Conservator of Forests to Senior Commissioner/Kerio, 31 July 1925, KNA ARC(FOR) 7/2/128, for a summary of the Department's criticisms of ESM.

6   'Report of the Select Committee of the Legislative Council appointed to consider Forest Royalties', 1919, KNA AG 4/919; Crown Advocate to Acting Chief Secretary, 23 April 1912 and Conservator of Forests to Attorney General, 3 November 1920, both KNA AG 4/2313; Nicholson to Colonial Secretary, 2 February 1928, KNA ARC(FOR) 7/2/128, Kenya's currency was counted in rupees until 1920, and in shillings and cents from 1921.

7   'ESM Ltd Forest Concession', unsigned, 1923, KNA AG 4/2332. Tannahill to Commissioner of Lands, 20 January 1921, and Acting Chief Secretary to Commissioner of Lands, 10 March 1921, both KNA ARC(FOR) 7/2/128.

8   ESM to Conservator of Forests, 26 February 1924, and Conservator of Forests to Senior Commissioner/Kerio, 31 July 1925, both in KNA ARC(FOR) 7/2/128.

9   'Grogan Forest Licence – Royalty Payments 1920–9', KNA ARC(FOR) 7/2/127; 'Grogan Forest Licence, 1921–8', KNA ARC(FOR) 7/2/128; 'Equator Saw Mills, 1923–9', KNA ARC(FOR) 7/1/41 II.

10   Grigg to Amery (Secretary of State), 12 November 1925, KNA ARC(FOR) 7/2/128; Governor's Deputy to Secretary of State, May 1926; Conservator of Forests to Tannahill (ESM), 25 July 1924; and Monthly Returns, 1924–9, all KNA ARC(FOR) 7/1/41 II.

11   'Grogan Forest Licence – Timber Payments, 1931–6', KNA ARC(FOR) 7/2/129.

12   E.M. Hyde-Clarke, 'Lembus Forest: Appreciation of the Position', 28 July 1938, KNA PC/NKU/2/1/31.

13   'Copy of Forest Lease, 1 March 1916', KNA AG 4/2313.

14   'ESM Ltd Forest Concession', 1923, KNA AG 4/2332.

15   Governor Coryndon, 'Definition of Native Rights', 12 December 1923, KNA PC/NKU/2/1/31.

16   E.M. Hyde-Clarke, 'Lembus Forest', 28 July 1938, KNA PC/NKU/2/1/31.

17   H.J.A. Rae(Forester), 'Lembus Right-Holders', 29 July 1938, and E.M. Hyde-Clarke, 'Lembus Forest', 28 July 1938, both KNA PC/NKU/2/1/31.

18   Londiani Forest Division Reports, 1931–6, KNA ARC(FOR)7/1/1 II.

19   H.J.A. Rae (Forester), 'Lembus Right-Holders', 29 July 1938, KNA PC/NKU/2/1/31.

20   Conservator of Forests to PC/Rift Valley, 11 April 1938, and PC/Rift Valley to DC/Baringo, 30 October 1940, both PC/NKU/2/1/31.

21   E.M. Hyde-Clarke, 'Lembus Forest', 28 July 1938, and H.J.A. Rae, 'Lembus Right-Holder', 29 July 1938, both KNA PC/NKU/2/1/31.

22   A.B. Simpson, 'Lembus Forest Area', 19 July 1949, KNA NKU/2/1/31; Denton (DO/Baringo) to Forest Officer/Londiani, 8 September 1952, KNA PC/NKU/2/13/3.

23   A.B. Simpson to Forester/Londiani, 19 May 1948, KNA PC/NKU/2/1/31.

24   A.B. Simpson to Forester/Londiani, 28 August 1948, KNA PC/NKU/2/1/31.

25   DC/Baringo to PC/Rift Valley, 13 May 1951, and DC/Baringo to Provincial Agricultural Officer/Rift Valley, 14 August 1951, both KNA PC/NKU/2/1/31.

26   PC/Rift Valley to Conservator of Forests, 22 May 1952, KNA PC/NKU/2/1/31.

27   J.M. ole Tameno to Chief Native Commissioner, 12 September 1952, and related correspondence, KNA PC/NKU/2/1/31.

28   DO/Eldama Ravine to DC/Baringo, 26 February 1952, and Solicitor General, 'Memo on Lembus', 15 November 1952, both KNA PC/NKU/2/1/31.

29   DO/Eldama Ravine to DC/Baringo, 26 February 1952; R.O. Hennings (ALDEV) to Colchester (Member for Forestry), 10 March 1956; PC/Rift Valley to Governor, 28 October 1955, all KNA PC/NKU/2/1/31. Graham (Acting Conservator of Forests) to Chief Native Commissioner, 17 September 1952, KNA PC/NKU/2/13/3.

30   'Minutes of meeting to consider the Future of the Lembus Forest', 24 February 1956, KNA PC/NKU/2/1/31.

References

ALDEV (1962). *African Land Development in Kenya 1946–62*. Nairobi: English Press.

ANDERSON, D.M (1982). Herder, settler, and Colonial Rule: a history of the peoples of the Baringo Plains, Kenya, *c*. 1890–1940. Unpublished PhD. thesis, University of Cambridge.

ANDERSON, D.M. (1984). Depression, Dust Bowl, Demography and Drought: the Colonial State and Soil Conservation in East Africa during the 1930s, *African Affairs*, **83** (332), 321–43.

ANDERSON, D.M. & MILLINGTON, A.C. (1987). The political ecology of soil conservation in anglo-phone Africa. In *African Resources: Appraisal, Monitoring and Management*, ed. A.C. Millington, A. Binns & S. Mutiso, Reading Geographical Papers Series. Reading University. (In press)

BEINART, W. (1984). Soil erosion, conservationism, and ideas about development in Southern Africa. *Journal of Southern African Studies*, **11** (2), 52–83.

BLACKBURN, R.H. (1974). The Okiek and their history. *Azania*, **9**, 139–57.

BRASNETT, N.V. (1942). Finance and the Colonial Forest Service. *Empire Forestry Journal*, **21**(1), 7–11.

CLIFFE, L. (1972). Nationalism and the reaction to enforced agricultural change in Tanganyika during the colonial period. In *Socialism in Tanzania: An Interdisciplinary Reader*, ed. L. Cliffe and J. Saul, pp. 17–24. Dar es Salaam: East African Publishing House.

ELIOT, C. (1905). *The East African Protectorate*. London: Edward Arnold.

GARDNER, H.M. (1942). Kenya forests and the War. *Empire Forestry Journal* **21**(1), 45–7.

GRAHAM, R.M. (1945). Forestry in Kenya. *Empire Forestry*, **24**, 156–75.

HELMS, D. & FLADER, S.L. ed. (1985). *The History of Soil and Water Conservation*, Washington DC: Agricultural History Society.

HUGHES, J.F. (1949). Forest and water supplies in East Africa. *Empire Forestry*, **28**, 314–23.

HUTCHINS, D.E. (1907). *Report on the Forests of Kenya*. London: HMSO.

HUTCHINS, D.E. (1909). *Report on the Forests of British East Africa*. London: HMSO.

JOHNSTON, H.H. (1902). *The Uganda Protectorate*, 2 vols. London: Edward Arnold.

KENYA, COLONYAND PROTECTORATE. (1950). *An Economic Survey of Forestry in Kenya and Recommendations regarding a Forest Commission*. Nairobi: English Press.

KENYA FOREST DEPARTMENT (1904–63). *Annual Reports*. Nairobi: Govt Printer.

KENYA LAND COMMISSION. (1934). *Kenya Land Commission (Carter): Evidence and Memoranda*, 3 vols. London: HMSO.

LOGIE, K.P.W. (1962). *Forestry in Kenya. A Historical Account of the Development of Forest Management in the Colony*. Nairobi: Govt Printer.

McCRACKEN, J. (1982). Experts and expertise in colonial Malawi. *African Affairs*, **81**(322), 101–16.

MATSON, A.T. (1972). *Nandi Resistance to British Rule, 1890–1906*. Nairobi: East African Publishing House.

MURRAY, N.U. (1982). The other lost lands: the administration of Kenya's forests, 1900–52. History Department Staff Seminar Paper, Kenyatta University College, Nairobi.

NICHOLSON, J.H. (1931). *The Future of Forestry in Kenya*. Nairobi: Govt Printer.

OFCANSKY, T.P. (1984). Kenya forestry under British colonial administration, 1895–1963. *Journal of Forest History*, **28**(3), 136–43.

POWELL, J.M. (1976). *Environmental Management in Australia, 1788–1914: Guardians, Improvers and Profit: an introductory survey*. Melbourne: Oxford University Press.

SORRENSON, M.P.K. (1968). *Origins of European Settlement in Kenya*. Nairobi: Oxford University Press.

STEBBING, E.P. (1922). *The Forests of India*, 3 vols. London: J. Lane.

STEBBING, E.P. (1937). *The Forests of West Africa and the Sahara*. London: Chambers.

STEBBING, E.P. (1941). Forestry in Africa. *Empire Forestry Journal*, **20**(2), 126–44.

THROUP, D.W. (1985). The origins of Mau Mau. *African Affairs*, **84**(336), 399–433.

UNWIN, A.H. (1920). *West African Forests and Forestry*. London: Unwin.

WALLER, R.D. (1985). Ecology, migration and expansion in East Africa. *African Affairs*, **84**(336), 347–70.

WARD, R. (1937). *Deserts in the Making: A study in the Causes and Effects of Soil Erosion*. Nairobi: Kenya Arbor Society.

PART FOUR

Consequences for conservation and development

Introduction

JOHN LONSDALE

Environmental crisis and demographic collapse are scarcely new to Africa. They are as old as the continent's ascertainable history. Memories of famine are among the more reliable sources which historians can use for dating the pre-colonial past. Africa's indigenous productive practices are premised on the inevitability of recurrent drought. Its ethnicity is generally based on the cultural elaboration of expert knowledge of local botany and climatic variation. In many regions local aesthetics have been moulded by the greater chances of survival one enjoys by being fat. Traditional political thought is shot through with the obligation of the fat to give succour to the famished, and with the need of the thin to give service in return. The new elements of Africa's contemporary crisis are the sustained population growth of recent years, the power of contemporary sovereign states and the demands of the international economic order.

In pre-colonial Africa there was an immensely varied relationship between environmental constraint and the human politics of survival. At one extreme, established polities could be destroyed by the collapse of their productive environment. Such seems to have been the fate of the Zimbabwe civilisation in the fifteenth century, and of a sucession of chiefships in the Angola hinterland throughout the pre-colonial era. Conversely, productive possibilities could be reconstructed through the very demands which existing regimes placed upon their peoples; the unusual and sustained prosperity of the Kuba kingdom of upper Zaïre is the outstanding example, but the role of Menelek's court in salvaging something from the disaster of the great Ethiopian famine of the 1890s also deserves to be remembered. It must have been true of many ruling establishments, as it was of the Bemba chiefdoms of Zambia, that their discussion was largely concerned with the 'organization of the food-supply, the exact type of soil in such and such a place, or the methods successfully used upon it' (Richards, 1939: 387).

271

Many pre-colonial African kingdoms flourished on their control of exchange between the specialist producers of essential commodities, agricultural, pastoral, sylvan and mineral. Their politics often institutionalised deals between complementary or federated sovereignties, with the interests of each economic sector being protected by courtly office or ritual shrine. Where disaster periodically strained such bargains, revolutionary movements might impose a stronger ideology of resource sharing, as in the West African Islamic theocracy of Macina, or a more ruthless hierarchy of resource dominance, as in Uganda's pastoral kingdoms or in Shaka's Zulu empire. There is no need to idealise the African past: economic crises were frequently solved by the forceful expropriation of one's neighbours' labour and resources.

But most Africans got along with adjoining groups who practised different cultural economies, without benefit of the distributional authority of a state. The pastoralists of eastern Africa, in the area studied by Hogg (Chapter 14) and more widely, developed intricate patterns of exchange, marriage and mutual obligation with their agricultural neighbours in a reciprocating network of reinsurance against disaster which only in the direst emergency demanded the audit of war. Gamaledinn's account (Chapter 16) of the contractual relations of the Afar, lowland pastoralists, with upland cultivators provides a classic example. Even here, however, one must beware of false premises about Merrie Africa in its Golden Age; it was wealthy farmers and herders who made the strongest alliances and the poor who were forced into debt bondage when starvation threatened. Insurance was an investment, and entitlement to its repayments was restricted to those who had been able to afford its prudential savings.

None of these varied political arrangements could avert periodic disaster; each ensured that some would survive, often enough at the price of a greater differentiation between the powerful and the poor, as the latter laboured on the solutions which the former controlled. Moreover, scarcely any productive system in pre-colonial Africa provided for its own intensification without the interruptions of long fallows for cultivated fields or the seasonal resting of pasture. Where production expanded it was almost always by territorial extension rather than technical intensification. African demography, like pre-industrial demography virtually everywhere, presented an alternating sawtooth pattern of rapid increases and sudden falls. 'Growth' in propitious times was a means to shore up survivial in lean years. Hard times created the reduced populations which could then resume the exploitation of resources which either survived better than the people who cultivated them, or multiplied faster than their herdsmen.

But now, on to the cyclical time of old Africa there has been grafted the exponential time of <u>modern man and the modern state</u>. Modern population growth, modern expectations of parents for the health and education of their children, modern public revenue and private banking systems, and not only their inflated salaries but also the worthy ambitions for the public good of the men who govern modern states, <u>all demand</u> the continuously intensifying exploitation of resources within frontiers <u>of settlement which are now scarcely open to further extension</u>. <u>Pre-colonial and colonial Africa were alike in that both were a mosaic of colonising societies</u>. Contemporary Africa has for the most part run out <u>of space, except in city slums</u>. <u>But just as</u> pre-colonial Africa was no Utopia, so also one must resist the fashionably easy judgement that <u>modern Africa</u> and its governance are entirely malign. Contemporary Africa is a product of a recent history which, like all history, is deeply ambivalent.

[margin note: new demands]

[margin note: OB J Q]

European colonies in Africa were conquest states which distanced alien rulers from indigenous subjects. But colonial rule also brought the transport and medical revolutions which put an end to both the famines of pre-colonial Africa and the epidemic scourges which colonial conquest had initially fanned. African nationalism gave birth to new ruling, urban, élites who were not much closer than their expatriate predecessors to rural peoples – but these had nonetheless been transformed, if sometimes but fleetingly, into citizenries. Citizens, as Areola argues in his chapter on Nigeria (Chapter 13), may have been persuaded that they are no more than tribesmen and thus excluded from the reformist politics of programme by the factional politics of personality. However, thanks to their former basis in specific ecologies, ethnic groups can also be the political champions of productive interests. The future is not entirely foreclosed by the recent past.

The chapters in this Part certainly show how difficult it is in Africa to work out a more sustainably productive politics of development. Their fundamental common theme is the absence of any politically coherent tradition, any inherited moral economy, which might discipline disputes and govern decisions about the use of Africa's resources and the distribution of their fruits. Colonial conquest states have not yet been fully nationalised. Areola's politicians surrender responsibility to visiting experts whom Adams (Chapter 15) sees as blind to local realities and ignorant of the local past, expert only in the employment of a disastrously inappropriate imported technology. <u>In the cases studied by Hogg and Gamaledinn</u> the past flexibilities of <u>pastoral survival are frustrated, if not indeed destroyed, whether by bureaucratic incomprehension or by</u> a revolutionary zeal which has intensified the ethnocentricity and crass *expropriation*

expropriations of imperial Ethiopia. To conjure up a more tolerable future for northern Nigeria's Bakalori irrigation scheme or for the Afar people of the Awash valley would no doubt be to succumb to wishful thinking against the facts. But the findings of Areola and Hogg suggest, in their very different ways, that as in pre-colonial Africa's past, so in contemporary Africa's future, varied, and perhaps unintended, accommodations between the environment and development are not impossible.

Areola shows how political apprehensions of crisis can give rise to environmentally appropriate legislation, lying unused now but nonetheless present in the accumulated and contradictory geology of the state, ready to be picked up and perhaps acted upon when a sufficiently powerful coalition of interests is next threatened. And it is perhaps too soon to dismiss the possibility that the irrigation schemes investigated by Hogg will not be reabsorbed into the flexible relations between fixed agriculture and transhumant pastoralism which have long characterised the area; in these, after all, the poorer herdsmen were always the first to have to accept the labourer's road of present indignity in the hope of a future re-entry to pastoralism. The politics of either potential future will not of course be easy. But that is not to say that they are in some predetermined way impossible. Africa's national economies are more and more integrated by the pressure on resources. Rural dearth is increasingly reflected in ungovernable urban shanty-towns and the politicians' terror of food riots. More positively, farmers both large and small are increasingly demanding the services which only the state can provide – and which the state, if it is to safeguard its foreign exchange earnings, must in fact provide – as their natural resources are depleted. And it is difficult to see how top-heavy projects which ride rough-shod over inherited ecological caution can for ever be financed against the growing experience of negative returns.

Small farmers and pastoralists cannot by themselves solve the problem of diminishing resources. Pauperised households are as destructive of the environment as greedy capitalists. For their own preservation Africa's statesmen will increasingly have to attend to the natural environment which sustains them both. A greater internal accountability[1] – the sentimental might dare to call it democracy – looks more and more to be the condition of Africa's survival. That does not mean that it will necessarily occur. But the countries which stand some chance of a future will be those in which political debate revolves, as it did in the past, around the organisation of the food supply, the of the soil in their divergent regions, and the productive ssary for its sustained exploitation.

Notes

1   For a general discussion, sadly lacking in an environmental dimension, see Lonsdale (1986). Readers will recognise at many points my intellectual debts to David Anderson, John Iliffe, Richard Waller and Neal Sobania. The best general history of Africa to give due weight to the questions of demography, production and power is Coquery-Vidrovich (1985) which, in its pessimism, perhaps exaggerates the disjunctions between village and state.

References

COQUERY-VIDROVICH, C. (1985). *Afrique Noire: permanences et ruptures*. Paris: Payot.

LONSDALE, J.M. (1986). Political accountability in African history. In *Political Domination in Africa: reflections on the limits of power*, ed. P. Chabal, pp 126–57. Cambridge: Cambridge University Press.

RICHARDS, A. (1939). *Land, Labour and Diet in Northern Rhodesia*. Oxford: Oxford University Press.

13

The political reality of conservation in Nigeria

OLUSEGUN AREOLA

In Africa the term conservation is most often associated with the provision of National Parks and game reserves and the protection of wildlife. In this area the aims of conservationists meet the desires of African governments to encourage the growth and maintenance of lucrative tourist industries. But conservation in the African context should not be seen merely in terms of nature conservation; it is also an important part of the reform process in land tenure systems, land-use patterns, and land management practices. It is primarily in relation to the control of man's exploitation of environmental resources that conservation has its greatest relevance for the governments of West Africa. In Nigeria, land reforms have long been the focus of concern over conservation, being viewed as the best insurance against abuse and misuse of land resources. At a general level, the goal of such reforms is a more controlled or guided use of the land and its resources to achieve sustained economic growth and to promote the well-being of the people. It is with this broader view of conservation as a reform process, linked to changes in land husbandry and land use, that this chapter will be concerned.

The social adjustments that any reform process may call for naturally make conservation a sensitive social and political issue. Therefore, in assessing the present extent of conservation awareness in Nigeria, and perhaps elsewhere in Africa, the two conditions stipulated by King (1977) as necessary to effect land reform in any area may be equally applicable to the introduction of conservation measures, namely: (i) a government or ruling class with the political wisdom, will and ability to effect land reform; and (ii) a populace that is aware of the necessity for reform and that has the determination and organisation to bring pressure to bear on government. The political process, because of its greater complexity and volatile nature, is perhaps more critical to the growth of the conservation-consciousness in Africa than, say, in the western world. In his discussion of the politics of conservation in Britain, Kennet (1974) dwelt on the politician's sensitivity or responsiveness to the interests of his 'base population', that is, those that vote for him and 'keep him in business'. This is a feature of a country where elections are fought, for the most part, on issues and on the personal qualities and abilities of contestants. In present-day Africa few democratically elected governments remain and, even in the past era of elected governments, elections in many countries have been fought not so much on issues as along ethnic and kinship lines. Thus, issues of conservation or land reform cannot be resolved principally on ecological arguments or by direct appeal to public opinion; other critical factors may be the extent to which the dominant socio-political groups feel affected by or concerned about such issues, and the extent to which governments are willing to override the objections and hostilities of the dominant ethnic groups towards conservation programmes.

The purpose of this chapter is to examine the political realities of conservation in Nigeria today, focusing upon both the governments' and the peoples' attitudes and actions. What have been the achievements and failures of Nigeria in conservation and other related fields? How willing are the people to accept and pay the social costs of necessary reforms? Is there enough political will to formulate and execute conservation-based programmes within the process of land reform and land-use control? Do African countries presently have the administrative capacity to implement policies that are sensitive to conservation? To answer these questions I will begin by examining the process of political decision-making in Nigeria, as it relates to conservation issues, taking the case of forest policies as a more detailed example. The difficulties of introducing and implementing conservation legislation will then be discussed, before considering the degree of awareness of conservation within Nigeria's development policies. Regrettably, my conclusions are pessimistic, for it will be shown that neither the political will on the part of government to implement conservation measures, nor the public awareness of the need to introduce such measures, are yet in evidence in Nigeria, and that Nigerian governments therefore continue to give inadequate attention to questions of conservation.

Conservation and political decision-making

After gaining political independence from the colonial powers in the early 1960s most African countries entered fully into the era of National Development Plans, with the encouragement of such bodies as the World Bank. However, as the case of Nigeria clearly exemplifies, in spite of the emphasis given to national planning, the major decisions subsequently taken by government have been, more often than not, reactions to rapidly changing circumstances and to crisis situations as they have arisen. Conservation programmes, like so much else, have suffered from these uncertainties, with the necessity of administrative response to problems created by environmental disasters acting as the impetus for a variety of largely piecemeal and often indirect measures.

The ecological education of the governments and the peoples of West Africa over the past two decades has come from such bitter experiences as the Sahelian drought of 1968–74 (Kowal & Adeoye, 1973; Mortimore, 1973; van Apeldoorn, 1981), the urban floods in Lagos, Ibadan and Warri in Nigeria (Areola & Akintola, 1980), flash floods in many *fadama* lands (Olofin, 1985), and the blowout of oil wells and oil spillage in the Niger Delta (Odu, 1977). Beyond these irregular but devastating crises, questions of environmental management have seldom, if ever, been debated. At the same time, the responsibility for motivating and implementing programmes for environmental protection has necessarily devolved more and more on the executive body of government, especially since Nigeria has for considerable periods been governed by the military rather than by elected representatives. Even in those periods when parliamentary government has existed, public debates on conservation have been sporadic, in consonance with the irregular occurrence of environmental disasters. An examination of the national development plans of Nigeria reveals the failure of the executive body to take a serious and long-term view of the problem of conservation. The country's environmental programme, for whatever it is worth, has been largely urban-centred with a virtual neglect of the rural environment.

The pre-independence Ten-Year Development Plan, 1945–56, laid the foundation in that it identified and focused on only three primary environmental issues, namely, health, water and town and country planning. A system of health inspectors was introduced which was very effective in ensuring that the people kept their surroundings and sources of drinking water clean. Under this environmental health scheme, mass vaccination and inoculation campaigns were mounted, for example, against the epidemic disease smallpox (Brown, 1955; Adejuwon, 1978). The concern about town and country planning was limited to the physical development of the towns (including the creation of Government Reservation Areas) and providing them with modern amenities. These initiatives in environmental sanitation taken by the colonial administration were allowed to die out in the post-independence period. The health inspector system had to be phased out as it became a tool in the hands of politicians for the victimisation of political opponents. In their longings for pipe-borne water most rural areas abandoned the simple but effective measures introduced by the colonial administration to maintain rural water supplies (Akintola & Areola, 1980).

The post-independence development plans have also concentrated on problems related to water supply, health facilities and town planning, with emphasis on housing, sewerage and refuse disposal. The establishment of a Ministry of Urban Development and Housing was one of the major outcomes of the Third Plan, 1975–80 (Federal Republic of Nigeria, 1975). This urban-centred focus of Nigeria's environmental programme is clearly a reflection of the preoccupation of the people and the political leadership with urban social and welfare issues. Political leaders have been too concerned with gaining and retaining power, not only in their respective home bases but also, and more importantly, at the centre. Thus, development efforts have been concentrated on social infrastructure and on highly visible projects and programmes that also yield quick results and which, therefore, would win them the broader support of the people. In this context, conservation measures can be seen to lack any immediate political utility.

The fact that political leadership and political groupings are polarised along ethnic lines may also constitute a barrier to the growth of conservation-consciousness, at times accentuated by Nigeria's federal system of government. Debates on environmental problems tend to be easily sidetracked by the manoeuvrings of various political leaders and groups, who may wish to use environmental issues to effect more favourable revenue allocations to their respective ethnic areas. This manoeuvring for federal funds has prevented states from taking decisive action to combat their local environmental problems. The argument is a familiar one: if the Federal government is spending so much money on drought relief in one part of the country, why should it not take on responsibility for erosion control in another part, and vice versa? Therefore, while awareness of and concern about the environment may have increased over recent years, environmental questions did not emerge as important issues during the political campaigns of the last civilian era, 1979–83. Despite the recurrence of environmental disasters affecting West Africa, political leaders seem to have successfully subordinated these issues, preferring to concentrate upon the seemingly overriding concern of holding control of political power at the centre. It is now widely recognised that by concentrating their efforts upon the competition for control of power at the centre, Nigeria's ruling élites have neglected their responsibilities to the people on many aspects of social, economic and environmental policy (Dudley, 1974, 1982; Nuoli, 1981).

The circumstances of political instability, transition and change that have prevailed in Nigeria over the past two decades have militated against the foundation of any coherent government approach to conservation. The urban focus of much policy and planning and the intense competition for political power have been dominating concerns. Yet even in those areas where conservation programmes were in existence from the colonial era, as in the case of forestry policies, the lack of government commitment and the consequent piecemeal implementation of policy have hindered the cause of conservation and threatened future programmes.

Forest policy

It is in the field of forestry that Nigeria has made the most conscious and discernible efforts at conservation. It was in the area of forest reservation that the colonial governments in West Africa set up their only coherent conservation-minded policy of lasting value. From its earliest stage colonial forest policy had the conservation of land and resources as a major objective (i.e. to protect the land and the forest and to conserve water). It was also clear that the objective was not to keep large areas of land unutilised, but rather to use and develop the land and resources under reserve in a rational manner to maintain their sustained yield (Adeyoju, 1970). Hence, the subsequent use of these reserves for lumbering, plantation forestry and wildlife management (Aubreville, 1949).

In spite of its laudable objectives, the policy of forest reservation was hampered by an indirect approach to the problem of conservation which sidetracked the broader problem of poor land management by the generality of land users. The legacy of the colonial era of legislated conservation has been to restrict subsequent conservation efforts in Nigeria to these publicly controlled lands. The introduction of modern land or resource management practices has only been adequately achieved on these expropriated lands, and the persistent problem for conservation has been the inability to carry conservation principles and practice from the reserves and publicly controlled lands to other areas. Indeed, the policy of forest reservation has not everywhere been popular. In the latter part of the colonial period and during the post-independence period, the forest reservation policy has had to make concessions to powerful group interests in many parts of Nigeria. In the savanna areas of northern Nigeria, the nomadic herders of the Bororo Fulbe, hard pressed for grazing land as they met stiffer competition from cultivators and as erosion reduced their erstwhile pastures, were assisted at the cost of the forest reserves. To appease this group, who could not be ignored because of their religious clout in the emirates, the government converted a number of savanna forest reserves into 'grazing reserves' located along the main migratory routes of the nomadic cattle (Buchanan & Pugh, 1955). A recent study (Federal Department of Forestry, 1984) has shown that the trend of dereservation of forests in this area still continues. The decline in the area of reserved forests is up to 3–5 per cent in Kano State, 8–14 per cent in Kaduna, 11–15 per cent in Bauchi and as high as 16–21 per cent in Sokoto. This has been brought about not only by the needs of grazing, but also by the establishment of large-scale agricultural development projects, especially since the creation of the River Basin Development Authorities in 1976 (see Adams, Chapter 15).

In eastern Nigeria, where land degradation was particularly serious, the colonial forest reservation policies proved extremely difficult to implement because of the high population density. Here, the colonial administration had to exercise compulsory land acquisition powers to create seven forest reserves. The local people vigorously resisted this forced reservation, and, indeed, no less than 539,263 ha of forest reserve or potential forest reserve were lost subsequent to gazettement (Rosevear, 1953).

An important feature of the forest reservation policy which has continued to affect conservation programmes in Nigeria is the policy of dual administration and management of the forests by the Federal Forest Department and other local authorities. Under the colonial system of indirect rule practised in Nigeria, this meant a sharing of powers between the colonial government and the Native Authorities, which extended to the administration of forest reserves. This system precluded any opportunity to develop a unitary forest policy in Nigeria which could have helped the cause of conservation in later years. The dual control of indirect rule has, in part, been carried into independent Nigeria's federal system of government, giving considerable power for the control and utilisation of land and its resources to regional governments. This has resulted in the emergence of a series of divergent forest policies, as each regional government has enacted its own forest programme in addition to that of the Federal Department of Forestry. However, in a general sense two motives or objectives appear to have dominated forestry until recently: namely, the economic one of developing local wood-based industries as part of the overall import-substitution policy of the government; and the welfare motive of providing employment and good livelihood for the local inhabitants. Although, judging from the forest policy of the Eastern region, there was 'an awareness of the modern concept of forestry involving multiple land use planning, provision of recreation and maintenance of good public relations' (Adeyoju, 1970), subsequent developments show that the economic motive has been uppermost in the considerations of the various regional, and later, state, governments. The proliferation of sawmills and secondary wood-based industries during the 1970s was glaring evidence of this. In 1970 there were already 133 officially registered sawmills in the country (Enabor, 1973) and the number rose to 348 in 1975 and to 580 in 1978 (Adeyoju, 1978). The increased level of lumbering activity throughout the country, encouraged by the growth of the sawmilling industry, proved difficult to monitor and control. Forest officers could not cope with the comparatively larger numbers of woodcutters, for aside from the sawmillers themselves, there were very many sawyers, individual farmers, land owners and 'middlemen' engaged in logging throughout the country. The illegal felling of trees and the overexploitation of forests, in the sense of removing immature trees, became a major difficulty. Added to these problems, the civil war of 1967–70 adversely affected forestry in eastern Nigeria. The drift of people back to the east increased pressure on land and on the few remaining pockets of forest reserve. In the north, a wave of dereservation of former forest reserves began after the civil war, with forest reserves being lost through encroachment and by the deliberate conversion to other forms of land use.

Against this mounting pressure on the forest reserves, the Forestry Departments have enjoyed some small success in the establishment of exotic and indigenous plantations, the introduction of an urban tree-planting campaign in the north that has now become an annual event to mark the United Nations World Environment Day, and the more significant UNDP and FAO supported savanna shelter belt programme, set up in the wake of the 1968–74 Sahelian drought as a measure to check wind erosion and desert encroachment (Adeyoju & Enabor, 1973; Enabor, 1977).

Implementation and legislation

Many of the difficulties faced by the forest services in Nigeria have to do with the lack of appropriate methods of ensuring policy implementation. As Adeyoju (1970) points out, in Nigeria emphasis has been placed on fiscal measures (protective tariffs, credit, etc.), rather than on legal measures for ensuring the implmentation of forestry policies. Nigerian governments have avoided the legal measures which have been adopted in many developed countries, which include legislation for the consolidation of land or prohibition of fragmentation, to establish new tenancy relationships, to provide for the compulsory acquisition of land, and to permit the control of the use of land in certain areas (zonation laws). More generally, the need for such legislation to enable the conservation and protection of the environment has been highlighted for Nigerians by the pollution of the delta region in connection with the workings of the oil industry.

Following the loud protests of the political leaders in the areas affected by oil pipe bursts and oil well blowouts in the delta region, the military government in the early 1970s initiated moves to enact an environmental protection law (Federal Republic of Nigeria, 1975, 1981). Apart from the enactment of one ineffectual decree (Decree no. 34: Oil in Navigable Waters Decree) nothing concrete was achieved, perhaps because, as many suspected, of the opposition of the oil companies and associated local vested interests and the concern of the government itself not to hinder the work of this vital sector of the economy. The creation of the delta area as a Special Development Area, with a board of management having responsibility for planning for the economic and physical development of the region, went some way towards appeasing local politicians. But the mere creation of a bureaucracy has not solved the environmental problems of the delta (Ikporukpo, 1983). During the civilian regime of 1979–82 the legislature, after much haggling, actually passed an Environmental Protection Agency Act (*New Nigerian*, 1 June 1982). However, this Act had not been signed into law by the President before the civilian regime was ousted from power – further controversy and discussion of the provisions of the Act apparently continued after it had been passed by the legislature, thereby delaying the signing. The debate on the Act was beclouded by arguments on the revenue allocation implications of conservation measures, as some legislators saw these as a means of channelling more federal funds to certain parts of the country. In this case, self-interest and a lack of honesty of purpose on the part of the legislators would appear to have prevented the country from taking a crucial step towards establishing a firm legal basis for conservation and environmental protection.

The only legislation enacted in Nigeria towards providing broader legal measures that might be made to serve the cause of conservation was the promulgation of the Land Use Decree (now Act) in 1978. The Land Use Act vests all land in the federal and state governments, thereby overturning traditional land ownership systems and tenancy relationships. The Act is basically a law designed to: (i) facilitate acquisition of land for public projects, and (ii) prescribe the maximum area of land that an individual can obtain in both the urban and rural areas. A land allocation committee has been set up in each local government area to administer the provisions of the Act, which is vigorously opposed by many vested interests, especially the traditional rulers and land owning families in the southern parts of Nigeria (Koehn, 1983; Francis, 1984; Udo, 1985). So far the Act has had very little impact on the land tenure situation, especially in the rural areas. In the urban centres, the provision requiring individuals and organisations to obtain certificates of occupancy on their land has turned out to be just one more hurdle in the protracted process of registering and getting approval for building plans (Agbola & Onibokun, 1985). Not surprisingly, most rural inhabitants regard the Land Use Act as meant principally for the cities and some criticise the federal government for regarding the land problems of Lagos and a few big cities as being typical of the whole country. The only category of rural inhabitants who are enthusiastic about the Act is those tenant farmers who stand to gain by it, although the threat posed to traditional tenancy relationships has resulted in civil unrest in some parts of the country (Udo, 1985).

The Land Use Act was never conceived as a conservation measure, nor was it brought about as a result of any careful assessment of Nigeria's resource management and environmental needs. Although enacted specifically as an instrument for regulating land acquisition and ownership, some commentators see within the Land Use Act the potential, with proper implementation, to handle conservation-related issues in an indirect manner and without the loud protests that would normally greet more direct measures. Adalemo (1978) sees the benefits that could be derived from the Act as including an end to land disputes, land speculation and arbitrary inflation of land values; the orderly development of urban areas; easier access to agricultural land for those actually engaged in agricultural production, with the possibility of consolidating fragmented farm plots and the encouragement of large-scale agricultural enterprises; and, most importantly in relation to conservation, the prevention of developments that threaten the local environment. Of course, many of these benefits have not yet been realised. Nevertheless, it is true that most African governments would rather adopt an indirect route to solving their land-use problems, and in this respect the Act offers a ready means of legislating for the implementation of conservation programmes.

Conservation and development

While the Land Use Act holds the potential for future conservation legislation, what of the current role of conservation within Nigeria's development policies? In the area of modern large-scale farming, the River Basin and Rural Development Authorities (formerly River Basin Development Authorities) now dominate the scene, and perhaps hold some promise of infusing conservation principles and measures in the rural areas in the absence of a general programme of land tenure and management reforms (but see Adams, Chapter 15). In the 1960s some regional governments had attempted to modernise agriculture through farm settlement schemes. These settlement schemes failed because of inadequate planning, poor administration and a lack of interest on the part of farmers (Olatubosun, 1971; Adegeye, 1974). The River Basin and Rural Development Authorities (RBRDAs), created by decree in 1976, have attracted a great deal more attention than the settlement schemes of the 1960s. The RBRDAs were conceived as suprastate development agencies, which by operating outside the state and local government structures would ensure the full and integrated development of entire regions, while avoiding some of the difficulties encountered by the earlier settlement schemes (Areola, Faniran & Akintola, 1985).

However, the RBRDAs have encountered a number of serious difficulties (Akinyosoye, 1984; Adams, 1985). The greatest danger to the life of the Authorities appears to be party politics, which nearly destroyed them during the civilian era from 1979 to 1983. At this time many unnecessary and ill-advised projects were established as a form of party patronage, while the cropping programmes of certain projects were dictated from above in total disregard of scientific and technical considerations. The military regime that came into power in December 1983 rescued the RBRDAs from the politicians, but the activities of the Authorities have subsequently been beset with new and perhaps, potentially more dangerous problems: financial difficulties, and serious discontent among the farmers on some key projects (Adams, 1985). The latter problem has been accentuated by the drought of 1983–4 which caused many rivers and *fadama* lands to dry up in the northern part of the country. Recent problems of drought and flood at several RBRDA projects in northern Nigeria have drawn attention to the shortcomings in environmental planning in these development schemes. As Adams indicates (1985, Chapter 15) some of the dams and agricultural projects under the RBRDAs were embarked upon without adequately detailed planning or design.

Inadequate data bases remain a major constraint on environmental and project planning not only in Nigeria, but throughout West Africa. While the project feasibility studies carried out by RBRDAs should mark an improvement in the data base on local land-use patterns (Areola *et al.*, 1985), this remains an area neglected by Nigerian governments.

The cause of sound environmental management within development projects in Nigeria, if it is evident at all, is upheld by the activities of international agencies. Lacking their own programmes for conservation and environmental management, successive Nigerian governments have come to depend very much upon the ideas, concepts and programmes suggested or recommended by consultancy units, international agencies and from the seminars, workshops and conferences organised by local research and professional organisations. Heavy reliance has been placed upon special commissions and *ad hoc* task forces in examining specific environmental problems and making recommendations on possible sol-utions, much of this stemming from international response to West Africa's various environmental 'crises' over the past two decades. Exter-nal organisations undertaking recent work of this sort in Nigeria include the Land Resources Division of the British Ministry of Overseas Develop-ment, which carried out soil and land evaluation studies over more than half of the country's land area; the United Nations Food and Agriculture Organisation (FAO), which has been very actively engaged in soil and land capability studies and project implementation in agriculture, fores-try, irrigation and livestock development; the United Nations Develop-ment Programme, which has often collaborated with FAO, especially in projects related to forestry and drought abatement and in providing and funding manpower training programmes; and the World Bank, which is currently helping to run many forestry and agriculture project monitoring and evaluation units in the country (Adeyoju, 1970; High, 1970; Ahsan, 1981; Idachaba, 1984).

The initiative in evaluating the environmental resources of Nigeria, and in assessing the impact of particular development programmes, there-fore remains, for the most part, with external bodies. The government of Nigeria seems more concerned with immediate 'development' than with the longer-term requirement for the conservation and protection of the environment. This apparent willingness to mortgage the future can be judged by the absence of complementary programmes or follow-up activities on the part of the Nigerian government to employ the resource data collected by international agencies. For instance, the recommenda-tions deriving from the British Land Resources Division studies and the FAO evaluation studies have been only very partially implemented. Failure to assess properly the environmental resources of an area, or to make thorough use of an assessment that may be available, has been just as responsible for the high failure rate of government development projects as have the more publicised shortcomings of bureaucractic bottlenecks, high overhead costs, poor staffing and management, and

low returns on investment (Osagie, 1983; Soyode., 1983; Andrea &
Beckman, 1986).

Within the process of development planning in Nigeria, then, issues
of conservation still have only a low priority. Development, particularly
that funded by external loans, is viewed by the government as a profit-
making economic venture. Any investment in conservation programmes
within a development project can seldom offer an immediate return,
either financially or in terms of political patronage, and so there seems
little incentive for federal or state governments to give greater consideration to the place of conservation within development. But the economic
difficulties confronting Nigeria in the 1980s may make it essential for
Nigerian perceptions and expectations of development projects to be
modified. Facing a mounting external debt problem, and in circumstances
where external sources of funding are likely to become less and less
accessible, Nigeria is already feeling the pinch of the financial squeeze.
It is perhaps timely to issue the warning that Nigeria cannot continue
to rely upon international agencies to finance her environmental and
conservation programmes, or, indeed, to conceive and plan them. The
government will have to recognise its responsibilities in this area, and
give greater priority to issues of conservation and environmental management.

Conclusion

King (1977) has recognised two modes of land reform: the evolutionary
and the revolutionary. Applying this to the Nigerian approach to conservation, it is clear that the revolutionary approach has been studiously
avoided. Neither the political leadership nor the mass public discontent
or awareness necessary to instigate revolutionary measures are to be
found in Nigeria. Whilst often realising the needs for reforms in land
use and the long-term benefits that would accrue, Nigerians seem unwilling to pay the current social costs of those reforms (see Bell, Chapter
4). Conservation, and the measures that might facilitate its implementa-
ion, may be 'a good thing', but no one is prepared to pay for it. They
are particularly unprepared to accept changes in systems of land ownership and traditional tenancy relationships. Nigerian governments, in their
turn, have not had the courage or conviction to take radical measures,
partly because of inadequate administrative capacity, but more crucially
because of the delicate relationship between political power and the
balance of ethnic or social groupings in different regions.

Having shied away from the revolutionary approach, Nigeria's government continues to adopt indirect measures in the field of conservation and environmental management, preferring to use surrogate agencies (international organisations) to undertake research and analysis, without showing any commitment to action. This 'evolutionary' approach is handicapped by a lack of political will on the one hand, and by the logistical problems of inadequate data bases for planning, poor administration and political instability on the other. The level of awareness of the need for conservation remains low, and so the Nigerian government has not yet been pushed to take up its full responsibilities in devising and implementing programmes for environmental protection. The shrinking of the forest reserve, the mounting anxiety over the problem of pollution in the Niger Delta, and the more general concerns over land-use practices and soil conservation throughout the rural areas, all indicate that such programmes are required. Yet, as Dasmann (1984) notes, if conservation and rural development are to progress, there is no alternative than to make individual governments face up to their responsibilities. International or intergovernmental agencies can only operate to the extent that the home governments allow them. In this era of military or one-party governments in Africa, the responsibility for motivating and designing conservation-based programmes must be largely that of the Executive body of government. The Nigerian government, along with the other governments of West Africa, remain preoccupied with their economic and balance of payment problems. The indications are that they will not act to introduce conservation programmes until their hands are forced once again, perhaps by a series of environmental disasters similar to the Sahel drought of 1968–74, or by a wave of social unrest prompted by an escalation in land disputes or hostilities in areas of competition between herders and farmers. The seemingly intractable nature of their national economic problems has made it difficult for African governments to make long-term plans, and the emphasis remains upon the search for quick solutions to the pressing problems of the moment. Programmes related to conservation, which characteristically do not yield immediate and tangible returns, do not enter into the present order of priorities. These are the harsh political realities of conservation in Nigeria.

References

ADALEMO, I.A. (1978). Land management in Nigeria: the promise of the Land Use Decree, 1978. In *Resources and Development in Africa*, vol.3, ed.

J.S. Oguntoyinbo, M.O. Filani & O. Areola, pp. 407–11. Lagos: Conference of the International Geographical Union.

ADAMS, W.M. (1985). River basin planning in Nigeria. *Applied Geography*, 5, 297–308.

ADEGEYE, A.J. (1974). Re-examination of the issues involved in the Farm Settlement Scheme of the Western State of Nigeria. *Oxford Agrarian Studies*, 3(2), 1–10.

ADEJUWON, J.O. (1978). Pests and diseases. In *A Geography of Nigerian Development*, ed. J.S. Oguntoyinbo, O. Areola & M.O. Filani, pp. 92–112. Ibadan: Heinemann.

ADEYOJU, S.K. (1970). *Forestry in the Nigerian Economy.* Ibadan: Ibadan University Press.

ADEYOJU, S.K. (1978). The conditions for new forest products industries in developing countries. Paper presented at the 3rd International Congress on 'Wood as a Resource in World Economics', Munich.

ADEYOJU, S.K. & ENABOR, E.E. (1973). *A Survey of the Drought affected Areas of Northern Nigeria.* Ibadan: Federal Department of Forestry.

AGBOLA, T. & ONIBOKUN, P. (1985). Institutional constraints on housing development in the urban areas of Nigeria: the case of the Land Use Decree and the building plan approval process. In *Urban Housing in Nigeria*, ed. P. Onibokun, Ibadan: Nigerian Institute of Social and Economic Research.

AHSAN, J. (1981). *Forest Management Planning in the Arid Zone of Nigeria.* Project Working Document no 8, UNDP/FAO/FGN. Development of Forest Management Capability. Lagos: Federal Department of Forestry.

AKINTOLA, F.O. & AREOLA, O. (1980). Pattern and strategy of public water supply in Nigeria. *Nigerian Journal of Economic and Social Studies*, 22(1), 41–52.

AKINYOSOYE, V.O. (1984). *River Basin Development Authorities and the Nigerian Food Economy: an overall assessment.* NISER Agricultural Policy research Report no.1. Ibadan: Nigerian Institute of Social and Economic Research.

ANDREA, G & BECKMAN, B. (1986). *The Wheat Trap; bread and underdevelopment in Nigeria.* London: Zed Press.

AREOLA, O. & AKINTOLA, F.O. (1980). Managing the urban environment in a developing country: the Ogunpa River Channelization Scheme in Ibadan City, Nigeria. *Environment International*, 3, 237–41.

AREOLA, O., FANIRAN, A. & AKINTOLA, F.O. (1985). The farmer-based small-farm schemes of the Ogun–Oshun River Basin Development Authority, Southwestern Nigeria. *Agricultural Systems*, 16, 7–21.

AUBREVILLE, A. (1949). *Climats, forêts et desertification de l'Afrique tropicale.* Societe d'Editions Geographiques, Maritimes et Coloniales, Paris, 4.

BROWN, A. (1955). Diseases as an element in the Nigerian environment. In *Land and People in Nigeria*, ed. K.M. Buchanan & J.C. Pugh, pp. 41–57. London: University of London Press.

BUCHANAN, K.M. & PUGH, J.C. (1955). *Land and People in Nigeria.* London: University of London Press.

DASMANN, R.F. (1984). The role of governments and international agencies in conservation and rural development. In *Traditional Life-styles, Conserva-*

tion and Rural Development. Commission on Ecology Papers, no.7, ed. J. Hanks, Geneva: IUCN.

DUDLEY, B.J. (1974). *Instability and Political Order*. Ibadan: Ibadan University Press.

DUDLEY, B.J. (1982). *An Introduction to Nigerian Government and Politics*. London: Macmillan.

ENABOR, E.E. (1973). The prospects of forest industries development in Nigeria. *Nigerian Geographical Journal*, **16**(1), 51–65.

ENABOR, E.E. (1977). The role of forestry in the amelioration of drought in Nigeria. *Nigerian Geographical Journal*, **20**(2), 153–64.

FEDERAL DEPARTMENT OF FORESTRY, NIGERIA (1984). *Manpower Study of the Forestry Sector in Nigeria*. Forestry Projects Monitoring and Evaluation Unit. Lagos: World Bank.

FEDERAL REPUBLIC OF NIGERIA (1975). *Third National Development Plan, 1981–5* Lagos: Govt Printer.

FEDERAL REPUBLIC OF NIGERIA (1981). *Fourth National Development Plan, 1971–80* Lagos; Govt Printer.

FRANCIS, P. (1984). For the use and the common benefit of all Nigerians: Consequences of the 1978 Land Nationalisation. *Africa*, **54**(3), 5–27.

HIGH, C. (1970). Land evaluation studies with special reference to Nigeria. In *Planning for Nigeria*, ed. K.M. Barbour. Ibadan: Ibadan University Press.

IDACHABA, F.S. (1984). Overview of the role of Agricultural Development Projects (ADP's) in government agricultural strategy. Keynote address delivered at the National Workshop on Crop Marketing and Input Distribution in Nigeria's Agricultural Development – Focus on the ADPs. Federal Agricultural Coordinating Unit, Ibadan.

IKPORUKPO, C.O. (1983). Environmental deterioration and public policy in Nigeria. *Applied Geograhy*, **3**, 303–16.

KENNET, W. (1974). The politics of conservation. In *Conservation in Practice*, ed. A. Warren & F.B. Goldsmith, pp. 465–75. London: Wiley.

KING, R. (1977). *Land Reform – A World Survey*. London: Bell.

KOEHN, P. (1983). State land allocation and class formation in Nigeria. *Journal of Modern African Studies*, **21**(3), 461–81.

KOWAL, J.M. & ADEOYE, K.B. (1973). An assessment of aridity and the severity of the 1972 drought in northern Nigeria and neighbouring countries. *Savanna*, **2**, 145–8.

MORTIMORE, M.J. (1973). Famine in Hausaland, 1973. *Savanna*, **2**, 103–8.

NUOLI, O. (1981). Progress versus reaction in Nigerian development. In *Paths to Nigerian Development*, ed. O. Nouli, pp. 192–216. Dakar: Codisira.

ODU, C.T.I. (1977). Oil pollution and the environment. *Bulletin of the Science Association of Nigeria*, **3**, 282–9.

OLATUBOSUN, D. (1971). The Farm Settlements – a case study of an agricultural project in Nigeria. *Bulletin of Rural Economics and Sociology*, **6**(1).

OLOFIN, E.A. (1985). Climatic constraints to water resource development in the Sudano-Sahelian zone of Nigeria. *Water International*, **10**, 29–37.

OSAGIE, E. (1983). Nigeria's economic development since independence. In *Development Economics and Planning*, ed. I.Z. Osayimwese, pp. 119–29. Ibadan: Dept of Economics, University of Ibadan.

SOYODE, A. (1983). Constraints on economic development in Nigeria. In *Development Economics and Planning*, ed. I.Z. Osayimwese, pp. 43–57. Ibadan: Dept of Economics, University of Ibadan.

ROSEVEAR, D.R. (1953). Vegetation, forestry and wildlife. In *The Nigerian Handbook*. Ibadan: Govt Printer.

UDO, R.K. (1985). *The Land Use Decree and its Antecedents* (University Lectures). Ibadan: University of Ibadan.

van APELDOORN, G.J. (1981). *Perspectives on Drought and Famine in Nigeria*. London: Allen & Unwin.

14

Settlement, pastoralism and the commons: the ideology and practice of irrigation development in northern Kenya[1]

RICHARD HOGG

Introduction

The most conspicuous changes in northern Kenya in recent years have been in the organisation of pastoralism. Pastoralism is becoming an increasingly part-time occupation. The wealthy, who also have access to the best jobs, tend to benefit the most from the changes, while the poor, who only have access to the worst jobs or no jobs at all, are thrust into ever increasing dependency (Dahl, 1979; Hogg, 1985a). The main reason for the changes has been the increasing intensity of national incorporation, which has increased the range of economic opportunities open to pastoralists and has led to the growth of permanent settlements. Yet government and donor agencies largely ignore these changes and continue to design their interventions in terms of an ideal model of pastoralism which, if it ever existed at all, has long since disappeared. In this paper I examine the reasons for the implementation and failure of one particularly important intervention, namely the development of irrigation agricultural schemes. I shall argue that official endeavours to conserve the range and to alleviate poverty have actually resulted in increasing the vulnerability of the people of the area to drought and its consequences of famine and pauperisation. Research on irrigation development was carried out in Isiolo, Turkana and Garissa Districts between 1982 and 1984 as part of a British Overseas Development Administration funded investigation of pastoralist responses to permanent settlement (Hogg, 1985c).

Ideology

Irrigation agriculture in northern Kenya was a response to an emergency situation in the 1960s and 1970s in which large numbers of pastoralists had been made destitute by war and drought, and to an increasing governmental concern over the effects of overstocking on the rangelands.

The prevailing orthodoxy was that destitution in pastoral areas was the inevitable result of an overloaded pastoral system, caused by human population increase, an 'ecologically unwise dependence on milk in a country where milk production should not be attempted' (Pratt & Gwynne, 1977: 40) and traditional range managment practices. In this view the only long-term way to eradicate destitution was for pastoralists to keep fewer livestock and to adopt new economic activities: 'destocking must be coupled with measures to reduce the number of pastoral people on the land. In some cases a remedy may be found in an irrigation scheme.' (Pratt & Gwynne, 1977: 39; cf. Brown, 1963, 1973; Allan, 1965; Konczacki, 1978; Sandford, 1983).

As long ago as the 1930s the colonial government had put forward the idea of irrigation schemes to provide grain to pastoralists in years of food shortage and as an alternative to food relief (Chambers, 1969). However, apart from the Perkerra scheme in Baringo District at which a number of destitute Il Chamus were settled, little or no attempt was made to develop irrigation agriculture in northern Kenya until after independence, when, with growing land pressure, the development of the agricultural potential of the arid and semi-arid lands (ASAL), which comprised over 80 per cent of the country, assumed increasing importance (Migot-Adholla & Little, 1981).

A Food and Agricultural Organization (FAO) survey of Turkana District in 1964, some three years after the 1960–1 drought, concluded: 'Although a population of 125,000 in an area of 24,000 sq. miles may not seem much agronomists agree that, in a purely pastoral economy, the district can only support a small fraction of this number . . . consequently, overgrazing has been going on for a long time causing a severe deterioration of the vegetation and a decrease of the stock carrying capacity.' As a result, 'no solution of the Turkana problem is possible by which all the people can continue their traditional way of life' (FAO, 1964: 7). The survey went on to outline the various development alternatives, such as the development of a fisheries industry at Lake Turkana, improvements to grazing and animal husbandry and, finally, the establishment of 'one or more pilot farms in the flood plains of the Turkwel and Kerio Rivers as a first step in the development of irrigated agriculture in Turkana' (FAO, 1964: 2).

The findings of the survey provided the basis for government and donor investment in irrigation agriculture in northern Kenya over the next 20 years. The objectives of this investment were:

(i)   to develop the food production potential of the semi-arid regions of Kenya with a view to decreasing food dependence on other parts of the country;

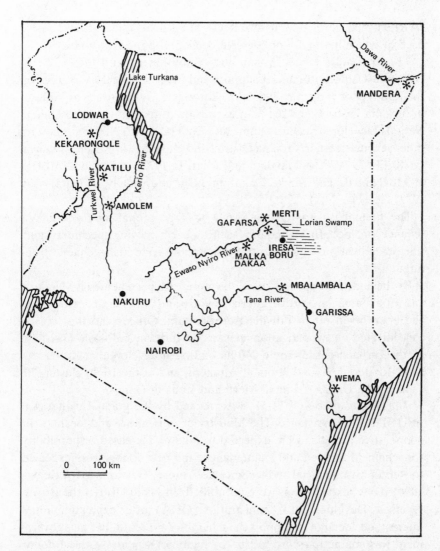

Fig. 14.1. Kenya: location of irrigation schemes.

(ii)   to provide an opportunity for destitute nomads to lead more stable and prosperous lives through irrigated agriculture and settlement;

(iii) to offset the destructive effects of the continuous encroachment of the desert (FAO/UNDP, 1977).

Irrigation agriculture

The government organisation primarily responsible for irrigation development was the Arid Regions Irrigation Development Project

(ARID). The development of ARID can be divided into three phases, each of which marked a progressive decline in project fortunes:

The first phase (1966–78) saw the establishment with MISEREOR (German Catholic) financial support and FAO technical assistance, of the initial pilot project in 1966 at Kekarongole, 30 km south of Lodwar in Turkana District, and the later expansion of the project, with United Nations Development Programme and FAO (UNDP/FAO) assistance to other schemes both in Turkana District and elsewhere in Northern Kenya (at Katilu in 1970, at Mandera and Merti in 1972, at Amolem in 1975, at Mbalambala and Malka Dakaa in 1976, and, finally, at Gafarsa in 1979) (see Fig. 14.1).

The first phase was characterized by large capital inputs, a heavy reliance on modern technology such as earth moving machinery and tractor cultivation, and a centralised authoritarian management structure.

By the end of the phase some of the more outlying schemes at Mandera and Mbalambala in North-Eastern Province and Wema in Coast Province had been hived off to Provincial Agricultural Offices and the project concentrated on two irrigation 'clusters' in Turkana and Isiolo Districts. At the Turkana cluster some 240 ha had been developed at Katilu, 35 ha at Kekarongole and 30 ha at Amolem, and at the Isiolo cluster, 70 ha at Malka Dakaa, 65 ha at Merti and 10 ha at Gafarsa.

The second phase (1979–81) was marked by the gradual withdrawal of UNDP/FAO assistance. The Ministry of Agriculture and local tenant cooperative societies were expected to take on increased responsibility for scheme operation and maintenance, and new donors were expected to step in with financial and technical assistance (Government of Kenya, 1984). These expectations were unfulfilled. In Isiolo District the British Overseas Development Administration (ODA), after expressing initial interest, decided not to support the schemes. As a result, because government was unable to afford to run the high cost schemes without donor assistance, the schemes rapidly declined. In Turkana District in 1982 the irrigated area at Katilu was only 194 ha and at Kekarongole only 15 ha. At Amolem there was no irrigation because of lack of diesel to run the pumps. In Isiolo District the schemes almost totally collapsed. Malka Dakaa and Merti functioned only intermittently and then only on a limited basis. For example, in his 1982 Annual Report the Cluster Manager recounts that after May there would be no diesel to run the pumps.

The third phase (1982–4) was marked by the continuing decline of the Isiolo Cluster of schemes. Only at Gafarsa, as the result of support from the European Economic Community (EEC), was there hope of any revival in scheme fortunes. By the end of the period the Catholic Mission at Merti had largely taken control of Merti scheme. At Malka Dakaa the scheme depended almost entirely on the intermittent efforts of the tenants to raise money to buy fuel and other inputs.

In Turkana District the schemes underwent a temporary revival as a result of Norwegian (NORAD) assistance. This assistance aimed to reduce operating costs by converting the schemes to basin irrigation and, at Amolem, a gravity fed irrigation system, and to encourage scheme self-management through a tenant cooperative society. In spite of their high costs – according to a recent report (Government of Kenya, 1984) the development costs of the three government schemes in Turkana amount to $61,420 per hectare or $21,800 per tenant household – none of the ARID schemes succeeded in achieving their most basic objective of providing destitute pastoralists with a viable alternative to pastoralism; indeed, almost invariably the destitute were the least able to benefit from scheme life, and were forced to depend on off-scheme interests (Hogg, 1983; Broche-Due & Störas, 1983).

Pauperisation

Those who first planned the irrigation schemes presumed that they were dealing with discrete economic sectors, so that pastoralists who settled at the schemes would eventually become full-time farmers. The assumption was that agriculture was inherently a more productive and secure way of life than pastoralism, with all its attendant risks and hardships. According to William Allan, a respected agricultural authority, whenever in the past pastoralists had been given the opportunity to settle they had willingly 'exchanged the freedom and austerity of nomadism for the greater security and routine labour of a sedentary or semi-sedentary way of life' (1965: 319).

The assumption, however, only partly reflected the attitude of the pastoralists themselves. While most of the pastoralists who settled at the schemes rather liked the idea of a settled life, especially since farming offered an opportunity to rebuild herds and flocks, they did not see settlement at a scheme as in any way a total commitment, and they continued to invest in livestock whenever they could. Such investment was not a reflection of poor farm productivity and general disillusion with farming – indeed, livestock investment was at its highest when farm productivity was at its peak – nor did it derive simply from a cultural attachment to livestock (although obviously people were attached to their livestock), but rather, a recognition that livestock appeared to be the most viable form of investment (Barth, 1973; Haaland, 1977; Sörbo, 1977).

Irrigation agriculture at the schemes could not offer the same kind of investment opportunities as livestock which increase naturally. In contrast, plots at the irrigation schemes could not be increased by investment of their product (crops), because the size of plots and crops produced were controlled by management, and were not freely exchangeable.[2] Farmers therefore had no alternative but to invest their occasional surpluses in off-scheme interests. Secondly, no family was prepared to invest all its assets in a single economic enterprise and especially one as obviously uncertain as irrigation agriculture. After the undeclared *Shifta*[3] war between Somalia and Kenya in the mid-1960s, which was followed by the droughts of the 1970s, the main strategy of both the wealthy and poor was to diversify economically in as many different ways as possible. People clearly perceived diversification to be the only way to insure themselves against drought and famine (cf. Dahl, 1979; O'Leary, 1980).

Irrigation agriculture was therefore always likely to encourage an expansion of livestock herds, the exact opposite of what was intended by those who established the schemes. It was only the poor performance of the schemes and the lack of any regular surpluses that effectively limited the rate of this expansion. Nevertheless, scheme performance in good years did allow for a slow accumulation of livestock, especially smallstock. In 1976, for example, very few Malka Dakaa farmers had any smallstock but by 1980 smallstock flocks were a common sight in the fields after harvest, and along the irrigation canals during the dry season. Women regularly carried home grass from along these canals and maize stalks from the fields to feed the young lambs and kids, and even calves. Brown (1980) reports a similar increase in flocks at Katilu scheme.

Increasing pressure on local grazing at the schemes was not, however, just the result of investment by farmers, but, more significantly, the result of the rapid transformation of nearly all the schemes into small towns, which attracted large numbers of non-farmers. Along the Turkwel, for instance, the population of Katilu scheme increased from almost nothing in 1970 to over 10,000 by 1980. Many of these were poor pastoralists attracted to the scheme because of the shops and opportunities for trade and wage labour. Others were fairly wealthy pastoralists who had moved near to the scheme because of opportunities to sell milk, and because of the protection proximity to the scheme offered against armed raiders. The overall effect was massive destruction of the forest along the banks of the Turkwel for building, stock enclosures, fuelwood and farm plots and localised heavy overgrazing by settlement herds and flocks (Broche-Due & Störas, 1983).

While the farmers were the main victims of this degradation they were not always the main culprits, for they could seldom afford to invest large amounts in livestock. The main livestock buyers were the shopkeepers, who were also often livestock traders, who bought up most of the available local livestock, and then grazed them near to the schemes prior to transport 'down-country'. When local conditions deteriorated the traders could afford to hire herders to take their livestock to stock camps. The poor, however, were generally trapped at the schemes with their few stock and because of their immobility were the first to suffer in any drought.

In the past, the movement of pastoral villages was largely dictated by the needs of the livestock. Nowadays, irrigation farming, wage labour and trade provide those settled at the schemes with alternative sources of income and subsistence. As a result, when local grazing is short all the settlement-based animals may be sent to mobile stock camps where they are herded by the young men while most people stay put. The conspicuous failure of the irrigation schemes, however, to generate either income or grain and hence reduce the need for livestock, meant that most poor farmers at the schemes still had to depend on their livestock to supplement their farm incomes. They were caught in a dilemma, for, quite apart from any labour problems they might experience, so long as they depended on the schemes for at least part of their subsistence/ income they could not move all their livestock away from the schemes. This basic restriction on the mobility of their livestock very often meant it rapidly declined in condition.

In contrast, the wealthy at the schemes who had access to secure incomes could send all their livestock to a stock camp. They did not need to keep their livestock nearby to supplement farm income or subsistence, because they had other economic resources they could draw on. Therefore, as soon as local conditions began to deteriorate they were quickly able to move their stock away to satellite stock camps. Similar processes have been noted elsewhere in Kenya among the Il Chamus (Little, 1985) and the Orma (Ensminger, 1984). I illustrate my argument with two case studies, one of Iresa Boru Township and the other of Gafarsa Scheme, in Isiolo District.

Case I – Iresa Boru Township

Iresa Boru is a small trade centre situated some 5 km south of the Ewaso
River and 40 km north east of Gafarsa (see Fig. 14.1). It has three shops,
a hospital dispensary, a primary school and a mosque. There is a dense
concentration of both people and stock in the roughly 30 km^2 grazing
area which surrounds the centre. Few people actually live in the trade
centre itself, but walk in from nearby villages in order to buy shop goods.

Just to the north of the shops is the Lorian Swamp. To the south is a
belt of *Sansevera* trees, and between the trees and the swamp a featureless
plain which is bare in the dry season, but which is covered with grass
in the rains. The borders of the swamp fluctuate with the seasons; when
the river is in full spate its flood waters almost reach the shops, but the
waters recede rapidly in the dry season, and indeed in severe drought
dry up altogether.

The swamp dominates the landscape. In spite of its importance as a
natural resource which provides all year round grazing and water, it is
a mixed blessing. It offers rich grazing but also contains dangers from
crocodiles, riverfluke, mosquitoes and tsetse fly. As a result cattle and
smallstock are not generally grazed far into the swamp. Throughout
much of the year, however, but especially in the dry season, there are
usually large numbers of stock grazing in the shallower waters.

There was not a permanent settlement at Iresa Boru prior to *Shifta*;
stockowners only visited the area in the dry season to water their animals
but did not linger, for the river held too many dangers for their stock,
especially from tsetse fly. In 1970, however, the National Christian Council of Kenya (NCCK) established a pilot scheme of 30 irrigated acres,
which attracted many destitute Boran families. In 1971 the first shop
was opened, and in 1973 a primary school was established and later a
dispensary opened. By 1973 the scheme comprised about 300 cultivated
acres. Since then farm production has been interrupted by frequent
droughts, in 1975–6, 1979–80 and 1983–4, and by flooding in 1977 and
1981. Nevertheless, in spite of the considerable risk that is involved, as
soon as one irrigation site is abandoned another site is established, for
stockowners in the area are keen to grow maize.

The central dilemma for Iresa Boru stockowners is to balance their
dependence on the swamp with the periodical needs of their livestock
to move away to dry grazing. They fully understand that grazing in the
swamp all year round leads to infestation by riverfluke, trypanosomiasis
and foot rot but, so long as they depend both on their milch stock and
on farming, there is little they can do about it. They just have to put up
with the risks. It is noticeable that the very wealthiest pastoralists avoid

the swamp, except in the dry season. When they buy goods from the shops, for example, they can afford to buy in bulk and to transport the goods back by donkey. The poor, by contrast, seldom have access to baggage animals, depend on shops to make daily purchases and on the swamp for its opportunities to farm and for its easy watering and herding. The presence of the primary school is also an attraction to the very poor, for with few animals their children are not needed for herding, and with education a child may possibly later acquire a job.

Iresa Boru is, in effect, a poor man's grazing area, a kind of pastoralist's 'slum', where few stockowners own more than 10–20 cattle, and most families have sons, brothers or a husband away in wage labour. Considering the scarcity of stock and the generally meagre supply of milk available, even in wet seasons, their adaptation to poverty is skilful, but is only possible at the expense of a decline in herd condition and the degradation of the local environment. Already the plain closest to the swamp has been denuded of trees, as people have cut them down to build their cattle and smallstock pens and for fuelwood. In the droughts of 1979–80 and 1983–4, when the swamp dried up and farming was no longer possible, it was the poorer stockowners who suffered most, because they were trapped by their poverty and immobility (Hogg, 1985a). The conflict between dependence on livestock and settled life at a scheme is particularly acute in time of drought. This was especially true at Gafarsa Scheme in 1979.

Case II – Gafarsa Scheme

Gafarsa has a population of about 1,600, dispersed over a number of pastoral villages which surround the scheme centre. The centre consists of a scheme camp, a primary school, a new dispensary and three or four small shops. The total area of settlement is about six square kilometres, with an overall density of roughly 280 persons per km².

Families move into and out of Gafarsa. The frequency and distance of such moves is largely dictated by the variable distribution of grazing for cattle and small stock, and the degree of dependence of families on maize. So in the rains some stockowners move out to the periphery, to be nearer to the grazing. The number and extent of these moves are restricted by the need to work their farm plots and/or to attend 'food-for-work'. As a result, wealthier livestock owners tend to live on the periphery, and the destitutes who are entirely dependent on agriculture or food relief nearer to the scheme centre.

Gafarsa residents prefer to keep stock away at the camps, for they are convinced that the area is not good for livestock, not just because good fodder is short but because, they say, the general air of the place causes stock to weaken. Only the very wealthiest residents, who have access to cash incomes and the necessary labour to look after their animals at stock camp (either because they can afford to keep sons from school/wage labour or because they can afford to hire herders), can afford to live apart from their livestock. Most others are forced to make frequent and difficult choices about the movements of their animals and their dependence on the scheme. When scheme productivity or food relief deliveries are interrupted whole families move to the stock camp. During drought the choice between moving and staying can be very difficult, and delay can result in destitution.

During the 1975–6 drought the choice for most residents was easy enough; most of the stock at the scheme stayed put, and largely survived off the stubble from the fields. In the 1979–80 drought the situation was very different. In 1979, in the lead-up to the drought, there was little or no farm production and the canal silted. At the time residents were extremely disillusioned with the scheme, and food relief deliveries were frequently interrupted. As a result most could see little point in keeping livestock at the scheme. The poorer stockowners, however, prevaricated and, as a result, many lost all their stock when the drought worsened. I describe below the different responses to the impending crisis of wealthy and poor stockowners at one village on the scheme periphery.

In 1979 Huka's village was located some three kilometres from the Gafarsa scheme, where most of its members also farmed. The wealthiest cattle owner, Huka, had over 60 cattle at the village, and others at stock camp. Most other stockowners in the village had only a few cattle. In early February Huka's family herd and those of poorer co-villagers pastured and watered to the south east of the village. Towards the end of the month a meeting of stockowners decided that the cattle would be better grazed in the direction of the river.

In early March there was little rain in the area, which meant the cattle, which numbered some 80–90, were taken to graze twice a day. During this period the younger married men of the village, all of whom also often attended 'food-for-work' at the scheme, took it in turns to herd during the early mornings. The children herded during the day.

The poor rains in March/April meant not only meagre milk yields, but a new herding regime, for the cattle were watered at the river only every other day so that they could take advantage of the good grazing in the opposite direction. To have both grazed and watered on the same day would have exhausted the cattle. An additional danger was the presence of lion near to the river, which necessitated the presence of adult herders when the cattle watered.

The use of married men to herd the cattle was resented by some who considered the danger of lion exaggerated and pleaded scheme commitments. By early May, as grazing conditions deteriorated near to the scheme, stockowners became increasingly worried about their cattle, especially their calves. Many complained that they were tied by their dependence on food relief at the scheme. They especially envied the freedom the Somali had to follow the rains.

As local conditions worsened Huka was able to maintain the condition of his animals by sending most of them to stock camp. He could do this because:

(i)   he had access to the labour of an adult grandson who herded the cattle at stock camp;

(ii) he was a wealthy man whose four adult sons were each earning good salaries in government jobs, and could afford to buy maize to compensate for falling milk yields.

Poorer stockowners had to keep many more of their animals at the scheme and so they were the first to be hit when drought struck.

These examples from Iresa Boru and Gafarsa illustrate the difficulties that the poor at the irrigation schemes have in achieving any long term economic stability. They lose out both in their investment in agriculture – because of poor scheme productivity – and their investment in pastoralism – because of settlement. Indeed, the outcome of nearly 20 years' irrigation development in Northern Kenya has been the creation of a highly unstable irrigation sector, which has had little significant impact on the problem of pastoral destitution. While some poor pastoralists have 'made it' via irrigation agriculture back into the pastoral sector, and even into retail trade, the majority have not. Rather, they have been forced to earn a living in the informal economy. The prospects for these poor families are increasingly bleak (see Dahl, 1979, on Isiolo Boran).

Conclusion

An overriding concern in the history of pastoral development in Kenya has been the danger of overgrazing as a result of 'overstocking beyond the carrying capacity of the land'. It was believed, almost as a matter of faith, by administrators and range planners alike, that the rangeland areas were vastly overstocked and overpopulated (Anderson, 1982; Homewood & Rodgers, Chapter 5). Attempts to institute grazing controls and to reorganise traditional land tenure systems were motivated as much by concern to conserve the land as by any strictly economic considerations. Indeed, the two went hand in hand: economic development in the pastoral areas was conceived of partly as an exercise in range conservation (Brown, 1963).

The development of irrigation agriculture in Northern Kenya was no exception, but part and parcel of a much broader strategy to reduce pressure on the range and to provide pastoralists with an alternative to what were generally considered the destructive effects of traditional pastoralism. In this it failed disastrously. If anything, the development of irrigation schemes has only encouraged the further marginalisation of a group of already poor pastoralists and significantly increased pressure on important dry-season grazing areas, areas of vital importance in times of drought.

While there are many reasons for the failure of irrigation schemes in Northern Kenya – high cost, poor management and organisation – perhaps the most fundamental is the failure to appreciate the high level of risk involved, and the difficulties many poor pastoralists experience in combining herd/flock management with settled farming. Irrigation in this marginal environment is heavily biased in favour of the wealthy. Without heavy subsidies it is just too expensive and/or risky for the poor. By reducing overheads and by simplifying scheme technology donors are not thereby increasing the chances of the poor to participate in a sustainable development activity, but merely ensuring that some families, mainly the richer ones, in some years, obtain reasonable returns from their plots; but such returns to them are a bonus, not their principal means of subsistence.

The problem of pastoral destitution stems from a variety of causes and not simply, as the conventional wisdom still dictates, from overstocking which causes degradation and destitution. Indeed, it can be argued that a number of rangeland areas, such as large parts of Turkana and most of Isiolo Districts, are under- rather than overstocked. In 1982, largely as the result of widespread stock raiding and the concentration of the population into famine camps, only half of Turkana District was populated (Ecosystems, 1983). Similarly in Isiolo District, large areas to the north of the Ewaso River were empty of both people and stock, and upwards of 40 per cent of Boran were living in small towns and irrigation schemes. Destitution has often had little to do with drought at all but has been a direct consequence of external interventions which have restricted mobility and cut off important dry-season grazing areas (see Gamaledinn, Chapter 16).

Developers and donors should recognise that there is no real economic alternative to pastoralism for the majority of the population in the arid areas of Kenya, and that the major emphasis of development should be in trying to preserve rather than destroy the mobility of pastoralists and their livestock (Hogg, 1985b). It makes little economic sense, and even less conservation sense, to try to settle pastoralists at irrigation schemes which neither government nor local people can afford to run, and which have the inevitable result of restricting mobility and creating localised dust bowls.

Notes

1   I am grateful to the Overseas Development Administration for funding my research in Kenya, to Paul Baxter for his comments on an earlier draft of this paper, and to Nikki Sandford for the map.
2   Barth has pointed out the peculiarities of livestock as capital, 'that saving and investment are necessary under all circumstances, the herd is perishable and must be replaced, and . . . such investment is possible without benefit of any economic institutions since one of the main products of the herds is lambs, calves, etc.' (1973: 12), in contrast with land which 'cannot be increased by investment of its product (crops) except where economic institutions exist to effect its conversion' (Barth, 1973).
3   *Shifta* is an Amhara word, which means robbers, outlaws and bandits. The *Shifta* war (1963–7) involved the Kenyan Army and irregular forces and sympathisers. It was essentially concerned to incorporate within a 'Greater Somalia' most of the Northern Frontier District of Kenya.

References

ALLAN, W. (1965). *The African Husbandman*. London: Oliver & Boyd.
ANDERSON, D.M. (1982). Herder, settler and colonial rule: a history of the peoples of the Baringo Plains, Kenya, *c.* 1890–1940. Unpublished Ph. D. thesis, University of Cambridge.
BARTH, F. (1973). A general perspective on nomad-sedentary relations in the Middle East. In *The Desert and the Sown*, ed. C. Nelson. Berkeley, California: Institute of International Studies, University of California.
BROCHE-DUE, V. & STORAS, F. (1983). *The Fields of the Foe – Factors Constraining Agricultural Output and Farmers' Capacity for Participation on Katilu Irrigation Scheme*. Bergen: NORAD/University of Bergen.,
BROWN, J. (1980). *A Socio-anthropological Survey of the Irrigation Schemes on the Turkwel River*. FAO, AG: DP/KEN/78/015. Rome: FAO.
BROWN. L.H. (1963) *The Development of the Semi-Arid Areas of Kenya*. Nairobi: Ministry of Agriculture, Govt Printer.
BROWN, L.H. (1973). *Conservation for Survival: Ethiopia's Choice*. Addis Ababa: Haile Selassie University Press.
CHAMBERS, R. (1969). *Settlement Schemes in Tropical Africa*. London: Routledge & Kegan Paul.

DAHL, G. (1979). *Suffering Grass: Subsistence and Society in Waso Borana.* Stockholm: Department of Social Anthropology, University of Stockholm.

ECOSYSTEMS (1983). *Turkana District Resources Survey Draft Report, vol II.* Nairobi: Ministry of Energy & Regional Development, Govt Printer.

ENSMINGER, J. (1984). Political economy among the pastoral Galole Orma: the effects of market integration. Unpublished Ph.D. thesis, Northwestern University.

FAO (1964). *Report on a Reconnaissance of the Agricultural Potential of the Turkana District of Kenya.* FAO, B-AG-010(22). Rome: FAO.

FAO/UNDP (1977). *Project Revision, Kenya, Irrigation in Arid Regions.* FAO, KEN/74/018/E/01/12. Rome: FAO.

GOVERNMENT OF KENYA (1984). *Evaluation of the Turkana Irrigation Cluster.* Nairobi: Ministry of Agriculture and Livestock Development, Planning Division.

HAALAND, G. (1977). Pastoral systems of production: the socio-cultural context and some economic and ecological implications. In *Landuse and development*, ed. P. O'Keefe & B. Wisner. London: International Africa Institute.

HOGG, R.S. (1983). Irrigation agriculture and pastoral development: a lesson from Kenya. *Development and Change*, **14**, 577–91.

HOGG, R.S. (1985a). The politics of drought: the pauperization of Isiolo Boran. *Disasters*, **9**(1), 39–43.

HOGG, R.S. (1985b). Re-stocking pastoralists in Kenya: a strategy for relief and rehabilitation. ODI Pastoral Development Network Paper 19c. London: ODI.

HOGG, R.S. (1985c). The socio-economic responses of nomadic pastoralists to permanent settlement and irrigation agriculture. Unpublished ODA ESCOR Report no.R3674.

KONCZACKI, Z.A. (1978). *The Economics of Pastoralism.* London: Frank Cass.

O'LEARY, M. (1980). Response to drought in Kitui District, Kenya. *Disasters*, **4**(3), 315–27.

LITTLE, P.D. (1985). Social differentiation and pastoralist sedentarization in Northern Kenya. *Africa*, **55**(3), 243–61.

MIGOT-ADHOLLA, S. & LITTLE, P.D. (1981). Evolution of policy towards the development of pastoral areas in Kenya. In *The Future of Pastoral Peoples*, ed. J. Galaty, D. Aronson, P. Salzman & A. Chouinard. Ottawa: International Development Research Centre.

PRATT, D. & GWYNNE, M. (1977). *Rangeland Management and Ecology in East Africa.* London: Hodder & Stoughton.

SÖRBO, G. (1977). Nomads on the scheme – a study of irrigation agriculture and pastoralism in Eastern Sudan. In *Landuse and Development*, ed P. O'Keefe & B. Wisner. London: International Africa Institute.

SANDFORD, S. (1983). *Management of Pastoral Development in the Third World.* Chichester: Wiley.

15

Approaches to water resource development, Sokoto Valley, Nigeria: the problem of sustainability

W. M. ADAMS

Introduction

In recent years there has been a growing awareness among development 'experts' (Chambers, 1983), of the importance of the natural environment, not simply as a constraint on possible action, but as part of the proper concern of development planning. In part this is the effect of the growth of environmentalism in the developed world in the 1970s (Sandbach, 1980; O'Riordan, 1981), in part a response to specific environment-related crises such as Sahelian drought and desertification. This interest has had two obvious results. First, there has been a realisation that the welfare of the poorest groups in poor countries, themselves the target of recent development concerns such as the basic needs approach (e.g. Stewart, 1985), is closely related to environmental quality (Mabogunje, 1984). Second, there has been a search for a new paradigm of development based on knowledge about the limitations and potentials of the natural environment. This search has expanded from the definition of limits and criteria for development based on ecology (Dasmann, Milton & Freeman, 1973), to attempts to define an alternative to existing productivist paradigms of development in the form of 'ecodevelopment' (Riddell, 1981; Glaeser, 1984; cf. Redclift, 1984). Probably the best known statement of the principle that development can *only* be based on the conservation of the environment is the *World Conservation Strategy* (WCS), launched in 1979 by the International Union for the Conservation of Nature (IUCN, 1980). This was based on the concept of sustainable development, and the premise that conservation and development were not alternatives or opposites, but were mutually dependent. According to the WCS, the conservation of resources and ecosystems was essential if development was to be sustained. It argued that

development and conservation operate in the same global context, and the underlying problems that must be overcome if either is to be successful are identical. *(IUCN, 1980: Section 2.20)*

307

In parallel with this concern about environmental issues in Third World development in general, there has been growing concern for environmental aspects of individual projects (Biswas, 1978; Stein and Johnson, 1979), as well as project appraisal procedures (Abel & Stocking, 1981; Ahmad & Sammy, 1985). In theory at least, quite detailed recommendations can be made about the appraisal of particular development projects and the problems associated with different kinds of schemes. However, to step away from theoretical planning structures and considerations into the real world of project implementation is a very different matter. Despite knowledge about how projects *ought* to be planned, in practice environmental considerations still get a low priority. Furthermore, despite the interest in 'ecodevelopment' as a concept, and the hopeful generalisations of the WCS, there has as yet been little or no progress with the infusion of ideas of environmental awareness, conservation, or sustainability into development programmes or policies. Without influence at this general policy level, small-scale piecemeal modifications of particular projects are of little value. Most environmental thinking in the development field remains remote and idealistic, and there is a large and serious gulf between development theorists and development practitioners, both in their frameworks of thought and their scales of analysis. Theorists tend to concentrate on general issues, be they macro-scale or related to single projects. They can be out of touch with the realities of project development, and their analyses may seem abstruse and irrelevant to decision-makers on the ground. Practitioners are necessarily more specific in their concerns, but frequently lack breadth of vision and an effective theoretical framework. They are constrained in what they say (and think) by political and commercial considerations. Communications between practitioners and theorists are poor, and the process of learning from past mistakes is slow, uninstitutionalised and ineffective. Questions about the environment in development are left unanswered, and frequently unasked.

It is important therefore to bridge the gaps between theory and practice, and between theorists and practitioners. It is also important to try to look beyond single projects at the effects of sets of projects or policies over time. Ideally, this should be done by detailed monitoring of current projects, and more attention should be paid to this by development agencies. Another way to do this is to look retrospectively at past development projects. It is important to go beyond a simple inventory of what was done and its effects (although studies of this sort are still uncommon enough to be important), to look at perceptions of the need for develop-

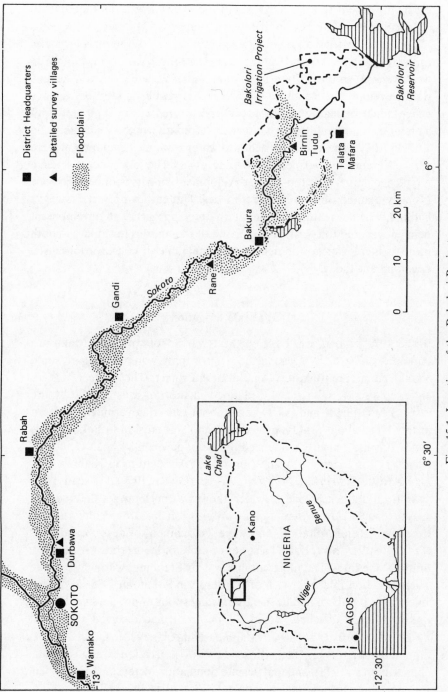

Fig. 15.1. Location of the Bakolori Project.

309

ment, the extent of knowledge about the environment, and the degree of learning from the development experience.

This chapter tries to do this by examining two different approaches to the development of the water resources of the Sokoto Valley in north-west Nigeria. In the 1970s a large dam and extensive irrigation scheme were developed at Bakolori (Fig. 15.1). Its problems, and the lessons which might be learned from its poor performance, are compared with a previous small-scale water conservation initiative in the valley between 1917 and 1921. The two approaches to water resource development were very different, and yet neither was successful. The more recent scheme is typical of large-scale top–down development, and its poor performance is easily blamed on these characteristics. The earlier project, however, had many of the features of the alternative approaches to development being advocated today. The comparison of the reasons for failure in both projects is relevant to the debate on sustainable or conservation-based development today.

Large scale irrigation

In the 1970s, a dam was built on the River Sokoto at Talata Mafara to impound the strongly seasonal flow and supply water to irrigate some 30,000 ha in the Bakolori Agricultural Project. The project was an enlarged version of a scheme planned in the previous decade by the FAO (FAO, 1969), and partly came about due to government concern in the 1950s about aridity, desiccation and soil erosion in Sokoto. This concern is most clearly evidenced by the paper in 1959 by D.G. Owen, Secretary for Irrigation in the Ministry of Agriculture in Kaduna, *The Dying River Systems of Northern Nigeria* (Owen, 1959). A 'dead' river system he defined as one in which there was no longer a defined dry-season course. Owen saw a clear progression from overcultivation to excessive erosion, siltation, and the encroachment of desert conditions (Owen, 1959). This followed a series of more or less alarmist statements on the same lines. The most notable was by Stebbing, who wrote of the 'silent and invisible' approach of the desert in Sokoto in 1935 (Stebbing, 1935: 510), but there had been earlier suggestions of progressive desiccation and desert advance (Bovill, 1921), and it had received a mention by Lord Lugard in *The Dual Mandate* (Lugard, 1922). Other authors argued that there was in fact little evidence of desiccation through climatic change (Jones, 1938), and that despite population increases, environmental conditions in Sokoto had not deteriorated in the 1950s (Prothero, 1962). Subsequent work in fact confirmed that increased sedimentation had occurred, although its effect was to increase flood heights in the Rima River and not cause desiccation (Ledger, 1961). There was some controversy over the 'dying rivers' paper. Harrison Church said in 1961 that, 'in my view the document was very controversial and I found that quite a lot of government people disagreed with it' (Harrison Church, 1961), however, it awakened ready responses in the government in Northern Nigeria in 1959. The Resident of Sokoto reported that the position of the Sokoto–Rima Basin was 'parlous in the extreme', and the Sultan thought the situation 'a matter of life and death to the Province's economy'. The Resident in Sokoto called for engineering skill and capital from Regional, Federal or international sources to prevent further silting of rivers, and the Native Authority noted 'with pleasure' that funds were being sought from the United Nations Special Fund for a survey.[1] The Food and Agriculture Organisation/International Cooperative Administration who were carrying out an agricultural survey of the Northern Region in 1960 recommended a reconnaissance survey of the whole river basin, and detailed survey of the floodplains to lead to a development plan for the Sokoto Valley.[2]

In 1962 the Sokoto–Rima Basin investigation was begun by the FAO, funded initially by the UN Special Fund, and from 1966 by the UNDP. Its ostensible aim was

to determine and map the natural resources of the area and develop plans for the stabilisation, diversification and increase of agricultural production.

(FAO, 1969)

However, the Sokoto Basin study was heavily biased towards the location of specific areas for irrigation. Only 10 per cent of man-months comprised work by socio-economists, and despite reiteration of the poor condition of land in the basin, the focus of the soil survey was solely on the location of irrigable areas. The volume *Land Use and Agronomy* in the basin was vague, lacked conclusions, and was not integrated into the rest of the report (Adams, 1983). Thus a government concern about desiccation (which was possibly misplaced), and evidence of increasing soil erosion in the Sokoto Basin, gave rise to an investigation whose report said very little about those problems. Indeed, in its brief reference to them, the FAO Report called for future 'watershed conservation measures and river basin studies and plans' (FAO, 1969, vol. 5: 87), the very purpose it was itself intended to fulfil.

However, although the FAO report failed to address the problem of soil erosion, it made clear suggestions about flood control and irrigation. A series of dams in the headwaters of the basin was recommended, plus irrigation in the downstream floodplain and adjacent to the dams. The first phase of development was to be a dam on the River Sokoto at Bakolori, and a 12,000 ha irrigation scheme on terrace and floodplain land just downstream. This idea was taken up in 1972 when an Italian company won the design contract. Their report was completed in 1974, although by that time they had also won the contract for construction and had already begun work (Adams, 1985a). The Bakolori Project was one of several large irrigation schemes begun at that time in Northern Nigeria, and followed a long but unsuccessful government involvement in a series of more or less experimental small irrigation schemes in Sokoto and elsewhere (Palmer-Jones, 1981, 1987). Bakolori exhibits a number of features typical of large-scale rural development schemes (Williams, 1981) and top–down development planning (Filani, 1981). Indeed, it is becoming known as a classic example of development failure. Some problems at least can be attributed to a failure of basic knowledge and environmental perception, others to a related failure to achieve stated development targets.

Two features of the project in particular show poor perception and knowledge. First, although the delicate relationship between floodplain farming (principally of rice and dry season vegetables) and river flooding had been clearly perceived since the 1920s, and had been identified again in 1969 by the FAO, the Bakolori Project was constructed without consideration of its impact on downstream farmers. The area of the scheme was over 2.5 times that suggested by the FAO, but the reservoir was not enlarged. The extra water for irrigation on the scheme was that earmarked for downstream rice farming, and without that allowance the wet season flood peaks needed to inundate the floodplain were reduced. The dam was completed in 1976, and by the early 1980s wet season cultivation had shifted from rice to the less productive mixture of guinea corn, millet and rice, and dry season vegetable gardening had ceased over extensive areas (Adams, 1985b).

A second example of poor appraisal is provided by the significant underestimate of the proportion of the project area already cultivated. The design studies suggested that 40 per cent of the scheme was unused or unclaimed by cultivators (Impresit, 1974, Section A vol. 3: 32), and on this basis a 5,000 ha commercial sugar estate and 2,000 ha cattle feedlot were planned, which greatly boosted the cost/benefit ratio of the scheme. In practice, occupancy was far greater, and the loss of land to engineering works (up to 20%) more than exceeded the unclaimed land area. Not only was a sugar estate impossible, but all cultivators had their holdings reduced in size.

Project development at Bakolori failed to match planned targets in several ways. The first concerned the timetable. The Contractor had claimed to be able to complete Bakolori inside six years, compared to the 15–20 years he estimated would normally be required (Tasso, 1978). This 'instant development' was the exact reverse of the slow and cautious approach recommended by the FAO (FAO, 1969, vol. 2: 4). Largely because of difficulties over land tenure and the expropriation of land for engineering construction (Bird, 1985; Adams, 1984) work fell behind. In 1980 only 2,700 ha were developed for irrigation (compared to the 17,000 ha planned, Impresit, 1974; Etuk & Abalu, 1982) and engineering construction finished in 1984, over four years late. Even at that time, however, substantial areas of the scheme lay idle because of land reallocation difficulties. These were made more serious by the failure in communication between scheme developers and farmers over the question of land expropriation and compensation, which led to repeated blockades of the project in 1979 and 1980 and a violent action by riot police in which many villagers were imprisoned, some injured and some killed (Adams, 1984).

There have also been problems with the economics of the Bakolori Project. Not only did project development fall behind, but the land tenure problems have meant that only part of the scheme has been irrigated, in 1980–1 only 38 per cent of the area (Etuk & Abalu, 1982). Also, yields have been poor, with maize only 22 per cent of the designer's prediction, wheat 42 per cent and rice 60 per cent (Etuk & Abalu, 1982, and project records). Furthermore, the large area of industrial crops such as tomatoes and groundnuts, which were given high priority by the designer as the raw material for agricultural processing industries, has not materialised. Groundnuts are grown, but are processed or eaten in the village, following the collapse of the national market in the 1970s. The Cadbury tomato paste factory at Zaria closed in May 1976, and no facilities have been established at Bakolori or in Sokoto.

One can therefore criticise Bakolori for its implementation in ignorance of the environment (the downstream impacts), ignorance of local socio-economic conditions (land tenure and land occupancy problems), an unrealistically rapid implementation schedule, ineffective communications and coercive relations with farmers related to the scale and speed of operations, unrealistic economic appraisal and unrealistic predictions about other essential related developments.

The classic solution to these kinds of shortcomings, which are fairly characteristic of 'top–down' development of this sort, is to advocate incremental, small-scale participant-led development projects (cf. Stohr, 1981; Chambers, 1983). It is, however, much easier to recommend such projects than to develop them in practice. This is demonstrated by a study of a previous approach to development in the Sokoto Valley. This appears to have some of these supposedly desirable characteristics, yet it too met with problems: indeed within a few years its effects were lost completely. It is instructive to examine this scheme in detail, to see why it failed, and the extent to which it is comparable with its grandiose successor.

Floodplain water conservation

The earlier developments in the Sokoto Valley also had their origins in Government concern about drought and desiccation. After the severe 1913 drought (Grove, 1973), the Resident at Sokoto again reported low rainfall in 1917,[3] low river flows in the River Rima and poor rice and sorghum yields:

The central and northern districts have suffered from the poor rainfall – their Guinea-corn crops along the Gulbin Rima and Gulbin Sokoto were practically complete failures. The stalks grew well but there was practically no grain in the ear. The same is true of the rice crop in Silame District – the river flood remained low and lasted so short a time that the grain had no chance to mature.

(Sokoto Annual Report, 1917)

The dry years of 1913 and 1917 led the Resident at Sokoto to believe that the area was undergoing progressive desiccation. In comments in the 1917 report the Governor of the Northern Region observed 'apparently the rainfall is not diminishing but merely oscillating'.[4] Indeed rainfall in Sokoto in 1918 was good (807 mm, MRT, 1979) and river flooding was extensive. However the Resident, while recognising inter-annual variations, maintained that the average rainfall recorded since 1904 (25–33 in) was 'less than any previous 15 year average in the preceding 10 centuries'. The symptoms of desiccation were, he felt, 'unmistakeable'.[5]

In pursuit of further information about desiccation in 1917, a District Officer, Harold Edwardes, made enquiries in Gandi District 'as to the progressive fall of the flood level of the Gulbin Sokoto and the consequent drying up of large lake areas in the valley of the river'. (Sokoto Annual Report, 1917). Tapkin Kuberi, near Gandi Village, was reported in 1918 to be practically dry, having been 'within living memory' 600 acres (240 ha) in extent, while a lake outside Yartsokua Village was also said to have dried up entirely for the first time ever (Sokoto Annual Report, 1917).

The Resident's perception in 1918 was of progressive desiccation causing low rainfall and poor river flooding and hence seriously reduced
foodcrop production. A solution was at hand. If a canal were cut (at an
estimated cost of £20–£30) through the bank of the river at Gandi the
Tapkin Kuberi could be reflooded the next year and a similar canal
would do the same at another site at Dawakawa. This could be just the
beginning:

The next step is to build a few dams with simple cement and timber sluices in
selected sites and by this means at trifling cost we can retain large areas of water
and use them for irrigation.   *(Sokoto Annual Report, 1918)*

The Resident saw a direct escape from the effects of desiccation via
irrigation. In his 1918 report he wrote:

The benefits that result from these works are various: evaporation, soakage,
irrigation, fisheries. As a means of combatting desiccation, it compares favourably with afforestation. Afforestation is slow, expensive and indirect in its results.
The benefits of this water storage are direct, and obtained at trifling cost. The
native idea of irrigation is primitive and laborious, but here there are considerable
areas which can be made available for irrigation by gravity. There is a dense
farming population close at hand, and if a single area were laid out as a beginning.
I feel sure it would be rapidly taken up.   *(Sokoto Annual Report, 1918)*

The belief in the efficacy of forests to control runoff and promote crop
growth by increasing humidity was widespread, being cited for example
by Lord Lugard (Lugard, 1922).

Work on the floodplain was begun in the dry season 1917–8, and the
Sokoto Native Administration, under Edwardes' direction, constructed
a series of small canals on dams along the valley from Dampo to Rabah
(Fig. 15.2):

By this means the river water has refilled a number of lakes and depressions
which have dried up at various times during the past 20 years or more, owing
to the continuous fall in the annual flood level of the Gulbin Sokoto and the
gradual failure of a number of tributary streams.   *(Sokoto Annual Report, 1918)*

These works, costing £217, were intended to increase storage in the
floodplain pools from 0.8m to 21m m^3 (Table 15.1). However, the rainfall
in the 1918 wet season was unexpectedly high (807 mm, MRT, 1979),
with river flooding more extensive than at any time in the previous thirty
years (Sokoto Annual Report, 1918). River gauging posts were set up
in 1918 for the first time, but the high river flows in that year were
unexpected. They scoured out the intake canals to the floodplain depressions so that the effective storage was reduced to about 13m m^3. Nonetheless, the Resident commented:

Table 15.1 *Water conservation works, 1917–18*

Date	Cost (£)	Proposed area (ha)	Proposed volume (m³)
1917 wet season (natural flood)	—	85	0.8m
1917–18 dry season	217	1,460	21m
1918–19 dry season	204	n.a.	31m

The abnormally high flood of 1918 would have refilled most of these depressions without any extraneous aid, but this does not detract from the value of the work which ensures their refilling by the annual floods and the replacement of water lost by evaporation even in the years of lowest flood water.

(Sokoto Annual Report, 1918)

The Resident pointed out that the area served by these works was 'precisely the area which has suffered so badly from drought during recent years'. In the 1918–9 dry season, further work was undertaken to increase storage in the floodplain to 31 m m³ (40m ha total area, see Table 15.1), and the Resident called in his report for help from the Public Works Department in the form of a foreman and masons to build headworks from local stone.

In the 1919 wet season the new dams withstood the flood; however, it was of reduced duration. The reservoirs at Kuberi, Kuriya and Dawakawa were insufficiently filled, and the total storage was less than planned (Table 15.2). However, Tapkin Natu near Bakura covered 2,500 acres (1,000 ha), and it was estimated that rice could be grown on 300–500 acres (120–200 ha). Edwardes reported that the lake at Gandi was now 11 miles (18 km) long (Edwardes, 1919). Rice cultivation in flooded areas was also recorded at Rabah and Tsamiya (Sokoto Annual Report, 1919), and it was claimed that 'thousands of cattle now remain on the farm instead of moving South in search of water', and that crops near Lake Natu 'should benefit from the humidity' (Sokoto Annual Report, 1919).

Table 15.2 *Actual and proposed storage in floodplain lakes*

Date	Proposed (m³)	Actual (m³)	Percentage of proposed storage actually achieved
1917 (natural flood)	—	0.8m	—
1918	21m	13m	62%
1919	31m	21m	68%

In 1920, the work of refilling floodplain depressions continued, and the Resident reported that a visit to Lake Natu had been 'most inspiriting' (Sokoto Annual Report, 1920), although problems were starting to emerge. Some of the people of Bakura grumbled that Tapkin Natu was now too deep for clap net fishing, although they also said their crops had been 'better than ever before', while an onion industry had sprung up (Sokoto Annual Report, 1920). Lugard wrote favourably of the work and was certainly pleased with the overall prospects:

For the remainder of the works I hear nothing but praise, and if we can introduce basin irrigation as suggested by the Director of Agriculture, the controls for which are now on order, the resulting benefits will be increased tenfold.

(Lugard, 1922)

Subsequent developments, however, were less happy. Edwardes left the Province under a cloud in 1921 having, while Acting Resident, exposed corrupt practices by the Sultan, and in the process broken the rule of never officially questioning a superior (Huessler, 1968; Palmer-Jones, 1987). There was widespread famine following crop failures in Sokoto in 1921 (Apeldoorn, 1981), caused not so much by low overall rainfall totals as by the early arrival of the rains in April followed by a long dry spell (Collins, 1923). The next year rainfall was high (35.41 in, 899 mm), and an inspection of the floodplain lakes in October 1923 by the irrigation engineer named Collins revealed extensive damage to the water conservation works. Of 14 embankments, six had been washed away and three cut by order. Only five remained intact (Collins, 1923). Collins thought the notion of water storage as a means of influencing the overall hydrology of the region of little value, and he stressed the problem of the uncertainty of the depth of flooding in the reservoirs. Thus, at Rabah (Fig. 15.2) the reservoir filled too rapidly for rice to be sown, because there was no way of controlling incoming water nor of drawing the reservoir down to give access to the inundated land. At Gora, two dams had breached, but 'the headman of the village said that the people did not desire them to be repaired or restored as they caused too much corn land to be flooded' (Collins, 1923). At the other extreme, the floods in 1923 were insufficient to fill Tapkin Angamba and Tapkin Sheyi through the canals Edwardes had made. At Tapkin Dambuchi near Tsamiya the dam had washed out and a large area of rice, planted because the farmers did not realize the area would not be flooded, was suffering water shortage (Collins, 1923). The most marked problems were at Tapkin Natu. The dam over the outfall of the lake was cut in April 1922 with official sanction following continued complaints about fishing and the flooding of guinea corn crops.[6] Collins commented:

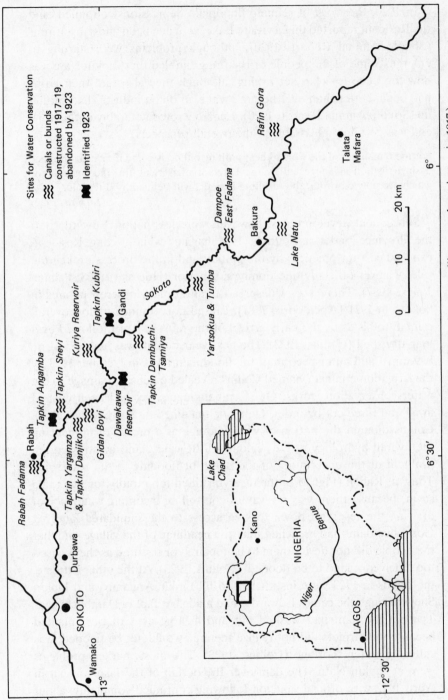

Fig. 15.2. Location of water conservation projects. (Note: spellings are those in use in 1917.)

From the point of view of the development of irrigation, it is a pity that this work was so hastily carried out, without a proper survey and without advising the people on the probable depth of water to be expected on surrounding land. The situation therefore will require careful handling and for a few years at any rate the lake must be left as it is. *(Collins, 1923: 23)*

Despite these problems, Collins clearly saw some potential for the development of irrigation in the Sokoto floodplain using the basins worked on by Edwardes, particularly Lake Natu. He recommended a thorough survey of the valley,[7] and compared it favourably with the Rima and Zamfara floodplains which he subsequently examined (Collins, 1924). However, the idea of an extensive survey of the Sokoto was not approved:

The Native Administration should not be advised to incur expenditure, in existing circumstances, on the survey of the Sokoto River Valley suggested by Colonel Collins as any scheme which may be carried out as a result of such a survey is sure to involve heavy expenditure. If there were any cheap means of transport available by which the produce of Sokoto could be conveyed to the principal markets or ports of Nigeria, such expenditure might well be justified, but there is not.[8]

Instead, the Secretary of the Northern provinces endorsed Collins' criticism of the attempt to store water without proper engineering structures:

It is obviously by no means advisable to attempt to carry out any further amateur schemes of 'water conservation' on the same haphazard lines hitherto adopted, the result of which has been in some cases to create among the inhabitants a profound distrust of projects for interfering with existing channels and lakes.
(Collins, 1924)

There was some approval for a further survey of smaller schemes in the Rima floodplain downstream of Sokoto,[9] but in the end further efforts were focussed on a small scheme at Kware based on the River Shalla near Sokoto.[10] Work began at Kware in 1925, and subsequently other small schemes were developed in the Rima floodplain (O'Reilly, 1983; Palmer-Jones, 1987).

Despite the potential for water development, Edwardes' projects were not a success. The immediate cause of failure is clear: there was far too little technical information about flooding patterns in the valley, and the approach to construction was amateur. Collins stressed the need for a complete topographic survey, river discharge data and proper masonry control structures. Without these the washing out of the bunds was to be expected.

Once Edwardes had been sent away from Sokoto, his projects fell into official disfavour, and their inherently solvable technical problems were not tackled. In time all trace of them effectively disappeared.

Conclusion

There are obvious similarities between the two approaches to development in the Sokoto Valley, the water conservation of 1917–21 and the
large-scale irrigation of the 1970s. In both cases, the initial concern
which started the development process was irrelevant to the nature of
the project eventually developed. Both started from the basic perception
that drought and desiccation were significant problems in the basin,
although in neither case did the project which emerged tackle these
directly. Of course, irrigation and water conservation both contributed
to some extent to the local alleviation of seasonal aridity, but neither
addressed the problems of rainfed cultivation or the deterioration of
land in the basin which were (and remain) the most pressing problems.
Instead, both projects focused on the development potential of the
floodplain and particularly the possibility of irrigation.

A second common feature of the two projects is the failure of technical
appraisal. In the case of Edwardes' work the problem was the lack of
survey data and engineering expertise, leading to breached bunds and
dry lakes. In the case of Bakolori, the engineering contractor made few
such errors (although there were problems of underdesigned irrigation
drains and consequent erosion and flooding problems, Adams, 1984).
Instead, it was in the areas of land use mapping and socio-economic
planning and management that the scheme was deficient and has fallen
most seriously into difficulties.

However, there are differences between the two approaches. The most
marked is their scale, and from this stems the chief difference in the
reason for their failure. The first project failed for lack of technical
expertise, both because it was conceived by a self-confessed amateur
(Edwardes), and because after 1921 he was posted away. Indeed, after
that, one might expect considerable disfavour to be shown to the project
whatever its effects (see Palmer-Jones, 1987, for discussion). However,
the scheme contained many of the characteristics of 'bottom–up' development, and with better technical and political support (such as might be
available six decades later) it might perform better today. The water
conservation project depended on an approach to cropping familiar to
floodplain farmers. It involved relatively small works at the village level.
In a number of cases the enlarged lakes were welcomed, and their demise
regretted. The project started small and developed year by year, and
despite technical criticism by the engineer Collins, there was clearly
potential in the water conservation approach.

By contrast, the problems of the Bakolori Project are not soluble by
the injection of more technical knowledge or government support, but

are a direct function of the scale and speed of development. The undoubted technical shortcomings stem from the deliberate increase in area (12,000 ha in the FAO Report of 1969, 30,000 ha built) and the abandonment of the slow and gradual approach. The shortcomings mostly concern environmental and socio-economic aspects of the project rather than its more obviously technical engineering aspects. These 'soft' disciplines had a typically lowly place in the process of project planning. In the case of Bakolori, they had little influence on the nature of project development, or indeed on the relations between developers and developed.

One sees, therefore, two different kinds of project failure in the Sokoto Valley. First, a *redeemable failure* in the earlier project. Here the problems could have been overcome had sufficient time and money been allowed, if the necessary technical inputs had been made, and had government interest been maintained. Second, *inherent failure* in the case of the Bakolori project. Its problems are not essentially soluble by any given set of policies because they stem from the very nature and scale of the development itself. This is not to say that the project is irredeemable, a waste of money whose costs outweigh its benefits (although it may prove so, Adams 1985b), but certainly the environmental impacts, the legacy of mistrust among farmers and consequent low cropping levels, the crippling capital cost (500m Naira, 21,000 Naira per ha) and costs of maintenance preclude any easy or gradual solution.

Therefore, if one wants to approach a definition of *sustainability* in development, the two projects in the Sokoto Valley – although both in their way failures – signpost the characteristics of sustainable and unsustainable development. Some of these are shown in Table 15.3. The list is not exhaustive, and not particularly original (see for example Stohr

Table 15.3 *Attributes of sustainable and unsustainable development*

	Sustainable	Unsustainable
Level of organisation	Local (village)	National/international
Scale	Smaller	Larger
Approach to existing technology	Adaptive	Transforming
Project identification	Local	Regional/national
Lead disciplines	Environmental, social	Engineering, economic
Approach to project development	Evolutionary and slow	Specific, planned and rapid
Approach to mistakes	Learn	Cover up or ignore

& Taylor, 1981, Chambers, 1983). The Sokoto Water Conservation project exhibits some sustainable characteristics, such as a measure of local organisation, adaptation of existing techniques and an evolutionary approach. Bakolori exhibits some unsustainable features, demanding sudden and large-scale transformation determined by external planning.

A fundamental characteristic of sustainable development must be the extent to which developers learn from their mistakes. Here the Sokoto Valley experience is instructive, for its seems that no appropriate lessons were learned from the early experiment with water conservation. Concern about desiccation persisted to the 1950s, but there is no evidence of any learning process in the way the problem was perceived, or any increased awareness of the effectiveness of particular kinds of development such as irrigation. Bakolori was designed and built by people in complete ignorance of what had gone before. The aims and effects of the earlier work were forgotten. That is at least one reason for the failings of the Bakolori Project, and indeed of most of the large-scale irrigation schemes developed in Northern Nigeria in the 1970s. It remains to be seen whether these will, in their turn, be properly appraised, and whether the lessons which they offer will be effectively learned and used to influence future planning. It should be possible, because the shortcomings are both significant and self-evident. If not, then mistakes will undoubtedly be repeated in the future. If development planning remains a practice without a memory, one must question whether it will ever be possible to reform the project planning process in such a way as to make a common cause of conservation and development.

Notes

1   Letter from Resident, Sokoto to Permanent Secretary, Ministry of Agriculture, Kaduna, 15 February 1960. IRR–15, Nigerian Archives, Kaduna.
    Notes on the Sokoto Investigation by the FAO/ICA Team, 3 November
2   1960. Appendix to Report on Agricultural Survey of the Northern Region of Nigeria, FAO/61/B 896–R.p.
3   Annual total 18.78 in or 477 mm compared to 414 mm in 1913 and an average of 710 mm from 1910–7 (MRT, 1979 Appendix 1; Annual Report 1917).
4   Letter from Secretary, Northern Province to Resident, Sokoto, 18 March 1919, SOKPROF 2/10 555/1918.
5   Letter from Resident, Sokoto to Secretary, Northern Province, 22 April 1919, SOKPROF 2/10 555/1918.
6   Letter from Resident, Sokoto to Secretary, Northern Provinces, 18 May 1922, SOKPROF 2/12.

7   The survey was estimated to require 12 months work by two expatriate surveyors, at a cost of £2,618.
8   Letter from Secretary, Northern Provinces to Chief Secretary, Lagos, 24 December 1923, SNP 972/1919/7.
9   Memo from Secretary, Northern Provinces to Chief Secretary, Lagos, 11 July 1924, SNP17 10708 vol. 2.
10   Memo from Resident, Sokoto Province to Secretary, Northern Provinces, 12 February 1925, SNP10708 vol. 2.

References

ABEL, N. & STOCKING, M. (1981). The experience of underdeveloped countries. In *Project Appraisal and Policy Review*, ed. T. O'Riordan & W.R.D. Sewell, pp. 253–5. Chichester: Wiley.

ADAMS, W.M. (1983). Downstream impact of river control, Sokoto Valley, Nigeria. Unpublished Ph.D. thesis, University of Cambridge.

ADAMS, W.M. (1984). Irrigation as hazard: farmers' responses to the introduction of irrigation in Sokoto, Nigeria. In *Irrigation and Tropical Agriculture: Problems and Problem-solving*, ed. W.M. Adams & A.T. Grove. Cambridge African Monographs no.3. Cambridge: African Studies Centre, University of Cambridge.

ADAMS, W.M. (1985a). River basin planning in Nigeria. *Applied Geography*, **5**, 297–308.

ADAMS, W.M. (1985b). The downstream impacts of dam construction: a case study from Nigeria. *Transactions of the British Institute of Geographers*, NS **10**, 292–302.

AHMAD, Y.J. & SAMMY, G.K. (1985). *Guidelines to Environmental Impact Assessment in Developing Countries*, London: Hodder & Stoughton.

APELDOORN, G.J. van (1981). *Perspectives on Drought and Famine in Nigeria*. London: Allen & Unwin.

BIRD, A. (1985). La participation des paysans dans l'élaboration et la mise en oeuvre des grands projets de mobilisation des resources en eau du Nigéria: Comparison du projet d'irrigation de Bakolori et du projet de réaménagement de Dadin Kowa. In *Les politiques de l'eau en Afrique: developpement agricole et participation paysanne*, ed. G. Conac, C. Savonnet-Guyot & F. Conac, pp. 550–66. Paris: Economica.

BISWAS, A.K. (1978). Environmental implications of water development for developing countries. *Water Supply and Management*, **2**, 283–97.

BOVILL, E.W. (1921). The encroachment of the Sahara and the Sudan. *Journal of the African Society*, **20**, 179–85.

CHAMBERS, R. (1983). *Rural Development: putting the last first*. Harlow: Longman.

COLLINS, M.R. (1923). A preliminary report on irrigation for the Sokoto River upstream of Sokoto, Part 1. SNP 10708 vol.II, Water Conservation, Sokoto. Nigerian Archives, Kaduna.

COLLINS, M.R. (1924). A preliminary report on irrigation in the Sokoto Province, Part II and III. SNP 17 10708 vol.II, Water Conservation, Sokoto. Nigerian Archives, Kaduna.

DASMANN, R.F., MILTON, J.P. & FREEMAN, P.H. (1973). *Ecological Principles for Economic Development*. Chichester: Wiley.

EDWARDES, H.S.W. (1919). Lake formation and desiccation in East Africa. *Geographical Journal*, **53**, 206–7.

ETUK, E.G. & ABALU, G.O.I. (1982). River basin development in Northern Nigeria: a case study of the Bakolori Project. *Proceedings of the 9th Afro-Asian Regional Conference of the ICID*, vol. II (Publ.026), pp. 335–46.

FAO (1969) *Soil and water resources survey of the Sokoto Valley, Nigeria: final report*. 6 volumes. Rome: FAO.

FILANI, M.O. (1981). Nigeria: the need to modify top–down development planning. In *Development from Above or Below*, ed. W.B. Stohr & D.R.F. Taylor, pp. 283–304. Chichester: Wiley.

GLAESER, B. (1984). *Ecodevelopment: concepts, projects and strategies*. London: Pergamon Press.

GROVE, A.T. (1973). A note on the remarkably low rainfall of the Sudan Zone in 1913. *Savanna*, **2**(2), 133–8.

HARRISON CHURCH, R. (1961). Discussion following paper, Problems of the development of the dry zone of West Africa. *Geographical Journal*, **127**, 187–204.

HUESSLER, R. (1968). *The British in Northern Nigeria*. Oxford: Oxford University Press.

IMPRESIT (1974). *Bakolori Project: first phase of the Sokoto Rima Basin Development, Final Report*. Rome: Impresit and Nuoro Castoro.

IUCN (1980). *World Conservation Strategy*. Gland, Switzerland: IUCN.

JONES, B. (1938). Desiccation in the West African colonies. *Geographical Journal*, **91**, 401–23.

LEDGER, D.C. (1961). Recent hydrological change in the Rima Basin, Northern Nigeria. *Geographical Journal*, **127**, 477–87.

LUGARD, Lord (1922). *The Dual Mandate in British Tropical Africa*. London: Frank Cass (1965 edition).

MABOGUNJE, A.L. (1984). The poor shall inherit the earth: issues of environmental quality in Third World development. *Geoforum*, **15**(3), 295–306.

MRT (1979). Sokoto Water Supply Extensions. Final Report. Unpublished report, MRT Consulting Engineers (Nigeria) Ltd.

O'REILLY, F.D. (1983). The Sokoto Valley Rice Project. Unpublished manuscript.

O'RIORDAN, T. (1981). *Environmentalism*. London: Pion Press.

OWEN, D.G. (1959). The Dying River Systems of Northern Nigeria. Unpublished manuscript, Ministry of Agriculture, IRR–115, Nigerian Archives, Kaduna.

PALMER-JONES, R.W. (1981). How not to learn from pilot irrigation projects: the Nigerian experience. *Water Supply and Management*, **5**(1), 81–105.

PALMER-JONES, R.W. (1987). Irrigation in Nigeria. In *Agricultural Development in Nigeria*, ed. M. Watts. (In press).

PROTHERO, R.M. (1962). Some observations on desiccation in North-western Nigeria. *Erkunde*, **16**, 112–9.

REDCLIFT, M. (1984). *Development and the Environmental Crisis: red or green alternatives?* London: Methuen.

RIDDELL, R. (1981). *Ecodevelopment*. Farnborough: Gower.

SANDBACH, F. (1980). *Environment, Ideology and Policy*. Oxford: Blackwell.

SOKOTO ANNUAL REPORTS (1917–20). *Annual Reports for Sokoto Province, Northern Nigeria*. Kaduna: Nigerian Archives.

STEBBING, E.P. (1935). The encroaching Sahara: the threat to the West African Colonies. *Geographical Journal*, **85**, 506–24.

STEIN, R.E. & JOHNSON, B. (1979). *Banking on the Biosphere? Environmental problems and practices of nine multi-lateral arid agencies*. Lexington, Mass: International Institute for Environment and Development.

STEWART, F. (1985). *Planning to Meet Basic Needs*. London: Macmillan.

STOHR, W.B. (1981). Development from Below: the bottom–up and periphery–inward development paradigm. In *Development: from Above or Below?*, ed. W.B. Stohr & D.R.F. Taylor, pp. 39–72. Chichester: Wiley.

TASSO, E. (1978). The Bakolori Project: a new approach to the implementation of large development projects. *New Civil Engineer*, 16 March and 30 March.

WILLIAMS, G. (1981). The World Bank and the peasant problem. In *Rural Development in Tropical Africa*, ed. J. Heyer, P. Roberts & G. Williams, pp. 16–51. London: Macmillan.

16

State policy and famine in the Awash Valley of Ethiopia: the lessons for conservation

MAKNUN GAMALEDINN

The increasing incidence of widespread famine among the peoples of the Sahel and northeast Africa has raised the issue of the responsibility of the state in matters of land-use planning in the most acute way possible. Some observers have placed the blame for the extent of the human disaster of famine on processes of environmental and climatic deterioration and population increase (e.g. Milas & Asrat, 1985). Rainfall decline since 1971 in many parts of the Sahel has made this analysis predictable. Moreover, the facts of environmental deterioration, especially in the form of deforestation, have been convincing, as far as the very weak statistical material allows (Grove, 1986). Since the Second World War Ethiopia has lost up to 70 per cent of its forest cover and the increased incidence of soil erosion has reflected this (Roundy, 1985). During the recent famine the image of an incompetent peasantry struggling to produce food by ineffective and destructive methods from a devastated environment has been assiduously cultivated by outside commentators. This image of incompetence has also been attached to a government which has been castigated for its failure over many years to provide effective and durable agricultural assistance in the famine-prone areas, as well as for its inequitable treatment of the victims of famine. Ignorant peasants and incompetent government therefore make up the popular image of Ethiopia's recent plight.

Such simplistic generalisations overlook both the ecological and the political complexities of Ethiopia, and give no account of the longer-term role of the expanding Ethiopian state in shaping the subsistence and environmental problems of the present. Since the beginnings of the expansion of the imperial Ethiopian state in the mid-nineteeth century, the tightening financial and bureaucratic grip of state controls and policies has steadily impinged upon the economies and ecologies of settled peasant farmers and pastoralist nomads (Pausewang, 1983; Pankhurst, 1986). The intrusion of centralised authority has, in fact, disrupted economic linkages between neighbouring groups and man–environment relationships within particular production systems, making the task of surviving climatic extremes a steadily more difficult proposition for many of Ethiopia's peoples. This has been increasingly apparent with the rapid extension of state economic controls since the Second World War. Over this period two new factors in state policy have had a powerful impact. Firstly, the institution of mechanised warfare has allowed the centre to dominate the subject nationalities more fully and to prosecute full-scale war against a growing number of secessionist movements. Secondly, both pre- and post-revolutionary governments have embraced 'development' plans for agriculture and embarked upon a number of large-scale agricultural and resettlement schemes. It is difficult to decide which of these two new aspects of state ambition has been more damaging for the peasantry. Both have had a totemic value in allowing the state to bolster notions of its own efficacy and *raison d'être* and in justifying the growth of bureaucracy. Both have promoted and prolonged famine conditions in the last two decades.

One of the groups worst affected by famine has been the Afar. Their fate, it is argued here, has had less to do with the direct effects of drought and soil erosion than with the direct erosion by the state of indigenous methods of resource conservation. Instead, the state has imposed its own preconceptions about resource utilisation based entirely on imported precepts. The devastating effect this process has had on the Afar people is illustrative of the much wider picture of the disintegration of the traditional relationship between pastoralist and environment which has occurred in recent years in Ethiopia and of which much of the famine mortality of the last two decades has been symptomatic. A very limited number of studies have focused on the impact of state policies on the Afar and other pastoral groups such as the Dasanetch, and their analyses are depended upon heavily in this chapter (Carr, 1977; Kloos, 1982). However, the more far-reaching consequences of the most recent bout of famine have elicited very little treatment beyond the purely journalistic, partly because of the lack of basic data. The experience of the entire period from 1971–85 does, nevertheless, on the basis of what information is available, assist in predicting the consequences of present trends in government policy affecting the interaction between people and environment.

Ecology and rural economy in the Awash valley

The Afar population in the Awash Valley numbers no less than 200,000. They inhabit an area which, by modern definition, has acquired a critical importance to the economy of Ethiopia, located between the Ethiopian

Highlands and the coast. Both the railroad to Djibouti and the main road link to the port of Assab in Eritrea pass through the areas inhabited by the Afar. The proximity of these arteries of communication has enhanced the potential for conventional economic development, and attempts to foster development have formed an important dimension of government policy since the early 1960s. In 1962 the Awash Valley Authority (AVA) was set up to supervise development in the valley, and subsequently established two settlement schemes. The intention was to settle Afar pastoralists on these irrigated agriculture schemes, under the management of the AVA (Caponera, 1956; Diebold, 1958). As part of this process, the government vested land ownership on the AVA, ignoring the traditional claims of the nomadic peoples. Under the control of the AVA, development in the valley took the form of large scale mechanised commercial enterprises, mostly managed by foreign agro-business in joint ventures with the state. The government's main concern at this stage was to acquire cash and commodities for its expanding military and civilian bureaucracy. Irrigation in the Awash Valley did increase the country's production of cotton and sugar, and was able to absorb a substantial migrant labour force. However, irrigation, the construction of dams and the government's drive for centralisation, interacting with a period of drought, produced a deplorable effect upon the nomads of the Awash (Gamaledinn, 1986).

A number of recent studies have indicated an explicit correlation between development policies, and drought and famine in Africa (Lofchie, 1975; Bail, 1976; Grove, 1979; Franke & Chasin, 1980). In the context of Ethiopia, the Great Famine of 1972–3 has been explained in terms of the feudal land tenure system of the Highlands (Shepherd, 1975; Hussein, 1976; Fitzgerald, 1980), and also, more specifically, by the encroachment on Afar pastures of irrigation schemes and the reduced river flooding caused by the construction of the Koka Dams (Bondestam, 1974; Flood, 1976; Kloos, De Sole & Lemma, 1981). We shall argue that there is an explicit connection between the government's irrigation development policy in the Awash Valley and drought and famine in the region. This is not to claim that drought is solely the creation of development policy; historical evidence demonstrates that drought is a recurrent phenomenon in this part of the world, and immediately prior to the Great Famine of 1972–3 the region had been hit by drought in 1958, 1964, 1966 and 1967 (Wood, 1977; Pankhurst, 1986). Yet, as Kloos suggests, there are strong indications from the case of Ethiopia that:

drought and famine do not always reflect cause–effect relationships and that the two may co-exist independently and often become linked only through politico-economic conditions. *(Kloos, 1982)*

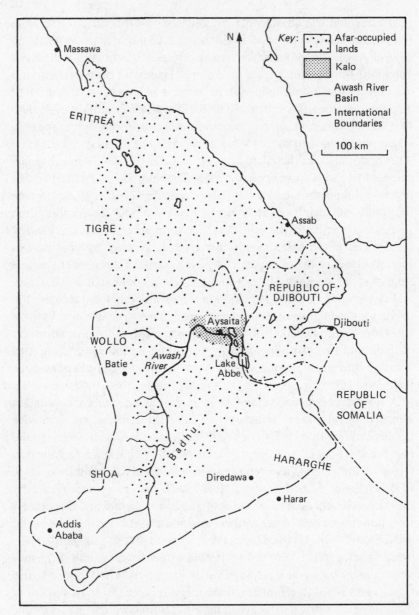

Fig. 16.1. The Awash River Basin.

Consequently, drought can be related, even if indirectly, to government policy. In the Awash Valley, the implementation of government development programmes has had a profound impact upon the rural economy and local ecology. These development initiatives, rather than improving the circumstances of the Afar, accentuated the impact of drought and thereby contributed to the effects of the Great Famine of 1972–3.

The Awash River basin lies between latitudes 8 °N and 12 °N, on the southern and eastern side of the Central Plateau of Ethiopia, extending between Addis Ababa in the west to the lowlands of the Aysaita Delta in the east. It covers an area of 120,000 km^2, but the Awash River and its tributaries effectively drain an area of only 70,000 km^2 (Fig. 16.1). The Awash River rises 70 km west of Addis Ababa, at an altitude of 3,000 m above sea level, and then flows for 1,200 km in a generally northerly direction before entering Lake Abbe at an altitude of 250 m. The average annual rainfall for the basin as a whole is 710 mm, but this rises to 1,000 mm in the upper basin and falls to 215 mm on the lower plains. The differences in average temperatures of approximately 29 °C on the lower plains and 13.5 °C on the plateau are equally striking. Thus, in the Awash basin, as elsewhere in Ethiopia, altitude is one of the major factors determining climatic conditions (Mariam, 1964; FAO–SF, 1965).

The vast area of the Awash Valley is populated by a diversity of ethnic groups, but it is the Afar, occupying the lower eastern portion of the valley along both banks of the river, who have been most affected by the activities of the AVA (Kloos, 1982). Within the region of the Awash Valley the economies of the various lowland pastoralist groups, including the Afar and their neighbouring highland agriculturalists, are essentially complementary. The Afar pastoralists utilise the areas close to the river banks during the dry season, and move their cattle to the escarpments during the rainy season, away from flooding and mosquitoes. Highland agriculturalists who cultivate small plots of land, and who are unable to graze their livestock, are known to have developed a contractual system with the Afar, who sell cattle to the Highlanders, and then act as herdsmen for the new owners. The Afar use the milk, but share any calves produced with the highland cultivators – the owners of the cows. This arrangement has satisfied both groups, since the Highlanders have a pressing need for oxen for ploughing (Mariam, 1964). Similar forms of cooperation are evident in reciprocal grazing arrangements between the Galla (Oromo) and the Afar. Alternatively, the Afar may pay an agreed amount, in either cash or kind, to graze their cattle on crop residues during the rainy season (Cossins, 1972). In sum, the economic systems of the various peoples of the Awash Valley are closely interconnected. These linkages cut across the ecological zones defined principally by altitude, the need to gain access to other zones providing the dynamic for these economic and social relationships.

Prior to the ecological changes brought about by planned irrigation development under the auspices of the AVA, the area utilised by Afar seasonal migrations ranged roughly from the foothills of the Highlands in the west to the Red Sea in the east. Movement to the south was contained by the Issa Somali. The area used therefore comprised much of the Awash Valley. The general pattern of migration followed the availability of seasonal grazing and water supply during the dry months from December to June. In the rainy period, from July to October, and thereafter, the Afar spread outwards to seasonal watering points and fresh pasture growth. In the crucial dry months the Awash River and its immediate environs provided the main sustenance for the Afar herds. The pattern of access to grazing and water supply was fairly similar for the middle valley area, *Badhu*, and the lower plains, *Kalo*, in that access was based upon clan control of the grazing area, but control of wells was in the hands of lineages and individuals. The significant difference was the existence in *Kalo* of a political structure which organised access to water, farming land and grazing, through a centralised system of cattle and forest managers (*malokti*, sing. *malak*) appointed by the Awsa Sultanate. The main functions of the livestock and pasture (including timber) *malokti* were: (i) to organise and coordinate all the controlled flooding and irrigation of pasture areas; (ii) to control and limit the entry of outsiders and to coordinate access for resident herds; and (iii) to organise and coordinate the treatment of cattle diseases or to isolate infected animals.

Within the Awash Valley there were three regional management units for livestock under this system, plus a separate unit for timber. Of these, two were located within the delta, and one in *Kalo*. The degree of access varied. The delta was highly restricted, and within the delta the north-central area, the home of the Sultanate's own cattle, was virtually an excluded area. The situation was more relaxed on the periphery of the delta, probably reflecting its more recent incorporation. Each of these regional units was run by several cattle *malokti* (or 'cattle fathers', *la hi Abba*) under a senior *malak* who reported directly to the Sultan through the deputy Sultan. According to a study conducted by Cossins (1973), there was one senior *malak* with 34 subsidiary *malokti*, and one senior *malak* for camels, goats and sheep (*gaali Abba*) with 19 subsidiary *malokti*, excluding eight *malokti* for timber (Cossins, 1973). Traditionally, *malokti* for livestock were recruited from the lineages within the management area, but in practice *malokti* were not restricted to their own clan areas. Within the lower plains, then, and particularly in the delta, a strict system of controlled access to grazing operated. The Lower Awash Valley was viewed by the Afar, including those from outside the valley, as a refuge in times of drought. The permanent Afar settlements in the delta area also provided food crops, which are significant during times of emergency.

In the middle valley, *Badhu*, the pattern was different. Here the semi-nomadic Afar normally move between dry season sites and wet season sites. These movements extend over 5 km to 30 km, and are undertaken once or twice a year. Most of the women, children and elderly stay as long as possible in their main homesteads, which are close to the river banks, although these are subject to flooding and mosquito infestation during the rainy season. The village sites are based on clan membership, although areas adjacent to irrigation developments have become more mixed with the influx of people from other clans. The wet season sites or villages, which are known as *Ganta*, normally include various clans who cooperate among themselves in watering their stock and possibly in protection against outside threats. Thus, the Afar of the middle valley are not pure nomads, but are transhumant, moving between two permanent sites, each long established. Nevertheless, patterns of occupancy are complex, due to the movement of part of the population to and from the two sites (Voelkner, 1974; Kloos, 1982).

In both the middle valley and the lower plains, the ultimate constraint on production within the traditional pastoral system was access to grazing, the availability of which was mediated by the amount of rainfall, but also by the degree of flooding of the Awash River, and in the lower plains by a sophisticated system of grazing control. These relationships are particularly important to our discussion, since recent ecological changes have had drastic effects. For the Afar, the major climatic characteristic of the region is the correlation between low mean annual rainfall, altitude, and river flooding. Rainfall is highly seasonal, confined to the 'small rains' (February/March), and the 'big rains' (July/August), which results in marked fluctuations in river discharge. Precipitation decreases and temperature increases with lower elevations. This is reflected in the vegetation zones which range from degraded montane savanna and forest on the High Plateau (2,500–3,000 m), to woodland and tree-savanna (1,200–2,500 m), and to predominantly tropical dry grass savanna and semi-desert interspaced with volcanic formations, basalt flows, and sand in the lowlands (Cossins, 1973). All of the numerous rivers draining the area from the Highlands to the west are subject to flash floods during the rainy season. In the lowlands, all but four of the Awash tributaries usually dry up after the rainy season.

These ecological constraints were met by the existence of a well-balanced system of land use, based on migration and transhumance, and reciprocal arrangements with the Highland cultivators which included grazing rights on crop residues, stock loans, and trading, especially in food. This last aspect is vital, because pastoralists in this region tend to meet almost half of their calorie requirement through agricultural products, and any disruption of the exchange pattern through which they acquire these foods therefore has an immediate and significant impact. To these adaptations we may add the internal adjustment mechanisms adopted by pastoralists when confronting drought (Dini, 1967; Helland, 1980).

The impact of irrigation development

In order to survive a dry season which can last from mid-September to mid-June, access to flooded grazing areas is crucial to the Afar pastoralists. Each pastoral group requires access to land which drains rapidly after flooding, and also to land which drains more slowly (Flood, 1976). The management of the pastures along the river banks, which constitute this most critical grazing area, has therefore been a central feature of the Afar pastoral system. The impact of irrigation development has been severe for the Afar precisely because it so drastically affected these river bank areas. The AVA absorbed parts of the flooded grazing area within the irrigation schemes themselves. The pattern of seasonal flooding was affected by changes in the regime of the Awash river, resulting from the regulation of the flow of water by the Koka Dams. Since 1960, three dams have been built on the Awash; Abu Samuel, Koka 1 and Koka 2. The purpose of Koka 1, the largest of the three, is to provide hydroelectric power for Addis Ababa. Impounding the river, and regulating a fairly steady release of water from the two Koka dams sharply reduced seasonal flooding downstream. It is estimated that:

The proportion of total annual Awash water discharged during the large rains (July–September) at Wonji fell from 84% prior to the dams to 35% after their completion in 1960. The new river flow pattern completely eliminated floods from the Upper Valley and significantly reduced them in the Middle Valley, though in the plains the Awash retains a more pronounced seasonal flow pattern, owing to the still unregulated tributaries.   *(Kloos, 1982)*

The most dramatic impact for the Afar came in 1972, when, under pressure from the AVA and the irrigation scheme farmers, the amount of water released from the reservoir between March and October was modified to allow for the cultivation of an additional 25,000 ha (Flood, 1976; Kloos, 1982). Commenting on this, Voelkner states that:

Before the intrusion of irrigated farming into the project area, the Afar way of life seemed to have been well balanced, with forage resources of the area provided by the rainfall and flooding of the river and necessitating only minimal amount of migration. This balance supported an even greater amount of livestock and population but any upset in this balance would naturally have the immediate effect (within 1 to 2 years) of reducing both. The effect of the latest drought (1972/73) may not have been as devastating had the river been allowed to flood as in its unregulated past and had the normally flooded area been available as grazing area to the Afar population. *(Voelkner, 1974)*

A substantial area of the Afar's best grazing was taken up by irrigation agriculture. By 1972, there were some 50,000 ha under irrigated agriculture, displacing some 20,000 pastoralists (Kloos, 1977). The irrigated land area was small in comparison to the size of the basin or the flat grazing area of the Awash, but this crucial belt was estimated by Goudie in 1972 to constitute '16% of the total size of the flat grazing originally available'. He continues, 'the position is more marked in the lower plains where 23% of the river flats are now used for irrigated cropping' (Goudie, 1972). Outside this belt, the Great Plains could not support a great number of people and livestock in both the dry and wet seasons. The removal of this strategic grazing zone also meant the blocking of migration routes and livestock watering points in Arsi at Nura Era, and in the Melka-Sedi and Awsa areas (Kloos, 1982).

The construction of irrigation schemes in the Awash Valley has had other, secondary effects upon the local ecology. Forage resources were significantly reduced by labourers clearing timber for use in construction, and for fuel. Even Awsa, which had a highly restricted system of protection under Sultan Alimirah, was not saved from this process (Kloos, 1977). In addition, woodcutting and charcoal production by farmers along the Addis Ababa–Assab and Batie–Assab roads, for use in the capital city and other large villages in the Awash River basin, resulted in large scale destruction of *Acacia* woodlands and deciduous bush vegetation in the wet-season grazing areas (Kloos, 1982).

The introduction of irrigated development disrupted both the traditional economy of the pastoralists and their pattern of life. The important dry-season gatherings that brought a large number of people together, and fostered social activities such as marriages, were disrupted. At the same time, 'new groups lacking amity have been thrust together, and conflict is high; whilst groups which before had many ritual links have sometimes been separated' (Flood, 1976). The cooperation between groups, which is linked to residential and genealogical patterns, is essential, particularly in the wet season when the clans move away from their residential areas; but this has been disrupted by forced out-migration.

The decline of this cooperation has brought conflict among the Afar, and between the Afar and their Highland neighbours, who began to limit reciprocal stock arrangements with the Afar (Cossins, 1972; Flood, 1976). This situation was undoubtedly exacerbated by the government's wider policy of centralisation which included the replacement of traditional markets by new ones in order to control and to tax nomads (Cossins, 1972). Land hunger among Highland peasants also rebounded upon the Afar pastoralists as farmers began to bring under cultivation more of the land which had hitherto been used by the Afar for grazing. These tensions between the Afar and their Highland neighbours led to open conflict, resulting in access to the Highlands being essentially closed to the Afar. This made 'getting to market and selling and buying . . . a problem of major proportions to the Afar' (Cossins, 1972).

Already struggling to maintain these market linkages when they were hit by drought, the Afar were compelled to sell livestock to purchase grain as livestock prices were falling fast. This 'very substantial' worsening of the exchange rate disrupted the Afar pastoralist's normal means of meeting his food requirements. As Sen states:

The characteristics of exchange relations between the pastoral and the agricultural economies thus contributed to the starvation of herdsmen by making price movements reinforce – rather than counteract – the decline in the livestock quantity. The pastoralist, hit by drought, was decimated by the market mechanism.   *(Sen, 1982)*

It was the intrusion of commercial agriculture and the disruption of pastoral processes which caused the overgrazing, seen by some as a basic cause of plant degradation in pastoral areas, and not the activities of the nomads themselves. Together with the failure of the 'small rains', this led inevitably to the devastating drought and famine of 1972–3. The disaster was compounded by the reduced river flooding over the preceding four years. The Afar were the first to be hit, and were among the refugees seeking help in Addis Ababa in December 1972. It was the Afar who lined the north–south highway through Wollo in early 1973, stopping cars and buses to ask for food (Green & Sinnshaw, 1973; Sen, 1982).

State response to famine

The famine of 1972–3 was an acute tragedy for the Afar. The extent of the human impact can only be estimated, but Bondestam (1974) has suggested that as many as 30 per cent of the Afar population perished. A report released in 1976 by the Inquiry Commission, which was established in the aftermath of the famine to investigate corruption and maladministration among officials of the Haile Selassie regime, claims that the central government was regularly informed about local conditions in the northern provinces from 1970 (Relief and Rehabilitation Commission (RRC), 1985). A proper and timely response could have saved thousands of lives lost in the famine. Instead, the government chose not to take any meaningful measures to mitigate the conditions. Local administrators and community leaders, whose concerns were expressed in their regular reports to their superiors in Addis Ababa, were left without any policy or guidance (RCC, 1985). The only response from the central government came in the form of the establishment of the Grain Deficits Study Committee (GDSC), to investigate the situation in November 1971. The GDSC was informed of the deteriorating situation in five provinces in Wollo, including Awsa Awraja province with its large Afar population (RRC, 1985), but lacked the resources to take decisive action.

The Provisional Military Administrative Council (PMAC), which replaced the Haile Selassie government in 1974, was faced with two major problems in the northern provinces; the first was a devastating famine, and the second a rebellion. The two problems were not unconnected. The government's priorities were to be determined by the nature and the orientation of the governing élites. Under Haile Selassie the central state had greatly expanded. This was necessitated by the governing élite's thirst for revenue and it was realised by reinforcing the position of the Amhara middle class. The educational system favoured Amhara language and culture. Those who replaced the *ancien régime* were moulded by this imperial ideology, and felt that they had transcended the existing national divisions. The demands of nationalities for self rule, which might have tackled some of the problems raised by drought, were rejected. Indeed, the slogan 'Motherland or Death' dominated much of the politics of Ethiopia in the mid-1970s and early 1980s and resources were directed to this centralising idea rather than to agrarian problems. Since 1974 the Ethiopian government has continued to allocate half of its annual budget to the military and its arms imports have risen by several hundred per cent in real terms (constant prices) over the 1970s. Furthermore, the continuation of war has led to the withdrawal of thousands of peasants from the production process. However, in March 1975 the PMAC instituted one of the world's most radical processes of land reform, which put an end to feudalism in Ethiopia. Afar leaders were at first jubilant in response to this reform, because the bill included a 'possessary rights' clause, which recognised the rights of nomads to traditional land. In May 1975, a meeting was held between the Afar leaders and the PMAC in Addis Ababa, prior to which the government had taken control of many of the irrigation projects in the Awash, including a farm managed by Afar elders with financial help from the Sultan of Awsa in the lower plains. During the meeting, the vice-chairman of the PMAC, Mengistu Haile Mariam, showed some understanding of the Afar plight when he referred to 'the double oppression of man and nature'. Afar delegates submitted a proposal to the PMAC calling for the establishment of an Afar state within Ethiopia. Only under such conditions, they argued, could development policies be successfully implemented. Negotiations between the PMAC and the Sultan ultimately failed, culminating in a revolt in June 1975, and the formation of the Afar Liberation Front (ALF). The government have subsequently tried to win Afar support by negotiation, but with little success.

In the aftermath of the 1972–3 famine both the government and its international supporters embarked upon the setting up of two types of relief programme. These were: (i) food-for-work programmes, which meant the provision of food in exchange for work on road building; (ii) a restocking programme, which was undertaken by the Ethiopian Livestock and Meat Board, with RRC and international support. These projects form the nucleus of the government's settlement schemes, along with the AVA sponsored schemes in Amibara in the middle valley and Dubti in the lower plains. In fact, it is difficult to describe the schemes properly as settlement schemes. They are, in reality, relief camps in perpetuity. These camps were set up temporarily, so the participants are not strictly settlers, yet they are unable to improve their lot sufficiently to make leaving the camp a viable option. Relief of this type has not assisted a return to normal life for these Afar pastoralists. Indeed, the settlers have become a part-time wage labour force on the growing number of state farms (Kloos, 1977).

In September 1977, the AVA was replaced by the Awash Valley Development Authority (AVDA). The settlement schemes were transferred to a Settlement Authority (SA), but the AVDA retained control of marketing. In 1979 both the AVDA and the SA, which carried out similar activities, were merged into the RRC. (RRC, 1985). This reorganisation made no difference to Afar nomads, because they were still excluded from the decision making process in the Awash. Yet the RRC's recent publication, *The Challenges of Drought*, boasted that the RRC, via the AVDA, prepared 10,000 ha of irrigated land for grazing, drilled seven water wells, and settled more than 900 families on 2,500 ha of irrigated cotton (RRC, 1985). It further states that it spent '10 m birr on water well programmes, on the building of new roads, the opening of trails in

Amibara, Alidghi, Gewani, Dubti, Ditbahari and Aysaita irrigated settlement and range development schemes' (RRC, 1985). The publication also mentions that the AVDA was able to settle 5,119 Afar families to grow cotton. However, it neglects to say how much land and investment has been allocated to the State Farms Authority in the Awash. All these figures regarding settlement projects require some qualification, as it is not clear whether they represent those who were put into relief camps after the 1972–3 famine, or whether they represent new settlers. Elsewhere in the same publication, the RRC admit that 'no new settlements were started after the merger' in 1979 (RRC, 1985).

The now chronic situation confronting the Afar with the recurrence of drought and famine in the 1980s demands a more far-reaching review of government policies in the Awash Valley. A reversal of the government's existing agricultural policies, emphasis on environmental rehabilitation and an end to the armed conflict in the region are seen by many as the only means to prevent a future disaster (Hancock, 1985). In the first place, this implies a structural readjustment between state-controlled agriculture and pastoralism in the Awash, and within the agricultural sector a greater commitment towards food crop production in place of cash crops. There are no signs that such adjustments are planned or intended. Instead, the emphasis of government response has been upon 'rehabilitation' within the confines of present structures, which since 1978 has taken the form of soil conservation programmes carried out by peasant associations, often under coercion. These measures have been criticised for failing to take account of the variety of agro-ecological conditions in Ethiopia, in some cases even being the cause of greater problems than those which the measures were intended to solve (Hancock, 1985), and they have done nothing to prevent the onset of famine in the 1980s. In the absence of any attempt by government to do more than respond belatedly to the symptoms of social disruption and economic dislocation, the continued recurrence of famine in the Awash is predictable.

Conclusion

Settled agrarian populations in the uncertain climatic conditions of Ethiopia have been subject to famine to some extent for many hundred years (Pankhurst, 1986). However, nomadic populations have until the post-war period been far less vulnerable and have conceivably been better adapted to the ecological extremes the climate entails. Recently, though, the disruptive effects of state intervention in all its aspects have imposed a proportionately even higher mortality on the more nomadic groups such as the Afar. Consequently, the history of the destruction of the nomadic pastoral economy of the Afar and other groups raises broader questions about the compatibility of pre-industrial agrarian economies of Africa with the modern state and about the future needs of African rural people. Highly adapted methods of conserving resources for a sustainable yield on the basis of long-accumulated empirical experience and orally-transmitted tradition now confront assumptions inherited by a powerful state apparatus. The critical characteristic of the imported concepts of land use and control used by the state is that they do not incorporate empirical experience gathered over time of the extreme rather than the average conditions which the agriculturalist and pastoralist are likely to encounter. Given that ecological survival hinges on the ability to survive extreme rather than average conditions, the designs of the state represent an elementary threat to rural producers who cannot fall back on alternative state income. In an extreme form, then, the Ethiopian famine raises the possiblity that the survival of the state in Africa (in its present form and with its ambitions for land control), and the survival of anything resembling the subsistence economies which evolved within the constraints of semi-arid Ethiopia, may be mutually exclusive.

The indications are that in responding to the recent extremity of famine the Ethiopian government has been more concerned with strengthening centralised control than with seriously seeking to ensure the security of the rural population against future climatic rigours. Instead of negotiating an end to a conflict which has both provoked and then prolonged a famine, the government has chosen to further assert its desire for control in the rural economy through large-scale resettlement and villagisation schemes. The net effect these schemes, ignoring their political or human rights aspects, has been to further intervene in the long-evolved relationship between people and the environment (Madeley, 1986). Precedents in Tanzania, South Africa and parts of the Soviet drylands indicate that such programmes, carried out without the benefit of a comprehensive knowledge of enviromental adaptation, have very little chance of success. Far from raising living standards, previous schemes of such an extensive kind have promoted rapid environmental degradation and subsequent out-migration to cities to seek alternative livelihoods. Both in South Africa and Tanzania, the two main precedents for large-scale resettlement, urban employment has been able to operate, to some extent, as a kind of ecological safety-valve. In Ethiopia there is no evidence that even this alternative would present itself.

The resettlement of alien northern peoples on the seasonal grazing lands of peasants in Keffa, Illubabor and Wollega has been carried out in complete ignorance of the environmental and cultural constraints pertaining in those regions, and under pressure of coercion. Similarly, coercive methods have been adopted in promoting soil conservation programmes in drought stricken areas. Ironically, only in parts of Tigrai outside government control have soil conservation programmes proceeded without encountering local resistance (N. Munro, personal communication). A National Park strategy originally set up by American consultants continues to be imposed, although only over a limited land area. In the Bale, Omo and Awash National Parks pastoralists have been excluded from essential seasonal grazing areas without consultation and movement has been seriously restricted (Turton, Chapter 8). In the Bale National Park peasants were encouraged to move by the simple expedient of putting their villages to the torch (Hillman, 1986). Two features of the behaviour of the state stand out in these instances and are surprisingly reminiscent of much of the colonial experience. Firstly, there has been an underlying assumption that the inherited expertise of the rural population must be inferior to the learned techniques at the disposal of the agents of the state. Secondly, the priority of the state in actually controlling rural population is seen to outweigh the (anyway ill-considered) ecological and human consequences of doing so. The cynical observer might simply conclude that the proponents of an urban-based ideology have no interest in incorporating the human and ecological complexities of the rural livelihood, and are unaware of the dangers incumbent in not doing so.

In practice the most damaging ambitions of the state, common to several other African governments, are those that discourage even the limited seasonal transhumance of essentially settled populations, let alone nomadism. Since these are often the only kinds of agricultural activity that can be practised in semi-arid areas without large capital inputs of fertiliser and equipment (which the economic condition of Ethiopia does not at present allow), further environmental deterioration seems inevitable. In other parts Africa the same motivations on the part of government, directed towards control and development, have helped to promote desertification in the most direct way, particularly through the building of waterholes and other irrigation schemes (Sinclair & Fryxell, 1985; Hogg, Chapter 14). These have been based on a total misunderstanding of, or indeed an unwillingness to understand, the adaptive complexities of societies which have evolved over a long period in regions of high climatic variability.

Determining whether government environmental policies are beneficial or harmful depends not so much on the political colour of the
government in question as on its responsiveness to the importance of
local conditions and needs. Central governments, especially those highly
centralised in ideology, commonly fail to recognise the importance of
interdependence of neighbouring areas and social groups. One ecological
region is often complementary to another, especially in dryland regions.
Effective use of a river floodplain or delta commonly implies reliance
on water supplied from remote rainfall catchments. Ethnic groups, differing greatly in their political and social organisations, may nevertheless
be interdependent economically, especially in times of climatic stress,
above all when droughts occur. Agriculturalist and pastoralist, highlander
and lowlander have operated within exchange systems which are to their
mutual benefit. Politicians and administrators remote from such areas,
and aid agencies all too often as well, fail to recognise such relationships,
and allow or even encourage development schemes which disrupt vital
ecological and economic linkages. In Ethiopia, as in much of the rest
of Africa, the arguments of engineers and economists, quantifiable in
financial terms, have been much more concrete and tangible and therefore more attractive than those of ecologists and social scientists who
cannot offer exactitudes and certainty. This fatal and facile attractiveness,
particularly to urban governing élites, as demonstrated by the sequence
of events over the last score of years in the Awash Valley of Ethiopia,
shows no sign of diminishing. It is proving to be destructive to land and
wildlife and tragic for the people of Africa.

References

BAIL, N. (1976). Understanding the causes of African famine. *Journal of Modern
    African Studies*, **14**, 517–21.
BONDESTAM, L. (1974). Peoples and capitalism in the north-lowlands of
    Ethiopia. *Journal of Modern African Studies*, **12**, 423–39.
CAPONERA, D.A. (1956). *Water Control Legislation: Report to the Government
    of Ethiopia*. FAO Expanded Programme of Technical Assistance, Report
    no.550. Rome: FAO.
CARR, C.J. (1977). *Pastoralism in Crisis: the Dasanetch and the Ethiopian
    Lands*. Chicago: University of Chicago Press.
COSSINS, N.J. (1972). *Green Heart of a Dying Land: a study of the new cotton
    wealth of the old Afar Sultanate of Awsa*. Addis Ababa: Sir Alexander Gibb
    & Partners/Huntings Ltd.
COSSINS, N.J. (1973). *No Way To Live: a study of the Afar clans of the northeast
    rangelands*. Addis Ababa: Imperial Ethiopian Govt, Livestock & Meat Board.
DIEBOLD, P.B. (1958). *Economic policies for expanding agricultural produc-
    tion: Report to the Government of Ethiopia*, Report no.926. Rome: FAO.

DINI, A. (1967). Un Fait Social Afar; le Fiema. *Pount*, **3**, 31–6.

FLOOD, G. (1976). Nomadism and its Future. In *Rehab: Drought and Famine in Ethiopia*, ed. Abdul Majid. London: International African Institute.

FAO-SF (1967). *Report on the Survey of the Awash River Basin, General Report, vol.1.* Rome: FAO.

FITZGERALD, W. (1980). Drought, famine and revolution: some political aspects of the Ethiopian drought. Unpublished MSc thesis, School of Oriental and African Studies, London University.

FRANKE, R. & CHASIN, B.H. (1980). *Seeds of Famine: Ecological desertification and the development dilemma in the Western Sahel.* Mountclair, Allerheld: Osman.

GAMALEDINN, M. (1986). The political economy of the Afar region of Ethiopia: a study in peripheral dynamism. Unpublished Ph.D. thesis, University of Cambridge.

GOUDIE, A.G. (1972). Irrigated land settlement: Ethiopia: informal technical report no.7. Rome: FAO.

GREEN, S. & SINNSHAW,T. (1973). *Famine in Wollo, a visit to drought affected areas, August 19–26.* Addis Ababa: World Bank.

GROVE, A.T. (1979). Desertification, man-made or natural? In *Symposium on Drought in Botswana.* ed. M.T. Hinchey, pp.71–4. Gaberone: National Museum of Botswana.

GROVE, A.T. (1986). The State of Africa. *Geographical Journal*, **152**(2) 193–203.

HANCOCK, G. (1985). *Ethiopia, The Challenge of Hunger.* London: Victor Gollancz.

HELLAND, J. (1977). *A Preliminary Report on the Afar.* Addis Ababa: ILCA.

HELLAND, J. (1980). *Five Essays on the Study of Pastoralists and the Development of Pastoralism.* Bergen: University of Bergen.

HILLMAN, C. (1986). The Bale National Park. Unpublished seminar paper, African Studies Centre, Cambridge University.

HUSSEIN, A.M. (1976). The political economy of famine in Ethiopia. In *Rehab: Drought and Famine in Ethiopia*, ed. Abdul Majid, pp. 9–51. London: International African Institute.

KLOOS, H. (1977). Schistosomiasis and Irrigation in the Awash Valley of Ethiopia. Unpublished Ph.D. thesis, University of California.

KLOOS, H. (1982). Development, Drought and Famine in the Awash Valley of Ethiopia. *African Studies Review*, **25**, 21–48.

KLOOS, H., De SOLE, G. & LEMMA, A. (1981). Intestinal parasitism in semi-nomadic pastoralists and subsistence farmers in and around irrigation schemes in the Awash Valley, Ethiopia, with special emphasis on ecological and cultural associations. *Social Science and Medicine*, **15B**(4), 457–69.

LOFCHIE, M.F. (1975). The Political and Economic Origins of African Hunger. *Journal of Modern African Studies*, **18**, 551–67.

MADELEY, J. (1986). Ethiopia's new villagers. *Geographical Magazine*, **48**(2), 25–32.

MARIAM, M.W. (1964). The Awash Valley – trends and prospects. *Ethiopian Geographical Journal*, **11**, 19.

MILAS, S. & ASRAT, M. (1985). Eastern Africa's spreading wastelands. *Desertification Control Bulletin*, **12**, 34–41. Nairobi: UNEP.

PANKHURST, R. (1986). *The History of Famine and Epidemics in Ethiopia prior to the Twentieth Century*. Addis Ababa: Relief and Rehabilitation Commission.

PAUSEWANG, S. (1983). *Peasants, Land and Society: a social history of Ethiopia*. Munchen: Weltforum.

RRC (1985). *The Challenge of Hunger*. Addis Ababa: Relief and Rehabilitation Commission.

ROUNDY, R.W. (1985). *Environmental productivity in pre-revolutionary Ethiopia: perennial vegetational resources*. Discussion Paper Series no.33, Centre for Development Area Studies. McGill University, Montreal.

SEN, A. (1982). *Poverty and Famines: an essay in entitlement and deprivation*. London: Oxford University Press.

SHEPHERD, J. (1975). *The Politics of Starvation*. New York: Carnegie Endowment for International Peace.

SINCLAIR, A.R.E. & FRYXELL, J.M. (1985). The Sahel of Africa: ecology of a disaster. *Canadian Journal of Ecology*, **63**, 987–94.

VOELKNER, H.E. (1974). *The social feasibility of settling semi-nomadic Afar on irrigated agriculture in the Awash Valley, Ethiopia*. Informal Technical Report, no.23. Rome: FAO.

WOOD, C.A. (1977). A preliminary chronology of Ethiopian droughts. In *Drought in Africa 2*, ed. D. Dalby, R.J. Harrison Church & F. Bezzaz. London: International African Institute.

INDEX